Standard Cataloging
for School and Public Libraries

Standard Cataloging
for School and Public Libraries

Third Edition

SHEILA S. INTNER
Graduate School of Library and Information Science
Simmons College
Boston, Massachusetts

and

JEAN WEIHS
Technical Services Group
Toronto, Ontario

2001
Libraries Unlimited
A Member of Greenwood Publishing, Inc.
Westport, Connecticut • London

Libraries Unlimited
A member of Greenwood Publishing Group, Inc.
88 Post Road West,
Westport, CT 06881
www.lu.com

Library of Congress Cataloging-in-Publication Data

Intner, Sheila S.
    Standard cataloging for school and public libraries / Sheila S. Intner and Jean Weihs.--
3rd ed.
        p. cm.
    Includes bibliographical references and index.
    ISBN 1-56308-781-2
        1. Cataloging--United States. 2. Cataloging--Canada. 3. Public libraries--United States.
4. Public libraries--Canada. 5. School libraries--United States. 6. School
libraries--Canada. I. Weihs, Jean Riddle. II. Title.

Z693 .I56 2001
025.3--dc21

                                                                    2001018615

10 9 8 7 6 5 4 3   EBA 04

Contents

Acknowledgments

The preparation of this book depended heavily on the assistance of many people who kindly agreed to read portions, offer suggestions and corrections, check citations, print data, and otherwise contribute their energy, knowledge, and time. The authors are very grateful to all of them. In particular, we wish to recognize and thank the following colleagues and friends: Paul Aloisio, Director, Technology Laboratory, Graduate School of Library and Information Science, Simmons College; Nita Dean, Manager, Public Relations, OCLC, Inc.; Robert Ewald, Senior Cataloging Policy Specialist, Library of Congress; Linda Gabel, Consulting Database Specialist, OCLC, Inc.; Jennifer Hartzell, Manager, RLG Corporate Communications; Betty Havrylik, Assistant Library Science Librarian, Graduate School of Library and Information Science, Simmons College; Oryst Iwanycky, Senior Systems Librarian, Information Technology Services, National Library of Canada; Bruce Chris Johnson, Team Leader, Cataloger's Desktop/Classification Plus Development Team and Senior Library Information Systems Specialist, Library of Congress; Maureen Killeen, Bibliographic Specialist, A-G Canada Ltd.; James M. Matarazzo, Dean, Graduate School of Library and Information Science, Simmons College; Joan Mitchell, Executive Director, OCLC Forest Press and Editor-in-Chief, Dewey Decimal Classification; Glenn Patton, Manager, Cataloging Products Department, OCLC, Inc.; Margaret Stewart, Chief, Standards and Support, Acquisitions and Bibliographic Services, National Library of Canada; Linda Watkins, Library Science Librarian, Simmons College; and Linda Willey, Assistant to the Dean, Graduate School of Library and Information Science, Simmons College.

Permission to reproduce data from copyrighted sources was granted to the authors by the Library of Congress, OCLC, Inc., the Research Libraries Group, and the H. W. Wilson Company.

Preface

This book is intended to help librarians and media specialists responsible for cataloging the materials collected by public libraries, learning centers, and school library media centers gain familiarity with the world of library cataloging by explaining its principles and standards. Students in library and/or information science programs who are learning to catalog materials also can benefit. Through better understanding of these foundations of practice, their application can be facilitated and standard catalog entries produced more easily; a result that the authors believe is both desirable and achievable. In no way are the fundamentals compromised to make the task simpler, but complications unlikely to be encountered on the job have been avoided.

Although one book of modest size cannot cover every detail, major considerations involved in managing bibliographic services for a public library, learning center, or school library media center, including decisions about cataloging and classification, shelving, catalogs and indexes are discussed. Computerization of bibliographic systems also is covered; both large networks and smaller, local systems. A chapter about management of the cataloging department and alternatives to cataloging materials in-house examines issues of importance to managers.

Four kinds of standards are explored: (1) rules used for descriptive cataloging, (2) subject heading lists, (3) popularly used classifications, and (4) computer data entry and communication protocols. Explanations are illustrated with examples from items in all formats. Some of the text in these general discussions is identical to that in *Special Libraries: A Cataloging Guide* (Libraries Unlimited, 1998). But selected topics treated in that book have been omitted; for example, specialized thesauri and classifications, which are infrequently used by public libraries, learning centers, and school library media centers. Other topics peripheral to the materials encountered in schools and public libraries (conference proceedings, technical reports, and continuations) have been covered only briefly, if at all.

Any errors in the text and figures are entirely the responsibility of the authors, who welcome readers' comments and corrections, which may be sent to them in care of the publisher.

Three appendixes to the main text include a selected bibliography, a glossary, and answers to the exercises in chapters 4, 5, 8, 9, 11, and 12.

The indexes to this book include topical and name indexes; and, for those who wish to study the examples more systematically, there is an index to the examples. The example index has four sections: (1) type of media, (2) description, (3) access points, and (4) classification.

Standard Cataloging for School and Public Libraries is meant to be readable and useful. It is intended to promote effective public services by making it easier for librarians, learning center specialists, and school library media specialists to implement standardized bibliographic services.

1

Introduction

The Dynamic Nature of Cataloging

The rules and standards used in library cataloging and classification are not static, but have evolved over time and continue evolving as attempts are made to resolve new access problems that arise. Precedent has played a key role in the shape of the rules and standards we now have, but major shifts occur from time to time, usually in response to expressed needs that emerge from the community of library practitioners. Often the shifts do not occur fast enough to satisfy them, and sometimes a change that solves one problem creates another. This is what happened when the code for descriptive cataloging was published in 1978. Even though the code enabled catalogers to create uniform, standard entries for all types of library materials that could be integrated into a single catalog, and resolved all but the most innocuous differences separating the British and North American versions of the previous code—both significant advances—it was extremely costly to implement in large libraries whose existing catalogs required extensive revision.

Many complaints were leveled at the *Anglo-American Cataloguing Rules,* second edition, most focusing on the cost of implementation. In 1988, ten years after its first appearance, a revised edition was published to incorporate into a single book the many changes that had occurred throughout the decade. Ten years later, in 1998, a second revision was published, this time both in a print edition and in electronic form, on a CD-ROM (i.e., a read-only laser optical disk). The process of revision continues, and from time to time packets of changes to the printed edition and new CD-ROMs containing updated content can be expected to be issued by the publishers. In 2000, a new packet of amendments was made available free of charge online (available via Internet at www.ala.org/editions/updates/aacr2) or for a small cost on paper (available via the Internet at www.alastore.ala.org). In the future, the two formats may not contain identical text, because updated text on CD-ROM is likely to be issued more frequently than updated text on paper.

Functions of the Catalog

The objectives of the various rulebooks, subject heading authorities, and classifications have not changed over the last century. In 1876, in celebration of the centennial of the United

States of America, Charles A. Cutter published his *Rules for a Dictionary Catalog.* It opened with a now-famous expression of the purposes of the catalog, which he called its objects:

1. To enable a person to find a book when one of the following is known:
    a) The author
    b) The title
    c) The subject

2. To show what the library has
    d) By a given author
    e) On a given subject
    f) In a given kind of literature

3. To assist in the choice of a book
    g) As to the edition (bibliographically)
    h) As to its character (literary or topical)[1]

Despite much research and analysis on cataloging questions since Cutter's time, his objects remain the definitive statement of what catalogers try to accomplish. Although they sound simple, Cutter's ideals of access have never been completely realized. They remain goals toward which to strive, achievable only in theory. The reason Cutter's objects are so difficult to attain is that the kinds of rules that promote the finding list function (i.e., finding a book when the author, title, or subject is known) work against the collocating function (bringing together or "collocating" the works by a given author, in a given subject, etc.) and vice versa. For example, if one copy of Beethoven's last symphony uses the title *Symphony No. 9* and gives the author's name as Luigi van Beethoven (as he occasionally signed himself) while another uses the title *Ninth Symphony* and gives the author's name as Ludwig van Beethoven, the following problems occur:

1. If we use the titles and names *exactly* as they appear on each of the scores, which promotes identification, neither the author entries nor the title entries will file in the same place.

2. If we use one form of the title and one form of the author's name for both scores, which promotes collocation, the entries will file neatly together, but we shall have used names and titles that cannot be found on the scores themselves.

Current cataloging and classification rules and standards come as close as they can to achieving these twin objectives of the catalog. The rules that pertain to headings for names, subjects, and series titles generally permit only one form to be used for all occurrences of each name, subject, or title. This brings together all the works by an author, all works on a particular topic, and all works in the same series, regardless of discrepancies in vocabulary, spelling, language, and other elements that could occur in expressing their names, subjects, or series. A special heading called a "uniform title" is created for works whose own titles on different versions vary (as in the previous example of the Beethoven symphony). The uniform title brings together all editions and versions of a title, just as the one permissible name, subject, and series title headings do.

The rules that pertain to the identification of a work, called its "bibliographic description" often require the exact transcription of data from the item being cataloged. This ensures that someone who uses the catalog record can match it exactly against a copy of the item it represents, ensuring that the correct item has been found. The same is true of a title heading made by using the same words as the title in the bibliographic description. When one work is published in many versions whose own titles vary, two title headings are made for each version cataloged: one that exactly matches the title on the item, thus helping searchers match them; and one authorized uniform title that collocates them in one place in the catalog.

Even in their imperfect state, catalogs accomplish a great deal. They are the keys to library, learning center, and media center collections everywhere, helping people find the materials they seek in any particular place. They help form links between collections, enabling one institution to share information and materials with others. Shelf arrangements also contribute to access by physically collocating materials that are related, first by subject, then within a subject by author, and finally by the titles of an author's work in a subject.

Good cataloging and classification accomplish two things. First, they do a better job as finding tools for their library, and second, they enable that library to link more effectively with its partners in local, county, state, regional, provincial, and national bibliographic networks. The ultimate goal is to make any title owned anywhere available to a person with a need for that material.

Development of national and international computer-based bibliographic networks such as the Online Computer Library Center (OCLC) in Dublin, Ohio, has made this goal a reality, at least for the tens of thousands of OCLC partners and the millions of titles in the network. The effectiveness of the network depends upon the uniformity of the information that goes into it, so that a desired item can be identified by any of the people who search for it. This not only facilitates interlibrary loans, but more important, it enables catalogers to share the task of cataloging. Once someone catalogs an item in the network, anyone else who buys that item can use the catalog record. This is called "derived" or "copy" cataloging. That sort of sharing sounds easy, but it can be completely confounded if two catalogers with the same item use different methods of describing it, each devising a different catalog record. Then the network's value as a sharing tool fails.

Why should public libraries, learning centers, and school library media centers care about computerized networks and problems of resource sharing? Many of these are self-contained entities that operate with little help from the larger library community. Sharing resources may not be a high priority. Two important changes in society now mandate a different approach. First, a combination of expansion and overlap in virtually all research areas has altered the boundaries of most disciplines. As a result, libraries seeking to serve small businesses need to collect legal materials, and learning centers seeking to provide enrichment for art classes will want information about computer graphics. Second, no individual library can afford to purchase and own all the information resources it needs to serve its public—not even large research libraries such as the University of Toronto or the New York Public Library. How much more difficult is it for a small public library or media center to have collections that cover all relevant topics and time periods in all desired formats? One way to increase a library's potential is to share holdings with network partners, receiving their cooperation in return. The only way to do this successfully is to have shareable cataloging information that is, by definition, in standardized form.

Understandably, local librarians' first priority is to serve their users. This may not be an easy task when users comprise different groups of people with dramatically different educational levels and intellectual needs. Everyone wants to have materials immediately, without waiting for cataloging or processing that takes time. Publishers and producers of the materials sometimes forget that their products will be stored in libraries or media centers, packaging them with end users and marketing displays in mind, not catalogers and library shelves. Inadequate packaging and labeling add pressure to the job of doing good cataloging.

Librarians in small public libraries and schools sometimes believe that the materials they handle are unlikely to be found in network databases. However, as these databases have grown larger and as network memberships have grown to include more school districts and community libraries, the proportion of successful searches for wanted materials has increased. At this writing, the OCLC network is logging approximately one million interlibrary loan requests in less than a month; most are satisfied promptly.

Good cataloging also has its own rewards. Small collections can be used to better advantage when they are well cataloged. Standard methods of cataloging and classification are intended to maximize the retrieval potential of materials and to help people using the catalog records locate what they need. Standard methods can be applied to all kinds of information resources, whether they are in the form of books, slides, sound or videotapes, or microcomputer software packages.

This book is dedicated to the proposition that standardized cataloging is the key that opens the door of better access to local information needs. The chapters cover each component of the cataloging process, including descriptive cataloging, subject headings, classification, and computer encoding. Each component is first discussed generally and then followed by one or more chapters describing individual standard tools for accomplishing those tasks; for example, Chapter 7 covers subject headings in general, and Chapters 8 and 9 cover the standard lists of subject headings used to do subject cataloging, *Sears List of Subject Headings* and *Library of Congress Subject Headings,* respectively. Chapter 10 covers classification in general, and Chapters 11 and 12 cover the standard classification systems, Dewey Decimal and Library of Congress (LC) classifications, respectively. Each chapter includes many illustrations, and a selected bibliography of essential tools and helpful manuals to assist librarians and media specialists in doing standard cataloging.

Cataloging-in-Publication

One of the most useful tools provided to catalogers by their national libraries is the preliminary cataloging published in most books and some nonbook materials called cataloging-in-publication or CIP (pronounced "sip"). Publishers and producers participating in the CIP program send galley proofs or other prepublication information to their national library. LC, although not legislated the U.S. national library, functions in fact as if it were and takes the same responsibilities for the United States. The national library catalogers perform all necessary research on CIP records' access points and call numbers, but only do skeletal bibliographic descriptions. Pagination cannot be completed because it is not final at the galley proof stage and it is not uncommon for titles and other descriptive elements to be changed between the galley proofs and the final publication of an item. CIP records are entered into national bibliographic databases and networks with identifying tags to show they are not full or complete. The national library also sends the CIP copy to the publisher or producer to be incorporated into the item being published. These CIP records usually appear on the back of the title page (called the verso), although occasionally they are found at the back of the book (called the colophon).

Local librarians and media specialists can use the CIP to select headings, determine titles proper, assign call numbers and, with the item in hand, complete an accurate bibliographic description. The careful, thorough work done by national library catalogers in establishing call numbers, name headings, and subject descriptors is usually trustworthy. However, sometimes mistakes are made or publishers change publishing data between the time the CIP record is prepared and the item is published. It may be necessary to make corrections in some records before including them in the catalog. It is particularly important to check CIP records that have not been done recently, because revisions to descriptive cataloging rules, subject heading lists, and classification schedules may have occurred since the CIP record was prepared. Figures in this and other chapters demonstrate some reasons why a local library would change CIP records.

In Figure 1.1, the CIP data lists "Includes index," but there is no index in this work. On the other hand, what appears to be an error—the listing of the compiler's name in CIP in a different form than found on the title page—is not an error; this bibliographic form of name was established from the way the compiler's name was published in her previous work. The source of information for Figure 1.1 is on the next page, 6.

FIGURE 1.1

This example is an illustration of:
- main entry under adapter
- edition statement
- publication date not listed, copyright date given
- multivolume work
- loose-leaf format
- quoted note
- marks of omission in quoted note
- edition note
- publication note
- corporate body added entries
- Canadian CIP data corrected
- British Library CIP
- 2nd level cataloging

```
Howarth, Lynne.
    AACR2 decisions & rule interpretations / compiled by Lynne C.
Howarth. -- 5th ed. -- Ottawa : Canadian Library Association,
c1991.
    2 v. (loose-leaf) ; 30 cm.

    "A consolidation ... which the Library of Congress, the
National Library of Canada, the British Library, and the National
Library of Australia have made to govern their use of the Anglo-
American cataloguing rules, second edition, 1988 revision"--Pref.
    Revised to March 1991.
    Co-published with: American Library Association, Library
Association.
    ISBN: 0-88802-237-9.

    1. Anglo-American cataloguing rules.  2. Descriptive cataloging
-- Rules.  I. Canadian Library Association.  II. American Library
Association.  III. Library Association.  IV. Title.

Recommended DDC: 025.32
Recommended LCC: Z694.C66 1991
```

Fig. 1.1—Continues

FIGURE 1.1 *(continued)*

(chief source of information)
        (title page)

AACR2

(information on verso)

Canadian Cataloguing in Publication Data

Howarth, Lynne

   AACR2 decisions and rule interpretations

5th ed.
"A consolidation of the decisions and rule
   interpretations which the Library of Congress,
   the National Library of Canada, the British
   Library, and the National Library of Australia
   have made to govern their use of the Anglo-
   American cataloguing rules, second edition,
   1988 revision (AACR2R)."--cf. Pref.
Revised to March 1991.
Co-published with: American Library Association,
Library Association.
Includes index.
ISBN 0-88802-237-9

   1. Anglo-American cataloguing rules.
I. Canadian Library Association II. American
Library Association III. Library Association
IV. Title.

Z694.C66   025.3'2   C91-090350-6

BRITISH LIBRARY CATALOGUING-IN-PUBLICATION DATA

Howarth, Lynne

   AACR2 decisions and rule interpretations.
   - 5th ed.
   I. Title
   025.3

   ISBN 1-85604-035-6

Published by the Canadian Library Association
200 Elgin Street, Suite 602, Ottawa, Ontario K2P 1L5
Copyright © 1991 Canadian Library Association
All rights reserved
ISBN 0-88802-237-9
Printed and bound in Canada

The CIP for Figure 1.2 is an example of a CIP that is no longer valid because of changes to the rules. The CIP for this book was produced while an earlier version of the cataloging rules was in force. Revisions to previous rules for descriptive cataloging have changed the main entry for this work. The source of information for Figure 1.2 is on the next page, 8.

FIGURE 1.2

This example is an illustration of:
- edition statement
- unnumbered series statement
- index note
- two ISBNs; the one given relates to the item in hand
- ISBN qualified
- Library of Congress subject heading
- added entry for original author
- additional title added entry
- prime marks in unabridged Dewey decimal classification number
- Library of Congress Classification number
- correction of LC CIP data due to rule revisions
- 2nd level cataloging

```
Chan, Lois Mai.
   Immroth's guide to the Library of Congress classification / by
Lois Mai Chan. -- 3rd ed. -- Littleton, CO : Libraries Unlimited,
1980.
   402 p. : ill. ; 23 cm. -- (Library science text series)

   Includes index.
   ISBN 0-87287-235-1 (pbk.).

   1. Classification, Library of Congress.  I. Immroth, John
Phillip.  II. Title.  III. Title: Guide to the Library of
Congress classification.

Recommended DDC: 025.4'33
Recommended abridged DDC: 025.4
Recommended LCC: Z696.U415 1980

N.B. There is no subject heading in Sears for this topic.
```

Fig. 1.2—Continues

FIGURE 1.2 *(continued)*

___

(chief source of information)
(title page)

(information on verso)

Based upon Immroth's *Guide to Library of Congress Classification*,
1st and 2d Editions,
© Barbara F. Immroth 1968, 1971
All Rights Reserved

**Immroth's Guide
to the
Library of Congress Classification**

© Libraries Unlimited, Inc. 1980
All Rights Reserved
Printed in the United States of America

Third Edition

No part of this publication may be reproduced, stored in a retrieval system, or transmitted, in any form or by any means, electronic, mechanical, photocopying, recording, or otherwise, without the prior written permission of the publisher.

LIBRARIES UNLIMITED, INC.
P.O. Box 263
Littleton, Colorado 80160

By
Lois Mai Chan

Library of Congress Cataloging in Publication Data

Immroth, John Phillip.
  Immroth's Guide to the Library of Congress classification.

   (Library science text series)
   Includes bibliographies and index.
   1.   Classification, Library of Congress.   I. Chan,
Lois Mai. II. Title. III. Title: Guide to the
Library of Congress classification.
Z696.U415 1980   025.4'33   80-16981
ISBN 0-87287-224-6
ISBN 0-87287-235-1 (pbk.)

Libraries Unlimited, Inc. • Littleton, CO • 1980

(information in several places)

LIBRARY SCIENCE TEXT SERIES

___

Figure 5.8 demonstrates both mistakes in CIP cataloging and the differences in two CIPs done by national libraries. The bibliographic form of the conference's name is correct in National Library of Canada's (NLC) CIP and incorrect in LC's CIP. NLC is correct in inferring that bibliographic references are spread throughout the book (LC's note suggests that they are gathered in one place). LC is correct in noting the index, a fact that NLC does not mention. NLC has made the optional decision to give added entries to the publishers, but has failed to trace the Canadian Library Association. Other differences, which include other title information, bibliographic form of personal name, and a publisher's note, will be mentioned when these subjects are discussed in later chapters.

Classification numbers assigned by LC and NLC also may differ. In Figure 6.6, LC has chosen to assign a classification number from its "F" schedule, whereas NLC preferred the "FC" schedule, which details Canadian history.

It is also important to check subject headings in the tracings to ensure that they are consistent with the latest edition of the subject heading list used by the library or media center. Note that the LC descriptor ANATOMY, HUMAN in the CIP tracing for Figure 5.9 has been changed in later editions of the subject heading list (see Chapter 9) to HUMAN ANATOMY since the CIP was produced.

The CIP for Figure 4.5 gives only one subject heading: COOKERY (POTATOES). There are 20 pages in this book about the history of the potato, potato museums, etc., that may be overlooked by someone searching for this information. A second subject heading, POTATOES, should be added to this record.

It is only in recent years that the British Library began using LC subject headings. Before that time, the British Library applied PRECIS headings, a computer-assisted subject heading system rarely used in North America. Figure 1.3 shows an example of a British Library CIP with this type of subject heading.

FIGURE 1.3

This example is an illustration of:
- all illustrations are colored
- width of book greater than height
- two ISBNs; the one given relates to the item in hand
- Library of Congress and Sears subect heading the same
- Dewey Decimal classification number
- British Library CIP
- 2nd level cataloging

```
Isaacson, Philip M.
   Round buildings, square buildings, & buildings that wiggle like
a fish / by Philip M. Isaacson. -- London : Julia MacRae, 1990.
   121 p. : col. ill. ; 23 x 25 cm.

   ISBN 0-86203-447-7.

   1. Architecture   I. Title.

Recommended DDC: 720.09 (N.B. updated to latest edition of DDC)
```

(chief source of information
(title page)

Round Buildings,
Square Buildings, &
Buildings That Wiggle Like a Fish

BY PHILIP M. ISAACSON

With photographs by the author

Julia MacRae Books
A DIVISION OF WALKER BOOKS

(information on verso)

Copyright © 1988 Philip M. Isaacson
All rights reserved
First published in the USA 1988
by Alfred A. Knopf, Inc.
First published in Great Britain 1990
by Julia MacRae Books
A division of Walker Books Ltd
87 Vauxhall Walk, London SE11 5HJ

Printed in Singapore

British Library Cataloguing in Publication Data

Isaacson, Philip M. 1924—
    Round buildings, square buildings, & buildings that
    wiggle like a fish.
    1. Architecture, to 1976 — For children
    I. Title
    720'.9

ISBN 0-86203-447-7 Hardback edition
ISBN 0-86203-468-X Paperback edition

In recent years, CIP records have listed the number of the edition of *Dewey Decimal Classification* that was used to classify the item. Note that the CIP for Figure 1.4 states "636′.93234—dc20" indicating that this work was classified using the 20th edition of Dewey. This number should be checked with the current edition to ensure its accuracy. The number in the current 21st edition is 636′.93592.

Classification numbers and subject headings taken from schemes other than those from the LC or Dewey are placed in square brackets in CIP tracings. This is demonstrated in the CIP for Figure 1.4, in which a subject heading and a classification number from the specialized tools published by the National Library of Medicine are listed as alternatives for specialized health science libraries. These can be ignored by general libraries because they do not need greater specificity in classification and subject cataloging.

FIGURE 1.4

This example is an illustration of:
- collection of works by different authors
- title main entry
- other title information
- edited work
- multiple places of publication
- publication date not listed, copyright date given
- detailed pagination
- bibliography and index note
- two ISBNs; the one given relates to the item in hand
- ISBN qualified
- Library of Congress, MeSH, and Sears subject headings
- added entry for editor
- unabridged Dewey, Library of Congress, and National Library of Medicine classification numbers
- Library of Congress CIP
- 2nd level cataloging

2nd level cataloging

```
Reshaping dementia care : practice and policy in long-term care
    / Miriam K. Aronson, editor. -- Thousand Oaks, Calif. : Sage,
    1994.
    xii, 179 p. ; 22 cm.

    Includes bibliographical references and index.
    ISBN 0-0-8039-5160-4 (pbk.)

Tracing with Library of Congress subject headings

    1. Senile dementia -- Patients -- Long-term care.
    2. Senile dementia -- Patients -- Long-term care -- United
    States.  I. Aronson, Miriam K.
```

Tracing with Medical subject headings (MeSH)

1. Dementia, Senile. 2. Long-Term Care -- organization & administration -- United States. 3. Long-Term Care -- in old age. I. Aronson, Miriam K.

Recommended DDC: 362.26
Recommended LCC: RC524.R47 1994
Recommended NLM: WT150 R433 1994

1st level cataloging

Reshaping dementia care / Miriam K. Aronson, editor. -- Sage, 1994.
  xii, 179 p.

  ISBN 0-0-8039-5160-4 (pbk.)

Tracing with Sears subject headings

1. Elderly -- Medical care. 2. Mentally ill -- Institutional care. I. Aronson, Miriam K.

Recommended abridged DDC: 362.2

(chief source of information)
(title page)

(information on verso)

For information address:

 SAGE Publications, Inc.
2455 Teller Road
Thousand Oaks, California 91320

SAGE Publications Ltd.
6 Bonhill Street
London EC2A 4PU
United Kingdom

SAGE Publications India Pvt. Ltd.
M-32 Market
Greater Kailash I
New Delhi 110 048 India

Printed in the United States of America

RESHAPING DEMENTIA CARE

Practice and Policy in Long-Term Care

Miriam K. Aronson
editor

SAGE Publications
International Educational and Professional Publisher
Thousand Oaks   London   New Delhi

Library of Congress Cataloging-in-Publication Data

Main entry under title:

Reshaping dementia care : practice and policy in long-term care / edited by Miriam K. Aronson
    p. cm.
    Includes bibliographical references and index.
    ISBN 0-8039-5159-0 (cl). — ISBN 0-8039-5160-4 (pbk.)
    1. Senile dementia—Patients—Long-term care. 2. Senile dementia Patients—Long-term care—United States. I. Aronson, Miriam K.
    [DNLM: 1. Dementia, Senile. 2. Long-Term Care—organization & administration—United States. 3. Long-Term Care—in old age. WT 150 R433 1994]
    RC524.R47 1994
    362.2'6—dc20
    DNLM/DLC   94-113

Similarly, materials cataloged as part of the LC's Annotated Card Program, described in connection with *Library of Congress Subject Headings,* Chapter 9, may include a summary of their contents in the body of the catalog record and specialized Annotated Card Subject Headings intended for children's materials given in brackets following the regular adult headings. Figure 1.5 shows cataloging for a picture book that includes Annotated Card headings. For public libraries, learning centers, and school library media centers catering to children and youth, these may be more useful than the regular adult headings. Decisions to adopt Annotated Card headings should be carefully weighed in such agencies.

FIGURE 1.5

This example is an illustration of:
- Library of Congress annotated card program
- statement of subsidiary responsibility
- edition statement
- unpaged book, paging supplied
- all illustrations are in color
- unnumbered series statement
- comparison of Library of Congress subject headings and LC annotated card subject headings
- added entry for illustrator
- optional addition of designation for illustrator
- series added entry in 2nd level cataloging
- prime marks in Dewey classification numbers
- Library of Congress CIP
- two levels of cataloging

2nd level cataloging

```
King-Smith, Dick.
   I love guinea pigs / by Dick King-Smith ; illustrated by Anita
Jeram. -- 1st U.S. ed. -- Cambridge, Mass. : Candlewick Press,
1995.
   [24] p. : col. ill. ; 26 cm. -- (Read and wonder books)

   ISBN 1-56402-389-3.
```

1st level cataloging

```
King-Smith, Dick.
   I love guinea pigs. -- Candlewick Press, 1995.
   [24] p.

   ISBN 1-56402-389-3.
```

The tracing with Library of Congress subject headings for 2nd level cataloging in an adult collection

```
   1. Guinea pigs as pets -- Juvenile literature.  I. Jeram,
Anita, ill.  II. Title.  III. Series.
```

The tracing with Annotated Card Program headings fo cataloging in a children's collection

   1. Guinea pigs.   2. Pets.   I. Jeram, Anita, III. Series.

The tracing for 1st level cataloging in either an adult or chi would omit "Jeram, Anita, ill". and "Series."

   Recommended DDC: 636'.935'92
   Recommended abridged DDC: 636'.935
   Recommended LCC: SF459.G9K55 1995

(chief source of information)
   (title page)

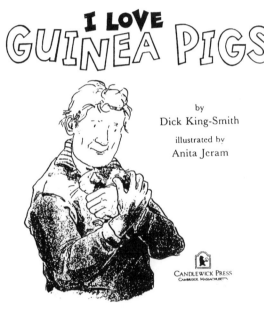

I LOVE GUINEA PIGS

by
Dick King-Smith

illustrated by
Anita Jeram

CANDLEWICK PRESS
CAMBRIDGE, MASSACHUSETTS

(information on verso)

Text copyright © 1994 by Foxbusters Ltd.
Illustrations copyright © 1994 by Anita Jeram

All rights reserved.

First U.S. edition 1995
First published in Great Britain in 1994 by
Walker Books Ltd., London.

Library of Congress Cataloging-in-Publication Data

King-Smith, Dick.
I love guinea pigs / by Dick King-Smith ;
illustrated by Anita Jeram.—1st U.S. ed.
(Read and wonder books)
ISBN 1-56402-389-3
1. Guinea pigs as pets—Juvenile literature. [1. Guinea pigs.
2. Pets.] I. Jeram, Anita, ill. II. Title. III. Series:
Read and wonder.
SF459.G9K55 1995
636'.93234—dc20   94-4880

10 9 8 7 6 5 4 3 2 1

Printed in Italy

The pictures in this book were done in line and watercolor.

Candlewick Press
2067 Massachusetts Avenue
Cambridge, Massachusetts 02140

(information on back cover)

READ
AND
WONDER
Read and Wonder Books

braries may set one of the following policies: accept CIP data as given, require further checking, or ignore it when other bibliographic sources are available. The decision should be based on the agency's need for accuracy and the alternative information sources available to them as well as the expertise of cataloging staff to improve the CIP records.

A Word About the Figures and Examples

The figures and examples included in this book have been chosen to illustrate various rules from the *Anglo-American Cataloguing Rules,* second edition, 1998 revision (AACR2-98) and, in some figures and examples, permitted options. For example, AACR2-98 rule 6.1C allows the optional addition of a general material designation (gmd) after a title proper, rule 25.5D after a uniform title. A library can choose to apply either one of these options, neither option, or both options. The figures for sound recordings illustrate all options involving the use of a gmd. (In the past, LC and NLC have chosen to list the gmd after the uniform title; since 1981, both have placed the gmd after the title proper.)

Some options illustrated in the figures and examples have not been adopted by the national libraries and, therefore, will not be found in their records. In other cases, the authors recommend LC, NLC, or both practices and have used it in all figures; for example, LC combines the bibliography note and index note into one note, a more economical method of conveying this information than the separate notes illustrated by examples in AACR2-98.

The figures in Chapter 1 have complete bibliographic records to demonstrate the use of CIP. Although the LC classification is not normally assigned to school and public library collections, it is included in these figures so that the whole CIP record will be understood.

No tracings or classification numbers are given in Chapters 2 through 6. Tracings are added beginning with Chapter 7 when subject analysis is discussed. Dewey Decimal Classification numbers are included beginning with Chapter 8. The authors have arbitrarily decided to assign unabridged Dewey numbers and LC subject headings to second-level cataloging records (that is, fuller records), and abridged Dewey numbers and Sears subject headings to first-level records (that is, simpler records). Individual libraries should make their own decisions about the level of subject analysis specificity needed for their collections.

In conclusion, the authors believe it is not difficult to do high-quality, standard cataloging. It just takes the right knowledge, a little confidence, and practice.

Notes

1.   Charles A. Cutter, *Rules for a Dictionary Catalog*, 4th ed. (Washington, DC: Government Printing Office, 1904), 12.

2

Decisions

A great many decisions have to be made before cataloging can begin, but the major decision—to adopt standard cataloging rules and practices—is the most important. Presumably, that commitment has motivated reading this book. As a result of the decision to do standard cataloging, the *Anglo-American Cataloguing Rules,* second edition, 1998 revision (AACR2-98) automatically becomes the standard for developing bibliographic descriptions and selecting headings associated with the description.[1]

Levels of Description

Unlike previous codes, which offered just one standard form of description, AACR2-98 prescribes three different standard styles, one of which must be selected by each institution for its original cataloging. These styles are called "levels." Level 1 bibliographic descriptions are the simplest and Level 3 are the most complex. Level 2 contains more information than Level 1, but less than Level 3. It is the style generally found in bibliographic utilities and, therefore, used for derived cataloging.

Level 1 descriptions may be sufficient for small general-purpose collections. Descriptions more detailed than Level 1 may contain more information than clients of those libraries and media centers require, and original cataloging at other levels will take more time to prepare and, therefore, cost more to produce. Still, although they satisfy AACR2-98's standards, Level 1 records are not considered full records by national bibliographic utilities. Therefore, the decision to use Level 1 should be made very carefully, considering not only a library's current needs, but its future needs, as well.

Level 2 requires that more rules be applied and more details be included in the records. This is the level usually chosen by middle- and large-sized general libraries whose clients use their catalogs for research purposes. Because bibliographic utilities require Level 2 description for their full-level bibliographic input standards (although simpler cataloging is acceptable also as long as it is appropriately identified), libraries and media centers that do derived cataloging will incur added costs if they remove data to conform to a chosen Level 1 standard. However, a library or media center can choose to have both Level 1 and Level 2 descriptions in the catalog. This also has some disadvantages. Inconsistent descriptions may inconvenience or frustrate searchers looking for information appearing in some records but not in all of them.

AACR2-98 Level 1 descriptions and less-than-full-level cataloging accepted by comput-erized networks are not defined in quite the same way. In fact, every library that uses any form of less-than-full cataloging—called *minimal level cataloging*—seems to have its own idea of what the records should contain. Some include one subject heading or two descriptive head-ings. Others do not permit either of these "luxuries."

Large research libraries, including the Library of Congress (LC) and the National Library of Canada (NLC), do minimal level cataloging for some of their materials, because otherwise their cataloging backlogs would become unmanageable. Together with a small but growing group of cooperating libraries known as the Program for Cooperative Cataloging (PCC), LC has helped develop a standard for less-than-second-level cataloging known as the "core" rec-ord. Core records include access points, all of which are expected to conform to current stan-dards for each heading type and include all associated authority work. The PCC aims to provide good catalog records containing enough strictly accurate data for searchers to be able to locate and identify the materials represented. In addition, the PCC formulated a set of values to guide its work and a training program to ensure that all cataloging contributed by participating librar-ies is of the same high quality as if it were full-level cataloging. The list of PCC libraries in-cludes some of the U.S. and Canada's most prestigious institutions. Yet, despite all efforts to define and produce quality products, some catalogers believe "good" cataloging means full rec-ords. They are not persuaded that core records can be good.

Level 3 is the fullest form of description, requiring that every applicable rule and bit of information be included in entries. It is not followed in many places, not even at the LC. It should never be adopted unless decision makers are certain it serves clearly defined purposes, because the work of adding extra information to catalog records is time-consuming and costly. Although it might be a worthwhile investment if the added information is used, it is wasteful if catalog users routinely ignore it.

In this book, it is assumed that most learning centers, school library media centers, and small public libraries will choose Level 1, Level 2, or something in between—call it enriched Level 1—as the most appropriate style. Most examples in this book are done at Level 2, but some are done at Level 1, and all are identified. Figure 2.1 illustrates Level 1, Level 1 enriched, Level 2, and Level 2 enriched cataloging. The first level enriched record lists other title infor-mation and a quoted note that enhances an understanding of the book's content. The second level enriched record states that the book is also available in French and gives the government catalog number that should be used if someone wants to purchase it. Second level enriched rec-ords seldom are found in public libraries and schools. The source of information for Figure 2.1 is on page 18.

FIGURE 2.1

This example is an illustration of:
- work emanating from a corporate body entered under personal author
- three joint authors
- optional addition of fuller form of personal name
- other title information
- publication date not listed, copyright date given
- descriptive illustration statement
- quoted note
- edition and history note
- note relating to numbers borne by the item other than ISBN/ISSN
- four levels of cataloging

1st level cataloging

```
Gillespie, D.I. (Douglas I.)
  Wetlands for the world / D.I. Gillespie, H. Boyd, and P. Logan.
-- Canadian Wildlife Service, c1991.
  40 p.

  ISBN 0-662-18517-X.
```

1st level enriched cataloging

```
Gillespie, D.I. (Douglas I.)
  Wetlands for the world : Canada's Ramsar sites / D.I.
Gillespie, H. Boyd, and P. Logan. -- Canadian Wildlife Service,
c1991.
  40 p.

  "The Convention on Wetlands of International Importance
Especially as Waterfowl Habitat (The Ramsar Convention)."
  ISBN 0-662-18517-X.
```

2nd level cataloging

```
Gillespie, D.I. (Douglas I.)
  Wetlands for the world : Canada's Ramsar sites / D.I.
Gillespie, H. Boyd, and P. Logan. -- Ottawa : Canadian Wildlife
Service, c1991.
  40 p. : ill., maps ; 28 cm.

  "The Convention on Wetlands of International Importance
Especially as Waterfowl Habitat (The Ramsar Convention)."
  ISBN 0-662-18517-X.
```

2nd level enriched cataloging

```
Gillespie, D.I. (Douglas I.)
  Wetlands for the world : Canada's Ramsar sites / D.I.
Gillespie, H. Boyd, and P. Logan. -- Ottawa : Canadian Wildlife
Service, c1991.
  40 p. : ill., maps ; 28 cm.

  "The Convention on Wetlands of International Importance
Especially as Waterfowl Habitat (The Ramsar Convention)."
  Also issued in French under title: Des zones humides pour la
Planete : sites Ramsar du Canada.
  DSS cat. no. CW66-115/1991E.
  ISBN 0-662-18517-X.
```

Fig. 2.1—Continues

FIGURE 2.1 *(continued)*

(chief source of information)
(title page)

Wetlands for the World:

Canada's Ramsar Sites

The Convention on Wetlands of International
Importance Especially as Waterfowl
Habitat (The Ramsar Convention)

D.I. Gillespie, H. Boyd, and P. Logan

Également disponible en français sous
le titre *Des zones humides pour la Planète : sites Ramsar du Canada*

A member of the Conservation and Protection family

(information on verso)

Published by Authority of the Minister of Environment
Canadian Wildlife Service
© Minister of Supply and Services Canada, 1991
Catalogue No. CW66-115/1991E
ISBN: 0-662-18517-X

Design: Ove Design Group

The Canadian Wildlife Service
    The Canadian Wildlife Service of Environment Canada handles wildl
matters that are the responsibility of the Canadian government. These inc
protection and management of migratory birds as well as nationally signifi
wildlife habitat. Other responsibilities are endangered species, control of in
tional trade in endangered species, and research on wildlife issues of natio
importance. The Service cooperates with the provinces, territories, Canadi
Parks Service, and other federal agencies in wildlife research and managem
    For more information about the Canadian Wildlife Service or its othe
publications, please write to:

Publications
Canadian Wildlife Service
Ottawa, Ontario
K1A 0H3

Figure 4.9 illustrates another occasion where a first level enriched record may be appropriate. The title proper "Where does the weirdness go?" does not reveal the true nature of the contents. If the subject headings shown in the CIP record on the title page verso are displayed in the public catalog together with the descriptive part of a Level 1 record, the searcher is likely to understand that quantum theory is the book's subject. However, if a public catalog does not make this connection in an easily understandable way (for example, if subject headings display on a different screen than the description), the subtitle should be added to the Level 1 record.

Subject Authorities

Choosing the right style for bibliographic description is not the only decision. Each cataloged item must also be indexed and catalog entries made for the subject headings or descriptors. Subject headings can (and should) also be standardized by selecting them from an internationally accepted published list known as a subject authority, because it provides compilations of authorized terms. The vast majority of libraries in the United States and Canada follows two general lists of subject headings: *Sears List of Subject Headings (Sears)*,[2] and the *Library of Congress Subject Headings (LCSH)*,[3] and their Canadian counterparts.[4]

Sears is a small list, contained in one volume the size of a rather lengthy book, and is used primarily in small schools and public libraries. Its broader, simpler headings may be appropriate for the materials collected by public libraries and schools. *LCSH*, however, may be a better choice if the public library or school has large numbers of materials on numerous topics, if the individual public library or school is part of a larger group sharing cataloging data that uses *LCSH*, if the library or school hopes to join such a group in the future, or if it wants to obtain its cataloging from outside sources likely to use *LCSH*. The initial decision to adopt one of the two lists, and any subsequent decision to change from one to the other should be made very carefully.

The aim of the subject index is to bring together enough work [to meet?]
the needs of searchers looking for material in the area, but not to ov[erwhelm]
works whose focus may be only marginally related to their interests. [If you]
were searching for something about bears. If the only subject [heading is]
ANIMALS, you could expect to retrieve many items about animals oth[er than]
those about bears; whereas, if both ANIMALS and BEARS were avail[able,]
bears would have the subject heading BEARS and those about other ty[pes would]
not, although works about many kinds of animals (including but not limit[ed to bears) would be]
indexed under ANIMALS. Given their relative sizes and numbers of a[vailable] [he]adings, if
Sears and *LCSH* were both used for the same collection, one could expect the *Sears* index to
bring together many more items than the *LCSH* index.

One can make the decision over which subject list to use by asking which one brings
together a better number of works—with "better" defined as not too many and not too few. The
answer will vary depending on one's view of the ideal number of retrievals per heading. Knowing that some topics, such as U.S. or Canadian history, will be heavily represented in any public
library or school library media center collection, the librarian or media specialist could make
the choice based on how well those large subject areas are treated; or, the librarian or media
specialist might decide to make the choice based on how well other subject areas are treated,
excluding the ones known to return large numbers of retrieved items.

Not only is *LCSH* a much larger compilation of terms than *Sears*, it tends to use the scientific or technical terms for topics. This may or may not be appropriate for the searchers who will
use the catalog. An elementary school covering grades K through 4 might want to avoid technical terms, but a secondary school or public library serving adults might find them acceptable. If
the group of searchers is heterogeneous, neither choice will be perfect for everyone, but it can
be geared to the needs of most searchers. Librarians and media specialists may have to assist the
rest in performing subject searches.

Despite its size and technical vocabulary, *LCSH* does not have all the terms needed to
index large specialized collections in some subject areas. Specialized subject heading lists
called thesauri are sometimes used in addition to, or in place of, *LCSH*. Thesauri often are sponsored by subject-oriented professional associations or leading libraries such as the National
Library of Medicine in Bethesda, Maryland, which sponsors the *Medical Subject Headings
(MeSH),*[5] or the Getty Art History Project in Santa Monica, California, which sponsors the *Art
& Architecture Thesaurus (AAT).*[6] Specialized thesauri are not discussed in this book, because public libraries and schools are unlikely to have the kinds of collections that require their
use. More information about them can be found in *Special Libraries: A Cataloging Guide.*[7]

Classification

Another important decision concerns the classification scheme selected to arrange materials on the shelves. Two standard general classification schemes dominate in the United States
and Canada: the Dewey Decimal and LC classifications.[8] In both countries, Dewey is the favor-
ite of school and public libraries regardless of their size. In Canada, the United Kingdom, and
many other Commonwealth countries, national libraries also use it for shelving their collections and arranging their national bibliographies. In the United States, however, LC, which
serves as the de facto national library, uses its own classification scheme. Many colleges and
universities began using it during the 1960s and 1970s when it seemed more appropriate and
economical for their larger collections, but Dewey is still used by large university research libraries, including those at the University of California Los Angeles, Northwestern University,
and the University of Illinois, as well as by special libraries and information centers; for example, AT&T Bell Laboratories and the Royal Bank of Canada.

...lly, local policies govern other marks added to classification numbers to create the ...ddresses for individual materials known as *call numbers.* shelf marks can include one or ...ore of the following: branch, collection designations (or both), cutter numbers, author letters, dates, volume numbers, etc. These are discussed in more detail in Chapter 10.

Integration of Catalogs and Shelving

Other decisions affect both the efficiency and effectiveness of catalogs and classifications. One is whether to interfile all catalog records, and another is whether to intershelve all materials. Integrating the catalog accomplishes the objectives of the catalog more fully than keeping several separate catalogs (and is our choice). It is also the method of choice for computerized networks.

Intershelving all materials has had its proponents and detractors. Studies show that *all* materials circulate better when they are intershelved, so it is recommended for your consideration.[9] Many librarians believe that the best information on some topics is contained in nonbook materials, but this information will be difficult to find and use if nonbook materials are kept out of sight in corners or locked cabinets, while books are shelved on open stacks in full view.[10]

In Chapter 3 we begin with a look at AACR2-98, the one standard set of rules for describing materials for the catalog.

Notes

1. *Anglo-American Cataloguing Rules,* 2nd ed., 1998 revision, prepared under the direction of The Joint Steering Committee for Revision of AACR (Ottawa: Canadian Library Association; London: Library Association Publishing; Chicago: American Library Association, 1998).

2. *Sears List of Subject Headings,* 17th ed., ed. Joseph Miller (New York: H. W. Wilson, 2000).

3. Library of Congress, Subject Cataloging Division, *Library of Congress Subject Headings,* 23rd ed. (Washington, DC: Library of Congress, 2000).

4. *Sears List of Subject Headings: Canadian Companion,* 5th ed., rev. by Lynne Lighthall (New York: H. W. Wilson, 1995); *Canadian Subject Headings,* 3rd ed., ed. Alina Schweitzer (Ottawa: National Library of Canada, 1992).

5. National Library of Medicine, *Medical Subject Headings* (Bethesda, MD: NLM, 1996).

6. *Art & Architecture Thesaurus,* 2nd ed. (New York: Oxford University Press, 1994).

7. Sheila S. Intner and Jean Weihs, *Special Libraries: A Cataloging Guide* (Englewood, CO: Libraries Unlimited, 1997).

8. *Dewey Decimal Classification and Relative Index,* 21st ed., ed. Joan S. Mitchell et al. (Albany, NY: OCLC-Forest Press, 1996); Library of Congress, Subject Cataloging Division, *Classification* (Washington, DC: Library of Congress, 1901-).

9. See, for example, Jean Weihs, *The Integrated Library: Encouraging Access to Multimedia Materials,* 2nd ed. (Phoenix, AZ: Oryx Press, 1991).

10. Sheila S. Intner, *Access to Media: A Guide to Integrating and Computerizing Catalogs* (New York: Neal-Schuman, 1984), 77, 136-138.

3

The Anglo-American Cataloguing Rules

Introduction

Building a standard cataloging record begins by describing the item you have according to a standard set of rules. The rule book for making this bibliographic description is *Anglo-American Cataloguing Rules,* second edition, 1998 revision.[1] The first edition, which appeared in 1967, was published in two versions, one for the British and one for the North Americans (i.e., Canada and the United States). The second edition, known as AACR2, was published in 1978 simultaneously by the three professional associations that sponsored it: the American Library Association, the Canadian Library Association, and the Library Association (United Kingdom). Since then, the second edition has been reissued twice, in 1988 and 1998, so that revisions made over the intervening years could be incorporated into a single text. An international body known as the Joint Steering Committee for Revision of AACR (JSC), supported by the three publishers, is officially responsible for all additions, deletions, and changes to the rules.

Cataloging rules must reflect the changing nature of library collections and of searchers' needs. To respond effectively to such changes, AACR has had a policy of continuous revision since its publication, a policy that was reaffirmed in 1992. The basic concepts and principles underlying its rules have not changed. Because the rule revision process is slow and deliberate, from time to time a library association publishes guidelines to answer a cataloging need more quickly than is possible through international negotiation. These guidelines are not rules; they frequently are designed to test new cataloging procedures likely be considered by the JSC when establishing formal rules.

AACR2-98, the current version of the rules, is available in four formats: (1) a clothbound book; (2) a paperback book; (3) in digital form on a CD-ROM disk, called AACR2-e; and, (4) unbound, prepunched pages, which a buyer who previously owned the rules in a loose-leaf binder edition can purchase to put in the old binder. However, new binders are no longer available. The clothbound book with its heavy-duty binding is intended for cataloging department staff likely to give it a great deal of use. Revisions must be added by cutting and pasting them into the book, or by making written notations. (Owners of the loose-leaf version not only found them easier to work with, but also to update.) The paperback book is intended for students or for library staff who refer to the rules only occasionally (e.g., for libraries and media centers that receive the bulk of their catalog records from a commercial cataloging service or a central processing unit, and catalog only items received directly). Revisions are accommodated in the same manner as with the clothbound book. The total number of users permitted to use a CD-ROM in a library or media center is regulated by the license. AACR2-e is also available as part of the Library of Congress's (LC) *Cataloger's Desktop* product.[2] One individual can license the CD-ROM for use, or several catalogers can share it if a library or media center purchases a site license.

At this writing, AACR2-e is identical to its printed counterpart. AACR2-e employs Folio-Bound Views software for access to the text, which is completely indexed, enabling catalogers to search by any word in the text. The chosen search words can be truncated and combined using Boolean operators (AND, OR, and NOT). Chapter numbers and rule numbers are searchable, as are the contents and index. Users of AACR2-e can "book mark" and highlight items by means of icons on a tool belt, similar to those found in other computer systems. Notes can be added to annotate the text, and links are available to help users move quickly through the text. Multiple windows can display different pages of text simultaneously. AACR2-e comes with a helpful "Quick Start" tutorial as well as a more general FolioViews tutorial that demonstrates all of its features.

Brief History of AACR

The second edition of AACR published in 1978 differed from the 1967 publication, AACR1, in several important ways. It had four main objectives: (1) to resolve the differences between British and North American usage so everyone could use the same rules, (2) to conform to developing international standards, (3) to facilitate the exchange of catalog records in computerized form, and (4) to accommodate identical cataloging information no matter what the physical form of the item being cataloged. Meeting these objectives was not a simple task, and understanding it requires knowing a little about AACR's history.

In 1908, the first set of international cataloging rules was devised by a group of British librarians working with a visiting party of American colleagues. The meeting of minds from opposite sides of the Atlantic Ocean was disrupted for a period during and after World War II, and the American Library Association unilaterally published a new code in 1949. But joint efforts were to resume before very long.

In 1961, due in large part to the efforts of the American theorist, Seymour Lubetzky, and others from around the world, an International Conference on Cataloguing Principles was convened in Paris. The meeting resulted in a statement of principles on which cataloging rules should be based, known afterward as the Paris Principles. Most of the delegates voted for the principles, although there were notable exceptions.[3]

Efforts following the Paris conference to forge an Anglo-American cataloging code resulted in the publication in 1967 of a code unified in name only: the *Anglo-American Cataloging Rules* (AACR1). Differences between the British on the one hand and United States and Canadian librarians on the other proved impossible to resolve, so the rules were published in two versions: a British text and a North American text. Even their titles differed, with the British using the "u" in *cataloguing* whereas the North Americans dropped it.

Despite the schism, a memorandum of agreement between the American Library Association and the Library Association (United Kingdom) provided the means for a continuing review of the rules. In 1974, an international body, the Joint Steering Committee for Revision of AACR, was formed to be the final authority on the content of the rules and their revision. One of its charges was to reconcile in a single work the North American and British texts. This goal was realized with the publication of AACR2, which was endorsed by the national library associations and libraries in Canada, the United Kingdom, the United States, Australia, and New Zealand. In addition, AACR2 has been translated into many foreign languages and adopted by a growing number of countries around the world.

Influence of International Standards

The result of JSC's labor was an integrated code that follows the rules of International Standard Bibliographic Description (ISBD). ISBD provided a uniform outline for describing all materials collected by libraries: eight elements of description and a system of punctuating them.

The elements of description were already familiar to catalogers and bibliographers as identifying elements. They included title, author, edition, publisher, etc. The order in which the elements should appear in catalog entries, however, was formalized into ISBD by authority of the International Federation of Library Associations and Institutions (IFLA) for use all over the world. IFLA's cataloging committee assigned the work on ISBD by forming working parties for various types of materials. Each working party had international representation. The first ISBD to be completed and published was the one for monographic books, called ISBD(M) for monographs.[4] Other ISBDs followed for serials and nonbook materials. Finally, a general guide, ISBD(G), was devised, which, although it was not the first, furnished a general outline to be followed in developing subsequent ISBDs and in revising those that already existed. The rule makers foresaw that changes would be necessary, so they wisely mandated reviews of every ISBD five years after publication.

The ISBD punctuation, often called confusing and superfluous by critics, was part of IFLA's efforts to make the catalog records of different countries understandable and interchangeable, either for entry into a computer or for use by catalogers who might not understand the language in which the entry was written. It is explained in greater detail in Chapter 4.

Accommodating Digitized Data

Three characteristics of AACR2 and its subsequent revisions accommodate the computerization of bibliographic information: its uniform structure for description, the system of punctuation, and the separation of description and access.

Computers are very literal in their interpretation of data—the way they recognize and manipulate it. When computer programmers write instructions for data entry and manipulation, they must account for all cases in which a particular set of characters will appear, so that the computer is not confused. Each part of the manipulation, no matter how complex, must be broken down into steps representing a single decision for the computer to make. Although it is possible to write complex instructions that tell the computer to do one thing if it encounters a book record and another if it encounters a musical score record (and, indeed, the MARC formats employ this strategy), the fewer irregularities are present, the simpler it is to write the instructions and the less possibility there is of error or misinterpretation. For these reasons, having a single, uniform structure for all bibliographic descriptions, regardless of the physical medium of the item involved, makes it easier to translate into a computer environment.

The punctuation mandated by ISBD and AACR2 also contributes to easy, uniform recognition of the elements of a bibliographic record regardless of its source, language, or the type of document it represents. This aids computers working on all sorts of records as well as helping human catalogers trying to decipher a bibliographic record in an unfamiliar language.

The advantages of the third characteristic are not so obvious. At first glance, separation of description from access might not seem to aid in computerization of bibliographic data. The rules of AACR1 instructed catalogers to begin cataloging by selecting a main entry for an item, and, then, to continue with its description. This procedure was based on the principle that the identification factor of prime importance was the author of a work. This principle worked well in the days when most books contained a single work written by a single person. But our world is now much more complex, and because we often encounter works for which authorship is difficult to determine precisely (who is the author of a video that takes many hundreds of people to create?) as well as bibliographic units that are capable of including many works in one item (laserdiscs, for example), many exceptions and alterations must be made to the basic principle.

The Magic Flute is an example of a work that has been published in various formats. Because Mozart wrote the music, there is no doubt that the bibliographic form of his name should be the main entry for a musical score of this work. Mozart also would be chosen for the main entry of a sound recording of this opera. On the other hand, a videorecording of *The Magic Flute* would be subject to the rule on works of mixed responsibility (see Chapter 4) that are entered under title. The reason for this is that, in addition to Mozart, others also have been responsible for the content of the work in which visual aspects are combined with sound to produce an opera that can be heard and seen.

Integrating All Forms of Material

The presence of a single order of elements of description for all materials regardless of their physical form was a revolutionary concept in the early 1970s. Up to that time, experts had believed that various kinds of physical forms were so distinct from one another that they had to be described differently. This belief turned out to be counterproductive and was superseded by a stronger belief that the informational content of any item could be described in the same terms. Most items have titles, sources of existence (places of publication, publishers or distributors from whom they may be obtained), dates, etc. When some experts said, "But nonbook media often have no names!" others answered, "Well, sometimes books have no names, and we will do the same thing for any nameless item." (A name is created for such an item by the cataloger.) Figure 3.1, a catalog record done at LC for a book published without a name on the title page, shows how this type of record looks when done in standard format.

FIGURE 3.1

```
Williams, Kit.
   [The bee on the comb] / Kit Williams. -- 1st American ed. --
New York : Knopf : Distributed by Random House, 1984.
   [32] p. : col. ill. ; 29 cm.

   Published without explicit title; author's hidden title: The
bee on the comb. Cf. Fine woodworking, no. 63 (Mar./Apr. 1987),
p. 6.
   Summary: The reader may discover the real title of this
allegory of seasons interwoven with the activities of a beekeeper
from clues hidden in the pages.
   ISBN 0-394-53817-X.
```

The application of the same bibliographic structure mandated by ISBD to all forms of material collected now or in the future by libraries furnished the integrated framework for description.

AACR2's developers also believed that headings chosen for items cataloged using the rules for description could be done in exactly the same way for any type of material. Certain special types of material, including but not limited to law-related works, religious works, art works, and musical works were singled out for unique treatments, but for the most part, catalogers simply choose the best headings for an item depending on the information given in its description.

Organization of AACR2-98

AACR2-98 is divided into two main sections. The first section covers description of items; the second covers their retrieval. Rules for retrieval involve the choice and form of headings, called access points, based on the description. The chapters in the first section are numbered in the ordinary way, from one to thirteen. The chapters in the second section, however, after a brief introductory chapter identified as chapter twenty, begin with twenty-one and are then numbered consecutively, twenty-two to twenty-six. This way, new chapters can be added to the first part without disturbing the numbering system of the second. Also, it is easy to remember that a chapter beginning with a two is from the second part of the book.

This mode of organizing the rules—description first, access second—was considered revolutionary when AACR2 appeared. Seymour Lubetzky, in particular, was critical of the apparent abandonment of the primacy of authorship in describing library materials.[5] But AACR2-98 is based on a belief that it is one thing to describe something, and another to decide which of its identifying elements should be headings in the catalog. The first heading chosen is called the *main* entry, and all subsequent headings are called *added* entries.

The first chapter in Part 1 contains rules that apply to all materials regardless of their physical form. At the end of Chapter 1 are rules for the cataloging of supplementary items; items made up of several types of materials, such as kits; and facsimiles, photocopies, and other reproductions. Subsequent chapters in Part 1 each cover a medium group, as follows:

Chapter 2:   Books, Pamphlets, and Printed Sheets

Chapter 3:   Cartographic Materials

Chapter 4:   Manuscripts

Chapter 5:   Music

Chapter 6:   Sound Recordings

Chapter 7:   Motion Pictures and Videorecordings

Chapter 8:   Graphic Materials

Chapter 9:   Electronic Resources

Chapter 10:   Three-dimensional Artefacts and Realia

Chapter 11:   Microforms

Chapter 12:   Serials

Chapter 13:   Analysis (parts of a larger work)

Although serials and analytics (the products of "analysis") are not physical formats, but are types of publications, each has common features that make them useful groupings for cataloging purposes. AACR2-98 is based on the principle that physical form governs the way things should be cataloged, a principle that has not gone unchallenged (see next section).

Another feature of AACR2-98 is the mnemonic numbering system of the rules. Each rule has a number in which the first digit stands for the chapter from which it comes and the second stands for the element of description to which it relates. (After the second number, a letter of the alphabet stands for each subelement within the element, and finer levels of detail are treated consistently, also.) If you want to find a rule relating to the title, the first element of description, it will be numbered x.1, in which x refers to the individual chapter involved. Because maps are covered in Chapter 3 and videorecordings in Chapter 7, a rule for map titles will be numbered 3.1, whereas a rule for video titles will be 7.1. This mnemonic numbering scheme enables the user to find things quickly as well as providing a shorthand method for referring to specific rules.

The Future of AACR

In October 1997, a conference was convened in Toronto to assist JSC in determining whether, in view of the present and future trends in information resources and information management, fundamental rule revision was appropriate and, if so, what the nature and direction of those revisions should be.[6] Called "The International Conference on the Principles and Future Development of AACR," it brought together 64 cataloging experts from 10 nations. Eleven of the participants were invited to write papers on specific topics that would serve as the basis for discussion. The papers were made available free of charge on an Internet Website, and a discussion list was established so that anyone who wished to do so could comment, ask questions, or pose additional issues to be considered. The discussion list had 650 participants from 18 countries and elicited a vigorous exchange of ideas.[7]

Delegates at the conference were assigned to a variety of discussion groups. Chief among the recommendations made by these groups were the following:

1. Add a clear statement of principles and the function of a catalog to the beginning of AACR.

2. Consider changing rule 0.24, stating that the physical form of an item being cataloged takes primacy over its intellectual content.

3. Revise the rules for cataloging serials substantively, including redefining "serial," altering rules about title changes, expanding options for information sources, allowing variations in transcribing data, and adopting a multilevel approach that considers content, physical format, and publication status.

4. Consider greater internationalization of AACR and the rule-making process.

Work proceeds on these matters as well as others.[8] The results of this conference could have as profound an effect on descriptive cataloging as the Paris Principles. Clearly, the goal of making all library cataloging interchangeable is expanding far beyond national borders or type-of-library boundaries, and the amount of new cataloging conforming to the rules is likely to grow.

Because rule revision is a slow process, new formats may appear in libraries and media centers before cataloging rules specific to that format have been developed. Figure 3.2 is an example of such a problem. This compact disc can be used in two ways: (1) as a sound recording that would be cataloged according to the rules in AACR2-98, Chapter 6, and (2) as an electronic resource that contains pictures and a video as well as music, and would be cataloged according to the rules in AACR2-98, Chapter 9. This is just one of the problems that JSC will consider in its future deliberations. In the meantime, catalogers are asked to try to fit these items, as much as possible, into the existing rules. The accommodation made in Figure 3.2 is to catalog the item as a sound recording because music is its main focus, and to give a system requirements note for its alternate use. The source of information for Figure 3.2 is on the next page, 28.

FIGURE 3.2

This example is an illustration of:
- sound disc with a CD-ROM component
- entry under performing group
- general material designation
- phonogram date
- optional omission of "sound" in extent of item (in 1st level example)
- accompanying material ephemeral and, therefore, not given
- publisher's number given in proper place in 2nd level example and in optional placement.as first note in 1st level example
- contents note
- physical description note for CD-ROM aspect
- system requirements note given after notes about sound disc
- two levels of cataloging

2nd level cataloging

```
Squirrel Nut Zippers (Musical group)
   Hot [sound recording] / Squirrel Nut Zippers. -- Carrboro, NC :
Mammoth, p1996.
   1 sound disc : digital ; 4¾ in.

   Mammoth: MR0137-2.
   Contents: Got my own thing now -- Put a lid on it -- Memphis
exorcism -- Twilight -- It ain't you -- Prince Nez -- Hell --
Meant to be -- Bad businessman -- Flight of the passing fancy --
Blue angel -- The interlocutor.
   May be used in a computer CD-ROM drive. System requirements:
minimum 8MB RAM; Macintosh system 7 or Microsoft Windows 3.1 or
greater; color monitor; double speed CD-ROM player.
```

1st level cataloging

```
Squirrel Nut Zippers (Musical group)
   Hot [sound recording]. -- Mammoth, p1996.
   1 disc : digital ; 4¾ in.

   Mammoth: MR0137-2.
   May be used in a computer CD-ROM drive. System requirements:
minimum 8MB RAM; Macintosh system 7 or Microsoft Windows 3.1 or
greater; color monitor; double speed CD-ROM player.
```

Fig. 3.2—Continues

FIGURE 3.2 *(continued)*

(information on container)

1 . . . . GOT MY OWN THING NOW
2 . . . . PUT A LID ON IT
3 . . . . MEMPHIS EXORCISM
4 . . . . TWILIGHT
5 . . . . IT AIN'T YOU
6 . . . . PRINCE NEZ
7 . . . . HELL
8 . . . . MEANT TO BE
9 . . . . BAD BUSINESSMAN
10 . . . . FLIGHT OF THE PASSING FANCY
11 . . . . BLUE ANGEL
12 . . . . THE INTERLOCUTOR

Recorded by Brian Paulson and Mike Napolitano.

℗ & © 1996 Mammoth Records. All Rights Reserved.
Unauthorized duplication violates applicable laws.
Mammoth Records The Broad Street Building, 101 B. Street, Carrboro,
NC 27510. Mammoth UK, 34-B Notting Hill Gate, London W11 3JQ.

0 35498-0137-2 0

CAUTION - EXPLOSIVE. USE ONLY UNDER ADULT SUPERVISION

DO NOT HOLD IN HAND AFTER LIGHTING

GOT MY OWN THING NOW * . . . (Mathus)

PUT A LID ON IT * . . . . (Maxwell)

MEMPHIS EXORCISM * . . . . (Mathus)

TWILIGHT * . . . . (Maxwell)

IT AIN'T YOU * . . . . (Mathus)

PRINCE NEZ * . . . . (Mathus)

HELL * . . . . (Maxwell)

MEANT TO BE * . . . . (Maxwell)

BAD BUSINESSMAN * * . . . (Mosher/Mathus)

FLIGHT OF THE PASSING FANCY * *
. . . . (Mosher/Mathus)

BLUE ANGEL * * . . . . (Mosher/Mathus)

THE INTERLOCUTOR * . . . . (Mosher)

* Shorty Brown Publishing Co., Inc./Strupt Throat Music, ASCAP.
* Hot Bat Sweet Publishing/Strupt Music, ASCAP.
* Saxaplex Publishing/Strupt Throat Music, ASCAP.

Computer Play Information
Requirements: Macintosh System 7 or Microsoft Windows 3.1 (or greater), double speed CD-ROM player,
minimum 8 MB RAM and color monitor. Insert disc into CD-ROM player and double click on README file for instructions.
(Warning: incompatible with some NEC drives). Multimedia program produced by Clay Walker.

(information on disc)

The next chapter examines the rules for description in greater detail.

Recommended Reading

Hill, Janet Swan. "More Than You Wanted to Know About How the Cataloging Rules Are Written." *ALCTS Newsletter* 4, no. 8 (1993): 93-95. Another perspective of the governance of the Joint Steering Committee will be found in "The Anglo-American Cataloguing Rules." *National Library of Canada Bulletin* 2, nos. 7 and 8 (July/August 2000): 11-12.

IFLA Study Group on the Functional Requirements for Bibliographic Records. *Functional Requirements for Bibliographic Records: Final Report.* München: K. G. Sauer, 1998.

Maxwell, Robert L., with Margaret F. Maxwell. *Maxwell's Handbook for AACR2R, Explaining and Illustrating the Anglo-American Cataloguing Rules and 1993 Amendments.* Chicago: American Library Association, 1997.

Reimer, John J., ed., *Cataloging and Classification Standards.* Binghamton, NY: Haworth Press, 1996; also published as *Cataloging & Classification Quarterly* 21, nos. 3 and 4 (1996).

Schottlaender, Brian E. C., ed. *The Future of the Descriptive Cataloging Rules.* Chicago: American Library Association, 1998.

Smiraglia, Richard P., ed., *Origins, Content, and Future of AACR2 Revised.* Chicago: American Library Association, 1992.

Weihs, Jean. "Interfaces: Cardinal Rule Change and the OPAC." *Technicalities* 19, no. 4 (April 1999): 1, 11-12.

———. "Interfaces: The Joint Steering Committee Plots the Future of AACR2." *Technicalities* 18, no. 1 (January 1998): 1, 6-8.

———. "Interfaces: Will the Toronto Tenets Replace the Paris Principles?" *Technicalities* 17, no. 5 (May 1997): 1, 6-7.

Weihs, Jean, with Shirley Lewis. *Nonbook Materials: The Organization of Integrated Collections.* 3rd ed. Ottawa: Canadian Library Association, 1989.

Notes

1.   Full citations for this standard rule book for description in the United States and Canada and major earlier editions include *Anglo-American Cataloguing Rules,* 2nd ed., 1998 revision, prepared under the direction of The Joint Steering Committee for Revision of AACR (Ottawa: Canadian Library Association; London: Library Association Publishing; Chicago: American Library Association, 1998) [hereafter AACR2-98]; *Anglo-American Cataloguing Rules,* 1988 revision, eds. Michael Gorman and Paul W. Winkler (Ottawa: Canadian Library Association; Chicago: American Library Association, 1988) [hereafter AACR2R]; *Anglo-American Cataloguing Rules,* 2nd ed., eds. Michael Gorman and Paul W. Winkler (Chicago: American Library Association; Ottawa: Canadian Library Association, 1978) [hereafter AACR2]; *Anglo-American Cataloging Rules, North American Text,* ed. Sumner Spalding (Chicago: American Library Association, 1967) [hereafter AACR1].

2.   *Cataloger's Desktop* [CD-ROM subscription, issued quarterly] (Library of Congress, Cataloging Distribution Service, 1997-).

3.   For a brief report of the Conference and the Principles, see the *Reader in Classification and Descriptive Cataloging,* ed. Ann F. Painter (Washington, DC: NCR-Microcard Editions, 1972).

4.   Two editions appeared: *ISBD(M): International Standard Bibliographic Description for Monographic Publications,* 1st standard ed. rev. (London: IFLA International Office for UBC, 1978); and, rev. ed. (London: IFLA Universal Bibliographic Control and International MARC Programme, British Library Bibliographic Services, 1987).

5.   For a good discussion of his objections to having rules for description precede those for headings, see his chapter in *The Making of a Code: The Issues Underlying AACR2,* ed. Doris Hargrett Clack (Chicago: American Library Association, 1980), 16-25.

6.   Jean Weihs, ed., *The Principles and Future of AACR: Proceedings of the International Conference on the Principles and Future of AACR, Toronto, Ontario, Canada, October 23-25, 1997* (Ottawa: Canadian Library Association; London: Library Association Publishing; Chicago: American Library Association, 1998).

7.   Jean Weihs, "Report on the International Conference on the Principles and Future Development of AACR, Toronto, 1997," *Feliciter* 44, no. 4 (Apr. 1998): 16-20.

8.   Documents on work emanating from the conference can be found at http://www.nlc-bnc.ca /jsc/index.htm.

4

Description

Decide What You Are Cataloging

Until and unless changes are made to AACR2-98's rule 0.24, the first step in cataloging any item is to decide *what* it is, in order to select the appropriate chapters of rules to apply to it. The physical form of the item determines which rules of AACR2-98 should be applied in doing the description. The first question to ask is: "Is this item made up of one part or more than one?" If there is just one part, next ask to which group it belongs, according to the following choices:

Chapter 2: Books, pamphlets, and printed sheets

Chapter 3: Cartographic materials (maps, globes, etc.)

Chapter 4: Manuscripts (including typescripts)

Chapter 5: Music

Chapter 6: Sound recordings

Chapter 7: Motion pictures and videorecordings

Chapter 8: Graphic materials (includes visual images of all kinds)

Chapter 9: Electronic resources

Chapter 10: Three-dimensional artefacts and realia (including toys, games, and "found" objects)

Chapter 11: Microforms

Chapter 12: Serials (items issued in parts intended to continue indefinitely)

The corresponding chapter, in conjunction with Chapter 1, has the rules needed to describe the item. When cataloging serials, Chapter 12 and Chapter 1 are all that are needed for print-on-paper items. If, however, the serial title is in any other physical form (such as a serially issued sound recording, videorecording, or electronic resource), three chapters will be used for the description: the appropriate chapter for the physical form, plus Chapters 1 and 12. This sounds complicated and does involve flipping to several different parts of AACR2-98, but it is not much more difficult in practice than cataloging a print-on-paper serial.

If the item consists of two or more pieces (excepting serials, of course), more questions need to be asked. The first is: "Are all the pieces in one physical medium?" Examples of this kind of item are multidisc sound recordings and CD-ROMs, and multivolume books. If the answer is "yes," proceed in the same way as if the item had only one part. Choose the appropriate chapter and begin.

If the answer is "no," another question must be answered. When a multipart item consists of pieces in more than one medium, there are two possibilities for cataloging: If one of the items is more important than the others, the item is cataloged by the chapter for the more important part, called the *predominant* piece, and the other pieces are considered accompanying material; if at least two pieces in different media are equal in importance, then the item is cataloged as a kit (or, if one uses the British interpretation of the rules, a multimedia item), using rule 1.10 (from Chapter 1) and the chapters appropriate to the media involved.

Importance is subjective. One useful rule of thumb if the relative importance of the pieces of a multipart item is in doubt is to consider whether each part of the item conveys the entire content of the item. If each does, none is most important, and the item is a kit. If none of the pieces conveys the entire content of the item, and to do so they must be used together, there is no predominant piece, and the item still is a kit. If, however, one piece conveys the entire content and the others do not, then that piece is more important than the others, and the catalog record should be made for it alone, with the other pieces treated solely as accompaniments. Figures 4.1 and 4.2 illustrate the different choices catalogers make in describing multipart items. Figure 4.1 shows a filmstrip and sound recording set in which the sound recording is considered more important because it is intended to be played with or without the filmstrip, whereas the filmstrip only contains pictures of the Gaspé that add minimally to the enjoyment of the music. This item is cataloged as a sound recording with accompanying filmstrip. The source of information for Figure 4.1 is on page 34.

Figure 4.2, page 32, shows a sound cassette, response sheets, a post test, and a teacher's guide set in which none of the parts conveys the entire content. There are references in the sound cassette to the response sheet and on the response sheet to the cassette; the post test needs both to be fully understood; the teacher's guide contains additional information on the topic. This set is cataloged as a kit.

Do not be confused if you see an LC-produced catalog record for a sound recording or printed item representing a multipart item that clearly is a kit according to the definition given here. Although the LC does collect materials that fit the definition of kits in AACR2-98, as a practical matter it has decided to select one part as being "predominant" and to catalog the rest of the parts as accompanying material. Other catalogers are not bound by this policy and can decide what an item is according to the AACR2-98 definitions.

FIGURE 4.1

This example is an illustration of:

- two-media set in which one medium is predominant
- bilingual item in which the title is in one language only so a parallel title is not given
- uniform title
- optional placement of the general material designation at end of title proper
- phonogram date
- accompanying material given in the physical description area
- physical description note
- contents note
- publisher's number note given in proper place in 1st example and in optional placement as first note in 2nd example
- 2nd level cataloging

```
Champagne, Claude.
   [Symphonie gaspésienne]
   Symphonie gaspésienne [sound recording] / Claude Champagne. --
Toronto : Mead, p1979.
   1 sound disc (19 min., 10 sec.) : analog, 33 1/3 rpm ; 12 in. +
1 filmstrip.

   May be played on mono or stereophonic equipment.
   Contents: Side 1. Study version -- Side 2. Listening version.
   Mead: SSC 1002.
```

Any of the following options can be used:
- the general material designation may be listed after the uniform title
- "sound" may be omitted from "1 sound disc"
- a statement of physical description may be added to accompanying material
- publisher's number may be listed as the first note

```
Champagne, Claude.
   [Symphonie gaspésienne. Sound recording]
   Symphonie gaspésienne / Claude Champagne. -- Toronto : Mead,
p1979.
   1 disc (19 min., 10 sec.) : analog, 33 1/3 rpm ; 12 in. + 1
filmstrip (100 fr. : col. ; 35 mm.)

   Mead: SSC 1002.
   May be played on mono or stereophonic equipment.
   Contents: Side 1. Study version -- Side 2. Listening version.
```

Fig. 4.1—Continues

FIGURE 4.1 *(continued)*

(chief sources of information)
(disc label)

(information on slipcase)

SYMPHONIE GASPÉSIENNE

claude champagne

This set consists of a record and a correlated filmstrip. The record offers two versions of the same music.

Side 1. Study Version — This side is designed to be played with the filmstrip. It presents a performance of the music with a distinctive electronic signal superimposed on the music to indicate when filmstrip frames are to be changed.

Side 2. Listening Version — This side presents the same performance without any electronic signals. It is designed solely for listening.

Instructions for record 1002 correlated with filmstrip SF1002.
  1. Load the filmstrip projector and advance to the frame that indicates when to start the accompanying record.
  2. Using the record side marked "audible signals"; start at the indicated filmstrip frame.
  3. Advance one frame at each electronic signal on the record.

The filmstrip
The photography in this filmstrip portrays the vitality of the life and land of the Gaspé region.

FIGURE 4.2

This example is an illustration of:
- kit
- publication and copyright dates unknown
- summary
- two levels of cataloging

2nd level cataloging

```
George, Miriam H.
   Reference books [kit] / author, Miriam H. George. -- Baltimore
: Media Materials, [19--]
   1 sound cassette, 30 identical response sheets, 1 post test, 1
teacher's guide ; in container 29 x 23 x 4 cm.

   Summary: The difference between abridged and unabridged
dictionaries and the use of cross references in information
searches are explained and specialized reference books
introduced.
```

1st level cataloging

```
George, Miriam H.
   Reference books [kit]. -- Media Materials, [19--]
   1 sound cassette, 30 identical response sheets, 1 post test, 1
teacher's guide.
```

(information on teacher's guide [the unifying piece])

The container is a standard box used for all Media Materials, Inc. packages of this size. All contents have title: Reference Books.

TITLE   REFERENCE BOOKS

AUTHOR   Miriam H. George, B.S.Ed.

APPROXIMATE LESSON TIME

40-45 minutes

PERFORMANCE OBJECTIVES
—Show students that dictionaries and encyclopedias have many uses.
—Practice in using guide words and cross references.
—Introduce students to the wealth of information found in atlases, *Readers' Guide, World Almanac, Dictionary of American History, Dictionary of American Biography, Current Biography, Who's Who in America, Twentieth Century Authors*, and *Familiar Quotations*.

SUMMARY
The difference between the abridged and unabridged dictionary is shown. The use of guide words in dictionaries and encyclopedias is stressed. The use of cross references in the card catalog, the Readers' Guide, and in encyclopedias is explained. Specialized reference books are introduced.

Also, do not be surprised to find interactive multimedia consisting of computer-video combinations cataloged either as electronic resources or as videorecordings, with the other type of material given as accompanying material. At this writing, AACR2-98 does not include rules for interactive multimedia materials. Assistance is available for U.S. catalogers (and others who wish to join them) in a set of guidelines approved by the American Library Association's Committee on Cataloging: Description and Access and published by the American Library Association, titled *Guidelines for Bibliographic Description of Interactive Multimedia*.[1] (Guidelines do not have the force of rules unless they are voted by the JSC.) They should not be applied to materials unless one is absolutely certain they meet all the tests of interactivity: (1) a computer must be used to access them; (2) access must be random, not sequential; (3) they must contain material in more than one medium; and (4) the user must be able to manipulate, add to, delete, change, or otherwise customize the content. Most electronic games and interactive stories that allow players or readers to write their own endings do not qualify as interactive multimedia, despite the elements of customization they contain. When in doubt, the guidelines specify that they should not be applied to the item.

Games, including handheld games with computer chips, puzzles, and dioramas are exceptions to the definition for kits. Although these kinds of items are usually comprised of many pieces in different media, they are considered single units and cataloged by the rules of Chapter 10. The AACR2-98 definition of a game is a set of objects designed to be played according to a set of rules.[2] Puzzles also fit this definition, because their pieces are designed to fit according to "rules." However, an item in several media that is not designed to be played or manipulated according to a set of rules is not a game and must be judged according to the other possibilities outlined previously. Dioramas (see Figure 4.3) are also made up of several pieces in different media, but are considered a single unit, based on their AACR2-98 definition: "A three-dimensional representation of a scene created by placing objects, figures, etc., in front of a two-dimensional painted background."[3]

FIGURE 4.3

Chief source of information (the item itself) has:
- the title and "Made in Indonesia" printed on the right hand corner of the background
- no other information is given

This example is an illustration of:
- diorama
- title main entry
- no statement of responsibility
- city of publication/manufacture not listed
- publisher and date of publication unknown
- summary
- 2nd level cataloging

```
Stages in rice culture [diorama]. -- Indonesia : [s.n., 19--]
    1 diorama (various pieces) : col. ; 90 x 60 x 30 cm.

    Summary: Shows lowland paddy rice culture from planting to
harvesting, threshing, and husking.
```

The important thing to remember about cataloging decisions is this: AACR2-98 operates on the assumption that, when in doubt, the cataloger's judgment is the ultimate authority. For that reason, you should not hesitate to exercise it. It is likely the cataloger has more training and experience in making these judgments than anyone else in the library or media center. It is better to make a judgment promptly that one decides, later, was not correct than to hold an item indefinitely until one gets help with it. A catalog record can be changed to reflect the change of mind, but patrons will have had access to the material.

Areas of Description

The ISBD structure for bibliographic description adopted by the Anglo-American cataloging community and incorporated into AACR2-98 has eight parts called *areas of description*. Learning these eight areas of description is absolutely essential to doing standard cataloging easily and quickly:

Area 1: Title and statement of responsibility

Area 2: Edition

Area 3: Material (or type of publication) specific details

Area 4: Publication, distribution, etc.

Area 5: Physical description

Area 6: Series

Area 7: Notes

Area 8: Standard number and terms of availability

Whenever cataloging any item, think in terms of the eight areas, beginning with the title. Not every area of description will be applicable to every item cataloged. For example, many items do not provide any information about the edition and, where it is not specifically stated on the item being cataloged, edition (Area 2) is left out of the description. This is also true of series information (Area 6) as well as notes (Area 7), most of which are optional. Material specific details (Area 3) are used in cataloging only a few of the media groups—serials in any physical form, electronic resources, maps, and music. However, because these kinds of materials are important components of many collections, it may be used often.

Quiz yourself about which area relates to which part of a description until you are perfectly sure that physical description is Area 5 and ISBNs (International Standard Book Numbers) are Area 8, and so on. When you know the eight areas, you will be able to use the mnemonic numbering scheme for the rules, because the first digit represents the chapter and the second digit represents the area of description, for example, rule 11.5 applies to a microform's (Chapter 11) physical description (Area 5).

Sources of Information

Think of descriptive cataloging as a puzzle with eight blank lines, each of which will be filled in according to the information appearing on the item being cataloged. There may be more information than you need or several competing sources of information on an item. Rules in AACR2-98 help different catalogers choose the same sources of information for cataloging purposes, if more than one source is likely to be present. They are numbered with a zero (.0) because they precede determining any of the areas of description, which are numbered one through eight (.1–.8). Rule 5.0B covers information sources for music, rule 9.0B covers information sources for electronic resources, and so on.

At the start of each chapter, in addition to indicating the *chief* source of information for the materials covered in the chapter, a list of *prescribed* information sources for each area of description appears. Area 1 has only one possible prescribed source for the information that goes into it—the chief source of information—because Area 1 is the most important piece of information in the entire description. People using the catalog record should be able to assume that it came from the chief source. If, for some reason, it does not—for example, because the chief source is missing from an item, or because there is no information at all on the item, which always is the case with realia—catalogers alert the user to that fact by putting the information supplied from elsewhere into square brackets and listing the source of the information in the notes (Area 7) shown in Figure 4.4.

Each area of description has specific information sources prescribed for it. Only Area 1 is limited to one source listed, the chief source. Data for all the other areas can come from any one of several sources listed. Information for Areas 5, 7, and 8 can come from *any* source, including reference tools or the cataloger's own personal knowledge. When information is taken from sources outside of those prescribed, square brackets are put around it to identify it. When appropriate, notes are made giving the sources of bracketed data.

FIGURE 4.4

This item is a mineral found in Payne Mine. When it arrived at the library, it was placed in a transparent container.

This example is an illustration of:
- realia
- naturally occurring object
- title main entry with supplied title
- source of title note
- edition and history note
- 2nd level cataloging

```
[Uraninite][realia].
    1 sample ; 5 x 7 x 6 cm. in container 8 x 8 x 8 cm.

    Title supplied by cataloger.
    From Payne Mine, Gatineau Park, Que.
```

The general principle followed by AACR2-98 about information sources is to *prefer information from the item itself over information from other locations.* Whenever a chapter covers a type of material that requires playback or projection equipment to access information on the item itself, alternatives are provided for catalogers who do not have that equipment available. Some media may have several choices for a chief source of information, such as a videocassette with opening and closing credits screens as well as labels pasted permanently on the cassette or a set of sound discs each of which has a label pasted permanently on the disc. Practical guidelines for choosing among them are furnished in the opening sections of each chapter. If you choose an alternative source as the chief source of information, it becomes the *chief source,* and information from it does not have to be bracketed, but the source should be listed in the notes (Area 7).

Cataloging requires making judgments: deciding what you are cataloging, choosing appropriate rules, choosing sources of information, and including or excluding information from those sources. Full-time catalogers become expert at making these judgments, yet they can and frequently do debate the "correct" interpretation of all sorts of details. In many cases, there is no one "correct" answer. It is a matter of making choices appropriate for the cataloger and the library or media center. AACR2-98 helps minimize the differences, but it cannot eliminate them entirely.

ISBD Punctuation

To understand and use bibliographic information from many lands in many languages, cataloging experts working under the authority of the IFLA have devised a system of punctuation that distinguishes each part of a catalog record. Unfortunately, when read all together at the beginning of each section, these punctuation rules seem terribly complicated. It is far easier to wait and put in the punctuation *after* the descriptive elements are assembled. Practicing putting in punctuation according to the standard format makes this mechanical part of preparing catalog records go much faster. Figure 4.5 illustrates the ISBD punctuation for a typical Level 2 description. You can imitate it for your own records, provided all the same elements are present, but if any element or subelement is missing, the punctuation will change, and you must consult AACR2-98 to find the correct marks. The source of information for Figure 4.5 is on the next page, 40.

FIGURE 4.5

This example is an illustration of:
- other title information
- distributor
- publishing date not listed, copyright date given
- index note
- Canadian CIP
- 2nd level cataloging

```
Reeves, Janet.
   One potato, two potato : a cookbook and more! / Janet Reeves.
-- Charlottetown, P.E.I. : Ragwood Press ; Distributed by General
Distribution Services, c1987.
   244 p. : ill. ; 23 cm.

   Includes index.
   ISBN 0-920304-70-2.
```

Fig. 4.5—Continues

FIGURE 4.5 *(continued)*

(chief source of information)
(title page)

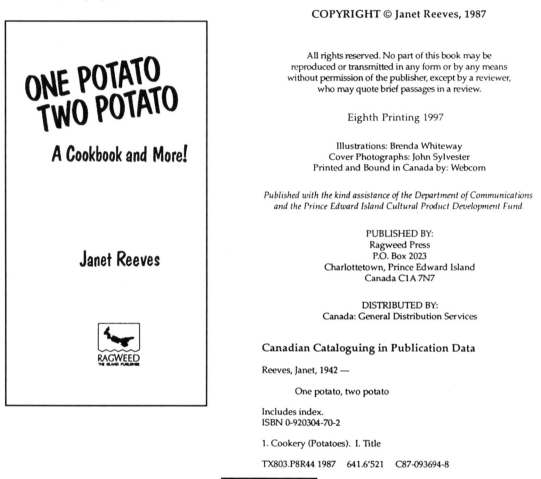

(information on verso)

COPYRIGHT © Janet Reeves, 1987

All rights reserved. No part of this book may be
reproduced or transmitted in any form or by any means
without permission of the publisher, except by a reviewer,
who may quote brief passages in a review.

Eighth Printing 1997

Illustrations: Brenda Whiteway
Cover Photographs: John Sylvester
Printed and Bound in Canada by: Webcom

*Published with the kind assistance of the Department of Communications
and the Prince Edward Island Cultural Product Development Fund*

PUBLISHED BY:
Ragweed Press
P.O. Box 2023
Charlottetown, Prince Edward Island
Canada C1A 7N7

DISTRIBUTED BY:
Canada: General Distribution Services

Canadian Cataloguing in Publication Data

Reeves, Janet, 1942 —

One potato, two potato

Includes index.
ISBN 0-920304-70-2

1. Cookery (Potatoes). I. Title

TX803.P8R44 1987   641.6′521   C87-093694-8

Keep in mind that to do their job, ISBD punctuation marks must precede the elements they identify in much the same way the statements in a computer program must tell the computer what kind of data it is going to receive before sending it (for example, to find a title or an author in a computerized catalog, many systems instruct searchers to enter statements such as "title=hamlet" or "au=shakespeare"). When a descriptive element or subelement is omitted, the punctuation that precedes it is also omitted, not the punctuation that follows it.

Area 1: Title and Statement of Responsibility

The first part of the puzzle to be filled in is the main title, called *title proper* in AACR2-98. It should be chosen from the chief source and then transcribed *exactly as it appears* on the item as to the order and spelling of the words, even if they are wrong. The reasoning behind precise transcription is to ensure that a catalog record can be matched to the item it represents, especially when several versions of a title or similar-sounding titles exist. When someone compares the catalog record with an item in hand or a listing in a bibliography, an exact match should be possible.

The layout and typography of the words on the chief source of information are used to determine where a title proper begins and ends. AACR2-98's rules aid in determining titles proper in some special cases that are encountered frequently; for example, if two separate versions of Charles Darwin's voyage appear in the two ways seen in Figures 4.6 and 4.7, then rules in Chapter 1 direct the cataloger to transcribe them as given: the first as *The voyage of the Beagle* and the second as *Journal of researches during the voyage of H.M.S. "Beagle."* When there is no rule to determine what should be done, just follow your instincts and make a choice. The worst thing that can happen is you will make a different choice than another colleague. If you discover the discrepancy at some future time, you can change the record to match your colleague's; or, perhaps the other person will decide to follow your lead.

FIGURE 4.6

This example is an illustration of:
- edition statement taken from outside prescribed sources (many libraries place such an edition statement in the note area, sometimes as a quoted note)
- publication date not listed, copyright date given
- numbered series statement
- index note
- 2nd level cataloging

```
Darwin, Charles.
    The voyage of the Beagle / by Charles Darwin with introduction
and notes. -- [2nd ed.]. -- New York : Collier, c1909.
    547 p. : ill. ; 20 cm. -- (The Harvard classics ; v. 29)

    Includes index.
```

(chief source of information)
   (title page)

THE HARVARD CLASSICS

EDITED BY CHARLES W ELIOT LL D

⁂

THE VOYAGE OF THE BEAGLE

BY CHARLES DARWIN

WITH INTRODUCTION AND NOTES

VOLUME 29

P F COLLIER & SON COMPANY
NEW YORK

(information on verso)

Copyright 1909

By P. F. Collier & Sons

Manufactured in U. S. A.

FIGURE 4.7

This example is an illustration of:

- edition statement taken from outside prescribed sources (many libraries place such an edition statement in the note area, sometimes as a quoted note)
- multiple places of publication
- publication date not listed, century uncertain
- 2nd level cataloging

2nd level cataloging for a Canadian library

```
Darwin, Charles.
   Journal of researches during the voyage of H.M.S. "Beagle" / by
Charles Darwin. -- [2nd ed. rev.]. -- London ; Toronto : T.
Nelson, [19--?]
   543 p. ; 16 cm.
```

2nd level cataloging for a U.S. library

```
Darwin, Charles.
   Journal of researches during the voyage of H.M.S. "Beagle" / by
Charles Darwin. -- [2nd ed. rev.]. -- London ; New York : T.
Nelson, [19--?]
   543 p. ; 16 cm.
```

(chief source of information)
     (title page)

Two aspects of the title proper that should not be transcribed exactly as they appear on the chief source are its capitalization and punctuation. Capitalization of all parts of the description follows standard rules contained in AACR2-98's Appendix A. Usually, in English language titles only the first word and proper nouns are capitalized, although there are cases when more capital letters are used. Different rules govern capitalization for other languages. Punctuation is not always transcribed as it appears, particularly when it might be confused with ISBD punctuation; for example, if a title begins with the marks of omission (...), hyphens will be substituted for them, so that a title such as: ... *Toward the limits of the universe* would be transcribed as: — *Toward the limits of the universe.*

Sometimes a work is published in two (and occasionally more than two) languages and has a title in both languages, as frequently occurs with Canadian government publications. Both of the titles, separated by a space-equal sign-space, are considered part of the title proper (see Figure 5.7). In other publications, however, a bilingual title does not mean that the material is a bilingual work. In Figure 4.8, despite the presence of a bilingual title on the title page, the book is not written in two languages (ᓄᓇᕗᑦ is pronounced "Nunavut" and translated into English is "Our land"). Most cataloging departments do not have the syllabic typeface to list the Inuktitut title as required for second-level cataloging, so first-level-enriched cataloging may be a simple, practical solution for titles with nonroman alphabets. The source of information for Figure 4.8 is on the next page, 44.

After the title proper, the rules suggest that a *general material designation* be given. The general material designation tells the catalog user in what physical format the work appears. AACR2-98 has two lists of permissible general material designations (gmds) on page 21. One list is for use by British catalogers; the other is for catalogers in Australia, Canada, and the United States. The two lists are an acknowledgement that, in other countries, library catalogs may be used differently or English words have different meanings, so catalogers must use the appropriate list for their location.

FIGURE 4.8

This example is an illustration of:
- bilingual title in a nonroman script
- publication date not listed, copyright date given
- unnumbered series statement
- series other title information
- contents note
- 1st level cataloging enriched

```
Weihs, Jean
   Nunavut : our land. -- M.O.D. Publishing, c1999.
   32 p. -- (Our country : provinces & territories)

   Glossary of English and equivalent Inuktitut words in roman
alphabet and in syllabics with pronunciation guide: p. 29.
   ISBN 1-89446109-6.
```

Fig. 4.8—Continues

FIGURE 4.8 *(continued)*

(chief source of information)
(title page)

(information on cover)

NUNAVUT: OUR LAND

OUR COUNTRY:
PROVINCES & TERRITORIES

ᓄᓇᕗᑦ

NUNAVUT

Jean Weihs
Illustrated by Cameron Riddle

M.O.D. Publishing
Mississauga, Ontario

(information on verso)

© 1999 Jean Weihs

ISBN: 1-89446109-6

Gmds are optional. In libraries consisting mostly of books, the gmd for books, *text,* is usually omitted and only gmds for other formats are used. If books are not your primary material, you may decide to use *text* along with all the others. Most important is that the use of gmds be consistent. Either all media (or all except one dominant medium, such as books, when a library or media center consists mostly of books) should be given a gmd, or none should, and a written policy should provide guidance to all catalogers. If you use gmds, then put them immediately after the title proper. An exception to this rule is made for uniform titles.

Following the gmd (or the title proper if no gmd is used) the rest of the title appears, called *other title information* by AACR2-98. This part of Area 1 is not required for Level 1 descriptions and may be skipped entirely if your policy is to do Level 1 cataloging. However, some titles are extremely brief. If the rest of the title (other title information) contains information that might be important to a catalog user, then it should be included. Figures 4.9, 4.10, present examples of other title information.

FIGURE 4.9

This example is an illustration of:
- other title information
- publishing date not listed, copyright date given
- detailed pagination
- bibliography and index note
- two ISBNs; the one given relates to the item in hand
- Library of Congress CIP
- three levels of cataloging

2nd level cataloging

```
Lindley, David.
   Where does the weirdness go? : why quantum mechanics is
strange, but not as strange as you think / David Lindley. -- New
York : Basic Books, c1996.
   xvi, 251 p. : ill. ; 26 cm.

   Includes bibliography (p. 227-240) and index.
   ISBN 0-465-06786-7 (pbk.).
```

1st level cataloging

```
Lindley, David.
   Where does the weirdness go?. -- Basic Books, c1996.
   xvi, 251 p.

   ISBN 0-465-06786-7 (pbk.).
```

1st level cataloging enriched

```
Lindley, David.
   Where does the weirdness go? : why quantum mechanics is
strange, but not as strange as you think. -- Basic Books, c1996.
   xvi, 251 p.

   ISBN 0-465-06786-7 (pbk.).
```

(chief source of information)
(title page)

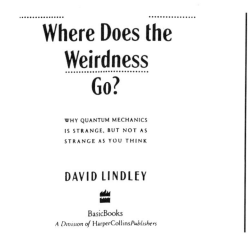

Where Does the Weirdness Go?

WHY QUANTUM MECHANICS
IS STRANGE, BUT NOT AS
STRANGE AS YOU THINK

DAVID LINDLEY

BasicBooks
A Division of HarperCollinsPublishers

(information on verso)

Copyright © 1996 by David Lindley.
Published by BasicBooks, A Division of HarperCollins Publishers, Inc.

All rights reserved. Printed in the United States of America. No part of this book may be reproduced in any manner whatsoever without written permission except in the case of brief quotations embodied in critical articles and reviews. For information, address BasicBooks, 10 East 53rd Street, New York, NY 10022-5299.

Designed by Elliott Beard

Library of Congress Cataloging-in-Publication Data
Lindley, David, 1956–
    Where does the weirdness go? : why quantum mechanics is strange, but not as strange as you think / by David Lindley.
        p.   cm.
    Includes index.
    ISBN 0-465-06785-9 (cloth)
    ISBN 0-465-06786-7 (paper)
    1. Quantum theory. 2. Physics—Philosophy. I. Title.
QC174.12.L54 1996
530.1'2—dc20
                                                    96-1049
                                                    CIP

FIGURE 4.10

This example is an illustration of:
- other title information
- publishing date not listed, copyright date given
- detailed pagination statement
- quoted note
- bibliography and index note
- two ISBNs; the one given relates to the item in hand
- ISBN qualified
- Library of Congress CIP
- 2nd level cataloging

```
Hofstadter,Douglas R.
   Metamagical themas : questing for the essence of mind and
pattern / Douglas R. Hofstadter. -- New York : Basic Books,
c1985.
   xxviii, 852 p. : ill., ; 24 cm.

   "An interlocked collection of literary, scientific, and
artistic studies"--Cover.
   Includes bibliographical references (p. 802-819) and index.
   ISBN 0-564-14540-5 (cloth).
```

(chief source of information)
(title page)

(information on cover)

METAMAGICAL THEMAS:

Questing for the Essence
of Mind and Pattern

DOUGLAS R. HOFSTADTER

BasicBooks
A Subsidiary of Perseus Books, L.L.C.

(information on verso)

Copyright © 1985 by BasicBooks, A Subsidiary of Perseus Books, L.L.C.

All rights reserved. Printed in the United States of America. No part of this book may
be reproduced in any manner whatsoever without written permission except in the
case of brief quotations embodied in critical articles and reviews. For information,
address BasicBooks, 10 East 53rd Street, New York, NY 10022-5299.

Library of Congress Cataloging-in-Publication Data

Hofstadter, Douglas R., 1945–
   Metamagical themas

   Bibliography: p. 802
   Includes Index
   1. Artificial intelligence 2. Intellect 3. Science—Philosophy
   4. Metamathematics 5. Self (Philosophy) 6. Amusements.
   I. Title
   Q335.H63 1985   001.53'5   83-46095
   ISBN 0–465–04540–5 (cloth)
   ISBN 0–465–04566–9 (paper)

METAMAGICAL THEMAS:

Questing for the Essence
of Mind and Pattern

DOUGLAS R. HOFSTADTER

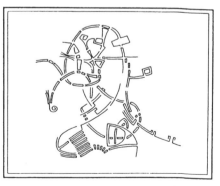

*An Interlocked Collection of
Literary, Scientific, and Artistic Studies*

FIGURE 4.11

This example is an illustration of:
- main entry under corporate body
- other title information
- responsibility not attributed in chief source of information
- edition statement taken from outside prescribed sources (many libraries place such an edition statement in the note area, sometimes as a quoted note)
- publication date not listed, copyright date given
- work consisting mostly of illustrations
- credits note
- edition and history note
- 2nd level cataloging

```
McMichael Canadian Collection.
    A heritage of Canadian art : the McMichael collection. -- [Rev.
and enl. ed.]. -- Toronto : Clarke, Irwin, c1976.
    198 p. : chiefly ill. ; 27 cm.

    Designed by A.J. Casson; biographies by Paul Duval.
    Previous ed. published in 1973 under title: A vision of Canada.
    ISBN 0-7720-1209-1.
```

(chief source of information)
(title page)

A HERITAGE OF CANADIAN ART

The McMichael Collection

Clarke, Irwin & Company Limited, Toronto, Vancouver

(information on verso)

Designed by A. J. Casson, LL.D., R.C.A.
Photography Hugh W. Thompson
Portraits of Artists by Joachim Gauthier, A.R.C.A., O.S.A.
Produced by Sampson Matthews Limited, Toronto

(information on page 16)

ACKNOWLEDEGMENTS

Paul Duval, well-known author of many books on Canadian art, contributed to the text for the introduction and is the author of each of the biographies. His assistance in the preparation of this book has been invaluable.

We are indebted to Bernhard Cinader F.R.S.C., an eminent Canadian scientist who prepared the text, *Woodland Indian Art*. He was among the first to recognize the aesthetic value of the contemporary art of the Woodland Indian, and to organize two of the first exhibitions of their work.

After eight trips to the Arctic to expand her special

© 1976 McMichael Canadian Collection
ISBN 0 7720 1060 X
Printed in Canada

16

(information on book jacket)

A Heritage of Canadian Art

an enlarged and revised study of
The McMichael Canadian Collection

Design by A. J. Casson

This new book about the famous McMichael Canadian Collection in Kleinburg carries all the impact of its highly acclaimed predecessor, *A Vision of Canada*. A completely new chapter on the Woodland Indians has been added, and sections on other indigenous Canadian cultures have been considerably expanded. A new introduction covers more fully the philosophy and history of the collection, and the works of art contained in it.

Vital Indian and Eskimo creations are presented alongside the work of the Group of Seven and their contemporaries. Masks and totems from the West Coast, stone carvings from the Arctic, magnificent landscapes of the Canadian wilderness, all combine to provide a rich record of our artistic heritage.

The book contains 1076 reproductions in black and white and 126 in full colour. Each facet of the collection is described by an expert, and sixteen individual biographies with full colour portraits of each artist by Joachim Gauthier supplement the text *(continued on back flap)*

Sometimes, if other title information is very long, it is put in the note area. In Figure 5.8, LC has chosen this way to deal with lengthy other title information in its CIP record.

The last part of Area 1 is the *statement of responsibility.* This is the place to transcribe the name(s) of the author(s), composer(s), artist(s), programmer(s), or other people or groups responsible for the overall content of the item, *provided* they appear "prominently" on the item being cataloged. Some catalogers interpret prominence as just appearing on the chief source or outer covering, but others choose to include only the names that appear in these places in large print, or that are identified as being important contributors to the work; for example, some catalogers do not give the names of writers of forewords, no matter how their names are displayed. If no names appear on the item, this element is omitted (see Figure 4.3).

Names that are important to the library or media center, but are not prominently displayed on the item being cataloged can be given in Area 7 (the note area) so that they can be used as headings, or if you want them to appear in the catalog record. Any name that is to be used as an access point must be given somewhere in the catalog record. If the name has not appeared in Areas 1 through 6, a note provides the basis for the access point. Some computerized catalogs have the capacity to search all fields of the record, so putting a name in the note field provides access without having to make a separate access point. For example, in Figure 4.11, A. J. Casson, an important Canadian painter, is listed as the book's designer on the verso and on the jacket. Usually, a book's designer is not noted on a catalog record; however, an art school media center may want to provide access to all of Casson's work in its collection. A library or media center may also want to note the contribution of Paul Duval who has written other books about Canadian artists. Because neither of these men is listed in the chief source of information, their addition to the catalog record is optional.

If more than one name is given for the same kind of contribution to the creation of the work—for example, if there are joint authors or joint producers—they are separated by commas. If more than one name is given but each is for different kinds of contributions to the creation of the work—for example, an author and an illustrator or a producer and a director—they are separated by a space-semicolon-space to indicate that they did not have the same kind of responsibility.

Level 1 descriptions are required to give only the first statement of responsibility (e.g., the author of a book, but not the illustrator; or the producer, production company of a film, or both, but not the director, writer of the script, etc.) if it differs from the item's main heading, or if there is no personal name main entry heading.

Area 2: Edition

If a specific edition is named on the prescribed sources of information for this area, it should be transcribed as it appears in the second area of description. The edition statement should be abbreviated if abbreviations for one or more of the words being transcribed are listed in AACR2-98's Appendix B or C. Figure 4.12, page 49, shows edition statements for different kinds of materials, using many abbreviations. Note that the statements, although abbreviated, transcribe the words in the order in which they appear and do not transpose them in any way.

Figure 4.12

1st ed.	(appears in item as: First Edition) (Note that if the item is a first edition, but is not labeled as such, no edition statement would be listed.)
2nd ed.	(appears in item as: Second Edition or as 2d Edition)
Colorized version	(appears in item as: Colorized version, Avanti Studios)
Rev. ed.	(appears in item as: Revised Edition)
2nd ed., rev. & enl.	(appears in item as: Second Edition, Revised & Enlarged)
2nd rev. and enl. ed.	(appears in item as: Second Revised and Enlarged Edition)
Release 3.1	(appears in item as: Release 3.1, 1999)
Large print ed.	(appears in item as: LARGE PRINT EDITION)
American ed.	(appears in item as: American Edition)
Book Club ed.	(appears in item as: Book Club Edition)

Area 3: Material (or Type of Publication) Specific Details

At this writing, four kinds of materials require use of Area 3: maps and other cartographic materials, printed music, electronic resources, and serials in all physical formats. Each of these types of material has its own information for this area, hence the name *material specific*. For maps and other cartographic items, the scale and, when found on the item, the projection and, optionally, a statement of coordinates and equinox are given; for music, the musical presentation; for electronic resources, when such information is readily available, the type of file and information relating to the number and size of files (for most items, this information is available only for files housed in a computer at a remote site, called "remote access" files); and for serials, the numbering of the first volume. Figures 4.13 through 4.16 illustrate the use of Area 3 for materials that require it.

FIGURE 4.13

This example is an illustration of:
- map
- main entry under corporate body
- general material designation
- other title information
- joint responsibility
- statement of scale and projection with optional addition of projection statement
- place, publisher, and date not listed on item; decade of publication known
- language note
- contents note
- 2nd level cataloging

```
Tungavik Federation of Nunavut.
    Inuit owned lands [map] : Nunavut / prepared by the Tungavik
Federation of Nunavut (TFN) and JLC Repro Graphic. -- Scale
1:3,000,000 ; Lambert conformal conic proj., standard parallels
at 49°N and 77°N central meridian of origin, longitude 95°W and
latitude 77°N. -- [S.l. : s.n., 199-]
    1 map : col. ; 109 x 100 cm.

    Legend in English, Inuktitut (both eastern and western
orthography), and French.
    Inset: Sanikiluao.
```

(information on the face of the map)

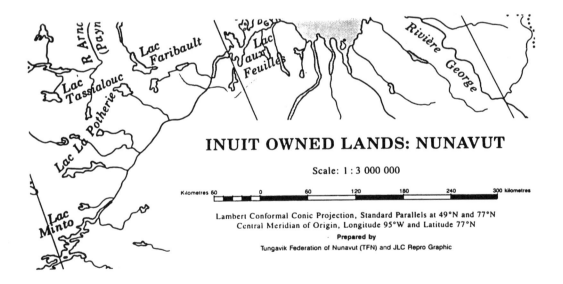

This legend is repeated in Eastern-Orthography Inuktitut, Western-Orthography Inuktitut, and French

NUNAVUT LEGEND

NUNAVUT SETTLEMENT AREA .... ————
   See Article 3 and Schedule 3.1 of the Agreement for full description

HIGH ARCTIC AREA EXEMPT FROM INUIT LAND OWNERSHIP....● ● ● ●
   See Section 19.2.6 and Schedule 19.1 of the Agreement for full description.

INUIT LAND QUANTUM

Regions	☐ Surface only excluding minerals Article 19.2.1b	▨ Surface and Subsurface including minerals Article 19.2.1a
North Baffin	31.026 sq miles	2.372 sq miles
South Baffin	23.941 sq miles	1.771 sq miles
Sanikiluaq	0 sq miles	1.001 sq miles
Keewatin	32.092 sq miles	5.040 sq miles
Kitikmeot East	13.790 sq miles	592 sq miles
Kitikmeot West	21.973 sq miles	3.852 sq miles
Nunavut Totals	122.822 sq miles	14.628 sq miles

   1 sq. mile - 2.5898 sq. kilometers

*(Regional totals above are larger than the negotiated quantum totals listed in Schedule 19.2 to 19.7 of the Agreement and the above are the actual amounts of land Inuit will own)

FORM OF TITLE
   See Article 19 of the Agreement for details, especially see
   Sub-section 19.2.1(a) and 19.2.1(b).

EXISTING MINERAL INTERESTS ON INUIT LAND
   See Section 19.2.2 to 19.2.4 of the Agreement for details.

INUIT OWNED LANDS WITHIN MUNICIPALITIES
   Not shown on this map. The following communities contain Inuit Owned Lands within their
   municipalities:

Iqaluit	Pond Inlet	Coppermine
Cape Dorset	Rankin Inlet	Cambridge Bay
Pangnirtung	Whale Cove	Taloyoak
Lake Harbour	Broughton Island	

   The Hamlet offices of the above communities have copies of maps showing Inuit Owned
   Lands within their municipality.

CROWN (PUBLIC) LANDS
   All other lands are Crown lands. Inuit have the right to hunt, trap, fish and participate in the
   management of all these lands. Please see the Agreement for more details.

TOTAL INUIT OWNED LANDS : 137,450 Square Miles

FIGURE 4.14

This work does not have a title page.

- -

The caption states:

> Symphony No. 4
> for Orchestra
> Jean Sibelius, Op. 63.

- -

The cover states:

> Miniature Score Edition
> JEAN SIBELIUS
> SYMPHONY No. 4
> in A minor
> Op. 63
> British & Continental Music Agencies Ltd.
> 125 Shaftesbury Avenue, London, W.C.2
> Printed In England

- -

Fig. 4.14—Continues

FIGURE 4.14 *(continued)*

This example is an illustration of:
- musical score
- uniform title
- optional placement of general material designation at end of title proper
- musical presentation statement (optional area 3)
- publication and copyright dates unknown
- 2nd level cataloging

```
Sibelius, Jean.
   [Symphonies, no. 4, op. 63, A minor]
   Symphony no. 4 in A minor, op. 63 [music] / Jean Sibelius. --
Miniature score. -- London : British & Continental Music
Agencies, [19--]
   1 miniature score (68 p.) ; 18 cm.
```

FIGURE 4.15

Chief source of information (the title screen) has:

Nutrition and Agriculture in Eighteenth-Century Europe
Compiled by Virginia S. Hanson.
Update 5.1   00/02/01

This example is an illustration of:
- electronic resource (remote access from central database)
- optional addition of fuller form of given names
- edition statement
- file characteristics statement
- nature and scope note
- mode of access note
- source of title note
- 2nd level cataloging

```
Hanson, Virginia S. (Virginia Susan).
   Nutrition and agriculture in eighteenth-century Europe
[electronic resource] / compiled by Virginia S. Hanson. -- Update
5.1. -- Electronic data (1 file : 650 records). -- 2000.

   Bibliography.
   Mode of access: METRONET.
   Title from title screen (viewed Mar. 31,2000).
```

FIGURE 4.16

This example is an illustration of:
- serial
- work emanating from a corporate body entered under title
- numeric and/or chronological, or other designation area
- open entry
- frequency note
- relationship with other serials note
- ISSN
- 2nd level cataloging

```
The American journal of distance education. -- Vol. 1, no. 1
   (1987)-    . -- University Park, Pa. : Office for Distance
   Education of the College of Education at The Pennsylvanis State
   University, c1987-
      v. ; 23 cm.

   Three no. yearly.
   Absorbed: Media and adult learning.
   ISSN 0892-3647.
```

(information on cover)

The Pennsylvania State University
College of Education

(information on back of first page)

©1987 The Pennsylvania State University.
All rights reserved. Published 1987
Printed in the United States of America

ISSN 0892-3647

(information on first page)

The American Journal of Distance Education
(Incorporating "Media and Adult Learning")

Editor: Michael G. Moore

 Published by the Office for Distance Education
of the College of Education at
The Pennsylvania State University
University Park, Pennsylvania

 Published with partial funding by
The Annenberg/CPB Project

The use of Area 3 is required for Level 1 cataloging, although some subelements previously listed are not, such as the projection of a cartographic item when that information is not readily available.

Area 4: Publication, Distribution, Etc.

Area 4 contains information about the location and name of the publisher or distributor of the item being cataloged and the date it was issued. For books, this information is called the *imprint.* Under the rules of AACR1, this area was identified as the "Imprint," but AACR2 broadened both its name and definition to accommodate materials that are not published like books.

Audiovisual materials are quite different. When a film or video is made, people in the industry say it is "produced." The act of production, however, is not the same as the act of distribution. For films and videos, the act of distribution is called "releasing" or, sometimes, just "distribution." Often two different companies "produce" and "release" a film or a video. Production for these materials is equivalent to the act of writing a book, and is recorded in Area 1, the statement of responsibility, or in Area 7, in the note associated with responsibility. The releasing agent, distributor, or both is named in Area 4, and is equivalent to the publisher of a book.

If there is just one publisher, the place in which it is located, its name, and the date the item was published or distributed are given. If the publisher is listed as having several locations, the first-named place always is given. However, if another place is listed more prominently, that place also is given. In addition, if neither the first-named place nor a more prominently named place is located in the cataloger's home country, a place in the home country, if one is listed, also is given.

In Figure 4.17, four places of publication are listed on the title page. The first of these—Melbourne—must be given in the catalog record. The second—Oakland—is given in a catalog record for U.S. libraries because it is the first-named place in the home country; "Oakland" is not given in a Canadian record.

FIGURE 4.17

This example is an illustration of:
- multiple places of publication
- work containing only one type of illustration
- unnumbered series statement
- contents note
- National Library of Australia CIP
- 2nd level cataloging

2nd level cataloging for a Canadian library

```
Kerr, Alex.
  Lost Japan / Alex Kerr. -- Melbourne, Victoria : Lonely Planet,
1996.
  269 p. : map ; 20 cm. -- (Lonely Planet journeys)

  Glossary: p. 264-269.
  ISBN 0-86442-370-5.
```

2nd level cataloging for a U.S. library

```
Kerr, Alex.
  Lost Japan / Alex Kerr. -- Melbourne, Victoria ; Oakland,
Calif. : Lonely Planet, 1996.
  269 p. : map ; 20 cm. -- (Lonely Planet journeys)

  Glossary: p. 264-269.
  ISBN 0-86442-370-5.
```

(chief source of information)
(title page)

LOST JAPAN

ALEX KERR

LONELY PLANET PUBLICATIONS
Melbourne • Oakland • London • Paris

(information on verso)

Lost Japan

Published by Lonely Planet Publications
   Head Office: PO Box 617, Hawthorn, Vic 3122, Australia
   Branches: 155 Filbert St, Suite 251, Oakland, CA 94607, USA
               10 Barley Mow Passage, Chiswick, London W4 4PH, UK
               71 bis rue du Cardinal Lemoine, 75005 Paris, France

Published 1996

Printed by SNP Printing Pte Ltd, Singapore

Translated and adapted from *Utsukushiki Nippon no Zanzo* (Shincho-sha, Tokyo, 1993), © Alex Kerr 1993

Author photograph by Philip Gostelow
Map by Trudi Canavan
Calligraphy by Alex Kerr

National Library of Australia Cataloguing in Publication Data

Kerr, Alex, 1952-
Lost Japan

ISBN 0 86442 370 5.

1. Kerr, Alex, 1952-
2. Japan – Civilization – 1945-
3. Japan – Description and travel.
I. Kerr, Alex, 1952 – Utsukushiki Nihon no zanzo
II. Title. III. Title: Utsukushiki Nihon no zanzo.

952.04

Text © Alex Kerr 1996
Map © Lonely Planet 1996

(information on cover)

If the item lists more than one publisher, the first-named publisher or distributor always is given. In many cases, that is all that will be required, but there are exceptions for which additional information is needed. As described previously, when another publisher is listed more prominently than the one first named, when the first-named publisher is located in a country foreign to the cataloger but a subsequently named publisher is located in the home country, two or three publishers will be given. There are some other exceptions, too, for which LC or NLC Rule Interpretations may be consulted.

If the item being cataloged does not list places or names of any publishers or distributors, the cataloger can supply the abbreviations [S.l.], [s.n.], or both in square brackets, meaning *sine loco* (without a place) and *sine nomine* (without a name), as substitutes (see Figure 4.13).

The date of publication or distribution—the third element of information included in this area—must always be given, even if the item bears no dates of any kind. There are only two exceptions to this rule; for obvious reasons, dates are not given to naturally occurring objects (see Figure 4.4), and unpublished materials are not given dates (see Chapter 6). Various kinds of dates are found on materials, including publication (or distribution) dates, copyright dates, printing dates, production dates, manufacture dates, etc. The preferred date for Area 4 is the date of *publication* or *distribution,* not the date of copyright, printing, production, or manufacture. If there are several dates, all of them publication or distribution dates, choose the one that matches the edition statement in Area 2. If there is still a choice among publication or distribution dates applying to one edition, choose the latest date for Area 4.

When there is no publication or distribution date given on the item, the next best choice for Area 4 is the copyright date. Nonbook materials are often copyrighted long before they are actually distributed, so some care should be exercised in selecting a very old copyright date for an item that clearly is a new distribution, such as might be found on a 1990s video production of a 1940s film. It is better to make an educated guess than to use a copyright date from the 1940s for a video that could not possibly have been made and distributed during that decade. The guessed date can be given in one of the following ways, depending on the degree of certainty that it is correct:

[1999] — the year is not in doubt, although its source is not one of the prescribed sources

[1999?] — the year is in doubt, although the cataloger is guessing it is 1999

[199-] — the exact year is in doubt, but the cataloger knows it is in the 1990s

[199-?] — the exact year is in doubt and although the cataloger guesses it is in the decade of the 1990s, he or she is not certain of it

A copyright date is identified by preceding it with a "c" or, in the case of some recordings, a "p," which stands for "phonogram" date.

In the absence of either a publication, distribution, or a copyright date, the date of manufacture (this is the printing date for a book) may be given in Area 4, but it must be properly identified as such.

When no dates appear on the item, the cataloger must make a guess, based on whatever information is available. One way to find a date is to look up the item in a reference work. Another is to consider the technology; for example, no microcomputer software would have existed before the 1970s, or television broadcasts before the 1940s. Sometimes one can glean clues from the item itself; for example, dress styles in photographs and other visual materials often can place the decade, if not the exact year, in which an item was made. As previously shown, AACR2-98 suggests a variety of means for expressing an approximate date, depending on one's degree of certainty and the time span.[4]

Figure 4.18 is an example of the use of research and common sense to determine an approximate date of publication. The preface is dated 1932 and the book's verso states that it is a wartime book, presumably a warning about inferior materials in its manufacture. This warning was prophetic because the pages of the book have turned brown. To what war does this statement refer? World War II is a logical assumption. In case a cataloger is unsure about paper production during the Korean or Vietnam wars, reference sources reveal that C. H. Best, a well-known scientist who participated in the discovery of insulin, was active professionally during World War II. This book was printed in the United States that entered the war in December 1941. Therefore, the dates 1942-1945 are the probable range of years in which this book was published. The source of information for Figure 4.18 is on the next page, 58.

FIGURE 4.18

This example is an illustration of:
- joint responsibility
- other title information
- edition statement taken from outside prescribed sources (many libraries place such an edition statement in the note area, sometimes as a quoted note)
- estimated date of publication
- both black and white and colored illustrations
- publication note
- index note
- 2nd level cataloging

```
Best, C.H.
   The human body and its functions : an elementary text-book of
physiology / by C.H. Best and N.B. Taylor. -- [Special ed.]. --
New York : H. Holt, [1942-1945]
   371 p. : ill. (some col.) ; 20 cm.

   "A wartime book". Pref. dated 1932.
   Includes index.
```

(information on verso)

(information on spine)

Title Proper

Author's Surnames

Special Edition

A WARTIME BOOK

THIS COMPLETE EDITION IS PRODUCTS IN FULL COMPLIANCE WITH THE GOVERN-MENT'S REGULATIONS FOR CONSERVING PAPER AND OTHER ESSENTIAL MATERIALS

PRINTED IN THE
UNITED STATES OF AMERICA

Chief source of information on p. 58.

FIGURE 4.18 *(continued)*

(chief source of information)
(title page)

THE HUMAN BODY
AND ITS FUNCTIONS

AN ELEMENTARY TEXT-BOOK OF PHYSIOLOGY

BY

C. H. BEST, M.A., M.D., D.Sc. (Lond.), F.R.S. (Canada),
F.R.C.P. (Canada)
Professor of Physiology and Director of the Department, Associate
Director of the Connaught Laboratories, Research Associate
in the Banting-Best Department of Medical Research,
University of Toronto

AND

N. B. TAYLOR, M.D., M.R.C.S. (Eng.), L.R.C.P. (Lond.),
F.R.C.S. (Edin.), F.R.C.P. (Canada)
Professor of Physiology, University of Toronto

NEW YORK
HENRY HOLT AND COMPANY

Level 1 records require only that the first publisher's name and the date be given.

Area 5: Physical Description

Physical descriptions are divided into four main elements: (1) the number and kind of pieces, called the *extent of item* that specifies the specific material designation (smd) and also can include duration for some media; (2) other physical details (such as illustrative matter in books, sound and color for visual materials, etc.); (3) dimensions; and (4) accompanying materials, if any. The physical details and dimensions vary with the medium as do the number and kind of pieces involved. Accompanying materials, which consist of additional pieces that are physically separate from the item being cataloged, are treated in the same manner for virtually all materials.

The extent of books is given as the number of pages, "pages" being the smd. "Pages" is by far the most frequently encountered smd for books, but it is not the only one. If a book has leaves (pages with text on only one side), then "leaves" is the smd. Each chapter of rules for individual media groups has different kinds of information to be given in this area, appropriate to the particular media groups involved.

As mentioned, books are described in terms of their pagination or, when there is more than one volume, in terms of the number of volumes. A special case is books issued with loose-leaf pages. For these items, only the number of volumes is given, with the word "loose-leaf" following in parentheses. Another special case encountered frequently enough to address here is the presence of plates in a book. Plates usually are not part of the regular sequence of pages. By definition, they are separate pages bound in with a text after it is prepared. Thus, plates are considered a separate part of the extent and are counted and listed after the regular pagination.

Electronic resources, sound recordings, and videos are described in terms of the number of disks, cartridges, cassettes, reels, or other carrier types. Motion pictures usually are described in terms of the number of film reels, although carriers other than reels may be encountered. Microforms, like motion pictures, may be described as reels of film, but they also can be fiches, opaques, etc. Because it is not possible to anticipate development of media formats, the rules in some AACR2-98 chapters allow catalogers to create an appropriate smd for an item when it cannot be described satisfactorily using one of the smds listed in that chapter. For example, Chapters 7, 8, 9, and 10 have such a provision, because visual and three-dimensional materials come in unusual shapes and forms, some of which have commonly accepted names to describe them.

The abbreviation "ill." is given for illustrations in printed materials and their reproductions; for example, microforms. Tables, illustrated title pages, and minor illustrations are not considered "ill." Optionally, specific types of illustrations may be given.[5] This option has been adopted for demonstration purposes in the figures and examples in this book.

Examples follow (Figure 4.19) of typical physical descriptions for materials covered by individual chapters of AACR2-98. Only the extent is required in Level 1 descriptions. However, some additional elements may need to be given in Level 1 records to alert users to necessary equipment, such as the dimensions of videodiscs or the disks associated with electronic resources. Notice, also, that the spelling of disc/disk varies for electronic resources: magnetic disks are spelled with a "k"; optical discs are spelled with a "c." Sound and videodiscs are spelled with the "c."

Figure 4.19

Books

[132] leaves ; 20 cm. (all unpaged leaves with no illustrations)

3 v. (124 p., 243 p., 222 p.) : ill., maps ; 28 cm. (multivolume set with pagination for each volume, an AACR2-98 option)

xvi, 245 p. ; 23 cm. (includes numbering of preliminary pages)

x, 245 p., [10] p. of plates : ill. ; 23 cm. (includes numbering of preliminary pages and total number of unpaged plates)

1 v. (loose-leaf) : ill., maps (some col.) ; 29 cm.

84 p. : all ill. ; 29 cm. (contains no text except captions)

84 p. : chiefly ill. ; 29 cm. (contains some text)

Fig. 4.19—Continues

FIGURE 4.19 *(continued)*

Nonbook Materials

    1 map : col. ; 60 x 80 cm.

    10 leaves : parchment ; 30 cm. (for a manuscript)

    1 score (27 p.) ; 32 cm. + 5 parts

    1 sound disc (60 min.) : digital, stereo. ; 4 3/4 in.

    4 videocassettes (60 min. each) : sd., col. ; 1/2 in.

    1 art original : oil on canvas; 45 x 60 cm.

    1 art print : engraving, col. ; 31 x 42 cm.

    1 electronic disk : sd., col. ; 3 1/2 in. + 1 user manual

    1 quilt : cotton, blue and yellow ; 120 x 100 cm.

    3 microfiches (100 fr. each) ; ill. (standard dimensions omitted)

        v. : ill. ; 28 cm. (open serial record, with no extent; note that three spaces are left for future entry of the number of volumes)

Area 6: Series

    If an item belongs to a series, the name of the series is given in this area. Like a title proper, the main title of a series is transcribed exactly as it appears on the item, even if you want to make a heading for it that is slightly different. When they are important for identification, statements of responsibility associated with a series may be given, also. If an International Standard Serial Number (ISSN) has been assigned to the series or a number within the series has been given to the item, this is included. Some items that appear regularly have both ISBNs and ISSNs, which makes it possible for catalogers to treat them either serially or monographically (see Figure 4.20). A policy should be developed for such materials, or should be determined on a case-by-case basis in the library or media center, depending on the types of materials involved and the needs of searchers.

    This area of description does not have to be included in Level 1 cataloging; you can omit it if that is your library's policy. However, if you think it is important to have the series title as an access point in your catalog, for example, if you think people will want to find all the titles in the series, you should give the series in the catalog record so the basis for the heading in the tracing and added entry is clear. The source of information for Figure 4.20 is on page 62.

FIGURE 4.20

This example is an illustration of:
- named conference
- entry under corporate body (name of conference)
- joint editors
- place of publication supplied
- bibliography and index note
- serial
- marks of omission
- open entry
- frequency note
- source of title note
- title information note
- relationship with other serials note
- ISBN and ISSN

2nd level cataloging as a monograph

```
Clinic on Library Applications of Data Processing(34th : 1997 :
     University of Illinois at Urbana-Champaign)
  Visualizing subject access for 21st century information
resources / edited by Pauline Atherton Cochrane, Eric H. Johnson
with the editorial assistance of Sandra Roe. -- [Urbana, Ill.] :
Graduate School of Library and Information Science, University of
Illinois at Urbana-Champaign, 1998.
  176 p. : ill. ; 24 cm.

  Includes bibliographical references and index.
  ISBN 0-87845-103-X.
```

2nd level cataloging as a serial

```
Clinic on Library Applications of Data Processing(University of
     Illinois at Urbana-Champaign)
  Papers presented at the ... Clinic on Library Applications of
Data Processing. -- 1980-    . -- [Urbana, Ill.] : Graduate
School of Library and Information Science, University of Illinois
at Urbana-Champaign, c1981-    .
     v. : ill. ; 24 cm.

  Annual.
  Title from half-title page.
  Each issue has a distinctive title.
  Continues: Proceedings of the Clinic on Library Applications of
Data Processing.
  ISSN 0069-4789.
```

Fig. 4.20—Continues

FIGURE 4.20 *(continued)*

(chief source of information)
(title page)

VISUALIZING SUBJECT
ACCESS FOR 21ST CENTURY
INFORMATION RESOURCES

Edited by
PAULINE ATHERTON COCHRANE
ERIC H. JOHNSON

with the editorial assistance
of Sandra Roe

GRADUATE SCHOOL OF LIBRARY AND INFORMATION SCIENCE
UNIVERSITY OF ILLINOIS AT URBANA-CHAMPAIGN
1998

(information on page opposite title page

VISUALIZING SUBJECT
ACCESS FOR 21ST CENTURY
INFORMATION RESOURCES

PAPERS PRESENTED AT THE
1997 CLINIC ON LIBRARY APPLICATIONS OF DATA PROCESSING
MARCH 2-4, 1997
GRADUATE SCHOOL OF LIBRARY AND INFORMATION SCIENCE
UNIVERSITY OF ILLINOIS AT URBANA-CHAMPAIGN

(information on page preceding title page)

CLINIC ON LIBRARY APPLICATIONS
OF DATA PROCESSING: 1997

(information on verso)

© 1998 The Board of Trustees of The University of Illinois
Manufactured in the United States of America
Printed on acid-free paper

ISBN 0-87845-103-X   ISSN 0069-4789

Area 7: Notes

With some exceptions, notes are optional, even when one does Level 2 or 3 cataloging; however, there are some notes a cataloger is directed to make in rules governing the other areas of description. One of the most frequently encountered examples of such required notes is that which must be made if the title proper is taken from outside the chief source or is made up by the cataloger. In the note, the cataloger explains where the name came from. "Title supplied by cataloger" and "Title from cover" are seen often in catalog records, explaining the source of bracketed titles proper. When cataloging electronic resources, notes explaining the source of the title proper, the source of the edition statement if different from the source of title proper, and the systems requirements are mandated and cannot be left out of the record, even for Level 1 descriptions.

To promote uniformity and consistency, the order in which notes should appear is laid out by AACR2-98. These basically follow the order of descriptive elements, with notes relating to titles given before notes relating to editions, notes relating to editions before notes relating to publication, distribution, etc. AACR2-98 does allow that a particularly important note may be the first written. The decision to place a particular note first should be made on a medium-by-medium basis, not item-by-item. For example, a decision has been made to give the publisher's or producer's number first for all sound recordings, not just for some. National standards do not recognize such decisions made locally; only when the change is approved by the appropriate national bodies will it be considered standard practice. In the United States, approval has been granted to give the publisher's or producer's numbers note for sound recordings first, but not the physical description note for videorecordings. "VHS" should not be given before other notes, but placed in the order set by AACR2-98 in rule 7.7B. Unlike LC, NLC follows the order of notes prescribed in AACR2-98.

Other notes that are important to make even when not required are the following:

1. *Physical description*: For some nonbook media, such as videorecordings and electronic resources, there is no other place to include important information about the hardware with which an item must be used. The physical description note is the place to tell people whether they need a VHS or Beta videocassette recorder, or an IBM-PC, or Macintosh computer. Even if it seems rather complicated and time-consuming to make this note, the information is essential and this is the only place in the catalog record where it might be put.

    Because AACR2-98 gives specific directions about information that can be listed in the physical description area, other useful information about physical details must be placed in the note area. For example, Figure 4.21 shows a note informing the catalog user that the book consists chiefly of photographs.

FIGURE 4.21

This example is an illustration of:
- title main entry with no statement of responsibility listed on the item
- other title information
- descriptive illustration statement
- all illustrations are in color
- illustration note
- index note
- also issued note (used for information about items not part of the collection)
- colophon as source of information
- 2nd level cataloging

Fig. 4.21—Continues

FIGURE 4.21 (continued)

```
The chateaux of the Loire : 66 locations, 291 photos. -- Blois,
   France : Valoire, 1997.
   127 p. : col.ill., geneal. table, map, ports. ; 27 cm.

   Consists chiefly of photographs.
   Includes index.
   Also issued in Dutch, French, German, Spanish, Swedish, and
other languages.
```

(chief source of information)
(title page)

(information in colophon)

Photographs by Editions Valoire
with the collaboration of P. Viard
and the assistance of Messrs. Berneron (p. 44 c) and Velut (p. 120 b, p. 97);
© Conseil Général du Loiret - Photos Dominique Chauveau (p. 12 a/b);
Photélico-Berger (pp. 14 b, 77 a); Héliflash (p. 19 b).
All rights reserved. Reproduction prohibited.
Printed in the EU. Legal deposit: 3rd quarter 1997.
ISBN 2-909575-03-9

2. *Contents notes*: These should be made whenever an item contains more than one *work*, such as a book of several short stories, a CD-ROM with two or more titles, or a microcomputer software package containing more than one program. If you have a 200-page book with one poem on each page, you may not want to make a contents note with 200 titles in it. Between the extremes of very few and a great many titles, the cataloger must use judgment. The decision should rest on an estimate of how many times people really want only one of the works, and how likely it is they can find it without the data in the catalog entry. Most people do not expect to find the names of individual poems listed in a library catalog, but hope to find individual short stories, plays, computer programs, musical suites, or other works of some length that could also be available individually. Another reason to make contents notes is to facilitate making added entries for the individual works. An added entry is not made for a title unless it is given somewhere in the catalog record. For example, a cataloger can choose to make added entries for all the items listed in the contents note in Figure 4.22, or select only pertinent items for added entry treatment. The source of information for Figure 4.22 is on page 66.

3. *Summaries*: These should always be made for items that are not available for browsing, or items having very little eye-readable information for the browser to use, unless the rest of the catalog record describes the subject content clearly. Films, videos, electronic resources, and other costly materials often are kept on closed shelves or stored in blank cans, boxes, or bags. If the searcher has to rely on the catalog record to decide if it is what they want, they should find enough information to make that decision. Summaries help a great deal (see Figure 4.23). Children's materials cataloged at LC under its Annotated Card Program automatically receive brief objective summaries to aid searchers in deciding whether a particular title is relevant to their needs. This program is discussed in greater detail in Chapter 9.

FIGURE 4.22

This example is an illustration of:
- electronic resource (CD-ROM)
- title main entry
- no statement of responsibility
- edition statement
- publication date not listed, copyright date given
- accompanying material
- systems requirements note
- source of title note
- contents note
- two levels of cataloging

2nd level cataloging

```
The 1999 Canadian encyclopedia [electronic resource]. -- Version
    5, World ed. -- Toronto : McClelland & Stewart, c1998.
    2 computer optical discs : sd., col. ; 4¾ in. + 1 user guide.

    Systems requirements: Windows 3.1 or Windows 95 or Macintosh
68040 and Power PC or higher; double speed CD-ROM drive.
    Title from title screen.
    Contents: Disc 1. The Canadian encyclopedia, The Columbia
encyclopedia (5th ed.), The Gage Canadian dictionary (recently
rev.), over 700 articles from Maclean's magazine, French-English
and English-French dictionary, Thesaurus, Timeline of Canadian
and world events, Canadiana quiz, CanuckletHead interactive quiz
-- Disc 2. The prime ministers.
```

1st level cataloging

```
The 1999 Canadian encyclopedia [electronic resource]. -- Version
    5, World ed. -- McClelland & Stewart, c1998.
    2 computer optical discs.

    Systems requirements: Windows 3.1 or Windows 95 or Macintosh
68040 and Power PC or higher; double speed CD-ROM drive.
    Title from title screen.
```

Fig. 4.22—Continues

FIGURE 4.22 *(continued)*

(information on disc)

Title screen on disc 1 states:
    The 1999 Canadian Encyclopedia:
        World Edition

Title screen on disc 2 states:
    The Prime Ministers

(information on insert)

User Guide advertises other versions of the
Canadian Encyclopedia

FIGURE 4.23

Chief source of information (the item itself) has:
- the title on a label affixed to the mount
- no other information is given

This example is an illustration of:
- transparency
- unpublished, unique item with a stated title and no indication of responsibility
- title main entry
- general material designation
- probable date
- audience level
- summary
- 2nd level cataloging

```
The Internal-combustion automobile engine [transparency]. --
   [1989?]
   1 transparency (7 overlays) : col. ; 26 x 20 cm.

   Intended audience: Grade 8 and up.
   Summary: Shows the fundamental structure and parts of a typical
six-cylinder, overhead-valve, internal combustion gasoline
automobile engine.
```

———————

4.   *Details of the library's copy*: This is the place to give whatever information is necessary about torn pages, special markings, autographs, other details, or all that do not apply to anyone else's copy of an item (see Figure 4.24). It is the place indicated by AACR2-98 for purely local information that you believe you must include, which is not universally applicable to that title.

5.   *Numbers on the item*: This note should not be confused with Area 8 (standard numbers). This is the place to give numbers other than the ISBN or ISSN that appear on an item; for example, videos often carry distributors' numbers and books often include LC Control Numbers (LCCNs). LCCNs once were used primarily for ordering LC printed catalog cards and the acronym stood for Library of Congress Card Number, but after the advent of online cataloging, the term was broadened to "Control" number and identifies LC's MARC records as well as their card counterparts. A library or media center should develop a policy about whether to list such numbers after giving careful consideration as to whether their usefulness for identification warrants the cost of adding them to catalog records.

FIGURE 4.24

This example is an illustration of:
- main entry indicated by typeface
- statement of subsidiary responsibility
- publishing date not listed, copyright date given
- all illustrations are in color
- unnumbered series statement
- audience level
- contents note
- copy being described note

2nd level cataloging for a Canadian library

```
Blum, Mark.
   Coral reef / photographs by Mark Blum ; text by Andrea Holden-
Boone. -- Toronto : Somerville House, c1998.
   32 p. : col. ill. ; 21 cm. -- (Eye to eye books)

   Audience level: ages 8-12.
   Includes Glossary (p. 31) and index.
   Library's copy has the 24 stereograph cards and viewer
detached and placed in back pocket.
   ISBN 1-894042-06-9.

N.B.  If a U.S. library wishes to indicate that this book has
also been published in the United States, a cataloger would add
the place of publication in square brackets, if known.  If the
place of publication cannot be ascertained, the publication,
distribution, etc., statement would read: Toronto ; United
States : Somerville House, c1998.
```

(chief source of information)
(title page)

Photographs By
Mark Blum

Text By
Andrea Holden-Booone

Somerville House Publishing
Toronto

(information on back cover)

(information on verso)

Copyright © 1998 by Somerville House Books Limited
Photographs © 1998 by Mark Blum

ISBN: 1-894042-06-9

Illustrated by Julian Mulock
Art Director: Neil Stuart
Design: FiWired.com
Printed in Hong Kong

Published simultaneously in the United States by
Somerville House, USA

Published in Canada by
Somerville House Publishing
a division of Somerville House Books Limited
3080 Yonge Street, Suite 5000
Toronto, Ontario M4N 3N1

This book includes:
- 3-D StereoFocus™ viewer
- 24 full-color sterogrpahic cards
  and a handy storage pocket
- 32 pages of facts, photos, and
  illustrations

For Ages 8-12
$13.95
Book printed in CHINA
Lenses manufactured in U.S.A.
Copyright©1998 Somerville House
Books Limited

Area 8: Standard Numbers and Terms of Availability

The final area of description is used for the ISBN or ISSN and the purchase price, rental fee, or other terms of availability for the item. No other numbers are given in Area 8; numbers other than the ISBN or ISSN are put in the note just described above. From their names, it appears that only books and printed serials have standard numbers, but they sometimes are given to other kinds of materials, particularly by publishers who produce nonbook materials as well as books. Most notably, ISBNs are assigned to some microcomputer software packages and videos, and ISSNs may be given both to nonbook and printed serials.

When there is no standard number, Area 8 can be left blank or only the terms of availability recorded, if desired. Terms of availability are optional and not required for any level of cataloging, but because they may be used by the circulation staff to determine the cost of a lost item, it may be important to record them. Prices fluctuate considerably over time and it might be better to consider recording the price of an item in the inventory record (usually in the shelflist) rather than in the catalog record when the two files are maintained separately. If they share a single file, as tends to be the case with integrated computer systems, the price in Area 8 becomes the inventory record.

Should the policy be to record prices in the catalog record, bear in mind the following two caveats:

1. If a purchased item was published or released more than two years earlier, the price given on the item may differ from the price at which it can now be purchased. The practice of LC and other cataloging agencies is to record the price only when cataloging an item within two years of its original publication or distribution date.

2. When the price is recorded, make sure it is the retail price, not a discounted price paid by your media center. For example, if the information on the item says $47.95 but your center receives a 30 percent discount from the supplier and only paid $33.56, record the higher price given on the item, not the actual price paid. Other media centers might receive a higher discount or no discount. What is important here is the price at which the item is listed by its publisher or distributor.

Data that should be added to the ISBN or ISSN are the type of binding (i.e., whether a book is bound with cloth or paper covers) and quality of the paper used (whether it has been treated to reduce acidity). These subelements will be given in parentheses following the ISBN or ISSN number, as follows:

ISBN 0-8389-0624-9 (alk. paper)
ISBN 0-8389-7809-6 (pbk.)

Punctuating Areas of Description

Each area of description is preceded by a period-space-dash-space (. —). AACR2-98 allows the option of starting certain areas with a new paragraph (Areas 1, 5, 7, 8). When this is done, the — punctuation is omitted before the area.

In the United States and Canada, it is customary when preparing catalog records to put Areas 1 through 4 together in one paragraph, Areas 5 and 6 in a second paragraph, and each note of Area 7 in a separate paragraph. Area 8 is also put in a separate paragraph. In some countries, it is customary to have all the elements of description in one paragraph, so it is useful to have the period-space-dash-space to separate and define them.

Within each area of description, other punctuation marks separate the parts of that area. Colons (:), semicolons (;), slashes (/), and commas (,) are used for several kinds of identification, whereas the equals sign (=) denotes the same data in another language, and the plus sign (+) identifies accompanying materials in the last part of Area 5. In Area 1, colons separate title proper from the rest of the title; in Area 4, they separate the place of publication from the name of the publisher; and in Area 5, they separate the extent and smd from other physical details. Slashes identify statements of responsibility in Areas 1, 2, 6, and 7. Within statements of responsibility, semicolons separate names when their types of responsibility differ, but commas are used when the responsibilities are the same, but shared by more than one person. A few examples follow, although they are merely possibilities; the way data are transcribed in the catalog record will depend on the exact words that appear on each item being cataloged:

1. A book written by one person, illustrated by another, and edited by a third party:

    / by Sheila S. Intner ; illustrated by Jean Weihs ; edited by John Robert Jones.
    (All the words given above appear on the title page as shown.)

2. A book written by all three:

    / by Sheila S. Intner, Jean Weihs, John Robert Jones. (The word "by" appears on the title page, with the names listed underneath.)

3. A book written by two people and edited by a third:

    / by Sheila S. Intner, Jean Weihs ; [edited by] John Robert Jones.
    (The words "edited by" do not appear on the title page and are supplied by the cataloger to explain Jones's contribution to the book.)

Whenever colons, semicolons, and slashes are used in ISBD punctuation, a space is put both before and after the mark. Commas and periods (called "full stops" in AACR2-98) only have one or two spaces after the mark, depending on how the mark is used, none before it. It may be difficult to decide whether a mark is part of ISBD punctuation or just an ordinary grammatical mark, as you might expect to find in the sentences of a summary note. Catalogers need not worry a great deal about errors in punctuation because most patrons do not notice them and these errors rarely affect retrieval.

Rule Interpretations

Helpful hints on applying the rules of AACR2-98 are given to catalogers by the policy makers at LC and NLC. These hints reflect the official policies of these bodies and are published by LC in its *Cataloging Service* bulletin, an inexpensive periodical produced twice a year. NLC, which once published its rule interpretations (RI) in a periodical titled *Bibliotech* has discontinued it, and now communicates RIs via the Internet.[6] Printed copies of Internet announcements are made available upon request. Although LC and NLC rule interpretations (LCRIs and NLCRIs) do not have the same authority as do the rules of AACR2-98, they carry the weight of the largest and most important originators of catalog records in the United States and Canada, respectively. In addition, the major computerized bibliographic networks follow them. Following LCRIs, NLCRIs, or both, or just using AACR2-98 and interpreting it on your own, is a matter of policy for your library or media center; however, a strong argument in favor of using LCRIs, NLCRIs, or both is that a more standard record will be produced because decisions are guided by national-level policies.

The more that derived cataloging records are changed, the more expensive the cataloging will be. However, a library or media center should consider whether a particular RI decision is best for its collection. For example, LC does not apply rule 21.0D1 to designate the function performed by a person named in a heading. You may want personal names categorized by function; for example, for picture book authors and illustrators, or to distinguish between authors and editors.

Summary of Areas of Description

To recapitulate, the cataloging record done at the second level of description should contain the following information whenever it is available from the appropriate sources of information on the item being cataloged (omissions for first level descriptions are given in parentheses):

1. Title proper, gmd if used, other title information, and statements of responsibility that appear prominently on the item. (Level 1 omits other title information and includes the first statement of responsibility only when it differs from the main heading or when there is a title main entry.)

2. Edition statement and a statement of responsibility for this edition. (Statement of responsibility is not given at Level 1.)

3. Material specific details are given for maps, music, electronic resources, and serials. (Some elements are omitted at Level 1.)

4. First place, name of publisher, and date of publication, distribution, etc., and, if appropriate, additional places, names, and dates are included. (At Level 1, only the name of the first publisher and the date of publication, distribution, etc., are required.)

5. Number and type (smd) of physical materials and for some media, duration, comprising the item being cataloged, other physical details, dimensions, and accompanying materials (if any) are given. (Only the number and type, and for some media, the duration, of physical materials comprising the item being cataloged must be given at Level 1.)

6. Series title and the number of the title being cataloged within the series are given. If needed for identification, a statement of responsibility for the series may be added. (The series area is omitted entirely at Level 1.)

7. Notes are optional, with some exceptions, regardless of the level of description being followed. But if a note is mandated or if the omission of a note would affect the use of the item, it is included in the catalog record.

8. Standard numbers (ISBN, ISSN) are given and, optionally, the terms of availability. (Terms of availability are omitted at Level 1.)

Figures 4.25 through 4.34, pages 72–81, present examples of the chief sources of information that might be encountered in a typical public library or school library media center. Try cataloging them according to first level description, then according to second level description. Completed descriptions are given in Appendix C.

FIGURE 4.25

(information on container)

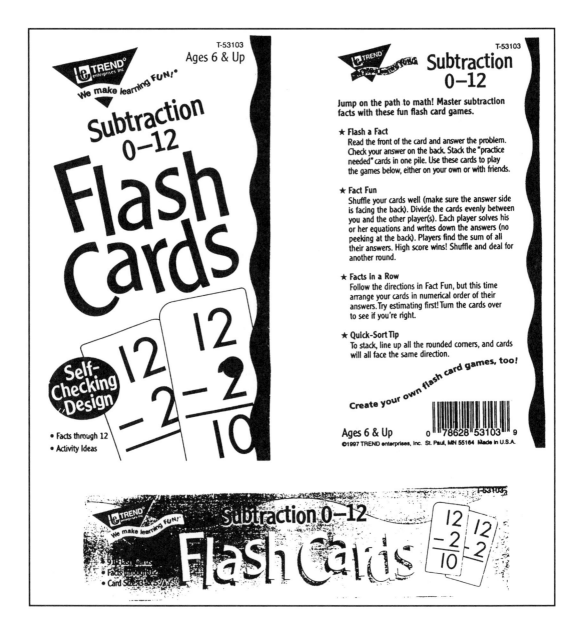

FIGURE 4.26

(chief source of information)
(title page)

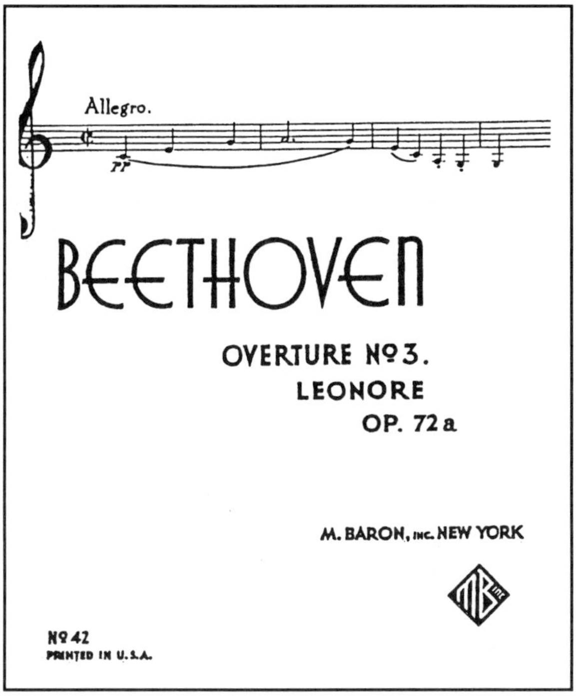

(Information on one of the last pages)

BARON ORCHESTRA SCORES

BACH, J. S.
131 VIOLIN CONCERTO in A minor
138 VIOLIN CONCERTO in E major
140 PIANO CONCERTO in D minor
141 CONCERTO in D minor, Two Violins
142 BRANDENBURG CONCERTO No. 1 in F major
143 BRANDENBURG CONCERTO No. 2 in F major
144 BRANDENBURG CONCERTO No. 3 in G major
145 BRANDENBURG CONCERTO No. 4 in G major
146 BRANDENBURG CONCERTO No. 5 in D major
147 BRANDENBURG CONCERTO No. 6 in B♭ major
148 SUITE (Overture) No. 2 in B minor
149 SUITE (Overture) No. 3 in D major
BEETHOVEN, L. Van
1 SYMPHONY No. 1 in C major, Op. 21
2 SYMPHONY No. 2 in D major, Op. 36
3 SYMPHONY No. 3 in E♭ major, Op. 55 (Eroica)
4 SYMPHONY No. 4 in B♭ major, Op. 60
5 SYMPHONY No. 5 in C minor, Op. 67
6 SYMPHONY No. 6 in F major, Op. 68 (Pastorale)
7 SYMPHONY No. 7 in A major, Op. 92
8 SYMPHONY No. 8 in F major, Op. 93
9 SYMPHONY No. 9 in D minor, Op. 125-(Choral)
150 OVERTURE PROMETHEUS, Op. 43
41 OVERTURE CORIOLANUS, Op. 62
42 OVERTURE LEONORE No. 3, Op. 72a
151 OVERTURE FIDELIO, Op. 72b
43 OVERTURE EGMONT, Op. 84
231 VIOLIN CONCERTO in D major, Op. 61
152 PIANO CONCERTO No. 1 in C major, Op. 15
153 PIANO CONCERTO No. 2 in B♭ major, Op. 19
154 PIANO CONCERTO No. 3 in C minor, Op. 37
155 PIANO CONCERTO No. 4 in G major, Op. 58
156 PIANO CONCERTO No. 5 in E♭ major, Op. 73 (Emperor)
157 TWO ROMANCES for Violin, Op. 40, Op. 50
BERLIOZ, H.
159 FANTASTIC SYMPHONY, Op. 14
158 HAROLD IN ITALY, Op. 16
44 OVERTURE ROMAN CARNIVAL, Op. 9
160 OVERTURE THE CORSAIR, Op. 21
45 OVERTURE BENEVENUTO CELLINI, Op. 23.
93 3 PIECES from THE DAMNATION OF FAUST
BIZET, G.
46 OVERTURE CARMEN
94 L'ARLESIENNE SUITE No. 1
95 L'ARLESIENNE SUITE No. 2
161 CARMEN SUITE No. 1
162 CARMEN SUITE No. 2
BOCCHERINI, L.
163 VIOLONCELLO CONCERTO in B♭ major
BORODIN, A.
164 SYMPHONY No. 2 in B minor
165 FROM THE STEPPES OF CENTRAL ASIA
96 POLOVETZIAN DANCES from PRINCE IGOR

FIGURE 4.27

(chief source of information)
(title page)

THE WORLD'S CLASSICS

══

BEN JONSON

Volpone, or The Fox
Epicene, or The Silent Woman
The Alchemist
Bartholomew Fair

══

Edited with an Introduction by
GORDON CAMPBELL

General Editor
MICHAEL CORDNER
Associate General Editors
PETER HOLLAND   MARTIN WIGGINS

Oxford   New York
OXFORD UNIVERSITY PRESS
1995

Oxford University Press, Walton Street, Oxford OX2 6DP
Oxford New York
Athens Auckland Bangkok Bombay
Calcutta Cape Town Dar es Salaam Delhi
Florence Hong Kong Istanbul Karachi
Kuala Lumpur Madras Madrid Melbourne
Mexico City Nairobi Paris Singapore
Taipei Tokyo Toronto
and associated companies in
Berlin Ibadan

Oxford is a trade mark of Oxford University Press

© *Gordon Campbell 1995*

First published as a World's Classics paperback 1995

British Library Cataloguing in Publication Data
Data available

Library of Congress Cataloging in Publication Data
Jonson, Ben, 1573?- 1637.
The alchemist/ Ben Jonson; edited with an introduction by Gordon
Campbell.
p.   cm. — (World's classics)
Includes bibliographical references and index.
I. Campbell, Gordon. II. Title. III. Series.
PR2605.A1 1995   822'.3—dc20   94-32779
ISBN 0-19-282252-7

(information on cover)

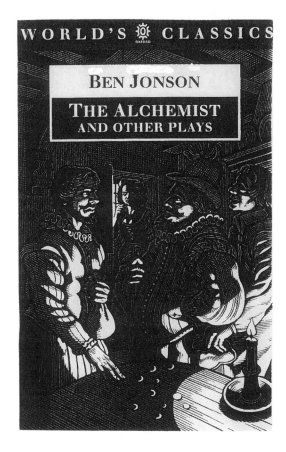

(information on verso)

FIGURE 4.28

(chief source of information)
    (title page)

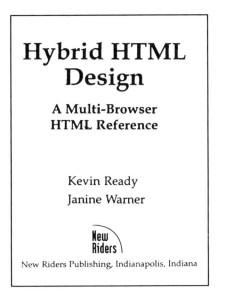

Hybrid HTML Design

**A Multi-Browser
HTML Reference**

Kevin Ready

Janine Warner

**New
Riders**

New Riders Publishing, Indianapolis, Indiana

(information on verso)

HYBRID HTML DESIGN

By Kevin Ready and Janine Warner

Published by:

New Riders Publishing
201 West 103rd Street
Indianapolis, IN 46290 USA

All rights reserved. No part of this book may be reproduced or transmitted in any form or by any means, electronic or mechanical, including photocopying, recording, or by any information storage and retrieval system, without written permission from the publisher, except for the inclusion of brief quotations in a review.

Copyright © 1996 by New Riders Publishing

Printed in the United States of America 1 2 3 4 5 6 7 8 9 0

Library of Congress Cataloging-in-Publication Data

CIP data available upon request

(disk in pocket on inside back cover)

FIGURE 4.29

(information on container)

Instructional booklet has title: Ladybird Key Words Reading Games and gives publisher and place of publication

FIGURE 4.30

(chief source of information)
(title page)

TORONTO'S TORONTO

A PHOTOGRAPHIC COLLECTION

Conceived and edited by j marc coté pouliot

Introduction by Barbara Frum

The Toronto Animation Partnership

The Coach House Press

(information on verso)

COPYRIGHT © 1988 THE TORONTO ANIMATION PARTNERSHIP
P.O. BOX 97, STATION A, TORONTO, ONTARIO, CANADA M5W 1A2

All rights reserved. No part of this publication may be reproduced, stored in a retrieval system, or transmitted in any form, or by any means, electronic, mechanical, photocopying, recording, or otherwise, without the prior permission of the publisher.

Manufactured in Canada

THE COACH HOUSE PRESS 401 (rear) Huron Street, Toronto, Ontario, Canada M5S 2G5

CANADIAN CATALOGUING IN PUBLICATION DATA

Main entry under title: Toronto's Toronto: a photographic collection
ISBN 0-88910-327-5
1. Toronto (Ont.) – Description – Views. I. Toronto Animation Partnership (Association).
FC3097.37.T67 1988   971.3'54104'0222   F1059.5.T684T67 1988   C88-093740-8

FIGURE 4.31

(chief source of information)
(container)

(information on other items in the kit)

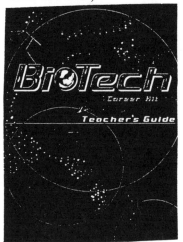

• What is Biotechnology?

• Over 50 Interviews with Biotech Workers.

•Is Biotech Right for You?

FIGURE 4.32

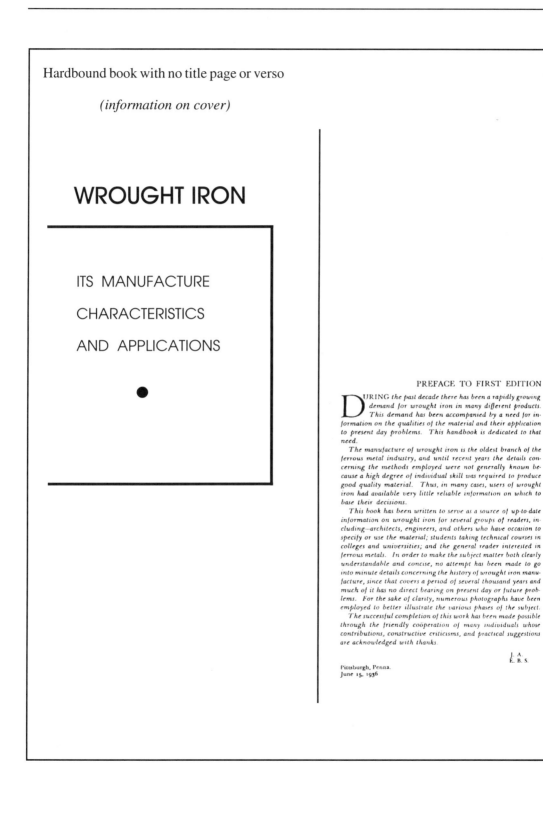

Hardbound book with no title page or verso

(information on cover)

WROUGHT IRON

ITS MANUFACTURE

CHARACTERISTICS

AND APPLICATIONS

PREFACE TO FIRST EDITION

DURING the past decade there has been a rapidly growing demand for wrought iron in many different products. This demand has been accompanied by a need for information on the qualities of the material and their application to present day problems. This handbook is dedicated to that need.

The manufacture of wrought iron is the oldest branch of the ferrous metal industry, and until recent years the details concerning the methods employed were not generally known because a high degree of individual skill was required to produce good quality material. Thus, in many cases, users of wrought iron had available very little reliable information on which to base their decisions.

This book has been written to serve as a source of up-to-date information on wrought iron for several groups of readers, including—architects, engineers, and others who have occasion to specify or use the material; students taking technical courses in colleges and universities; and the general reader interested in ferrous metals. In order to make the subject matter both clearly understandable and concise, no attempt has been made to go into minute details concerning the history of wrought iron manufacture, since that covers a period of several thousand years and much of it has no direct bearing on present day or future problems. For the sake of clarity, numerous photographs have been employed to better illustrate the various phases of the subject.

The successful completion of this work has been made possible through the friendly coöperation of many individuals whose contributions, constructive criticisms, and practical suggestions are acknowledged with thanks.

J. A.
E. B. S.

Pittsburgh, Penna.
June 15, 1936

FIGURE 4.33

(chief source of information)
     (title page)

CALCULUS MADE EASY:

BEING A VERY-SIMPLEST INTRODUCTION TO
THOSE BEAUTIFUL METHODS OF RECKONING
WHICH ARE GENERALLY CALLED BY THE
TERRIFYING NAMES OF THE

DIFFERENTIAL CALCULUS
AND THE
INTEGRAL CALCULUS

(information on verso)

BY
SILVANUS P. THOMPSON, F.R.S.

COPYRIGHT

First Edition 1910.
Reprinted 1911 (twice), 1912, 1913.
Second Edition 1914.
Reprinted 1915, 1917; with corrections 1918 (twice).
Revised and enlarged, 1919.
Reprinted 1920, 1921, 1922, 1924, 1927, 1931, 1936, 1940, 1942, 1943.
Third Edition 1946.

THIRD EDITION

MACMILLAN AND CO., LIMITED
ST. MARTIN'S STREET, LONDON
1946

(information from publisher's note)

For the new edition the book has been reset, and the diagrams modernised. Mr. F. G. W. Brown has been good enough to revise the whole of the book, but he has taken great care not to interfere with the original plan. Thus teachers and students will still recognise their well-known guide to the intricacies of the calculus. While the changes made are not of a major kind, yet their significance may not be inconsiderable. There seems no reason now, even if one ever existed, for

It must, however, be emphatically stated that the plan of the original author remains unchanged ; even in its more modern form, the book still remains a monument to the skill and the courage of the late Professor Silvanus P. Thompson. All that the present reviser has attempted is to revitalize the usefulness of the work by adapting its distinctive utilitarian bias more closely in relation to present-day requirements.

FIGURE 4.34

(chief source of information)
(title page)

THE
OPERA
LIBRETTO
LIBRARY

The Authentic Texts of
the German, French, and Italian Operas
with Music of the Principal Airs

With
the Complete English and German, French, or Italian
Parallel Texts

AVENEL BOOKS
NEW YORK

(information on verso)

Copyright © 1980 by Crown Publishers, Inc.

Copyright © MCMXXXVIII, MCMLXVI, MCMXXXIX, MCMLXVII by Crown Publishers, Inc. *La Forza del Destino* copyright MCMXVIII by Oliver Ditson Company. *Cavalleria Rusticana* copyright MCMXIX by Mary Emma S. Macy. *Götterdämmerung* copyright MCMXXVI by Oliver Ditson Company. All rights reserved.

This edition is published by Avenel Books, distributed by Crown Publishers, Inc.
  d e f g h
1980 EDITION

ISBN 0-517-318830

Recommended Reading

Association for Library Collections & Technical Services, Committee on Cataloging: Description and Access. *Guidelines for Bibliographic Description of Reproductions.* Chicago: American Library Association, 1995.

Ferguson, Bobby. *Cataloging Nonbook Materials: A Blitz Cataloging Workbook.* Englewood, CO: Libraries Unlimited, 1999.

Geer, Beverley, and Beatrice L. Caraway. *Notes for Serials Cataloging,* 2nd ed. Englewood, CO: Libraries Unlimited, 1998.

Map Cataloging Manual. Washington, DC: Library of Congress, 1991.

Marker, Rhonda J., and Melinda Ann Reagor. "Variation in Place of Publication: A Model for Cataloging Simplification." *Library Resources & Technical Services* 38 (January 1994): 17-26.

Olson, Nancy B. *Cataloging Motion Pictures and Videorecordings.* Lake Crystal, MN: Soldier Creek Press, 1991.

———. *Cataloging Computer Files.* Lake Crystal, MN: Soldier Creek Press, 1992.

Saye, Jerry D., and Sherry L. Vellucci. *Notes in the Catalog Record: Based on AACR2 and LC Rule Interpretations.* Chicago: American Library Association, 1989.

Smiraglia, Richard P. *Describing Music Materials,* 3rd ed. Lake Crystal, MN: Soldier Creek Press, 1997.

Tucker, Ben. "The Limits of a Title Proper, or, One Case Showing Why Human Beings, Not Machines, Must Do the Cataloging." *Library Resources & Technical Services* 34 (April 1990): 240-244.

Urbanski, Verna, with Bao Chu Chang and Bernard L. Karon. *Cataloging Unpublished Nonprint Materials: A Manual of Suggestions, Comments, and Examples.* Lake Crystal, MN: Soldier Creek Press, 1992.

Notes

1.   American Library Association, Interactive Multimedia Guidelines Review Task Force, *Guidelines for Bibliographic Description of Interactive Multimedia* (Chicago: American Library Association, 1994).

2.   AACR2-98, 618.

3.   AACR2-98, 617. Dioramas should not be confused with models, which also are three dimensional, but are representations of real things (see AACR2-98, 620), although both are cataloged by the rules of Chapter 10.

4.   AACR2-98, 41.

5.   AACR2-98, 77.

6.   NLCRIs can be found at http://www.nlc-bnc.ca/catalog/aacr/econtent.htm.

5

Access

Introduction

Description is only the first step in the process of making catalog records. The next step, a most important one, is choosing the headings under which the description will appear in the catalog. Rules for choosing headings are contained in Part 2 of AACR2-98. Chapter 21, the first full chapter in this section of AACR2-98 (Chapter 20 is a brief introduction to Part 2) is "Choice of Access Points"; it deals with deciding which elements of the description should become headings. These rules explain how to select the names, titles, or combinations of names and titles that will, if searched in the catalog, result in finding the description from which they are chosen.

All but one of the remaining chapters in Part 2 of AACR2-98 are devoted to rules for putting the headings chosen using Chapter 21 into the proper form. There are chapters on how to construct headings for personal names (Chapter 22); geographic names (Chapter 23); names for entities made up of groups of people acting together known as *corporate bodies* (Chapter 24); and conventional titles assigned to works that may appear with varying titles even though the work is the same, called *uniform titles* (Chapter 25). (One of the best-known uniform titles is *Mother Goose.*) Some classical music known primarily by the generic name of their compositional types, such as symphonies, concertos, etc., are also given uniform titles as are statutes and regulations that may be published variously as collections, selections, or individual items. Figures 5.1 and 5.2, are examples of works that have been published with varying titles proper and that have been identified for collocation purposes by a uniform title.

Sometimes, even though a derived or CIP record contains a uniform title, a library or media center need not have this uniform title for the work in its catalog record, because the library or center does not intend to add other editions and translations of the work to its collection. An example of such a case is shown in Figure 5.3, where the uniform title in LC's CIP record does not differ much from the book's title. It is likely that a searcher using either title would find this item in the library or media center's catalog.

FIGURE 5.1

This example is an illustration of:
- atlas
- uniform title
- chief statement of responsibility as part of title
- statement of subsidiary responsibility
- statement of scale (mathematical data area)
- work containing only one type of illustration
- language note
- edition and history note
- publication note
- bibliography note
- 2nd level cataloging

```
Blaeu, Joan.
   [Atlas maior. Selections]
   Blaeu's the grand atlas of the 17th century world /
introduction, captions and selection of maps by John Goss ;
foreword by Peter Clark. -- Scales vary. -- London : Studio
Editions, 1990.
   1 atlas (224 p.) : 100 col. maps ; 39 cm.

   Introd. and commentary in English, maps in Latin.
   Maps originally published in Atlas major. Amsterdam, 1662.
   Published in co-operation with Royal Geographical Society
London.
   Includes bibliographical references (p. 224).
   ISBN 1-85170-400-0.
```

(chief source of information)
(title page)

(information on verso)

BLAEU'S
THE GRAND
ATLAS

OF THE 17TH CENTURY WORLD

INTRODUCTION, CAPTIONS AND
SELECTION OF MAPS BY JOHN GOSS
FORMERLY CARTOGRAPHIC ADVISOR TO SOTHEBY'S

FOREWORD BY PETER CLARK
KEEPER, ROYAL GEOGRAPHICAL SOCIETY LONDON

PUBLISHED IN CO-OPERATION WITH
ROYAL GEOGRAPHICAL SOCIETY LONDON

STUDIO EDITIONS
London

The original maps in
Blaeu's The Grand Atlas of the 17th Century World
first appeared in
Dr Joan Blaeu's *Atlas Major*
Published in Amsterdam in 1662

This edition published 1990 by Studio Editions Ltd.
Princess House, 50 Eastcastle Street
London W1N 7AP, England

Copyright © Studio Editions Ltd., 1990

Text. Copyright © John Goss, 1990

All rights reserved. This publication may not
be reproduced, stored in a retrieval system,
or transmitted, in any form or by any means
electronic, mechanical, photocopying,
recording or otherwise, without the prior
permission of the publishers.

ISBN 1 85170 400 0

Printed and bound in Hong Kong

FIGURE 5.2

This example is an illustration of:
- musical score
- uniform title
- optional placement of general material designation at end of uniform title
- two statements of subsidiary responsibility
- publication date not listed, copyright date given
- renewal copyright date not given (Library of Congress and National Library of Canada rule interpretations)
- publisher's number note
- 2nd level cataloging

```
Liszt, Franz.
    [Rhapsodies hongroises, piano. No. 2; arr. Music]
    2me rhapsodie hongroise / Franz Liszt ; edited and fingered by
Louis Oesterie ; easier arrangement by Franz Bendel. -- New York
: G. Schmirmer, c1908.
    1 piano score (16 p.) ; 30 cm.

    Publisher's no.: 20664.
```

(information from caption title page)

(cover page)
(This is advertising, not a series statement.)

FIGURE 5.3

This example is an illustration of:
- other title information
- subsidiary responsibility not attributed in chief source of information
- publishing date not listed, copyright date given
- detailed illustration statement
- series statement
- statement of responsibility note
- contents notes
- Library of Congress CIP
- series qualified (in CIP data)
- 2nd level cataloging

```
Mohen, Jean-Pierre.
    Megaliths : stones of memory / Jean-Pierre Mohen. -- New York :
Harry N. Abrams, c1999.
    175 p. : ill. (chiefly col.), map ; 18 cm. -- (Discoveries)

    Translated from the French by Dorie B. and David J. Baker.
    Glossary: p. 160-165.
    Includes bibliographical references and index.
    ISBN 0-8109-2861-2 (pbk.).
```

(chief source of information)
(title page)

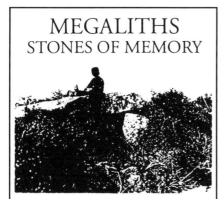

MEGALITHS
STONES OF MEMORY

Jean-Pierre Mohen

DISCOVERIES®
HARRY N. ABRAMS, INC., PUBLISHERS

(information on collophon)

Translated from the French by Dorie B. and David J. Baker

For Harry N. Abrams, Inc.
Editor: Sharon AvRutick
Typographic designers: Elissa Ichiyasu, Tina Thompson
Cover designer: Dana Sloan
Text permissions: Barbara Lyons

Library of Congress Cataloging-in-Publication Data

Mohen, Jean-Pierre, 1944–
  [Mégalithes. English]
  Megaliths : stones of memory / Jean-Pierre Mohen.
    p.   cm. — (Discoveries)
  Includes bibliographical references and index.
  ISBN 0–8109–2861–2 (pbk.)
  1. Megalithic monuments. I. Title. II. Series : Discoveries (New York, N.Y.)
GN790.M7313   1999
930.1'4—dc21   98-50716

Copyright © Gallimard 1998
English translation copyright © 1999 Harry N. Abrams, Inc., New York
Published in 1999 by Harry N. Abrams, Incorporated, New York
All rights reserved. No part of the contents of this book may be reproduced
without the written permission of the publisher.
Printed and bound in Italy by Editoriale Lloyd, Trieste

(information on cover)

There are more than 75 books in the DISCOVERIES® series.
For a complete list, please contact the Sales Department:

These four chapters cover all the possibilities for main and added entries chosen from a bibliographic description. If you wonder why elements such as dates and control numbers are not mentioned here, remember that the searching of entries under numeric elements such as ISBNs and dates is a recent development in access points. These are features of computerized systems, and have not been treated by cataloging rules. Someday it may be necessary to have rules for choosing numeric access points, too.

Chapter 26, "References," describes four different types of references that are made to assist catalog users—see, see also, name-title, and explanatory references—and how they should be made for the names of persons, geographic locations, corporate bodies, and uniform titles. The chapter also discusses references to added entries for series and serials, and the use of references in place of added entries.

Main and Added Entries

Headings are divided into two kinds—main and added entries. The only difference between them is that the first and most important heading chosen is designated as the main entry; all the others are added entries.

Main and added entries are distinguished for several reasons. The main entry is important for catalogs providing only one heading per item represented, because it usually is the heading chosen. Most media center and public library catalogs, however, have several headings for each item represented—author, title, and subject—so the importance in distinguishing between main and added entries is diminished.

Another reason for distinguishing between main and added entries in older card catalogs, particularly if the cards were handwritten or individually typed, is that to save writing or typing, full information might be given only on the main entry card. Added entry cards in these catalogs then contained an abbreviated form of the entry, with the instruction to use the main entry for more information.

The most important reason today for retaining the main entry concept is that shelf marks are derived from the main entry. Shelf marks (also called book marks, book numbers, cutter numbers, and call letters) are added to the classification numbers to form call numbers so that items can be placed on a media center's or library's shelves in a meaningful order. If we stopped differentiating between main and added entries, rules for the consistent creation of cutter numbers or call letters would be needed, because using titles as the source would not produce the same kind of shelf arrangements.

The Anglo-American tradition of cataloging followed by U.S. and Canadian librarians is the legacy of an eighteenth-century British librarian named Anthony Panizzi. It operates on the assumption that the creator of a work is its most important identifying feature. For this reason, in AACR2-98, main entry usually is assigned to the creator of a work, but it is not the only possibility.

Choosing Main Entry

There are three types of main entry, one of which is appropriate to every item cataloged:

1. A personal author or creator.

2. A corporate body author or creator.

3. A title.

Only one individual person, corporate body, or title can be named as the main entry. There are no "joint" main entries, even if an item being cataloged has two co-equal authors, such as the well known operettas of William S. Gilbert and Arthur Sullivan.

The easiest choice of main entry occurs when only one person is responsible for the content of an item. That person is chosen as its main entry. There are exceptions to this rule: If the item comes from a corporate body (called *emanating* from the corporate body by AACR2-98), other rules govern the choice of main entry and the person might *not* be chosen as main entry, although that person would be named as an added entry. Figure 5.4 shows a work of this type, for which a title main entry is more appropriate according to Chapter 21. Another exception applies to compiled or edited works, in which the true creators are the authors of the various pieces, such as *The Ark in the Garden,* collected by Albert Manguel (Figure 5.5 The source of information is on page 90). Editors and compilers are not the same as authors or creators, and AACR2-98 avoids using editors and compilers for main entry.

FIGURE 5.4

This example is an illustration of:
- edited work
- title main entry
- edition statement more accurately stated on the verso
- multiple places of publication
- detailed pagination
- contents note

2nd level cataloging for a Canadian library

```
The Oxford companion to English literature / edited by Margaret
    Drabble. -- 5th ed. rev.-- Oxford : Oxford University Press,
    1998.
    viii, 1154 p. ; 24 cm.

    Includes a chronology, a list of the Poets Laureate, and a list
of the winners of literary awards.
```

2nd level cataloging for a U.S. library

```
The Oxford companion to English literature / edited by Margaret
    Drabble. -- 5th ed. rev.-- Oxford ; New York : Oxford
    University Press, 1998.
    viii, 1154 p. ; 24 cm.

    Includes a chronology, a list of the Poets Laureate, and a list
of the winners of literary awards.
```

(chief source of information)
(title page)

(information on verso)

THE OXFORD COMPANION TO ENGLISH LITERATURE

REVISED EDITION

EDITED BY
MARGARET DRABBLE

Oxford New York
OXFORD UNIVERSITY PRESS
1998

Oxford University Press, Great Clarendon Street, Oxford ox2 6DP
Oxford New York
Athens Auckland Bangkok Bogota Buenos Aires Calcutta
Cape Town Chennai Dar es Salaam Delhi Florence Hong Kong Istanbul
Karachi Kuala Lumpur Madrid Melbourne Mexico City Mumbai
Nairobi Paris Sao Paolo Singapore Taipei Tokyo Toronto Warsaw
and associated companies in Berlin Ibadan

Oxford is a registered trade mark of Oxford University Press

Published in the United States
by Oxford University Press, Inc., New York

© Margaret Drabble and Oxford University Press 1985, 1995

First edition 1932
Second edition 1937
Third edition 1946
Fourth edition 1967
Fifth edition 1985
First revision 1995
Second revision 1998

British Library Cataloguing in Publication Data
Data available

Library of Congress Cataloging in Publication Data
Data available

ISBN 0-19-866233-5

FIGURE 5.5

This example is an illustration of:
- compiled work
- item with many separately titled parts, different authors for these parts, and a collective title for the item as a whole
- title main entry
- other title information listed at head of title proper
- date inferred from the copyright date of the individual parts
- contents note
- Canadian CIP
- 2nd level cataloging

```
The ark in the garden : fables for our times / collected by
   Alberto Manguel. -- Toronto : Macfarlane Walter & Ross,
   [1998?]
   63 p. : ill. ; 19 cm.

   Contents: A Christmas lorac / Margaret Atwood -- The ark in the
garden / Timothy Findley -- Come, said the eagle / Neil
Bissoondath -- The axe and the trees / Jane Urquhart -- From
plus-fours to minus-fours/ Rohinton Mistry -- The banana wars /
Yves Beauchemin.
   ISBN 1-55199-030-X.
```

Fig. 5.5—Continues

FIGURE 5.5 *(continued)*

(chief source of information)
        (title page)

Fables for Our Times

The Ark in the Garden

Collected by

Alberto Manguel

Macfarlane Walter & Ross
Toronto

(information on verso)

Macfarlane Walter & Ross
37A Hazeelton Avenue
Toronto, Canada M5R 2E3

Canadian Cataloguing in Publication Data

Main entry under title:
    The ark in the garden: fables for our times

ISBN 1-55199-030-X

1. Political satire, Canadian (English).* 2. Canadian fiction (English) - 20th century.* 3. Canada - Politics and government - 1993-   -Humor.* I. Manguel, Alberto, 1948-

PS8375.A74 1998   C813'.5408'0358   C98-932031-6
PR9197.8.A74 1998

Macfarlane Walter & Ross gratefully acknowledges financial support for its publishing program from the Canada Council for the Arts, the Ontario Arts Council, and the Government of Canada through the Book Publishing Industry Development Program.

Printed and bound in Canada

(table of contents)

The special rules about items created by more than one person or corporate body, in which all of them share the same creative function, such as writing a book, drawing a poster or a cartoon, writing a computer program, or composing a musical piece, are called rules for *shared responsibility* in AACR2-98. The rules direct the cataloger to choose as main entry the person or body having the greatest amount of responsibility, if that can be determined. When it cannot be determined that one person or body made the greatest contribution to the creation of the work, the one named first on the chief source of information should be chosen, unless many are listed. ("Many" in this case is defined by AACR2-98 as four or more.) For example, catalogers have determined that Jacob Grimm is the first named of the two co-equal Brothers Grimm and is, therefore, the main entry of all their works. To collocate all of Grimm's tales, he must be selected as main entry even if he is not named separately on a particular item.

The chief way to determine whether one person has a greater amount of responsibility is to see how the statement of responsibility is worded. If the chief source on an electronic resource says, "Programmed by Bill Atkinson, with the assistance of members of the Macintosh staff," you can conclude that the contribution by the Macintosh staff is less important than Atkinson's. Sometimes the more important person's name is given in larger type than the others (see Figure 4.22); sometimes it is set apart from other names on the page, screen, or label; sometimes all the other names will be in alphabetical order, except for that one. All of these are devices for showing the greater importance of one person among a group of creators. If none of these devices is present, you can assume that all the parties named have equal responsibility.

When you have more than one co-equal creator, count them. If there are two or three, main entry is assigned to the first named. If there are four or more, none is chosen as main entry, and the title is selected as main entry instead. The principle behind this *Rule of Three* (a library-wide rule of thumb you will encounter elsewhere) is that people are not likely to know the name of the first or, indeed, any one of the creators of a work that has so many co-creators; therefore, the title is a better primary access point.

More special rules, called rules for *mixed responsibility,* explain how to choose between people who perform different creative functions for an item being cataloged, such as writing and illustrating a book, drawing and coloring a cartoon, programming and designing a micro-computer file, or composing and arranging a musical piece. For the most part, the rules lean toward authors of words rather than illustrators (except for items that are entirely or mostly pictures), composers of music rather than arrangers or writers of lyrics, and artists rather than other contributors when works of art are being considered. Some kinds of items, such as films and videos, usually are the product of many different kinds of creative effort—producing, directing, acting, costuming, music, etc.—not three or fewer. If this is the case, then none of the several possibilities is chosen for main entry. Instead, the item receives a title main entry.

What if the item does emanate from a corporate body, or a corporate body is named "author" on the chief source of information? Do we automatically use that corporate body name as main entry? The answer is an emphatic "No!" Rule 21.1B2 limits the use of a corporate body as main entry to six specific cases:

1. When the item is an internal document of the corporate body, such as the catalog of one's library or media center, or the membership directory of an association.

2. When the item is an administrative document, such as the budget of the organization or an annual report. Even though these documents are prepared for external distribution, they are, nonetheless, a reflection of the body itself.

3. When the item represents the collective thought of the body, such as the minutes of a meeting or reports of a committee. Figure 5.6 illustrates such a report.

FIGURE 5.6

This example is an illustration of:
- main entry under corporate body
- two statements of other title information
- marks of omission to shorten lengthy other title information
- same organization responsible for intellectual content and publication
- detailed pagination statement
- bibliography note
- two levels of cataloging

2nd level cataloging

```
Kansas Library Network Board. Preservation Committee.
   Saving the past to enrich the future : a plan for preserving
information resources in Kansas : report ... to the citizens of
Kansas. -- Topeka, Kan. : The Board, 1993.
   vi, 52 p. : ill. ; 28 cm.

   Includes bibliography: (p. 39-45).
```

1st level cataloging

```
Kansas Library Network Board. Preservation Committee.
   Saving the past to enrich the future. -- The Board, 1993.
   vi, 52 p.
```

(chief source of information)
    (title page)

Saving the Past to Enrich the Future

A Plan for Preserving Information Resources in Kansas

Report of the Kansas Library Network Board's
Preservation Committee to
the citizens of Kansas

Published with support from the
National Endowment for the Humanities,
Division of Preservation and Access

Published by the Kansas Library Network Board
March 1993

(information on back cover)

Published with support from the National
Endowment for the Humanities

Kansas Library Network Board
300 SW 10th Street, Room 343
Topeka, KS 66612-1593
(913) 296-3296

4. When the item represents the collective effort of a voyage, expedition, or a conference. If, however, the event has no official name, it does not meet the full definition
of a corporate body, which is "an organization or a group of persons that is identified
by a particular name and that acts, or may act, as an entity."[1] Figures 5.7 and 5.8
show examples of named and unnamed conferences (more likely to be encountered
these days than a voyage or expedition). The source of information for Figure 5.7 is
on page 94; and on page 96 for Figure 5.8.

FIGURE 5.7

This example is an illustration of:
- bilingual item
- unnamed conference
- title main entry
- edited work
- two other title information statements
- extensive other title information optionally given in the note area
- detailed pagination
- title information note
- language note
- statement of responsibility note
- Library of Congress CIP
- two methods of cataloging

2nd level cataloging in a unilingual catalog

```
Dewey decimal classification : francophone perspectives : papers
   from a workshop presented at the General Conference of the
   International Federation of Library Associations and
   Institutions (IFLA) Amsterdam, Netherlands, August 20, 1998 /
   edited by Julianne Beall and Raymonde Couture-Lafleur. --
   Albany : Forest Press, 1999.
   vii, 58, 60, vii p. ; 23 cm.

   Added title page title: Classification décimale Dewey :
perspectives francophones.
   English and French.
   Sponsored by the IFLA Section on Classification and Indexing.
   ISBN 0-910608-67-9.
```

2nd level cataloging in a bilingual catalog

```
Dewey decimal classification : francophone perspectives /
   edited by Julianne Beall and Raymonde Couture-Lafleur =
   Classification décimale Dewey : perspectives francophones /
   préparées par Julianne Beall et Raymonde Couture-Lafleur. --
   Albany : Forest Press, 1999.
   vii, 58, 60, vii p. ; 23 cm.

   Papers from a workshop presented at the General Conference of
the International Federation of Library Associations and
Institutions (IFLA) Amsterdam, Netherlands, August 20, 1998.
   Sponsored by the IFLA Section on Classification and Indexing.
   ISBN 0-910608-67-9.
```

Fig. 5.7—Continues

FIGURE 5.7 *(continued)*

(chief source of information)
(title page)

Dewey Decimal Classification
Francophone Perspectives

Papers from a Workshop
Presented at the General Conference
of the International Federation of
Library Associations and Institutions (IFLA)
Amsterdam, Netherlands
August 20, 1998

**Edited by Julianne Beall
and Raymonde Couture-Lafleur**

Sponsored by the
IFLA Section on Classification and Indexing

FOREST PRESS
A Division of
OCLC Online Computer Library Center, Inc.
Albany, New York
1999

Classification décimale Dewey
Perspectives francophones

Communications d'un Atelier
présentées à la Conférence générale
de la Fédération Internationale des
Associations de Bibliothécaires
et des Bibliothèques (IFLA)
Amsterdam, Pays-Bas
20 août 1998

**Préparées par Julianne Beall et
Raymonde Couture-Lafleur**

Atelier organisé par la
Section de classification et indexation de l'IFLA

FOREST PRESS
A Division of
OCLC Online Computer Library Center, Inc.
Albany, New York
1999

(information on verso)

Library of Congress Cataloging-in-Publication Data

Dewey decimal classification--francophone perspectives : papers from
a workshop presented at the General Conference of the International
Federation of Library Associations and Institutions (IFLA) Amsterdam,
Netherlands, August 20, 1998 / edited by Julianne Beall and Raymonde
Couture-Lafleur .
    Forest Press, 1999.
        p.   cm.
    Added title page title : Classification décimale Dewey--perspectives
francophones
    "Sponsored by the IFLA Section on Classification and Indexing."
    English and French.
    ISBN 0-910608-67-9
    1. Classification, Dewey decimal--Congresses.   2. Library science--
French-speaking countries--Congresses.   I. Beall, Julianne, 1946-   .
II. Couture-Lafleur, Raymonde, 1934-   .   III. International Federation
of Library Associations and Institutions. Section on Classification and
Indexing.   IV. IFLA General Conference (64th : 1998 : Amsterdam,
Netherlands)
Z696.D7D495   1999   99-35669
025.4'31--dc21   CIP

FIGURE 5.8

This example is an illustration of:
- named conference
- main entry under corporate body
- other title information
- multiple places of publication and publishers
- detailed pagination
- publishing note
- bibliography and index note
- Library of Congress and Canadian CIPs

2nd level cataloging for a Canadian library

```
International Conference on the Principles and Future of AACR
     (1997 : Toronto, Ont.)
  The principles and future of AACR : proceedings of the
International Conference on the Principles and Future of AACR,
Toronto, Ontario, Canada, October 23-25, 1997 / Jean Weihs,
editor. -- Ottawa : Canadian Library Association, 1997.
  xi, 272 p. ; 28 cm.

  Co-published by American Library Association and Library
Association.
  Includes bibliographies and index.
  ISBN 0-88802-287-5.
```

2nd level cataloging for a U.S. library

```
International Conference on the Principles and Future of AACR
     (1997 : Toronto, Ont.)
  The principles and future of AACR : proceedings of the
International Conference on the Principles and Future of AACR,
Toronto, Ontario, Canada, October 23-25, 1997 / Jean Weihs,
editor. -- Ottawa : Canadian Library Association ; Chicago :
American Library Association, 1997.
  xi, 272 p. ; 28 cm.

  Includes bibliographies and index.
  ISBN 0-8389-3493-5.
```

Fig. 5.8—Continues

FIGURE 5.8 *(continued)*

(chief source of information)
(title page)

The Principles and Future of AACR

Proceedings of the
International Conference
on the Principles
and Future Development
of AACR

Toronto, Ontario, Canada
October 23–25, 1997

JEAN WEIHS
Editor

CANADIAN LIBRARY ASSOCIATION / Ottawa
LIBRARY ASSOCIATION PUBLISHING / London
AMERICAN LIBRARY ASSOCIATION / Chicago
1998

(information on verso)

Published by
AMERICAN LIBRARY ASSOCIATION
50 East Huron Street, Chicago, Illinois 60611
CANADIAN LIBRARY ASSOCIATION
200 Elgin Street, Ottawa, Ontario K2P 1L5
LIBRARY ASSOCIATION PUBLISHING
7 Ridgmount Street, London WC1E 7AE

Library Assocation Publishing is wholly owned
by The Library Association

Library of Congress Cataloging-in-Publication Data
International Conference on the Principles and Future Development of
AACR (1997 : Toronto, Ontario, Canada)
    The principles and future of AACR / Jean Weihs, editor
        p.   cm.
    "Proceedings of the International Conference in the Principles and
Future Development of AACR, Toronto, Ontario, October 23-25, 1997
American Library Association, Chicago and London, 1999."
    Includes bibliographical references (p.   ) and index.
    ISBN 0-8389-3493-5
    1. Anglo-American cataloguing rules—Congresses. 2. Descriptive
cataloging—United States—Rules—Congresses. 3. Descriptive
cataloging—Great Britain—Rules—Congresses. 4. Descriptive
cataloging—Canada—Rules—Congresses. 5. Descriptive cataloging —
Australia—Rules—Congresses. I. Weihs, Jean Riddle. II. Title.
III. Title: Principles and future of Anglo-American cataloguing rules.
Z694.15.A5155   1997
025.3'2—dc21   98-34562
Canadian Cataloguing in Publication Data
International Conference on the Principles and Future Development of
AACR (1997 : Toronto, Ont.)
    The principles and future of AACR : proceedings of the International
Conference on the Principles and Future Development of AACR.
Toronto. Ontario. Canada. October 23-25, 1997
        Co-published by American Library Association and Library Association
        Includes bibliographical references.
        ISBN 0-88802-287-5
    1. Anglo-American cataloguing rules—Congresses. 2. Descriptive
cataloging—United States—Rules—Congresses. 3. Descriptive
cataloging—Great Britain—Rules—Congresses. 4. Descriptive
cataloging—Canada—Rules—Congresses. 5. Descriptive cataloging—
Australia—Rules—Congresses. I. Weihs, Jean, 1930- II. American
Library Association. III. Library Association. IV. Title. V. Title:
Principles and future of Anglo-American cataloguing rules.
Z694.15.A5158   1997   025.3'2   C98-901015.5
British Library Cataloguing-in-Publication Data
A catalogue record for this book is available from the British Library
ISBN 1-85604-303-7

5. If the item is a sound recording, film, or video, *and* the responsible corporate body does more than just perform it. This rule involves a difficult principle, that of judging when a performing group does something that qualifies as *more than mere performance,* that is, something we would call *creation.* One difference lies in the way classical and popular music, especially jazz, are performed. When classical music is performed, the notes are expected to be played the way they were written by the composer. Although different classical performers playing the same work may sound different to music lovers, essentially they all are playing the same notes, and following the composer's notations on when to play loud and soft, fast and slow.

   When popular music, especially jazz, is performed, improvisation normally is part of the performance. The "writing" of jazz or popular music may be just a melody or set of beats from which the performer is supposed to create a performance. The same is true of videos or films of some kinds of performances, such as rock concerts. This rule is not applicable to all performers, but those who act together as a group and have a name, such as the rock group Kiss. It would not apply to several individual performers who just happened to be put on the same program for a recording date or a concert.

6. When the item is a map or other cartographic representation and the corporate body involved is responsible for more than just publication. A good example of this kind of corporate body main entry is the National Geographic Society, which often does much more than just publish maps. It may finance the expedition to explore the territories, hire and direct the staff who do the actual cartographic work, and perform other functions as well.

When an item comes from a corporate body, but does not fit into any of these categories, it should not be given a corporate body main entry. It should be treated as if it did not emanate from a corporate body and, if there were a person or persons named in the item as its creator, one of them would be the main entry. If we suspected that someone not named in the item was responsible for its existence, we could name that person. According to AACR2-98, we should name as main entry "the personal author, the principal personal author, or the *probable* personal author."[2] [Emphasis added]

When do we apply the third option, title main entry? The easiest way to answer this question is to say that title main entry is chosen when there is no person or corporate body that is both principally responsible for the creation of the item *and* permitted to be chosen main entry by the rules. The most frequently encountered cases are

1. When there is no known creator.

2. When there are more than three creators sharing equal amounts of the same type of responsibility for the item, if their contributions are the same (see Figure 5.9). The source of information for Figure 5.9 is on the next page, 98.

FIGURE 5.9

This example is an illustration of:
*   item with more than three authors
*   title main entry
*   other title information
*   marks of omission
*   statement of subsidiary responsibility
*   publication date not listed, copyright date given
*   detailed pagination statement
*   all illustrations are in color
*   width of book greater than height
*   index note
*   Library of Congress CIP
*   two levels of cataloging

2nd level cataloging

```
Melloni's illustrated review of human anatomy : by
   structures--arteries, bones, muscles, nerves, veins / June L.
   Melloni ... [et al.] ; illustrated by the authors. --
   Philadelphia : Lippincott, c1988.
   vii, 268 p. : col. ill. ; 23 x 31 cm.

Includes index.
ISBN 0-397-50956-1
```

Fig. 5-9—Continues

FIGURE 5.9 *(continued)*

1st level cataloging

```
Melloni's illustrated review of human anatomy / June L. Melloni
    ... [et al.]. -- Lippincott, c1988.
    vii, 268 p.

    ISBN 0-397-50956-1
```

(chief source of information)

  (title page)

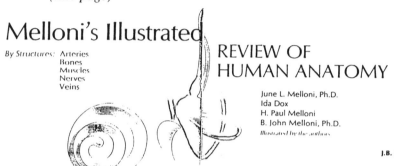

Melloni's Illustrated

By Structures: Arteries
               Bones
               Muscles
               Nerves
               Veins

REVIEW OF
HUMAN ANATOMY

June L. Melloni, Ph.D.
Ida Dox
H. Paul Melloni
B. John Melloni, Ph.D.
Illustrated by the authors

J.B. Lippincott Company   Philadelphia
London   Mexico City   New York
St. Louis   São Paulo   Sydney

(information on verso)

Acquisitions Editor: Lisa A. Biello
Developmental Editor: Delois Patterson
Design Coordinator: Michelle Gerdes
Cover Designer: Stephen Cymerman
Production Manager: Carol A. Florence
Production Editor: Rosanne Hallowell
Production Coordinator: Barney Fernandes
Compositor: McFarland Graphics
Text Printer/Binder: Kingsport Press
Cover Printer: The Lehigh Press, Inc.

Copyright © 1988 by Biagio John Melloni, Ph.D.
Copyright under the International Copyright Union

All rights reserved. No part of this book may be used or reproduced
in any manner whatsoever without written permission from Biagio
John Melloni, Ph.D., 9308 Renshaw Drive, Bethesda, Maryland 20817.
Printed in the United States of America. For information write
J.B. Lippincott Company, East Washington Square, Philadelphia,
Pennsylvania 19105.

1   3   5   6   4   2

LIBRARY OF CONGRESS
Library of Congress Cataloging-in-Publication Data

Melloni's illustrated review of human anatomy : by structures—arteries,
bones, muscles, nerves, veins / June L. Melloni . . . [et al.] ; illustrated
by the authors.
        p. cm.
    Includes index.
    ISBN 0-397-50956-1
    1. Anatomy, Human—Atlases.   2. Anatomy, Human—Outlines, syllabi,
etc.   I. Melloni, June L.   II. Title: Illustrated review of human anatomy.
QM25.M45 1988
611'.0022'2—dc19   88-722
                                                              CIP

3. When the item emanates from a corporate body, but does not fall into one of the six categories enumerated in AACR2-98's rule 21.1B2 and has no personal author (see Figure 5.10). The source of information for Figure 5.10 is on the next page, 100.

4. When the work is produced under "editorial" direction (see Figure 5.4).

FIGURE 5.10

This example is an illustration of:
- electronic resource accessed through Internet
- work emanating from a corporate body entered under title
- file characteristics area
- place of publication not stated in sources of information, but known
- mode of access note
- source of title note
- also issued note (used for information about items not part of the collection)
- 2nd level cataloging

```
ISBD(ER) : international standard bibliographic description for
    electronic resources. -- Electronic data. -- [London] :
    International Federation of Library Associations and
    Institutions, 1999.

    Mode of access: World Wide Web. URL:
http://www.ifla.org/VII/s13/pubs/isbd.htm.
    Title from title screen (viewed on Aug. 31, 1999).
    Also issued in printed ed.
```

Fig. 5-10—Continues

FIGURE 5.10 *(continues)*

(chief source of information)
     (title screen)

IFLA **IFLANET** ——— Search   Contacts
International Federation of Library Associations and Institutions
Activities & Services

ISBD(ER):
International Standard Bibliographic Description
for Electronic Resources

Continued

CONTENTS

Introduction

Preliminary notes

Scope, purpose and use
Definitions
Comparative outline of the ISBD(G) and the ISBD(ER)
Punctuation
Sources of information
Language and script of the description
Abridgements and abbreviations
Capitalization
Examples
Misprints
Symbols, etc

Specification of elements

1. Title and statement of responsibility area
2. Edition area
3. Type and extent of resource area
4. Publication, distribution, etc., area
5. Physical description area
6. Series area
7. Note area
8. Standard number (or alternative) and terms of availability area

Appendices

A. Multi-level description
B. Bi-directional records
C. Recommended general material designation, resource designations and specific material designations with their definition
D. Recommended abbreviations for use in English language records based on ISBD(ER)

http://www.ifla.org/VII/s13/pubs/isbd2.htm   8/31/99

Choosing Added Entries

Some added entries are mandated by the rules for main entry. A rule will state something such as: "In this event, choose A as the main entry and make an added entry for B." (If whatever is described as *this event* is not the case, then the cataloger might be instructed to make B the main entry, and to make an added entry for A.)

Any added entry can be made if a cataloger thinks it is needed by users of the catalog, with one proviso: Names or titles should not be used as added entries if they are not mentioned anywhere in the bibliographic description. Notes are made about variant titles, titles of the parts of an item, or secondary statements of responsibility, so that they can be selected as headings for additional records for the item.

This is not true of the *main* entry. A name or title can become the main entry of an item even if it never appears anywhere in the bibliographic description. Uniform titles are constructed by catalogers, and thus rarely appear as transcriptions. Furthermore, when an item is erroneously attributed to someone on the chief source of information, but the cataloger knows who truly created it, the rules of AACR2-98 prescribe giving the main entry to its true creator (or its *probable* creator, if the cataloger is not certain). In any event, the cataloger should not use the erroneous heading when it is known to be incorrect.

Several kinds of added entries are made routinely, covered by AACR2-98 rules 21.29 and 21.30. They include the following kinds of headings:

1. Joint authors, composers, or other kinds of creators.

2. People making other types of creative contributions, such as illustrators or editors of books, librettists of operas, or performers of recorded classical music.

3. Corporate bodies, provided they are named prominently on the item and they do not function solely as publishers, distributors, or manufacturers.

4. Titles proper for items having a personal or corporate body name main entry, or a uniform title main entry. (Title added entries are not made for nondistinctive titles, such as *Concerto no. 1* or *Mood 4,* that depend on the name of the composer or artist for identification.)

5. Variations of the title proper found on the item.

6. Analytical titles; that is, titles for individual works on an item containing multiple works, such as an integrated software package, an anthology of plays, or an album of songs.

7. Series titles.

To recapitulate, the first, most important heading for a title being cataloged is called its main entry, and all other desired headings are called added entries. Names, titles, and combinations of names and titles included in the record can be selected as headings. The only exception is the main entry, which need not appear in the record.

One way to ensure that you are selecting the correct main entry is to pose a series of questions that will guide you through the process. The following eleven questions and two caveats form a decision tree that you may find useful.

1. Does the item emanate from a corporate body? No? Proceed to Question 8. Yes? Go to Question 2. (If in doubt, assume that the answer is no and proceed to Question 8.)

2. Is the item an administrative work dealing with the body itself? Yes? Assign a corporate body main entry. (If more than one corporate body is involved, follow the rules for multiple personal authors, below.) No? Go to Question 3.

3. Is the item one of the designated types of works in rule 21.1B2b? Yes? Assign a corporate body main entry. (If more than one corporate body is involved, follow the rules for multiple personal authors, below.) No? Go to Question 4.

4. Does the item record the collective thought of the body? Yes? Assign a corporate body main entry. (If more than one corporate body is involved, follow the rules for multiple personal authors, below.) No? Go to Question 5.

5. Does the item record the collective activity of an event? Yes? Assign a corporate body main entry. (If more than one corporate body is involved, follow the rules for multiple personal authors, below.) No? Go to Question 6.

6. Does the item result from the collective activity of a performing group as a whole that goes beyond mere performance? Yes? Assign a corporate body main entry. (If more than one corporate body is involved in the performing, follow the rules for multiple personal authors, below.) No? Go to Question 7.

7. Is the item cartographic, and does the responsibility of the corporate body go beyond publication/distribution? Yes? Assign a corporate body main entry. (If more than one corporate body is involved, follow the rules for multiple personal authors, below.) No? Go to Question 8.

8. Is the work by one or more persons? No? Assign a title main entry. Yes? Go to Question 9.

9. Is one person the sole creator or principal creator of the work? Yes? Assign that person as main entry. No? Go to Question 10.

10. Are two or three persons equally responsible for the creation of the work? Yes? Assign the first-named as main entry and give added entries for the rest. No? Go to Question 11.

11. Are more than three persons responsible for the creation of the work? Assign a title main entry and give an added entry for the first named person.

    CAVEAT No. 1: Questions 10 and 11 assume that all creators have made the same kind of contribution to the creation of the work, such as writing a book, painting a picture, or programming a computer file. Answers given are for *shared* responsibility. Consult special rules for *mixed* responsibility to determine the relative weight of differing types of contributions to the creation of a work, such as writing and illustrating a children's book (AACR2-98 rules 21.8-21.17). In general, the Rule of Three is applied both to the types of contribution and the number of persons or bodies sharing a single type. If either of those elements exceeds three and none are indicated as predominant, a title main entry should be assigned.

CAVEAT No. 2: Editors are not considered "creators" of the works they edit. Instead, an edited work containing contributions by one or more "authors" is considered the collective work of those authors, whether persons, corporate bodies, or both; and whether the "authorship" involves writing, composing music, painting pictures, etc. When a work such as a bibliography is compiled, the compiler is considered equivalent to an author, even if the term applied to the compiler on the title page is "editor."

Forms of Headings

Personal Names

Two basic principles underlie the rules in AACR2-98 for the form into which a personal name heading is put:

1. The form of name used for the heading should be that which is most familiar to most users of the catalog.

2. In most cases, there should be only one heading for a single individual. This principle ensures that all the works of an author or creator will be brought together in one place (or, collocated) in the catalog.

The first principle—that the most commonly known form of a person's name be chosen as the one used for the heading—seems logical, but it is the reverse of the principle on which AACR1's rules were based. AACR1 required that catalogers determine the fullest form of a person's real name and use that, with their birth and death dates as well as the one and only heading for the person. If a person used a pseudonym, catalogers still were to seek out the real name and use it in the fullest form they could find. *1984* was entered under Eric Arthur Blair, not George Orwell, and *Manhattan* was entered under Allen Stewart Konigsberg, not Woody Allen. Furthermore, initials or appellations were not permitted as headings; instead, an item was entered either under the person's real name or under the title of the work being cataloged if the real name could not be ascertained. The reason for this practice was that the fullest form of the name was considered to be the most authoritative form and the least likely to be incorrect or mistaken for someone else. We mention this because many catalogs may still contain older forms of names. If the catalog is automated, a decision on name forms will be mandated, and many call numbers will need to be changed.

AACR2-98, however, goes back to Charles Cutter's idea that the headings in the catalog should match what most searchers expect to find there; therefore, it instructs catalogers to use the name by which the person is most commonly known and, in certain cases, permits more than one form of name to be used simultaneously. AACR2-98 also permits pseudonyms, initials, and appellations to be used as headings if they are how an individual is most commonly known.

Although the AACR2-98 principle is a welcome change for searchers, it poses some problems for catalogers. How do they determine the most commonly known name for a person who uses more than one? It seems relatively easy to choose a form for someone long dead, someone who cannot introduce changes. Catalogers just count the number of times each possible form of name appears on the published works and use the one that appears most frequently. Living or contemporaneous creators, however, may continue to change the styles of their names or the names they use for publication or production, and what once was most commonly encountered may not remain so indefinitely. AACR2-98 devised a new rule to address this problem: "If a contemporary author uses more than one pseudonym or his or her real name and one or more pseudonyms, use, as the basis for the heading for each work, the name appearing in it. Make references to connect the names."[3] This solution enables catalogers to stop worrying about how many times a person's name changes or how frequently a particular form of name appears for a person who has what AACR2-98 calls "separate bibliographic identities."[4]

Naturally, when a person's name appears in more than one form on their works, a cataloger should make cross-references for the form(s) of name that are not used as headings. If a searcher looks under a form that is not used, for example, for Konigsberg in place of Allen, that person will be led to the form that is used. And if more than one name heading is used for a single creator, cross-references should be made that will lead searchers looking under any one heading to the others.

Fortunately for catalogers, most creators do not produce multiple works under multiple names. The form of name established when an individual's first work is cataloged often will remain the only authoritative heading needed in the catalog for that person.

If AACR2-98 did not subscribe to the second principle—the desire to bring all works by one creator using a particular name together under one heading—it would be very easy to create headings. All a cataloger would have to do is copy whatever appeared on the item being cataloged. In cases in which no name appeared, a reference work might be consulted (remember, a main entry heading can be created for a name that does not appear anywhere in the bibliographic description). The result of such a policy, however, would be to fragment the works of a single person under multiple headings. Author Jean Weihs offers an example. Jean Weihs has written books under three forms of name: one using her second given name and her first married name—Jean Riddle; then one using her second given name, her first married name, and her second married name—Jean Riddle Weihs; then using her second given name and her second married name—Jean Weihs. If, in addition to these three, she also used her first given name—Barbara—with any of these combinations and also published under her maiden name, Northgrave, the various forms of name blossom from three to a possible eight. Her works would be scattered in multiple places in the Ns, Rs, and Ws. Sometimes, the bibliographic form of name is established differently by different national libraries. A good example of this is in the CIPs for Figure 5.8. LC has "Weihs, Jean Riddle" whereas NLC has "Weihs, Jean." LC and NLC have a formal policy for the establishment of the names of corporate bodies, but this agreement does not cover personal names.[5]

In the eighteenth and nineteenth centuries, it was common to conceal one's identity using only initials or appellations, such as "A Learned Gentleman" or "A Lady of Leisure." In recent years, a well-known example of hidden identity is the book *Primary Colors,* whose title page reads "by Anonymous." The identity of the author eventually was revealed, but the title page does not include it (at least, not as of this writing) even though another book by the same author proclaims him "Author of *Primary Colors.*" Reissues of older works and subsequent editions might be produced today using the real names of their creators, particularly if they have become classics or if the individuals are well known in other contexts. Some modern works are produced with their creators' names written as initials or nicknames in some editions and as full forms or given names in others.

There are other cases of different names or forms of names for the same individual, also. For the most part, the rules of AACR2-98 attempt to bring together under one name form all of the different possibilities, to make it easier for searchers to find all the works of an individual under one heading; that by which the individual is best known.

Corporate Bodies

The preceding paragraphs also pertain to corporate bodies. Generally, only one heading should be used for a single corporate body. When a corporate body decides to change its name, however, it may also become a new body. Changes are more likely to be substantive in the case of a corporate body, resulting in the presence of more than one heading in the catalog for a corporate body that has evolved over time.

Using the most commonly known form of name as the authoritative form applies for corporate bodies as well as for people's names, but the application is a little different. For corporate bodies, the name used by the group on its stationery, official documents, and publications is considered the most commonly known form of its name. Sometimes, problems occur when a corporate body decides to update its image by creating or modernizing its logo using initials or similar graphic devices intended merely to attract attention. Rules defining substantive changes to a corporate body name intend to eliminate the creation of multiple headings for a body undergoing a change of this kind, such as from I.B.M. to IBM. (This is a hypothetical example. The heading for IBM is really International Business Machines Corporation, but cross-references to it should be made from the initials with and without the periods.) Sometimes a corporate body will announce its intention to be known by a different name, such as the University at Albany, State University of New York did when it changed from State University of New York at Albany.

The most complicated problem about corporate body names is caused by the fact that some corporate bodies are parts of larger entities or parent bodies. Smaller units within these entities are known as subordinate bodies. Determining whether the name of a subordinate body should include that of the larger entity is a complex problem, made even more difficult when there is more than one layer of bureaucracy between the parent entity and the subordinate unit. Using the example of the Committee on Cataloging: Description and Access (CC:DA)—the committee that governs AACR2-98 in the United States—there are two intervening layers of hierarchy between the parent entity, the American Library Association (ALA), and the subordinate body, CC:DA:

1.   American Library Association (parent body)

2.   Association for Library Collections & Technical Services (subunit of the parent body, called a "division" by the parent body)

3.   Cataloging and Classification Section (subunit of the division)

4.   Committee on Cataloging: Description and Access (subunit of the section)

Generally, if the name of a corporate body implies that it is a subordinate unit—clearly the case with a "committee," "division," "section," "office," "bureau," etc.—then the name of the higher body is included. AACR2-98 instructs catalogers to include the name of the lowest unit of hierarchy that can stand alone, provided it is a unique identification. For CC:DA, the only higher body that needs to be added is Association for Library Collections & Technical Services (ALCTS). The authoritative name form for CC:DA is, thus: *Association for Library Collections & Technical Services. Committee on Cataloging: Description and Access.* "Cataloging and Classification Section" is not used as the access point because it is a subordinate body (the word "section" implies subordination). It also is not needed in the hierarchy because no other section of ALCTS has a committee by this name.

The Cataloging and Classification Section of ALCTS has a Policy and Research Committee, but its authoritative heading would not be *Association for Library Collections & Technical Services. Policy and Research Committee* because another section within ALCTS, the Serials Section, also has a committee by that name. Each one must be identified uniquely. The authoritative form of the Cataloging and Classification Section's Policy and Research Committee is, therefore: *Association for Library Collections & Technical Services. Cataloging and Classification Section. Policy and Research Committee.*

Before a 1990 referendum among its members voted to change the division's name, ALCTS was known as the Resources and Technical Services Division of ALA. Because that name implied subordination (because it contained the word "division"), the heading for CC:DA was not given before 1990 as *Resources and Technical Services Division. Committee on Cataloging: Description and Access.* Instead, it had to be given as *American Library Association. Committee on Cataloging: Description and Access.* Unfortunately, these distinctions are nearly as confusing to catalogers as they are to patrons seeking corporate body headings in the catalog. The best help for patrons is a policy of making cross-references to any potential search term and programming local catalog search software to match any word or combination of words in corporate body headings and retrieve all sets that include the requested terms.

Many corporate bodies consisting of multiple units already have established name forms listed in the LC *Name Authority File* and NLC *Canadiana Authorities,* which help catalogers meet the challenge of determining these complex headings. NLC has a formal agreement with LC regarding the establishment of Canadian corporate names. These names used by LC in current cataloging are formulated according to the AACR2-98 forms for names established by NLC. If LC or a U.S. institution participating in LC's Name Authority Cooperative Program (NACO) does not find an authority for a Canadian corporate name, NLC establishes the heading and creates an authority record at their request. NLC is not a full member of NACO because of its bilingual cataloging policy.[6]

Geographic Names

Geographic names are also used in headings for the catalog. It is easy to imagine the confusion that would result if different forms of name were used for the same geographic entity. A nation that is at once a familiar friend and our cohort in the development of cataloging rules is a good example: Should we use Britain, Great Britain, or United Kingdom as the authoritative heading for the territory inhabited by our colleagues across the Atlantic? Choosing headings for places located in a non-English-speaking country between the English name form versus the vernacular name form (e.g., Florence/Firenze) and for place names in languages written in non-roman characters, such as Chinese or Russian, adds to the need for consistent rules to govern the way geographic name headings are made.

The rules of Chapter 23 instruct catalogers to use English forms for place names if there are such forms in general use; if not, the vernacular form in the official language of the country is preferred.[7] When place names change, catalogers are instructed to use as many names as are required by the rules in Chapter 24 for government names, additions to corporate and conference names, or other corporate body name headings.

Sometimes one name is used for more than one geographic location (e.g., Cairo, Egypt, and Cairo, Illinois). To distinguish place names properly, AACR2-98 includes rules for additions to place names. Generally, additions are made only for places smaller than a country. Additions differ for various countries, with one group comprising Australia, Canada, Malaysia, and the United States. Localities within these places are augmented by the addition of the name of the state, province, territory, etc.

The countries of the British Isles—England, the Republic of Ireland, Northern Ireland, Scotland, and Wales as well as the Isle of Man and the Channel Islands—form a second group, for which local place names are augmented by the addition of the appropriate country or island name. This same practice applies to countries of the world other than those in the group named above, including the individual nations which once were part of the Union of Soviet Socialist Republics and Yugoslavia.

Other special rules deal with place names that require more specific identification or special kinds of identification, such as two or more localities with identical headings even after the appropriate additions are made (Saint Anthony, Hennepin County, Minnesota, and Saint Anthony, Stearns County, Minnesota), or communities within cities (Hyde Park, London, England, and Hyde Park, Chicago, Illinois), or names involving political jurisdictions [for example, Distrito Federal (Brazil)]. These rules and their interpretations in LCRIs and NLCRIs can be consulted in the event an item being cataloged requires establishing that kind of heading.

Uniform Titles

For most works, there is only one edition or production and one title that identifies it. These works cause no problems. When used as headings, they are simply transcribed as they appear on the work itself: the title proper. A few works, however, do not appear once, but are produced and reproduced many times over long spans of years, and their publishers or producers do not always use the same title proper to identify them. *Mother Goose* is a good example, because its title might appear in any one of the following ways (as well as others not listed):

Brian Wildsmith's *Mother Goose*

The Illustrated Mother Goose

My Little Mother Goose

The Golden Book of Mother Goose

Works of the kind that may appear in many different forms depending on the producer's or publisher's whim are given a single title by catalogers called a *conventional* or *uniform title,* so that they will all file together in the catalog. The most widely used uniform titles are found in AACR2-98's Chapter 25, along with rules for assigning a uniform title to a work the cataloger thinks should have one.

Uniform titles are common among seven types of works:

1. Classic works, especially anonymous ones, that appear in many editions and versions.

2. Musical works, which may have generic titles such as "Symphony," or that may appear in different versions, some original and complete, whereas others are arrangements or selections from the whole.

3. Religious works, such as the Bible, the Koran, or prayer books used by people of different faiths, which often appear with variant titles.

4. Laws.

5. Works that may appear in complete form or only in part, such as the complete Bible, selections from it, or just one book.

6. Works appearing in several physical formats, such as plays that may be printed as books and performed on films, videorecordings, and sound recordings.

7   Translated works, when the library or media center includes them in more than one language.

Titles proper of these works often vary.

When cataloging these kinds of works, the cataloger wants to have one title heading under which all versions, editions, and formats appear, so that someone searching in the catalog can select the one wanted from among all the library's holdings of that work. Uniform titles should not be made for every work that exists in more than one version unless multiple versions, editions, or formats are represented in the catalog or are likely to be added to it. Some works, however, such as the Bible, may require the addition of uniform titles to the catalog record because of the requirements of cooperative cataloging networks, even though your information center may own only one edition, version, or format.

Authority Files

Once name headings have been established, catalogers might want to keep records of the headings, cross-references, and sources of information used to establish them. Such records are called *authority files.* Large libraries that do a great deal of original cataloging often keep authority files, but because they are costly and time consuming to maintain, smaller libraries and media centers that do very little original cataloging may not do so.

Catalogers can look to LC and NLC for help in deciding on authoritative forms of names because these libraries maintain extensive authority files and issue lists of the name headings they establish. As mentioned previously, when faced with a new or unfamiliar name, catalogers can consult LC's *Name Authority File* or NLC's *Canadiana Authorities* for an already-established heading for the person, corporate body, or place name in question (see Figures 5.11 and 5.12). These tools are available directly from the two libraries, or indirectly as part of the services offered to customers of central, cooperative, or commercial cataloging services, and other sources.

FIGURE 5.11   Library of Congress authority record for a personal name.

```
ARN:    1131636
Rec stat: c        Entered:      19840524
Type:      z       Upd status:  a     Enc lvl:    n      Source:
Roman:             Ref status:  n     Mod rec:           Name use: a
Govt agn:          Auth status: a     Subj:       a      Subj use: a
Series:    n       Auth/ref:    a     Geo subd:   n      Ser use:  b
Ser num:   n       Name:        a     Subdiv tp:         Rules:    c
   1   010     n  84048778
   2   040        DLC   c DLC   d DLC
   3   005        19860703135455.4
   4   100 10  Intner, Sheila S.
   5   670        Her Access to nonprint materials, 1984:  b CIP t.p. (Sheila S.
Intner)
   6   670        Her Circulation policy in academic, public, and school
libraries, c1986:  b CIP t.p. (Sheila S. Intner) data sheet (b. 1935)
```

FIGURE 5.12   National Library of Canada authority record for a corporate body.

```
Leader                nz  22      n   4500

005              19990714104132.0
008              980122nneacnnnaabn            a ana

016      a       $a1003-K-9881E
110 2    a       $aCanadian Council for Health and Active Living at Work

040              $aCaOONL$beng$cCaOONL$dCaOONL
042              $anlc

410   2          $aCCHALW

670              $aWalk and roll, c1998:$bp. 2 (CCHALW)

710 25           $aConseil canadien de la santé et de la vie active au
                 travail$0(CaOONL)1003-K-9881F
```

Summary

Access is the process of choosing and formulating access points, or headings, under which a bibliographic description can be found in the catalog. The rules for choice and form of access points are contained in the second part of AACR2-98. Chapter 21 contains rules for choosing headings; chapters 22 through 25 provide rules for putting the choices into the proper form.

Catalogers choose two kinds of headings: main and added entries. Main entries differ from added entries only in that they are the first and most important access point chosen, and they would be the only one if the catalog did not have more than one access point for each work. The rules in Chapter 21 concern choice of main entry for the most part, but there also are rules to help in determining which added entries should be made after deciding on the main entry.

There are three kinds of main entries: persons, named groups of people acting together called corporate bodies, and titles. Our cataloging tradition operates on the assumption that the creator of a work is its most important identifying feature; therefore, if a work has a single or primary creator, this person usually is chosen as its main entry. The main exception to this rule is for works emanating from a corporate body. If that is the case, one must look at the type of work before choosing the corporate body as main entry. AACR2-98 puts strict limits on works that can be given a corporate body main entry. When a work emanates from a corporate body but is not among the types that can have corporate body main entries, it will be treated as if it did not emanate from the body and will be given an author or title main entry, depending on the information that appears on the item. If you encounter several creators, there are additional rules for choosing among them. Multiple creators can share a single kind of contribution to the item, such as joint authorship of a book, or different kinds, such as composing music and writing lyrics for a song. In AACR2-98, the former is called *shared* responsibility; the latter is called *mixed* responsibility.

Title main entries are chosen when there is no known creator; when there are too many co-equal creators; when an item emanates from a corporate body, but is not the type of work to which a corporate body main entry or author entry can be assigned; or when an item is produced under editorial direction.

Added entries chosen usually include people or corporate bodies other than the creator who contributed to the existence of the work, and titles found on or associated with the work. When the work belongs to a series, the series title can be chosen as an added entry.

Once the main and added entries are chosen, the names, titles, or both must be put into proper form so that the same name or uniform title heading will appear in only one way in the catalog. Separate chapters in AACR2-98 give rules for formulating personal names (Chapter 22), geographic names (Chapter 23), corporate body names (Chapter 24), and uniform titles (Chapter 25). Uniform titles are agreed-upon titles constructed by catalogers used as headings when works appear with many different titles proper. Because these varying titles proper would file in different places in the catalog, the uniform title is added to bring them together under a single heading. A user then can see all the library's holdings of a work and select the one wanted. Cross-references can be made to link related headings that might otherwise not be obvious to a catalog user. Chapter 26 furnishes rules for making them.

One final note: When choosing *added* entry access points, remember that AACR2-98 encourages catalogers to select any name or title they believe might be searched by someone using their catalogs. The only requirement is that the reason for the selection must be apparent from the bibliographic description. A note must be made for a desired added entry in Area 7 if the name or title does not appear elsewhere in the description.

In Figures 5.13 through 5.18, information from chief sources is reproduced. Choose the main and added entry access points you would want for your catalog. Those chosen by LC catalogers appear in Appendix C, along with explanations of the AACR2-98 rules used to make the choices.

FIGURE 5.13

Pertinent information from chief source of information (title page):

LIBRARY TECHNICAL SERVICES
OPERATIONS AND MANAGEMENT
EDITED BY IRENE P. GODDEN

(Book contains 7 essays by different authors plus an introduction by Godden and the statement: Library and Information Science Series)

Main entry: _____

Added entries: _____

_____

_____

FIGURE 5.14

Pertinent information from chief source of information (title page):

The Loma Prieta
(San Francisco/Monterey Bay)
Earthquake Emergency Response & Stabilization Study

Prepared for the Federal Emergency Management Agency
United States Fire Administration

Prepared by the National Fire Protection Association
Fire Investigations Department

Main entry: _____

Added entries: _____

_____

_____

FIGURE 5.15

Pertinent information from chief source of information (title page):

PLAN OR DIE!
10 KEYS TO ORGANIZATIONAL SUCCESS

TIMOTHY NOLAN, Ph.D.
LEONARD GOODSTEIN, Ph.D.
J. WILLIAM PFEIFFER, Ph.D., J.D.

(Preface states that this book was previously published under the title
Shaping Your Organization's Future)

Main entry:_____

Added entries: _____

_____

_____

FIGURE 5.16

Pertinent information from chief source of information (title screen of an Internet document):

The Art of Physics
Artists Who Depict the Forces of Nature
A Bibliography of Their Works Briefly Annotated

compiled by
Jean Miller
James Stewart
Leah Macdonald
Barbara Lewis

Main entry:_____

Added entries: _____

_____

_____

FIGURE 5.17

Pertinent information from chief source of information (title page):

THE SESAME STREET MOTHER GOOSE

(Information from verso: Copyright 1976 Children's Television Workshop ... "Sesame Street" and the "Sesame Street" sign are trademarks and servicemarks of Children's Television Workshop ... published by Random House, Inc.)

Main entry:_____

Added entries: _____

_____

_____

FIGURE 5.18

Pertinent information from chief source of information (title page):

ABUSE & NEGLECT OF OLDER ADULTS: A Discussion Paper
by L. McDonald & A. Collins for the Family Violence Prevention Unit, Health Canada,
published by Health Canada

Main entry:_____

Added entries: _____

_____

_____

Recommended Reading

Authority Control in the 21st Century: An Invitational Conference, March 31-April 1, 1996. Dublin, OH: OCLC Inc., 1996. Available online at http://www.oclc.org/oclc/man/authconf/confhome.htm.

Bierbaum, Esther Green. "A Modest Proposal: No More Main Entry." *American Libraries* 25 (January 1994): 81-84.

Carlyle, Alyson. "Fulfilling the Second Objective in the Online Catalog: Schemes for Organizing Author and Work Records into Usable Displays." *Library Resources & Technical Services* 41, no. 2 (April 1997): 79-100.

Clack, Doris Hargrett. *Authority Control: Principles, Applications, and Instructions.* Chicago: American Library Association, 1990.

The Future Is Now: Reconciling Change and Continuity in Authority Control: Proceedings of the OCLC Symposium, ALA Annual Conference, June 23, 1995. Dublin, OH: OCLC Inc., 1995.

Kaskus, Marie A., and Dawn Hale, eds. *Outsourcing Cataloging, Authority Work, and Physical Processing: A Checklist of Considerations.* Chicago: American Library Association, 1995.

Shoham, Snunith, and Susan S. Lazinger. "The No-Main-Entry-Principle and the Automated Catalog." *Cataloging & Classification Quarterly* 12 (1991): 51-67.

Smith, David, et al. *Using the New AACR2: An Expert Systems Approach to Choice of Access Points.* Rev. ed. London: Library Association, 1993.

Talmacs, Kerrie. "Authority Control." In *Technical Services Today and Tomorrow,* 2nd ed. Ed. Michael Gorman. Englewood, CO: Libraries Unlimited, 1998, p. 129-139.

Taylor, Arlene G. *The Organization of Information.* Englewood, CO: Libraries Unlimited, 1999.

Tull, Laura, et al. "Establishing Geographic Names." *Cataloging & Classification Quarterly* 10, no. 3 (1990): 3-17.

Notes

1. AACR2-98, 312.

2. Ibid.

3. Ibid., 384-385.

4. Ibid., 384.

5. Correspondence, September 21, 1999, with Margaret Stewart, Chief, Standards and Support, Acquisitions and Bibliographic Services, National Library of Canada.

6. Ibid.

7. AACR2-98, 434.

Special Applications of AACR2-98

Introduction

Public library and school library media center collections do not contain many unusual materials of the sort held in more specialized collections (historical materials in manuscript, recordings of various types, unpublished materials, sets, serials, etc.), but they may include a few such items, and these might require in-house original cataloging. Also, although introductory cataloging textbooks tend to focus mainly on the description of monographic books, leaving the task of addressing more complex issues involved in describing nonmonographic works to more advanced and specialized works, this text promises not to compromise relevance for simplicity. Therefore, this chapter focuses on three special types of materials and explains how AACR2-98 is applied to them: ongoing publications such as serials and series; unpublished materials; and nonbook formats.

Description of Serials

Serials include both *periodicals* and *continuations*. Periodicals are issued frequently (generally more than once a year), at regular intervals, and include materials such as journals, magazines, and newspapers. Continuations consist of less frequently issued items, irregularly issued items, or both, such as annuals and occasional papers.

To qualify for the AACR2-98 definition of a serial, a publication must satisfy two requirements—first, it must be issued in parts; second, the publisher's intention must be to continue issuing the parts forever. Problems result from a cataloger's inability to judge both requirements. It is impossible to predict with certainty that the parts of a title, once publication is initiated, will never cease being issued; or, conversely, that once a publisher stops issuing the parts of a particular title, it will never resume issuing them at some future time. Nevertheless, choosing to call a title "serial" means the cataloger has decided to assume that the parts will continue to be issued indefinitely into the future.

Although AACR2-98's definition does not specifically say it, the parts in which the serial is issued are all expected to bear the same name and no other. It is understood that publications bearing different names would not usually be interpreted as parts of the same title. (The title issue will be discussed again in connection with series and sets.) When a title changes, the item is considered a new publication for which a new cataloging record must be made.

Rules in AACR2-98 establish when to consider that a title has changed and when a change can safely be ignored, eliminating unnecessary work. For example, catalogers would not make a new record for a change in title from *The Universal Songfest Bulletin* to *Universal Songfest Bulletin* or from *County and State Education News* to *County & State Education News* (these are imaginary titles). A title is considered to have changed, according to AACR2-98, ". . . if any word other than an article, preposition, or conjunction is added, deleted, or changed, or if the order of the first five words (the first six words if the title begins with "A," "An," or "The") is changed."[1] Clearly, the imaginary examples just given are cases in which the title changes did not involve changing the first five significant words (excluding the initial article) in a substantive way. They would not need new catalog records.

It gets more difficult to decide if a title has changed when it goes from something such as the *THE Magazine* to *Technological Horizons in Education Magazine,* or vice versa. A great many title change problems arose in the past several decades with acronyms, perhaps not so much from a conscious wish to change these titles as from the desire of the rather staid scholarly societies that issued them (or their public relations staff) to modernize their images.

Title changes may or may not occur in conjunction with breaks in publication pattern. For example, when the American Library Association's Resources and Technical Services Division changed its name to Association for Library Collections & Technical Services, it also changed the name of its periodical newsletter from *RTSD Newsletter* to *ALCTS Newsletter,* without any break in the issuing of the parts. (For years, the Serials Section of this division has given a series of annual awards for title changes to highlight, in a humorous way, their displeasure with them. The year the RTSD-to-ALCTS title change occurred, it won the section's ultimate award, reserved for library and information science serials, known as "The Snake in the Grass Award.") But it is also possible for a serial title to cease publication for a while and, later, when the publisher decides to resume publication, reissue it under a different title. The new title will be given a new catalog record, and, unless the cataloger is extremely knowledgeable or the first issue of the new title is explicit about its name change, that record may lack a link to the previous title. Sometimes, however, publishers are careful to retain the same title for the resumption of a ceased serial even when they alter its contents and physical characteristics (size, illustration, etc.).

Underlying the description of serials is the concept that all parts of a title must be included in the description for that title. It means that serial descriptions are always open, unfinished, and in flux (commonly called "open entries"). This does not happen with monographic items, because by definition they either are complete when received for cataloging or they will be completed within a reasonable period of time when their descriptions can be filled out and finished. Elements in a serial record that may be expected to change over time, such as the names of editors, authors and titles of articles, etc., usually are omitted from the description to minimize the number of times the catalog record needs updating. LC, which does second-level cataloging for books, does only first level (sometimes with enrichments) for serials. This policy decision makes the records briefer and less informative, but also means the cataloging will be less costly and time-consuming, both in its initial preparation as well as in its ongoing maintenance.

AACR2-98 mandates that the first (or earliest available) issue of the title should be the source for bibliographic data. One advantage of doing this is that the place and name of the publisher need not change even when the reality differs. (Acquisition librarians might find this inconvenient, but the argument can be made that it is correct, even if it no longer reflects a current situation.) Combining the rule that says the earliest issue is the basis for cataloging with the rule that a new catalog record must be made if the title changes means that cataloging for serials that go through title changes is divided among several records. Links must be established through notes and cross references for other titles to which any one catalog record might be related, as shown in Figure 6.1. The source of information for Figure 6.1 is on the next page, 118. Under AACR1 rules, the latest issue of a serial was the basis for its catalog record, and all the earlier titles were subsumed under the newest one. If this rule were applied to the example in Figure 6.1, the cataloging for the same group of titles would look like Figure 6.2. (Some librarians still prefer those rules.)

FIGURE 6.1

This example is an illustration of:
- serial
- work emanating from a corporate body entered under title
- numeric and/or chronological, or other designation area
- publication date not listed, copyright date given
- closed entry
- multivolume work
- frequency note
- variations in title note
- relationship with other serials note
- bibliography and index note
- 2nd level cataloging

```
ASHRAE handbook & product directory / American Society of
   Heating, Refrigerating and Air Conditioning Engineers. --
   1973-1980. -- New York : ASHRAE, c1973-1980.
   8 v. : ill. ; 29 cm.

   Composed of alternatively issued vols. with subtitles:
Fundamentals; Applications; Equipment; and Systems.
   Annual.
   Continues: ASHRAE guide and data book.
   Continued by: ASHRAE handbook; product directory section
continued by: ASHRAE product specification file.
   Includes bibliographic references and index.
```

Fig. 6.1—Continues

FIGURE 6.1 *(continued)*

(chief source of information)
(title page)

ASHRAE HANDBOOK
&
PRODUCT DIRECTORY

1973 SYSTEMS

*An Instrument of Service
Prepared for the Profession
containing*

A TECHNICAL DATA SECTION OF REFERENCE MATERIAL PERTAINING TO SYSTEMS FOR HEATING, REFRIGERATING, VENTILATING, AND AIR-CONDITIONING, AND BASED ON—ASHRAE TRANSACTIONS—THE INVESTIGATIONS OF THE ASHRAE RESEARCH PROGRAMS AND COOPERATING INSTITUTIONS—AND THE PRACTICE OF THE MEMBERS AND FRIENDS OF THE SOCIETY; COMPLETE INDEX TO TECHNICAL SECTIONS OF ALL CURRENT VOLUMES; A PRODUCT DIRECTORY SECTION CONTAINING MANUFACTURERS' ADDRESSES, PRODUCT SOURCES, AND MANUFACTURERS' CATALOG DATA CONTAINING ESSENTIAL INFORMATION CONCERNING MODERN EQUIPMENT.

(information on verso)

COPYRIGHT 1973
BY THE

AMERICAN SOCIETY OF HEATING, REFRIGERATING
AND
AIR-CONDITIONING ENGINEERS, INC.

PUBLISHED BY THE
AMERICAN SOCIETY OF HEATING, REFRIGERATING
AND
AIR-CONDITIONING ENGINEERS, INC.
345 EAST 47TH STREET, NEW YORK, N. Y. 10017

(information from preface)

The 1973 Systems volume of ASHRAE Handbook & Product Directory (formerly ASHRAE Guide and Data Book) is another step forward in the continuing effort of ASHRAE to present the most complete and up-to-date source of reference data on air conditioning, heating, ventilating, and refrigerating.

A complete index to the technical data in this volume, the 1972 Equipment and 1971 Applications volumes of ASHRAE Guide and Data Book, and the 1972 ASHRAE *Handbook of Fundamentals*, is included in this volume (immediately following this Preface). Chapter titles for the four current books are included inside the front cover.

FIGURE 6.2

This example is an illustration of:
- serial
- work emanating from a corporate body entered under title
- numeric and/or chronological, or other designation area
- publication date not listed, copyright date given
- open entry
- frequency note
- variations in title note
- relationship with other serials note
- bibliography and index note
- ISSN
- 2nd level cataloging

```
ASHRAE handbook / American Society of Heating, Refrigerating
   and Air Conditioning Engineers. -- 1981-     . -- Atlanta :
   ASHRAE, c1981-     .
       v. : ill. ; 29 cm.

   Composed of alternatively issued vols. with subtitles:
Fundamentals; Applications; Equipment; and Systems.
   Annual.
   Companion volume to: ASHRAE product specification guide.
   Previous titles: ASHRAE handbook and product directory; ASHRAE
guide and data book.
   Includes bibliographic references and index.
   ISSN 1041-2344.
```

(chief source of information)
(title page)

ASHRAE HANDBOOK
1981 FUNDAMENTALS

An Instrument of Service
Prepared for the Profession
containing

A TECHNICAL DATA SECTION OF REFERENCE MATERIAL PERTAINING TO SYSTEMS FOR HEATING, REFRIGERATING, VENTILATING, AND AIR CONDITIONING, AND BASED ON—ASHRAE TRANSACTIONS—THE INVESTIGATIONS OF THE ASHRAE RESEARCH PROGRAMS AND COOPERATING INSTITUTIONS—AND THE PRACTICE OF THE MEMBERS AND FRIENDS OF THE SOCIETY: COMPLETE INDEX TO TECHNICAL SECTIONS OF ALL CURRENT VOLUMES.

PUBLISHED BY THE
AMERICAN SOCIETY OF HEATING, REFRIGERATING
AND
AIR-CONDITIONING ENGINEERS, INC.
1791 TULLIE CIRCLE NE, ATLANTA, GA 30329

(information in preface)

The 1981 Fundamentals volume of the ASHRAE HAND-BOOK is the latest step in a continuing effort to provide the most comprehensive and current source of reference data on air conditioning, heating, ventilation, and refrigeration. This volume replaces the 1977 Volume. Also see the ASHRAE Product Specification File, a companion volume to the HANDBOOK. It contains a Product Directory, Catalog Data Section, Publications Catalog, and other useful information. The File will be revised annually to update and expand this information.

A complete index to the technical data in this volume, as well as the 1980 Systems, 1979 Equipment, and 1978 Applications volumes, is included (immediately following the preface). Chapter titles for the four current volumes are listed inside the front cover.

Errata for the 1980 Systems Volume follows the Technical Data Section (page ER1). Errata for the 1981 Fundamentals Volume will be included in the 1982 Applications Volume.

In preparing this volume, the HANDBOOK Committee has had the valuable cooperation of many of the Technical Committees, under the general guidance of the ASHRAE Research and Technical Committee.

Technical Committees are charged by the Research and Technical Committee with the responsibility for review and updating of HANDBOOK Chapters within their area of interest.

The specific Technical Committee (TC) for each chapter is indicated in a footnote at the bottom of the first page of the chapter.

(information on verso)

COPYRIGHT 1981

BY THE
AMERICAN SOCIETY OF HEATING, REFRIGERATING
AND
AIR-CONDITIONING ENGINEERS, INC.

ISSN appears on later volumes

According to LC rule interpretations for cataloging serials, Area 1 includes only the title proper, a gmd if the title is one of the media for which LC uses them, and the first statement of responsibility if there is one and it differs from the main entry of the work. For many serials, this means just the title proper. Figure 6.3 shows bibliographic data and corresponding Area 1, done according to LC's policies.

Area 2 for serials contains the same information as for nonserial items and is formulated in the same way. When a newspaper, for example, is published in different versions for local and distant markets (such as *The New York Times* local edition for metropolitan New York and non-local edition for other U.S. cities), the statements identifying each edition are given in Area 2. Journals may have varying editions for specific readerships, in various languages, or in different formats, all of which would be given in this area. AACR2-98 lists five types of data that belong here: local editions; special interests; special formats; languages; and reprints or reissues. The information is transcribed exactly as it appears in the item.

Area 3 was originally designed with printed serials in mind as the place to record the numbering and dating of individual issues. After these data are given, they are followed by a hyphen and four spaces to indicate that the area is unfinished. If the serial "dies," the closing numbering and dating will be added in those spaces. Here are some commonly encountered interpretations of data for Area 3:

The first issue of a magazine says "Issue number 1"
>   Area 3: Issue no. 1---- .

The last issue of the same magazine says "Issue number 101"
>   Area 3: Issue no. 1-101.

The first screen of an electronic periodical says "Volume 1, number 1, 1999"
>   Area 3: Vol. 1, no. 1 (1999)---- .

The first screen of an electronic periodical says "Volume 1, number 1, January 1999"
>   Area 3: Vol. 1, no. 1 (Jan. 1999)---- .

The rules assume that numbering will not change over the life of a serial, but things don't always work that way. Sometimes a publisher will begin by numbering each issue sequentially, but find, later on, that it is advantageous to supply readers with volume numbers as well as issue numbers. This happened with *Library Hi-Tech,* shown in Figure 6.4, which continues to supply both its old and new numbering systems.

The date in Area 4, like the numbering in Area 3, is followed by a hyphen and four spaces to make room for an eventual end date. This structure demonstrates the unfinished status of the title. Similarly, the number of pieces in the extent is omitted, because it will change as each issue, volume, reel, cassette, or other physical part is published (see Figure 6.3).

Notes encountered frequently in serials records include some common to monographs, such as the source of data for title proper (often taken from the cover), but others are unique to serials, such as the frequency of issue, which AACR2-98 mandates should be given as the first note. Another note unique to serials is the "relationship with other serials" data, in which the cataloger can record earlier and later titles, mergers and splits, absorptions, supplements, and other information.

FIGURE 6.3

ISSN 0737-8831

Consecutive Issue 5; Vol. 2, No. 1/1984

LIBRARY HI TECH

PUBLISHER
C. Edward Wall

EDITOR-IN-CHIEF
Nancy Jean Melin

ASSOCIATE EDITORIAL DIRECTOR
Thomas Schultheiss

MANAGING EDITOR
Linda Mark

EDITORIAL ASSISTANTS
Karen Bell
Susan Gooding
Jon Hertzig

ADVERTISING
Eileen Parker, *Advertising Manager*
Mary Beth Bimber, *Advertising Assistant*

PRODUCTION
Peggy Cabot, *Production Supervisor*
Bronwyn Beeler, *Production/Layout*
Rebecca McDermott, *Production Assistant*

DESIGN
Bronwyn Beeler
Eileen Parker

Published quarterly: Spring (published April); Summer (published July); Fall (published October); Winter (published January).

Subscriptions are $39.50 per year; $36.00 per year for each additional subscription, same customer; Foreign subscriptions (including Canada and P.U.A.) are $46.50 per year. Single issues, $12.50; individuals may subscribe for $19.50 per year.* Combined subscriptions to Library Hi Tech Journal and Library Hi Tech News (11 issues per year) are $90.00 per year. Individuals may purchase a combined subscription for $54.00 per year.* Send all subscription orders, changes of address, and claims to Pierian Press, P.O. Box 1808, Ann Arbor, MI 48106: (313) 434–5530.

*(Individual subscriptions must be paid by personal check or money order and deliverable to home address only.)

LHT accepts advertising for products or services applicable to libraries/information centers or of interest to those involved with information management. LHT reserves the right to reject any advertisement which is deemed inappropriate to the advertising profile of the periodical or which, in view of the Editors, features misinformation, distortion of facts, or exaggerated claims. Direct advertising correspondence to Eileen Parker, P.O. Box 1808, Ann Arbor, MI 48106. Rates upon request. (313) 434–6409.

Reader letters and queries may be forwarded directly to the Editor at 42 Grandview, Mt. Kisco, NY 10549, or call 914/666-4099. Editorial specialists are identified at the back of the journal and should be consulted for matters relating to potential and submitted manuscripts as appropriate.

Library Hi Tech is unique as a current guide to all available and forthcoming technologies applicable to libraries and information centers; as a single source reviewing related literature in periodicals, books, reports, studies and conference proceedings; as a major journal of practical articles related to all available and forthcoming technologies. LHT evaluates, describes, and reports on the selection, installation, maintenance, and integration of systems and hardware. Library Hi Tech is indexed in *Current Index to Journals in Education*.

FIGURE 6.4

This example is an illustration of:
- serial
- work emanating from a corporate body entered under title
- other title information
- numeric and/or alphabetic, chronological, or other designation area
- open entry
- same organization responsible for intellectual content and publication
- frequency note
- source of title note
- ISSN
- 2nd level cataloging

```
Ex libris news : newsletter of the Ex Libris Association. --
    No. 1 (spring 1987)-      . -- London, Ont. : The
    Association, 1987-
        v. ; 28 cm.

    Two issues yearly.
    Title from caption.
    ISSN 0833-4278.
```

Cataloging according to Library of Congress policy

```
Ex libris news. -- No. 1 (spring 1987)-      . -- London, Ont. :
    The Association, 1987-
        v. ; 28 cm.

    Two issues yearly.
    Title from caption.
    ISSN 0833-4278.
```

(chief source of information)
   (title on first page)

EX LIBRIS NEWS ..... Newsletter of the Ex Libris Association

Supported by funds from NEW HORIZONS FOR SENIOR CITIZENS

Spring 1987 (Number 1)   ISSN 0833-4278

The standard number for serials, which is entered in Area 8, is the International Standard Serial Number (ISSN). It consists of two groups of four digits each, separated by a hyphen. Among other data considered standard and entered here is the key-title, a unique identifier applied to every serial recognized by the International Serials Data System (ISDS). ISDS is an international program of serials identification similar to ISSN, but it is sponsored by UNESCO's UNISIST program (Universal System for Information in Science and Technology), whereas ISSN is sponsored by IFLA.

Description of Series

Another type of material that can be collected is a group of items that appear one at a time very much like monographic books, but continue to be issued over long periods of time. If each item in the group has its own title in addition to the common title, the group of items qualifies as a "series" or, more specifically, a "monographic series."[2] When a monographic series contains numbers, it qualifies as a type of serial.[3] It is easy to see why catalogers have problems distinguishing serials and series—even the definitions in AACR2-98 overlap and fail to clarify them completely.

Sometimes, librarians also deal with materials called "sets." Sets are not defined or discussed by AACR2-98. The concept of a set comes from the world of publishing, not the world of cataloging. Materials issued in sets will fit into the definition of a multivolume monograph or a monographic series, depending on the structure of the titles. If they are simply multivolume monographs, a group of items will have one catalog record that encompasses them all. If they are a monographic series, more complicated decisions will govern their treatment.

If a group of items is a true series, it can be treated in two ways: monographically or serially. The decision is a matter of local policy, and it should be considered very carefully when it is made. All series can be treated alike, or selected series can be treated differently, depending on how people may be expected to search for them and use them. When a series is treated monographically, records are made for each individual item, with one element—Area 6—used to give the series data: title, number of the item within the series, ISSN, etc.

When a series is treated serially, it means that the catalog record relates solely to the series, including the title statement, edition, publication data, physical description, etc. Until the series ends, some data elements will be left open, as it is in serial records, such as the dates of publication and total number of volumes. Information about individual volumes, if included in the record at all, appears in the notes, generally in the form of a contents note giving the titles of the individual volumes and requires updating as each new volume appears.

Treating each part of the series individually provides more data and greater searchability. Treating all items together as one unit in one catalog record minimizes the amount of data it contains and the work to prepare it; therefore it is more economical and efficient as well as less costly. Figure 6.5 shows a catalog record for a monographic series and Figure 6.6 an example of a record for one of the works in the series if the decision were made to catalog each item separately.

FIGURE 6.5

This example is an illustration of:
- monographic series
- title main entry
- place of publication supplied
- publishing date not listed, copyright date given
- open entry
- descriptive illustration statement
- index note
- contents note
- Canadian CIP data
- two levels of cataloging

2nd level enriched cataloging

```
Records of our history. -- [Ottawa] : Public Archives Canada,
   c1982-
      v. : col. ill., facsims., col. maps ; 28 cm.

   Includes indexes.
   Contents: Dreams of empire : Canada before 1700 / André Vachon,
Victorin Chabot, André Desrosiers -- Taking root : Canada from
1700 to 1760 / André Vachon, Victorin Chabot, André Desrosiers --
Colonial identities : Canada from 1760 to 1815 / Bruce G. Wilson
-- A future defined : Canada from 1849 to 1893 / George
Bolotenko.
```

1st level cataloging

```
Records of our history. -- Public Archives Canada, c1982-
      v.
```

FIGURE 6.6

This example is an illustration of:
- item in monographic series cataloged separately
- other title information
- place of publication supplied
- publishing date not listed,copyright date given
- detailed pagination
- descriptive illustration statement
- unnumbered series statement
- index note
- ISBN qualified
- Canadian CIP data
- 2nd level cataloging

Wilson, Bruce G.
   Colonial identities : Canada from 1760 to 1815 / Bruce G.
Wilson. -- [Ottawa] : National Archives of Canada, c1988.
   xii, 236 p. : col. ill., facsims., col. maps, music ; 28 cm.
-- (Records of our history)

   Includes index.
   ISBN 0-660-12721-0 (pbk.).

(chief source of information)
      (title page)

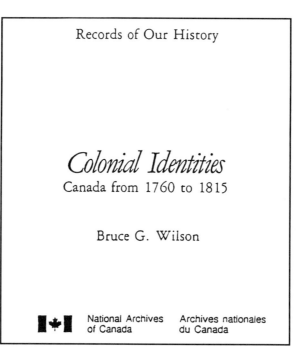

Records of Our History

Colonial Identities

Canada from 1760 to 1815

Bruce G. Wilson

National Archives of Canada   Archives nationales du Canada

(information on verso)

° Minister of Supply and Services Canada 1988
Available in Canada through
associated bookstores
and other booksellers

Cat. No.: SA2-129/3-1988-1E
ISBN: 0-660-12721-0
Canada: $24.95
Other countries: $29.95

Canadian Cataloguing in Publication Data

Wilson, Bruce G., 1946–
   Colonial identities: Canada from 1760 to 1815

   (Records of our History)
   Issued also in French under title:
   Identités coloniales.
   DSS cat. no. SA2-129/3-1988-E (bound)
   DSS cat. no. SA2-129/3-1988-1E (pbk.)
   ISBN 0-660-12666-4 (bound): $34.95 ($41.95, foreign)
   ISBN 0-660-12721-0 (pbk.): $24.95 ($29.95, foreign)
1. Canada—History—1763–1791—Sources.
2. Canada—History—1760–1763—Sources.
3. Canada—History—1791–1841—Sources.
I. National Archives of Canada. II. Title. III. Series.
FC410.W54 1988 971.02 C88-099000-7
F1032.W54 1988

To summarize, when a series is treated collectively, description will be handled as follows:

Area 1:   Series title proper, gmd, other title, and responsibility data relating solely to the series as a whole.

Area 2:   Edition statement relating solely to the series as a whole.

Area 3:   Not applicable for a monographic series unless the format is cartographic, musical, or electronic resource.

Area 4:   Initial publication date and a hyphen, plus four spaces for an end date when the final volume in the series is issued.

Area 5:   Three blank spaces and the smd; generally include in other subareas solely that data applying to the series as a whole, not to individual volumes.

Area 6:   Not applicable unless the series being cataloged is, itself, part of another series.

Area 7:   If access to individual volumes is desired, give their titles in a contents note.

Area 8:   ISSN (or, if it has one, an ISBN) solely for the series as a whole; do not use for ISBNs on individual volumes in this area, but include them with the title to which they relate in the contents note, if desired.

"Generic" Titles

When rules for interpreting titles proper are applied to serials, it is not unusual for the titles of different serial publications to be identical generic terms like "Bulletin" or "Directory." These titles also may function as main entries. Thus, a file results with many different publications bearing the same main entry title. Catalogers resolve the conflict by applying uniform titles to distinguish what would otherwise be identical titles for different works—exactly the opposite of the original function of uniform titles to bring together differing titles for the same work.

AACR2-98 rule 25.5B allows for additions to be made to uniform titles to resolve conflicts, but the rule merely says one should add an "appropriate" word or phrase, leaving the choice of which word or phrase to use to catalogers. Catalogers and reference librarians have long debated the relative merits of specific elements as the appropriate qualifier. Catalogers favor adding places of publication, which tend to be more concise and require less work to establish properly than the names of sponsoring bodies. Reference librarians favor adding the names of sponsoring bodies because they believe searchers find it to be more useful information than the publisher's locations. Figure 6.7 shows the two possible uniform titles for a "generic" title proper. The source of information for Figure 6.7 is on page 128.

LC and NLC rule interpretations instruct North American catalogers to add the place of publication. Some libraries and media centers may find that this results in questions about where to find particular titles and may want to make name-title added entries for sponsoring bodies and the titles to accommodate users.

FIGURE 6.7

This example is an illustration of:
- serial
- uniform title main entry for a title that has the same title as other serials; two records with alternative qualifiers
- numeric and/or alphabetic, chronological, or other designation area
- first issue lacks designation
- open entry
- frequency note
- source of title note
- quoted note
- numbering and chronological designation note
- ISSN
- 2nd level cataloging

```
Access (Ontario Library Association)
    Access. -- [No. 1] (autumn 1994)-      . -- Toronto : Naylor
Communications, 1994-
        v. : ill. ; 28 cm.

    Three issues yearly.
    Title from cover.
    "Official publication of the Ontario Library Association".
    Numbering irregular autumn 1994 to winter 1996.
    ISSN 1201-0472.


Access (Toronto, Ont.)
    Access. -- [No. 1] (autumn 1994)-      . -- Toronto : Naylor
Communications, 1994-
        v. : ill. ; 28 cm.

    Three issues yearly.
    Title from cover.
    "Official publication of the Ontario Library Association".
    Numbering irregular autumn 1994 to winter 1996.
    ISSN 1201-0472.
```

Fig. 6.7—Continues

FIGURE 6.7 *(continued)*

(chief source of information)
   (Title page substitute: analytical title page)

Ontario Library Association
100 Lombard St., Suite 303
Toronto M5C 1M3
(416) 363-3388
FAX (416) 941-9581 or
(800) 387-1181
E-Mail: moorel@gov.on.ca

Published for the members of the Ontario
Library Association three times per year, *Access*
furthers the continuing education activities of
the Association. The magazine is a forum on
issues, a source of ideas for the improvement of
librarianship in Ontario and a touchstone for
the trends that will affect the future development of the profession.

Executive Director: Larry Moore
Deputy Director/Communications:
   Jefferson Gilbart, CAE
Deputy Director/Programs: Maureen Cubbarley
Membership: Toni Porter
Publications Assistant: Theresa Lung

The Official Publication Of The Ontario Library Association OLA

Table of Contents

SPECIAL REPORT:
The Virtual Library

On The Cover... Tall Ships sailed into Collingwood last summer and
helped the local library raise $27,000. *Photo courtesy of Georgian Bay '94*

Access is published by Naylor Communications Ltd. 6th Floor, 920 Yonge Street, Toronto,
ON, M4W 3C7 Tel: (416) 961-1028 Fax: (416) 924-4408.

Publisher: Robert Thompson

Editor: Lori Knowles   PUBLISHED OCTOBER 1994/861

Sales Manager: Tim German

Sales Representatives: Barb Tate, Bob Graham, Cyndi Brown

Practical Issues

Making the basic decision to treat items in a series all together or individually has implications that go beyond descriptive cataloging. The number and kinds of access points made subsequently also depend on this choice as well as the way individual items will be indexed and classified. If the combined decision factors are seen as a continuum, the two extremes can be described as follows:

> Choice No. 1—One record for all: Make this choice if all the volumes in a series should stand together in one place on the shelf for client convenience; if searchers would be likely to seek them using the same subject terms; and if the unique titles of individual volumes were less important to searchers than the common series title.

> Choice No. 2—One record for each individual item: Make this choice if each volume would be used in different ways by different clients; if searchers would use different search terms; or if the individual volumes would be expected to be in different places on the shelves.

Serials (and series treated as serials) may not be classified at all in some libraries and media centers. Instead, they are shelved in alphabetical order by title in a separate section instead of being intershelved with books on the same subjects. The potential benefits of grouping serials by form (making it easier to find something if one knows it is a serial) must be weighed against the potential benefits of keeping them together with materials on the same subject (making it easier to find more material on a particular subject), particularly when searchers tend to do a lot of browsing at the shelves, as is common in public libraries and school library media centers.

Describing Unpublished Materials

Internally produced documents such as reports, lectures, and similar items are sometimes found in public library and media center collections. Some look very much like their published counterparts, with covers, title pages, tables of contents, etc.; but others could be extremely informal—file folders containing memos, letters, minutes of meetings, or other assorted items; taped recordings of speeches, presentations, or interviews; or, possibly, databases of information concerning special projects or research studies. No matter what their origins or outward appearances, these materials can be important parts of a collection and should be treated with as much care as any published items.

Verna Urbanski[4] suggests answering the following questions before making decisions about cataloging unpublished items:

- Why do we have this item and why is it being kept?

- How long will the item be retained?

- Does the library have other materials similar to this and, if so, how were they handled?

- Is this item part of an ongoing collection?

- Is there a way to capture ephemeral information that may not be available later?

- Can information be authenticated?

- Does the source of information contain obvious errors?

Urbanski's questions are aimed at choosing the appropriate route to follow for cataloging. Decisions should be informed by knowledge of what an item is and why it was put in the collection. Also, the length of time the item can be expected to remain in the collection will help decide about the level of cataloging it should receive. Generally speaking, items intended for long-term retention warrant more detailed treatment than items with a short shelf life. Urbanski's third question implies that locating similar items and examining their treatment would reveal the presence of a *de facto* policy already in place; whereas the fourth suggests that any ongoing collection has policies and new additions must follow them.

So far, the answers to these four questions help to determine the existence of previously made cataloging policy decisions applying to the item in hand; or, if none have been made, identifying the kinds of characteristics that would help to determine the correct treatment for it. Urbanski's last three questions move beyond "how to catalog" to the next matter: how complete and trustworthy is the bibliographic data on the item? Speed is an essential factor in obtaining the best possible data. When an unpublished item comes across one's desk, a background check needs to be done at once if cataloging is to be done. Otherwise, by the time one asks who created the item and why, when was it done and where, or what was its intended use, no one may be able to answer. The people involved might have moved on to other projects and neglected to leave a paper trail. They may have been hired temporarily as consultants, or been an ad hoc team assembled for a limited time. In the worst-case scenario, no one can identify the item or provide information for cataloging.

When unpublished material is common in a collection, it is useful to develop a form for identifying the data elements needed for cataloging. Units that regularly generate such documents (e.g., school departments that retain student projects or local history librarians who acquire minutes of town meetings) might be encouraged to fill out the data form when they prepare a document, or attach it to the item with as much information as they can provide. Or, the form can be used by catalogers to gather basic information immediately on receiving an unpublished item, without waiting to identify it until it is cataloged.

In the long run, if an item will be retained and used in the same manner as published material receiving full cataloging, the fact that it was not published should make no difference. If specific types of unpublished materials will continue being added to the collection, establishing policies for their cataloging, classification, and indexing will speed the process and ensure consistent treatment for related items. In the paragraphs that follow, the most critical descriptive elements likely to differ from published materials are described.

Data Sources: Unpublished items can lack traditional bibliographic data sources entirely, such as title pages, title screens, labels, and other equivalents mentioned in AACR2-98. When this is the case, flexibility needs to be exercised in choosing alternatives, which might be the item itself, taken as a whole, the cover or first page, or a reference source. Equally important as making the choice of chief source is indicating it in the catalog record by means of a note, so that data can be verified by a searcher trying to match a retrieved document against a catalog record.

Even when a chief source is present, the data on it—not needed for identifying and marketing the item to potential buyers, sellers, or users—may not be given in the expected manner. Abbreviations, initials, and shorthand notations of various kinds may be provided in place of full titles, names of people or groups responsible for the item, etc. Errors in spelling and wording may be suspected, or may be obvious to the cataloger. Work to authenticate and verify data may be needed. Nonetheless, catalogers must work with what they have, and AACR2-98 is very specific in mandating that even errors must be transcribed, although they can be corrected. If a person's name is misspelled on a title page, it is transcribed as given, but corrected—"by Jean [i.e., Joan] Thurston." If Ms. Thurston's name was given on the title page as "J.T.," it can be augmented as follows: "by J[oan] T[hurston]." And, if the cataloger knows, having talked to

Ms. Thurston, that she is solely the editor, not the author, "[edited]" is added before the word "by," as follows: "[edited] by J[oan] T[hurston]." When a searcher sees "by J.T." on the title page, it will match up to the statement of responsibility with its bracketed information which, although more complete and more informative, does not match what they see on the page.

Supplying Titles: In supplying titles, the best rule of thumb is to keep the construction as simple and direct as possible, and not add unnecessary words. For example, if a videotape of a special assembly about lunar rocks contains no title screens or labels, one might call it "Lunar rocks," not "Videorecording of an assembly about lunar rocks," or "Assembly on lunar rocks," or "Lunar rocks assembly," which contain extra words. The name of the school and the event will be part of be the main entry of the item, so it need not appear as part of the title, and the fact that the item is a video will appear in the general material designation immediately following the title. Unless there is a compelling reason to incorporate other elements into a constructed title proper (such as having keyword searching available solely for titles proper), they can and should be omitted.

Edition Statements: One might think that unpublished items cannot possibly have multiple editions, but documents can go through drafts, be updated and revised, amended, or otherwise altered. When statements on an unpublished item indicate that these kinds of changes have been made, they are interpreted in the same manner as ordinary edition statements on published works and belong in Area 2.

Publication, Distribution Information: The most obvious difference from published materials is that there is no "publication, distribution" information for unpublished materials. The publisher's or distributor's place and name are omitted. However, based on the rationale that dates are too important an element of description to omit entirely, the date of an item's creation is given in Area 4 for unpublished materials (see Figures 6.8 and 6.9). The sole exception to the rule of including a date is the case of naturally occurring objects that have not been packaged for commercial distribution—no date is given for those objects (see Figure 4.4).

Series Statements: Although series statements are not generally associated with unpublished materials, they can appear. Series titles are useful as access points when an ongoing project or program generates a flow of items with their own titles proper as well as that of the series. Examples are lecture and concert series, in which each lecture, concert, or presentation has its own title proper as well as the title of the series. (Take care not to mistake an item issued in parts all bearing the same title—a serial—as a monographic series.) When an "official" series title doesn't appear on the individual items, but the library or media center would benefit from having it, one can be constructed using the name of the project, program, or presentation series. Once established, catalogers are obliged to track the title as they would any other heading, in a series title authority file.

Notes: Catalog records for unpublished materials benefit from having useful notes. However, a few notes that haven't been highlighted previously in this book merit mention here. Notes relating to the origins of the item may be especially useful to searchers who have forgotten why a particular document was created. Similarly, when the names of contributors to the item are not "prominently displayed," but they could be searched, the notes are the place to record them so access points can be created. Finally, any numbers found on unpublished items should be recorded in notes, especially if notes are, themselves, searchable. These numbers, often overlooked or ignored on published materials, can include identifiers important to the library or school, and should be given as found on the item.

Urbanski also mentions notes relating to title variations, accompanying materials and supplements, audience, summary, contents, and copy-specific information as well as "with" notes, which link records made for parts of an item.[5] These should be kept in mind and used as needed when cataloging unpublished items.

FIGURE 6.8

This example is an illustration of:
- unpublished item
- work emanating from a corporate body entered under title
- title proper is acronym
- other title information
- more than three corporate bodies responsible for intellectual content
- marks of omission
- descriptive illustration statement
- 2nd level cataloging

```
WHMIS : workplace hazardous materials information system /
   Mohawk College, produced by the Physical Services
   Department ... [et al.]. -- 1991.
   43 p. : ill., forms ; 28 cm.
```

(chief source of information)
  (title page)

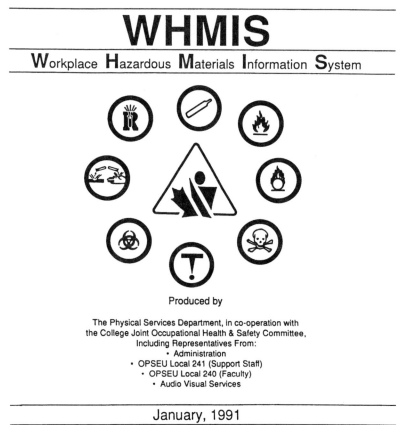

FIGURE 6.9

Chief source of information (the item itself) has:

----

on the bottom of the item: made by L.H. Smith 1988

----

no other information is given

This example is an illustration of:
- model
- unpublished, unique item with a stated creator
- option of fuller form of given names added to name in heading to distinguish it from headings that would otherwise be identical
- supplied title
- optional omission of the specific material designation "1 model" in the physical description area
- source of title proper note
- summary
- 2nd level cataloging

```
Smith, L.H. (Leslie Harold).
   [Canal lock system] [model] / made by L.H. Smith. -- 1988.
   2 pieces : wood and glass ; 60 x 20 x 30 cm.

   Title supplied by cataloger.
   Summary: With or without the use of water, demonstrates both
manual and automated systems for assisting the passage of a boat
through different water levels.
```

Access points are created in the same manner for unpublished items as for published materials, as are subject descriptors and classification numbers. AACR2-98 does not contain any special instructions for creating access points for unpublished materials. The first question to be answered in determining main entry, "Does this item emanate from a corporate body," may, however, be of critical importance. If the answer is "yes," items such as internal policies, other official statements, minutes of meetings, etc., all would receive corporate body main entries. Research reports and external databases (such as data from an experiment conducted by a school's faculty members or a piece of music composed by a member of the school orchestra) would not qualify, because these are not administrative works nor do they reflect activity shared by the whole body. When the answer is "no," the next option is to seek a person entirely or primarily responsible for the intellectual or artistic content of the item.

Access to unpublished materials is enhanced considerably when added entries are made liberally. This gives searchers every opportunity to locate materials via related names and titles. Title added entries for supplied titles are not usually made because searchers are unlikely to know what title has been assigned in the catalog department, but title added entries for titles appearing on an item can be good sources for keywords. Depending on the value of the documents, it might be appropriate to ignore AACR2-98's "rule of three" and make added entries for more than three personal or corporate body authors, editors, sponsors, etc. Similarly, subject descriptors can be assigned to express all relevant topics of interest, because knowledge of the persons or bodies associated with the item could fade although need for the item continues.

Subject access through classification is unaffected by the absence of publication. Because it is content-related rather than object-related, classification is no more difficult for unpublished items than for published ones.

Principles in
Cataloging Nonbook Materials

Decades of experience with materials in different formats that libraries and media centers collect has led catalogers to develop additional principles on which to base cataloging decisions. These principles are explored a little further in this section.

Data Sources: The principle governing the choice of places from which to take bibliographic information is always to prefer information closest to the material itself. For example, catalogers prefer title screens to labels on a videocassette and prefer the labels pasted permanently to the videocassette over any box or case in which the cassette was packed. The preferred places from which cataloging information should be gathered can require viewing the contents of an item such as a videorecording or an electronic resource, but doing so requires the equipment with which the medium is associated. When the equipment is not available, alternative information sources must be used. AACR2-98 provides for alternatives to title screens and the like, and when one is chosen the cataloger need not use brackets on the information taken from them, but the data may differ from what would have been found in the preferred place. For that reason, catalogers should ensure that those using their catalog records know where they found the information given in it, and make notes about their data sources.

Titles: Nonbook items, particularly those packaged in small physical carriers, can bear abbreviated titles or acronym versions of longer titles that would not fit in the space available for identifying data. The principle to be followed here is to acknowledge the importance of multiple titles. They should be described in the notes and traced.

Title interpretation for selected nonbook materials requires special rules. Musical scores and recordings can have generic titles similar to those discussed in connection with serials, although the terms involved denote types of compositions (such as symphony, concerto, or cantata). These titles are given special title proper constructions and uniform titles to aid in their identification and retrieval.

Catalogers unfamiliar with music may be confused in deciding whether a title is generic or distinctive. It is done by removing the following elements and examining what is left after they are gone: the composer's name or other statements of responsibility; the key in which the music is written; the series number; the number within the body of the composer's works, known as an opus number; or, the number within a well-known list of the composer's works (for Mozart, this would be a Köchel number). *Beethoven's Ninth Symphony* sounds as though it is distinctive, but if one removes the name of the composer and series number, one is left with only "Symphony." *Chopin's Fantasy Impromptu,* on the other hand, is distinctive, because when one removes the composer's name, one is left with "Fantasy Impromptu," which is more than the name of the compositional type (in this case, a fantasy).

When a title is generic, elements that would normally be excluded from title proper (serial number, opus number, key signature, etc.) are added to form a more identifiable title proper. When a title is distinctive, they are excluded from title proper and recorded as other title information, after the appropriate ISBD punctuation. Figures 6.10 and 6.11 show the way titles proper and uniform titles should be constructed for generic and distinctive musical titles. Notice the placement of the general material designation in the two examples.

FIGURE 6.10

This example is an illustration of:
- sound disc (compact disc)
- bilingual item in which title on chief source of information is in one language only
- uniform title
- optional placement of general material designation at end of title proper
- statement of subsidiary responsibility
- publication date not listed, decade certain (copyright date given in the accompanying materials note cannot be assumed to be the date of the production of the compact disc; it only refers to the content of the program notes)
- accompanying material given in note area
- publisher's number given in optional placement as first note
- performer note
- 2nd level cataloging

```
Beethoven, Ludwig van.
    [Concertos, violin, orchestra, op. 61, D major]
    Violin concerto in D major, op. 61 [sound recording] /
Beethoven ; cadenzas by Kreisler. -- Middlesex, England : EMI,
[199-]
    1 sound disc (43 min., 47 sec.) : digital, stereo. ; 4 3/4 in.

    EMI: LG0233.
    Itzhak Perlman, violin; Philharmonia Orchestra, Carlo Maria
Giulini, conductor.
    Program notes in English, German, French, and Italian by Basil
Deane, c1981.
```

(chief source of information)
(label on disc)

(information on program notes

```
BEETHOVEN
VIOLIN CONCERTO IN D MAJOR, Op. 61
(Cadenzas by Kreisler)
ITZHAK PERLMAN (Violin)
PHILHARMONIA ORCHESTRA
conducted by
CARLO MARIA GIULINI
LG 0233
```

LUDWIG VAN BEETHOVEN
(1770 – 1827)

Concerto for Violin and Orchestra in D major, Op. 61
Konzert für Violine und Orchester D-dur, Op. 61
Concerto pour violon et orchestre en Ré majeur, Op. 61

1 I: Allegro ma non troppo (Cadenza/Kadenz/ | 24'19|
     Cadence: Kreisler)
2 II: Larghetto   [19'28|
     III: Rondo (Allegro)
     (Cadenza/Kadenz/Cadence: Kreisler)

Producer/Produzent/
Directeur de production:
Suvi Raj Grubb

Balance Engineer/
Tonmeister/Ingénieur du son:
Michael Gray

Cover photo/Foto Titelseite/
Photo en couverture:
Christian Steiner

℗ 1981 Original sound
  recording made by
  EMI Records Ltd.
©
Printed in Japan/
Imprimé au Japon
Made in Japan
EMI Records Ltd. Hayes
Middlesex England

Itzhak Perlman
(Violin/Violine/Violon)

Philharmonia Orchestra

Conductor/Dirigent/Chef d'orchestre
Carlo Maria Giulini

ITZHAK PERLMAN
CARLO MARIA GIULINI
BEETHOVEN: VIOLIN CONCERTO
PHILHARMONIA ORCHESTRA

FIGURE 6.11

This example is an illustration of:
- sound cassette
- bilingual item in which title on chief source of information is in one language only
- uniform title (in 2nd level example)
- optional placement of general material designation at end of uniform title (in 2nd level example) and at end of title proper (in 1st level example)
- city of publication not listed, country given
- publication date not listed, century certain
- optional omission of "sound" in extent of item (in 1st level example)
- accompanying material given in note area (in 2nd level example) and in the physical description area (in 1st level)
- publisher's number given in proper place in 2nd level example and in optional placement as first note in 1st level example
- variations in title note
- edition and history note given as a quoted note
- performer note
- two levels of cataloging

2nd level cataloging

```
Handel, George Frideric.
  [Messiah. Sound recording]
  Messiah / George Frideric Handel. -- Holland : Philips, [19--]
  3 sound cassettes : analog, stereo.

  Title on container: Messiah = Messiah.
  ''Complete original version.''
  Heather Harper, soprano; Helen Watts, contralto; John
Wakefield, tenor; John Shirley-Quirk, bass; Ralph Downes, organ;
Leslie Pearson, harpsichord; William Lang, trumpet; London
Symphony Choir, John Aldis, chorus master; London Symphony
Orchestra, Colin Davis, conductor.
  Program notes in English and French by A. David Hogarth.
  Philips: 7300500-7300502.
```

1st level cataloging

```
Handel, George Frideric.
  Messiah [sound recording]. -- Philips, [19--]
  3 cassettes + 1 booklet of program notes.

  Philips: 7300500-7300502.
  London Symphony Orchestra, Colin Davis, conductor.
```

(information on cassette)   *(information on container)*

(information on program notes)

Handel Messiah
Haendel Le Messie

Heather Harper soprano soprano   London Symphony Choir
Helen Watts contralto contralto   Choeurs Symphoniques de Londres
John Wakefield tenor tenor   John Aldis
John Shirley Quirk bass basse   Chgorus Master / Maître des choeurs

Ralph Downes organ orgue   London Symphony Orchestra
Leslie Pearson harpsichord clavecin   Orchestre Symphonique de Londres
William Lang trumpet trompette   Colin Davis
                                         Conductor Direction

The principle followed for selecting which contributors to name in the statement of responsibility is that the contribution must be made to the work as a whole, not solely a part. Generally, this is interpreted to mean recording the names of the writers of texts, composers of musical works, programmers of computer programs, painters of pictures, producers and directors of motion pictures and videorecordings, etc. Others responsible for contributions that constitute just a part of a work, such as arrangers of musical works, casting directors, costumers, composers of film scores, and performers are given in the note area, and two notes are specially designated for cast and credits. When in doubt about where to record the name of a contributor, use the note area.

Publication, Distribution Information: Unlike books, which tend to be released for distribution as soon as they are printed and bound, some nonbook titles are held for periods of time before they are released and marketed. The principle followed in choosing data for this area is to look for who distributes the title, not who produced it. "Production" for films and videos is equivalent to "creation," whereas publication is called "release." Information that should be given in this area is the information about release and distribution—the year reflecting when a particular title is available on the market to be acquired. If the dates on an item indicate that a significant gap occurred between the time it was produced and released, a note should be made to explain it. Figure 6.12 illustrates this point. (Notice that the main entry of this item is Charlie Chaplin. Although it is unusual for an individual to be principally responsible for a mixed responsibility item such as this, it is not impossible.)

Physical Description: Information relating to physical description is found in three places in catalog records: the gmd (Area 1), the physical description (Area 5), and the notes (Area 7). Gmds are solely a word or phrase alerting catalog users to the fact that the title they are looking at is in a particular format. One might think the physical description area would contain the greatest detail, but, following the model of books, only selected kinds of information are included in it, with the rest placed in the notes. Catalogers give basic information for the physical carrier (the smd), other selected details such as the presence of sound and color, and the dimensions of the carrier, if they are not standard to the type. (When dimensions are standard to the carrier, they are omitted.) Other important information goes in the note area. A description of necessary hardware, in particular, is given in a carefully constructed systems requirements note (see Figure 6.13). Electronic resources accessed on local computers from external locations have no physical description, for obvious reasons.

Notes: Nonbook materials are likely to benefit from many notes, particularly those already mentioned here and in Chapter 4. The principle to be followed here is to take the time to make these notes, based not only on what is required by rules for other areas of description, but what would be helpful to the person using the catalog record. The frequency with which nonbook materials are held in closed stacks or reading areas lacking the hardware for browsing recommend following a policy of being generous in making notes.

FIGURE 6.12

This example is an illustration of:
- videorecording
- responsibility attributed to one person with no collective title for its components
- publication date not listed, copyright date given
- unnumbered series statement
- cast note
- publication, distribution, etc., note
- physical description note
- 2nd level cataloging

```
Chaplin, Charles.
   The kid [videorecording] ; The idle class / music composed,
written, produced and directed by Charlie Chaplin. -- New York :
Key Video, c1989.
   1 videocassette (ca. 86 min.) : sd., b&w ; ½ in. -- (Centennial
collection)

   Cast: Charlie Chaplin, Edna Purviance, Jack Coogan (The kid);
Charlie Chaplin, Edna Purviance (The idle class).
   Originally released in 1921.
   VHS Hi-fi.
```

(information on cassette label)

The Kid/
The Idle Class

Cat. No. 3002   **Recorded in HI-FI.**
Approx. 86 Min.

(information on container)

FIGURE 6.13   System Requirements Notes

For an electronic resource in a remote location:
System requirements: Requires Adobe Acrobat reader, 3.0 or higher

For an electronic resource stored in the library or media center:
System requirements: Intel Pentium processor or equivalent; Windows 95, 98, or NT Workstation 4.0; 16 MB RAM (32 recommended), 57 MB free hard disk space; VGA video (296-color minimum); CD-ROM drive.

For an interactive multimedia disc:
System requirements: Philips Interactive compact disc (CD-I) player with monitor.

For an Internet resource:
Mode of access: Metronet.

Catalogers cannot rely greatly on LC's leadership in cataloging nonbook materials, because its coverage for these materials tends to be incomplete in comparison with its coverage of books. When it was active, LC's Audiovisual Section often based its cataloging on publishers' data, similar to what is used for CIP, instead of viewing published items in hand. Moreover, because the Audiovisual Section was disbanded several years ago, new LCRIs for nonbook materials have not been issued, nor existing ones updated. Thus, catalogers might look more profitably for leadership and guidance to specialized professional organizations such as Online Audiovisual Catalogers, the Music Library Association, the ALA Map and Geography Round Table, etc.

Cataloging Internet Resources

A brief word about Internet resources may be helpful for catalogers in libraries and media centers trying to prepare catalog records for such materials. Internet resources, many of which are serials, are described using rules for cataloging remote electronic resources, plus the rules for serial publications when applicable. Although most elements in the catalog record for Internet resources are the same as they would be for any other type of material, the following elements differ.

- The type of file is given as "material specific" data; in addition, if the resource is a serial, the usual numbering and dating information will also be given.

- The method of access is given in a note called the "Mode of Access" note. This may include the electronic address of the item, known as the Uniform Resource Locator (URL).

- The URL is given as an access point, also, even if it means repeating it a second time. Actual access may be enhanced by making the URL a direct link to the resource, so the user only has to point the computer cursor at it and click on it to be transferred to the material itself.

- The date the electronic resource was viewed for cataloging purposes is helpful to give, not only if the record is based on an issue other than the first, but for every resource, because electronic resources tend to update more often than other forms of material. NLC has issued a rule interpretation advising this practice.

Creating data for identifying and accessing Internet resources is known as creating *metadata.* The use of a special word to describe the elements of a bibliographic record for Internet resources makes these resources appear mysterious and difficult to handle to some catalogers. By using the good judgment applied in cataloging other formats and helpful manuals that interpret descriptive cataloging rules for the form,[6] an Internet resource should not be much more difficult to catalog than any other type of item. At the same time, minimizing the complexity of cataloging Internet resources is not appropriate, either. It takes familiarity with how materials in this form are likely to appear as well as how to navigate the Internet in finding them to make cataloging Internet resources appear routine. Figure 5.10 is an example of the cataloging of an Internet resource.

The OCLC network sponsors a cooperative project known as CORC (Cooperative Online Resource Catalog) whose members are building a shared database of metadata for selected Internet resources to be used in libraries. CORC also provides subject-oriented lists of metadata called *pathfinders* to aid librarians in doing reference work. As the CORC project progresses and grows, catalogers are learning to create and use metadata effectively.

Application to Internet resources of library cataloging rules creates a familiar kind of metadata that might be called "library metadata," but library rules are not the only ones. Some of the other schemes being used to create metadata include the Text Encoded Initiative (TEI), Encoded Archival Description (EAD), and Dublin Core. Each scheme has a following; for example, the EAD is used primarily by archives and archivists. The Dublin Core is used to identify Internet resources by both librarians and nonlibrarians. It has 15 elements: title, creator, subject, description, publisher, contributor, date, type, format, identifier, source, language, relation, coverage, and rights. All the elements are optional; all can be repeated (more than one title, more than one creator, subject, etc.); all can be displayed in any order; and all can be enriched with added information. Databases using the Dublin Core are being built in many countries of the world, including the CORC project described previously.

Conclusion

Ultimately, the issues of patron need and convenience must be balanced with the institution's need to conserve resources and economize. If catalog records do not provide access to the information in collections of serials, unpublished titles, and nonbook materials, either reference staff or the patrons themselves must expend the time and money to find it. Who does the work, how long it takes, and how much it costs will vary according to the cataloging decisions made at this point in the workflow. One way to decide how to handle these materials is to ask if alternatives are available to these materials for the information they contain. If the answer is no, it indicates a priority for the best treatment they can be given. If the answer is yes, one could ask whether they are truly necessary to collect.

Recommended Reading

Boydston, Jeanne M. K. et al., eds. *Serials Cataloging at the Turn of the Century.* New York: Haworth Press, 1997.

CONSER Cataloging Manual and Updates. Washington, DC: Library of Congress, 1993- .

CONSER Editing Guide. Washington, DC: Library of Congress, 1991- .

Fecko, Mary Beth. *Cataloging Nonbook Resources: A How-To-Do-It Manual.* New York: Neal-Schuman, 1993.

Geer, Beverley, and Beatrice L. Caraway. *Notes for Serials Cataloging,* 2nd ed. Englewood, CO: Libraries Unlimited, 1998.

Hirons, Jean, and Judy Kuhagen. "Revisions to Library of Congress Rule Interpretations for Serials and Series." *The Serials Librarian* 30, no. 1 (1996): 49-58.

Hsieh-Yee, Ingrid. *Organizing Audiovisual and Electronic Resources for Access: A Cataloging Guide.* Englewood, CO: Libraries Unlimited, 2000.

Interactive Electronic Serials Cataloging Aid (ESCA). Available online at http://www.library .nwu.edu/iesca.

Intner, Sheila S. "Access to Serials," "Serials Catalog Records: Image and Reality," and "Modern Serials Cataloging." In *Interfaces: Relationships Between Library Technical and Public Services*, 77-92. Englewood, CO: Libraries Unlimited, 1993.

Johnson, Bruce Chris, ed. *Guidelines for Bibliographic Description of Reproductions.* Prepared by the Committee on Cataloging: Description and Access of the Association for Library Collections & Technical Services. Chicago: American Library Association, 1993.

Jones, Wayne, ed. *Serials Canada: Aspects of Serials Work in Canadian Libraries.* Binghamton, NY: Haworth Press, 1996.

The Journal of Internet Cataloging. Binghamton, NY: Haworth Press, 1996- .

Liheng, Carol, and Winnie S. Chan. *Serials Cataloging Handbook: An Illustrative Guide to the Use of AACR2R and LC Rule Interpretations,* 2nd ed. Chicago: American Library Association, 1998.

Olson, Nancy B. *Audiovisual Materials Glossary.* Dublin, OH: OCLC, 1988.

———. *Cataloging of Audiovisual Materials and Other Special Materials.* 4th ed. Eds. Sheila S. Intner and Edward Swanson. DeKalb, IL: Media Marketing Group, 1998.

The Serials Librarian: The International Journal of Serials Management. Binghamton, NY: Haworth Press, 1971- . [quarterly]

Shubert, Steven Blake. "Subject Access to Serial Publications in Toronto Bank Libraries." *Special Libraries* 82, no. 1 (1991): 33-39.

Tools for Serials Catalogers: A Collection of Useful Sites and Sources. Vanderbilt University Library. Available online at http://www.library.vanderbilt.edu/ercelawn/serials.html.

Urbanski, Verna et al. *Cataloging Unpublished Nonprint Materials: A Manual of Suggestions, Comments, and Examples.* Lake Crystal, MN: Soldier Creek Press, 1992.

Weihs, Jean, and Shirley Lewis. *Nonbook Materials: The Organization of Integrated Collections.* 3rd ed. Ottawa: Canadian Library Association, 1989.

Notes

1.   At this writing, a proposal to change the definition of "serial" in AACR2-98 has been put before the Joint Steering Committee and its approval is expected at the Committee's next meeting. The new definition reads as follows: "A bibliographic resource issued in a succession of discrete parts, usually bearing numbering, and usually having no predetermined conclusion. Examples of serials include journals, magazines, electronic journals, continuing directories, annual reports, newspapers, newsletters of an event, and monographic series." The text in this chapter is based on the existing definition, which, while worded in more restrictive language, does not differ in principle.

2.   AACR2-98, p. 314.

3.   AACR2-98, p. 622, definition 1 of Series.

4.   AACR2-98, p. 622, definition of Serial.

5.   Verna Urbanski, et al., *Cataloging Unpublished Nonprint Materials: A Manual of Suggestions, Comments, and Examples* (Lake Crystal, Minn.: Soldier Creek Press, 1992), p. ix-x.

6.   Ibid., p. 8-10.

7.   Nancy B. Olson, ed. *Cataloging Internet Resources,* 2nd ed. (Dublin, Ohio: OCLC, 1997-   ). Available at http://www.purl.org/oclc/cataloging-internet.

7

Subject Authorities

Introduction

Completing the descriptive cataloging, which includes making a bibliographic description, choosing access points from it, and putting them into proper form to be used as headings, is half the battle of cataloging. It is the half that deals with works as physical entities—books, videos, electronic resources, etc.—and identifies them in terms appropriate to the physical format in which the work is manifested. Next, the cataloger must consider the content of the work, which is defined, identified, and represented in terms of subject matter.

There is no AACR2-98 for *subject cataloging,* the phrase describing the assignment of subject headings to a work. Instead, the words used to represent the subject matter of an item being cataloged and chosen for use in the catalog may be taken from different sources, depending on the policies of the individual library. Those who wish to use standard terminology can take their subject cataloging terms from published lists of words accepted by the cataloging community for use as subject headings in the catalog. These *subject authorities* are much like the name authorities discussed in Chapter 5 and are referred to as *controlled* terms or *controlled vocabularies.* All catalogers do not use the same list, and even those who do don't always use their list in the same manner.

Catalogers who prefer using the terminology found in the materials being cataloged create lists of terms from title words. It would be difficult to publish these words in lists of authorized terms because no one can predict or control the words an author will choose. For this reason, unauthorized title words used as subject headings are referred to as *uncontrolled* terms or *uncontrolled vocabularies.* Computer-based catalogs frequently are programmed to search title words, despite the fact that they are not authorized, to add a richer vocabulary to the authorized terms in subject authorities. To maximize the possibility of finding desired materials, both types of subject terms should be used.

The most important tools for using subject authorities in doing subject cataloging are guidelines published by national libraries and committees of national professional associations. Published guidelines do not have the force of AACR2-98, however, although many catalogers follow their lead. LC's subject guidelines are extensive and complex, growing out of its own need to codify its subject cataloging policies and practices. Individual policy decisions are issued internally as memoranda and, since 1989, have been compiled into loose-leaf notebooks for sale to interested parties (see Figure 7.1).[1] LC made the compilation available to the cataloging community in response to requests for help from the field. New subject headings appear in

LC's *Cataloging Service* bulletin as well as in updates to its subject heading list, *Library of Congress Subject Headings* (LCSH), which is issued in book form in a new edition every year.[2] Computerized versions of LCSH are available online and on CD-ROM disks, and an offline version can be obtained on microfiche.

FIGURE 7.1   Sample page from <u>Subject Cataloging Manual: Subject Headings</u>

Editions H 175

LC practice:
1. General rule. Assign the same subject heading or set of subject headings to all editions of a single work that are present in the LC Database and that have an imprint date of 1981 or later.

> *Exception:* If the content of a new edition of a work changes so significantly that its scope and focus are entirely different from earlier editions, assign the headings required to designate properly the contents of the edition being cataloged regardless of the headings assigned to the other edition(s). If the variation in content is slight, however, assign the same heading(s) to all post-1980 editions.

For general cataloging procedures, definition of the term **edition**, and guidelines for retaining identical classification numbers for various editions of a work, see D 450.

LC practice:
2. Changing subject headings on earlier editions. When a decision is made to assign different headings to a new edition from those assigned to the earlier edition(s) for reasons other than those described as exceptions above, change the headings of all other editions of the work in the LC Database that have an imprint date of 1981 or later, so that they match those assigned to the new edition.

Follow the procedures described in D 240 for the correction of subject headings in existing bibliographic records.

Do not change the headings on editions having an imprint date earlier than 1981.

Subject Cataloging Manual: Subject Headings   *H 175 Page 1*
                                                                 February 2000

ALA's guidelines, which usually come from subcommittees of the Subject Analysis Committee of the Cataloging and Classification Section of the Association for Library Collections & Technical Services (a division of ALA), tend to be much shorter and less specific, because they are designed for a broad cross-section of settings, not a single library or media center.[3] Some special library groups also publish guidelines for subject analysis and lists of specialized terms to be used for subject cataloging the literature in their fields.

The volume containing *Sears List of Subject Headings* includes rules for applying the terms it authorizes, which, for the most part, are similar to LC's policies and practices. Among the more important differences is the number of headings that can be assigned.

Subject cataloging is the same as indexing, although the bibliographic unit differs. It is difficult to see why library catalogers don't refer to what they do as indexing, but they don't. The only obvious differences between subject cataloging and indexing are the units being indexed and the intended purpose of the products. Indexers work on one of two types of units: either the text of a single book, for which they prepare an index that is part of that book, or articles from journals, for which they are preparing ongoing periodical indexes such as the *Readers' Guide to Periodical Literature,* or similar tools. Periodical indexes are used by people searching for information on a particular subject in articles published in magazines, journals, or similar publications. (Periodical indexes also list authors' names and article titles.) Because the same principles apply to all types of indexing, including subject cataloging, the same search skills are employed in retrieving indexed material, whether from card catalogs, online catalogs, or online reference databases.

Subject catalogers usually work on items they have cataloged—almost exclusively monographic items (i.e., complete in one unit)—and instead of preparing extensive indexes containing many terms, they seek to assign a very limited number of terms—from one, considered by Cutter to be ideal, to a maximum of five—to describe the entire contents of the work. Years ago, catalogers used to assign a maximum of three subject headings per item, but that "Rule of Three" fell out of favor when it became clear that searchers wanted and needed more subject headings. The advent of computers made it easier to maintain both the larger catalogs that resulted and the related subject authority files. Subject catalogers substituted a "20 percent rule" for the Rule of Three, in which a heading was assigned if it was determined that 20 percent of the material in an item being cataloged was about a particular topic. The application was straightforward; for example, if 20 pages of a 100-page book were about lemons, the subject heading LEMONS would be assigned; but if only 10 pages of that book were about lemons, or if 20 pages of a 200-page book were about lemons, it would not. In the latter cases, either the book would receive a broader heading covering lemons and other types of fruit (such as CITRUS FRUITS or just plain FRUIT), or it might be ignored entirely if too many other specific headings were assigned to the book. After LCSH went online in 1988, LC's policies have tended to become even more generous, with some works receiving more than the five heading limit implied by the 20 percent rule.

To sum up, subject catalogers and indexers do, basically, the same thing, but subject catalogers provide summary access to whole books, videos, and other items they are cataloging by assigning a small number of terms to them; periodical indexers provide deeper access to individual articles within magazines or journals by assigning a similar or larger number of index terms to these smaller bibliographic units; and back-of-the-book indexers provide the deepest access of all by assigning a very large number of terms—often numbering in the hundreds—to the text of one book (or other item being indexed).

The purpose of subject headings, regardless of their number, is to make the contents of the item to which they are assigned available to users of the subject catalog. Principles of indexing apply to subject cataloging even though the process of assigning headings is not called indexing and the purpose is to furnish headings for a catalog and not the more detailed type of access afforded by published indexes.

Principles of Indexing and Subject Cataloging

Recalling Cutter's *objects of the catalog* (see pages 2–3), the catalog is to show what the library has if a searcher is interested in a subject as well as to collocate all items on a single subject. These two objectives—the finding list objective and the collocation objective—apply to subject headings and subject catalogs as well as to authors, titles, and editions. Here, also, the two objectives conflict, causing problems that make ideal catalogs impossible to achieve.

An index is designed to lead searchers to desired material. Indexes, like catalogs, can be arranged in different ways, such as by the names of authors or titles (called, obviously, author or title indexes), or by subjects arranged in alphabetical or classified order. People in the United States and Canada are most familiar with alphabetical subject indexes because this is how North American library catalogs usually are arranged. Classified indexes can contain the same terms, but they are arranged in *subject* order, with the broadest topics first, followed by related, but narrower topics, in a logical organization for each major subject division.

In a classified catalog, the entire catalog might be divided into a few sections or main classes; for example, HUMANITIES, NATURAL SCIENCES, and SOCIAL SCIENCES. NATURAL SCIENCES would be the broadest term used for the second section, followed by individual scientific disciplines: ASTRONOMY, MATHEMATICS, PHYSICS, CHEMISTRY, BIOLOGY, GEOLOGY, etc. In turn, CHEMISTRY would be followed by still smaller topics, such as ORGANIC CHEMISTRY and INORGANIC CHEMISTRY, etc. It is easy to see the contrast with an alphabetical, or dictionary, catalog such as those in most media centers and public libraries. There, these same topics would be arranged as follows: ASTRONOMY, BIOLOGY, CHEMISTRY, GEOLOGY, HUMANITIES, INORGANIC CHEMISTRY, MATHEMATICS, NATURAL SCIENCES, ORGANIC CHEMISTRY, PHYSICS, and SOCIAL SCIENCES. HUMANITIES seems oddly placed, sandwiched in between GEOLOGY and INORGANIC CHEMISTRY, and five of the natural science disciplines and one subdiscipline appear before the heading for natural sciences as a whole. To someone accustomed to a classified catalog, this would seem peculiar. Classified catalogs usually are arranged with classification numbers, which are symbolic representations of topics and subtopics.

A hybrid type of subject catalog, partly classified and partly alphabetical, also has been devised, called an *alphabetico-classified* catalog. In such a catalog, principal headings are in classified order, but within each level of hierarchy, subheadings are arranged alphabetically. In an alphabetico-classified listing, one might find the following:

        HUMANITIES
          ART
          LITERATURE
          MUSIC
            HARMONY
            MELODY
            RHYTHM
              DYNAMICS (MUSIC)
              TEMPO
          RELIGION
        NATURAL SCIENCES
          ASTRONOMY
            COMETS
            PLANETS
            STARS
          CHEMISTRY
          PHYSICS
            MECHANICS
            OPTICS
            THERMODYNAMICS
        SOCIAL SCIENCES

Different levels of hierarchy are shown by means of indentations, but other devices, such as thumb tabs or guide cards, color coding, etc., can be used when indentations are difficult or inconvenient to display; and there is no requirement to identify the hierarchical levels at all.

The arrangement of the index terms is open to question, but there are standard principles that guide the choice of terms and their assignment. The following points are essential to a good index or subject catalog:

1. Synonyms may not be used simultaneously as headings in a single catalog. If the terms CELEBRITIES and FAMOUS PEOPLE were both used as subject headings, which one would a searcher select for *Lifestyles of the Rich and Famous,* the television series focusing on these people? Some episodes might be filed under CELEBRITIES, while others could be filed under FAMOUS PEOPLE. Librarians rely on subject authorities to avoid the inadvertent use of two headings that mean the same thing. If both terms are likely to be searched, both may be listed, but only one is authorized for use; the other term will have a cross-reference to the one actually used.

2. Words used for subject headings should have one clear and precise meaning. Consider the word BARS. Does it refer to the metal rods used in construction? Or does it refer to the pieces of furniture in which people keep things related to drinking alcoholic beverages or the places at which people obtain alcoholic beverages? Or, even, to the things one sees on maps? Subject authorities avoid using words that have more than one meaning wherever they can. When they cannot, they add something that indicates the specific meaning intended. There is no doubt about what is meant if BARS is qualified: BARS (ENGINEERING), BARS (FURNITURE), BARS (GEOMORPHOLOGY), and BARS (DRINKING ESTABLISHMENTS).

3. The meaning of terms used as subject headings should fit, precisely, the topic they describe. They should not be open to interpretation or be more or less specific than the topic they represent. If CALCULATORS is used as a heading, it should be defined to include all materials about what we currently term calculators, but none about computers, which, though they manipulate numbers, are a different type of machine. In fact, this is the case in *Sears List of Subject Headings,* in which the scope note at CALCULATORS says: "Use for materials on present-day calculators or on calculators and mechanical computers made before 1945. Materials on modern electronic computers developed after 1945 are entered under **Computers.**"[4]

4. Each subject heading term should be discrete with respect to all others at the same topical level. There are different levels of topical hierarchy among subject headings; for example, SCIENCE, CHEMISTRY, INORGANIC CHEMISTRY, and MOLECULAR STRUCTURE may all be subject headings, but they represent scientific topics at different levels of specificity (i.e., broadness or narrowness). There must be clearly defined rules for using one term or the other. Problems occur when there are overlaps in meaning between subject headings at the same level of hierarchy, such as BIOLOGY, CHEMISTRY, and BIOCHEMISTRY, or these three subjects together with MEDICINE and BIOMEDICAL ENGINEERING. When all these words are used in the same catalog or subject authority, they must be defined carefully so that each represents a discrete territory and a cataloger assigning the terms or a person using the catalog can understand what the boundaries between them are.

David Judson Haykin, a well-known and respected head of LC's subject division in the 1950s, codified the principles that should apply to subject heading assignment at LC. They are based, for the most part, on Cutter's ideas, and remain to this day the definitive expression of our basic assumptions about subject heading practice:

> *The Reader as the Focus.* All other considerations, such as convenience and the desire to arrange entries in some logical order, are secondary to the basic rule that the heading, in wording and structure, should be that which the reader will seek in the catalog.

> *Unity.* A subject catalog must bring together under one heading all the books that deal principally or exclusively with the subject, whatever the terms applied to it by the authors of the books and whatever the varying terms applied to it at different times. Therefore, the cataloger must choose with care the term to be used and apply it uniformly to all the books on the subject.

> *Usage.* The heading chosen must represent common usage or, at any rate, the usage of the class of reader for whom the material on the subject within which the heading falls is intended.

> *English vs. Foreign Terms.* Foreign terms should be used only under [limited] conditions: 1) when the concept is foreign to Anglo-American experience . . .; and 2) when, especially in the case of scientific names, the foreign term is precise, whereas the English one is not.

> *Specificity.* The heading should be as specific as the topic it is intended to cover. As a corollary, the heading should not be broader than the topic; rather than use a broader heading, the cataloger should use two specific headings which will approximately cover it.[5]

Evaluating Subject Catalogs

Subject catalogs can be evaluated using the following criteria:

1. *Recall.* The quality of recall refers to the amount of material that a searcher retrieves when using the headings in the catalog. To be "good," a catalog should promote recall, but not too much of it; in other words, it should give searchers enough material in response to their inquiries, but not overwhelm them. If every movie in a very large collection of videorecordings of made-for-television movies had a different subject heading, the recall would be very low (i.e., one item) for any one subject heading. If all the items had the same heading, like TELEVISION MOVIES, the recall would be very high; that is, the searcher would retrieve all of them at once when searching that heading. These are the extremes between which a balance must be sought. Things that are related should be grouped together, to satisfy the collocating feature of the catalog and ensure that someone using the subject heading will recall all items related to the particular subject in which they are interested, but the search should not be so wide that *everything* is included in it. Items that are not related to the subject should be excluded.

2. *Relevance.* The quality of relevance refers to how well materials retrieved using a particular subject heading or set of subject headings match the searcher's needs. Obviously, a "good" subject catalog will receive high marks for relevance. The more specific a searcher is, the more likely it is that what is found will be relevant to that person's needs. If a searcher wants something about computer programming and uses the subject heading PROGRAMMING (ELECTRONIC COMPUTERS), it should be possible for the searcher to recall every item in the collection about that subject. However, the assignment of PROGRAMMING (ELECTRONIC COMPUTERS) might be limited to items entirely about this subject, but not to items with a chapter or two or a section about it. Using PROGRAMMING (ELECTRONIC COMPUTERS) would not retrieve these latter items, even though they contain relevant material. If the broader subject heading COMPUTERS were added to the original search under PROGRAMMING (ELECTRONIC COMPUTERS), the searcher might retrieve more items having a chapter or two about programming, but this larger batch of material will contain a great deal of material having nothing to do with programming; for example, covering hardware, computer architecture, network design, and other irrelevant subjects. The quality of relevance tends to decrease as the amount of recall increases. These two qualities are said to have an *inverse relationship.*

3. *Precision.* Precision is the ability to specify exactly what is wanted, without having to use broader subject headings representing other things as well. Imagine that the searcher in our previous example was really interested only in items about programming in BASIC, a particular programming language. Using the subject heading PROGRAMMING (ELECTRONIC COMPUTERS) would retrieve material on all programming languages, including BASIC. If, however, the searcher used the subject heading BASIC (COMPUTER PROGRAM LANGUAGE), it would allow for much more precision than if one can only choose COMPUTERS or PROGRAMMING (ELECTRONIC COMPUTERS). Precision varies with the specificity of terms as well as with their definition and application. Precision will be affected by the presence of overlapping and ambiguous terms.

The decision to add subdivisions to subject headings also affects precision. One type of subdivision might specify form. If a searcher wants only computer-aided instruction about BASIC programming, that searcher would not want to retrieve catalog records for books, videos, or sound recordings about it. If the catalog does not specify the physical format of an item as part of its subject headings, then all the records with the subject heading BASIC (COMPUTER PROGRAM LANGUAGE) would have to be scanned to find items of interest. A form subdivision added to this heading, BASIC (COMPUTER PROGRAM LANGUAGE)—COMPUTER-ASSISTED INSTRUCTION, would collocate items with the same topic and format making a very specific search much more efficient in a large file with many items on this subject.

However, specifying physical format by means of subheadings added to primary subject headings conflicts with the concept that information is important regardless of its form. There are reasons why achieving maximum precision in subject headings is not always desirable; for example, when searching small collections, one might be unable to retrieve anything if overly precise (or specific) headings are used.

4. *Exhaustivity.* This quality refers to the indexing level; that is, the amount or the depth of subject cataloging that the cataloger is willing to do for the materials in the collection. Some catalogers are willing to give each item being cataloged only one

subject heading. This is the broadest summary level of indexing. Others may give up to three or five headings, both common practices, covering the overall subject matter of each item—still a summary level of indexing, but with greater flexibility. Some catalogers might wish to furnish subject headings for each chapter of a book or each part of an electronic resource. This is a deeper level of indexing, furnishing greater exhaustivity. The highest marks for exhaustivity would go to the catalog furnishing subject headings for every idea contained within an item as well as for its form, genre, language, and other pertinent features.

5. *Ease of Use.* Two kinds of people use the subject catalog: staff members who assign subject headings to materials, search the catalog to answer questions, or both, and clients (frequently referred to as *end users*), who use the catalog by themselves. The subject heading system should be easy for both kinds of people to use.

6. *Cost.* A "good" subject catalog should maximize value in the sense that the most service possible is provided for the money spent on it. It also must be affordable. Subject cataloging can be costly, especially if a library or media center wants to assign as many subject headings and cross-references as possible to each item. Evaluating the expenditures must be done by considering their impact. If, in our hypothetical agency, the money spent results in superb service and end users have no difficulty finding what they want without having to ask for assistance, freeing the reference staff for other duties, it may be exactly the way the agency should spend its budget. If the expenditures do not result in extraordinary service and end users have to ask for help just as frequently, then the cost would be deemed too great for the amount of service being provided.

    Another consideration is the cost of producing the product; that is, for staff members to do the cataloging. A subject system that enabled a computer or members of the clerical staff to do all or most of the work would be less costly than one that required the librarian or media specialist to do it. This is an important consideration when choosing a subject heading system.

    Cost is relative and there are no standard measures for high- and low-cost cataloging. However, it is not difficult to measure increases and decreases in costs and resulting services, as long as objective measures of service are devised (e.g., "better" service = fewer requests for assistance with searches; or, "better" service = an increase in use of materials with no more than a 2 percent increase in requests for assistance with searches). Then, experiments to find an optimal balance for their agencies between cost and service can be done.

This list of evaluative criteria indicates that there is a give-and-take in producing and using subject catalogs. One criterion cannot be used by itself to measure the worth of a catalog, and all must be put into a reasonable balance to achieve good service at bearable cost. There are no magic formulas to decide how deeply to index or how many cross-references to make. Glaring faults should be obvious to a concerned practitioner and problems can be understood more clearly when considered in light of this list of catalog features.

Problems of the Subject Catalog

Conflict among the subject catalog's objectives occurs when different terms are used to express one topic (a common response to changes in the meaning and usage of words over long periods of time or between the works of different authors); when topics overlap; when the number of records recalled in an average search is much too great or too small; and, perhaps most critical of all, when authorized headings and searchers' vocabularies do not match. A person looking up a subject using a term that is not present in the catalog either as a subject heading or a cross-reference will find nothing. To promote the finding list feature of the subject catalog, all words used by searchers and authors should be present as headings. But if all subject terms found in published works and commonly used by searchers were acceptable as subject headings, how would all the works on a single subject be brought together? To promote the collocating feature, all the synonymous and quasi-synonymous terms must be brought together with a few carefully defined terms, and the specificity of these terms should result in a reasonable number of retrieved items containing information relevant to the searcher's needs.

These conflicts have no one resolution. Public libraries and school library media centers tend to promote the collocating feature at the expense of the finding list feature by using a limited number of terms from a published list—the *controlled vocabulary*—as headings. Although not required to do so, catalogers generally limit the number of cross-references made to those recommended by the particular list from which they obtain their terms, and in some places not even those references are made. Reasons put forth to justify such policies include, first, that subject cataloging operations are faster and less expensive that way (and the agency cannot afford anything else); and, that the catalog already is too large and complicated without adding more unused terms to it, although disappointed searchers who get no response to a term can look it up in the authority list itself to check whether they used an acceptable term, or ask for help from a librarian or media specialist.

Now, however, computers offer new solutions that can promote the finding list feature without disturbing collocation to any great extent. Computers enable catalog users to search terms found in titles, summaries, or other areas in bibliographic descriptions containing information about the content of works in "natural language" in addition to the designated subject headings. Computers permit searching any word of a subject heading, called a subject "keyword," even if it is not the first word of a primary heading, or if it occurs in a subheading. This was not possible with card catalogs, in which only the word in the filing position (called the "lead term") could be searched.

Additional retrieval capabilities made possible when subject catalogs are computerized include the following:

- Searches with partial data (e.g., if an asterisk stands for any letters, COMPUT* can retrieve both COMPUT*ERS* and COMPUT*ING*, while *COMPUT* can retrieve both of those plus *MICRO*COMPUT*ERS* and *MINI*COMPUT*ERS).*

- Saving search requests and using them in more than one database or catalog.

- Combining more than one subject heading into complex requests (e.g., COMPUTERS **AND** ART, or MUSIC **AND** POPULAR **NOT** JAZZ), or combining a subject heading with other bibliographic elements in a single search (e.g., SU=SYMPHONIES **AND** AU=MOZART).

- Accessing the catalog from outside the agency via telecommunications systems.

- Accessing local acquisition and circulation data as well as catalog records, so a searcher can determine not only whether the item is present in the catalog, but its availability status as well.

- Accessing external databases and catalogs via larger computing networks.

This list does not exhaust current possibilities. The boundaries among search capabilities that require the use of a particular kind of subject vocabulary and those that only need a properly programmed computer system are blurring.

The use of computers has not led to the discontinuation of controlled vocabularies as some predicted in the 1980s; rather, it has led to intensified efforts to enhance subject recall potential by developing the ability to search other data elements likely to express subject content and to improve subject vocabularies.

Before one can enrich them, however, subject headings must be chosen for the works cataloged. Following is a brief discussion of the way subject catalogs are created and maintained.

Subject Lists Used by Libraries

North American public libraries and school library media centers frequently use one of two general subject headings lists with their Canadian supplements: *Sears List of Subject Headings* (Sears) and its *Canadian Companion,* or *Library of Congress Subject Headings* (LCSH) and its Canadian counterpart, the NLC's *Canadian Subject Headings.*[6] These are discussed in detail in Chapters 8 and 9; however, a quick look at the process of using these subject authorities is appropriate here.

General subject heading lists are important for libraries that collect materials in most, if not all, subject areas. Schools and public libraries tend to have general collections, with information on almost any subject one could name. Except for the largest of these libraries, most of the individual items in them cover topics having a relatively large scope within the disciplines and subjects. Few of the items being cataloged are about a single, tiny part of a topic, such as the antennae of ants. There may be books, films, or recordings about ants, or possibly even about the antennae of insects, but not solely about the antennae of ants. Thus, the subject heading ANTS or INSECTS might be expected to match the scope of the holdings.

If a school specializes in entomology, it might buy materials describing the different parts and aspects of ants. Therefore, it might not be very useful to have all of them subsumed under the single subject heading ANTS, particularly if students using the collection were interested solely in finding works about ant antennae, wings, or food-gathering activities. When the holdings in a particular subject area become very large and detailed, a general subject heading list may not divide headings into sufficiently narrow categories to satisfy most searchers' needs. For this reason, there also are specialized lists of terms called *thesauri.* Thesauri usually are limited to a single subject or discipline and contain detailed terms for dividing a large group of items in one subject area into manageable parts.

Individual agencies, whether serving schools or the public, may choose to use both a general subject heading list for topics outside the areas of specialization *and* a thesaurus for those subject areas in which its holdings are particularly rich and large. Doing so, however, creates certain problems that must be resolved; for example, what will happen when the thesaurus has a different but synonymous term for the same topic found in the general list? And what will happen if the terms are similar, but not identical? One option is to devise policies that mandate resolutions for anticipated problems, thus enabling multiple subject authorities to be interfiled in the same catalog. Solutions to such problems are suggested and analyzed by Mandel and by Petersen and Molholt.[7] A second option is maintaining two or more separate catalogs, but because patrons tend to search only one file, it is less effective.

The use of both LCSH and Sears by one agency is rare, although Sears was designed so that terms from LCSH could be added if a cataloger needed them and wanted to do so. The main difference between Sears and LCSH is their size and, by virtue of their relative sizes, the specificity of the headings they contain. LCSH is an extremely large list in which topics are broken down into a large number of narrow categories. Quite a few LCSH headings are subdivided, some twice or three times. By contrast, Sears is a much smaller list containing broader terms, few of which are subdivided into narrower categories. Other differences between Sears and LCSH are their terminology, availability, updating methods, and cost.

- *Terminology.* Sears uses simple vocabulary appropriate for children and nonspecialists using school library media centers and local public libraries. LCSH uses more complex and technical terminology geared toward knowledgeable researchers, such as those employed by LC.

- *Availability.* At this writing, Sears is available in book form or on magnetic tape in MARC or Wilson-tagged format. LCSH is available online, on CD-ROM or floppy disks, in microform, and in book form.

- *Updating.* Sears issues new editions frequently but does not disseminate changes between editions. LCSH is updated continuously, and its updates can be obtained immediately by online users, or weekly, quarterly, or annually by offline users, depending on which of LC's products they choose to buy.

- *Cost.* The basic LCSH list is more costly than the basic Sears list, but to arrive at a total cost for either one, the expenses of additional tools—updates, subdivisions, and application policies—and the costs of working with each list and supplying reference assistance to searchers when it fails, must be considered and evaluated. It might seem that the gap between LCSH and Sears can only widen if these elements are added, but that is not necessarily the case. For example, the assignment of LCSH headings in CIP and network member records lowers the cost of working with LCSH considerably, unless similar sources for Sears's headings are available. Total cost packages are more difficult to assess, but they reflect values that are more realistic than the price tag of the basic tool alone.

Sears and LCSH also share selected features: They use similar grammar and syntax, cross-referencing, and subdivision techniques (see Figure 7.2). Both omit name headings and recommend using a standard AACR2-98-compatible name authority file for them. Application principles and practices are similar; thus, someone familiar with one can use many of the same techniques in working with the other.

Maintaining Subject Catalogs in Libraries and Media Centers

Maintaining the subject catalog is an important part of the process of furnishing subject access to library materials. We saw how differently alphabetic and classified subject catalogs are arranged. In the United States, the alphabetical arrangement was the legacy of Charles Cutter, along with his objects of the catalog. Cutter believed that, in a democracy such as the United States, the catalog should be easy to use, even for a novice. Classified catalogs presume the searcher knows how a subject is divided, and will know the level of hierarchy in which the topic being sought is located. An alphabetically arranged subject file does not require this knowledge. To make it as easy for beginners as for experts to search the subject catalog, catalog records are filed in alphabetical order (or, as Cutter called it, *dictionary* order).

Several policy decisions about the maintenance of the subject catalog should be made and publicized to those who use it. One of the most important of these decisions is whether to interfile subject entries with those for authors and titles. When card catalogs were the rule, the choice usually was a function of the size of the file and the ease with which people could search it. After the advent of computers, even large catalogs tend to be interfiled, because the computer does the "legwork" of searching and filing. If, however, searchers must select the subject heading, subject keyword, title, title keyword, or name index when they enter a search term, as is common with local computer systems, it is equivalent to dividing the file. The person must remember to search other files if their first attempts do not produce desired results.

FIGURE 7.2   Comparison of Sears and LCSH (excerpts)

Sears

Education (May subdiv. geog.)   370
   Subdivisions listed under this heading may
   be used under other education headings where
   applicable.
   UF   Instruction
         Pedagogy
         Study and teaching
   SA   types of education [to be added
         as needed], e.g. Vocational
         education; classes of persons
         and social and ethnic groups
         with the subdivision *Educa-
         tion*, e.g. **Deaf—Education;
         African Americans—Educa-
         tion;** etc.; and subjects with
         the subdivision *Study and
         teaching*, e.g. **Science—Study
         and teaching** [to be added as
         needed]
Education—Aims and objectives   370.11
Education and church
   USE   **Church and education**
Education and radio
   USE   **Radio in education**
Education—Curricula   375
   UF   Core curriculum
         Courses of study
         Curricula
         Schools—Curricula
   SA   types of education and schools
         with the subdivision *Curricu-
         la*, e.g. **Library education—
         Curricula** [to be added as
         needed]
   NT   **Articulation (Education)
         Colleges and universities—Cur-
         ricula
         Curriculum planning
         Library education—Curricula**
Education—Data processing
   USE   **Computer-assisted instruction**
Education—Developing countries
         370.9172
   UF   Developing countries—Education
Education, Elementary
   USE   **Elementary education**
Education—Experimental methods
         371.3
   UF   Activity schools
         Experimental methods in educa-
         tion
         Progressive education
         Teaching—Experimental methods
   SA   types of experimental methods,
         e.g. **Nongraded schools;
         Open plan schools;** etc. [to
         be added as needed]
   NT   **Experimental schools
         Nongraded schools
         Open plan schools
         Whole language**

LCSH

Education   *(May Subd Geog)*
   ₍L₎
   UF   Children—Education
         Education, Primitive
            [Former heading]
         Education of children
            [Former heading]
         Human resource development
         Instruction
         Pedagogy
         Youth—Education
   SA   *subdivision* Education *under names of
         denominations, sects, orders, etc.,
         e.g.* Jesuits—Education; *and under
         special classes of people and various
         social groups, e.g.* Blind—
         Education; Mentally handicapped
         children—Education; Children of
         migrant laborers—Education; *also
         subdivision* Study and teaching
         under special subjects, e.g. Science
         —Study and teaching; *and headings
         beginning with the word*
         Educational
   — Aims and objectives   *(May Subd Geog)*
         ₍LB41 (Essays)₎
      UF   Aims and objectives of education
            Educational aims and objectives
            Educational goals
            Educational objectives
            Educational purposes
            Goals, Educational
            Instructional objectives
            Objectives, Educational
            Purposes, Educational
   — Curricula
         ₍LB1570-LB1571 (Elementary
         schools)₎
      UF   Core curriculum
            Courses of study
            Curricula (Courses of study)
            Schools—Curricula
            Study, Courses of
      BT   Instructional systems
      SA   *subdivision* Curricula *under names
            of individual educational
            institutions, and under types of
            education and educational
            institutions, for listings of
            courses offered, or discussions
            about them, e.g.* Harvard
            University—Curricula; Technical
            education—Curricula;
            Universities and colleges—
            Curricula
      NT   Articulation (Education)
            Combination of grades
            Curriculum change
            Curriculum enrichment
            Curriculum planning
            Disability studies
            Gay and lesbian studies
            Lesson planning
            Men's studies
            Schedules, School
            Student evaluation of curriculum
            Teacher participation in curriculum
               planning
            Women's studies
   — — **Law and legislation**
         (May Subd Geog)
         BT   Educational law and legislation
   — **Data processing**
         ₍LB1028.43₎
      UF   Computer uses in education
            Computers in education
            Educational computing
            Microcomputer uses in education
            Microcomputers in education

Another policy issue concerns cross-references. It may be difficult to keep track of cross-references and to change them should it become necessary to do so. This is not because of any inherent difficulty in cross-references themselves, but because they tend to proliferate rapidly—one heading may have several cross-references, each of which may have several of its own as well. Decisions must be made about making them and how extensively they will be done.

One thing searchers do not like to encounter is a cross-reference that leads nowhere. To illustrate, suppose there is a cross-reference from BUSINESS to PROMOTERS. As long as there are materials listed under the subject heading PROMOTERS, that is a helpful reference. But as soon as the last item bearing the heading PROMOTERS is discarded, not only does the heading itself become obsolete in the catalog, but all of its cross-references do, also, among them BUSINESS. If the reference is not removed, it leads people to a heading that, although usable, no longer produces any materials present in the catalog. This is called a *blind reference.* Policies for maintaining the cross-reference structure should prevent this from happening.

One group of librarians believes that cross-references serve a purpose quite apart from leading searchers to materials filed under related headings, namely, that of teaching them about related subjects. According to these people, all cross-references given in the subject heading list should be present in the catalog whether they lead to any entries or not. (If such a policy is followed, it might be helpful if catalogers added notations to recordless headings explaining that there are no holdings on those topics.) Other librarians believe the cost of creating and maintaining a "living" cross-reference structure (called a *syndetic* structure) is not warranted by the use made of it.

At one end of the spectrum, every term that searchers might conceivably employ is present in the catalog either as an authorized heading or a cross reference, whether it is given in the subject authority or not. At the opposite end of the spectrum, cross-references are omitted entirely, with exceptions made solely for a limited number of terms catalogers believe are absolutely essential. Most librarians and media specialists take a centrist position, making the cross-references recommended by their subject authority, but excepting terms determined to be unnecessary. Each cataloger must weigh the various alternatives—to include all, some, or no cross-references—and arrive at a viable policy for its searchers and its catalog. Some may find it necessary to decide about cross-references on a case-by-case basis, but it is more efficient to systematize the policy so individual decisions are not necessary.

Finally, there are implications for maintenance in the way subject headings are filed. Two different arrangements of subject headings are furnished by the rules used at LC,[8] and those published by ALA.[9] LC's filing rules, which are used to file LCSH, distinguish between different kinds of subject heading forms and types of subdivisions, whereas ALA's do not. Sears's headings are filed by the ALA rules. Figure 7.3 illustrates how the use of each method would cause an identical group of headings to be arranged.

Figure 7.3

Filed by the LC (1980) Filing Rules	Filed by the ALA (1980) Filing Rules
Art—16th century	Art—16th century
Art—Adaptations	Art—Adaptations
Art—Themes, motives	Art, Aegean
Art—Australia	Art, American
Art, Aegean	Art, Ancient
Art, American	Art and anthropology
Art, Ancient	Art and industry
Art, Comparative	Art—Australia
Art, Modern—17th-18th centuries—History	Art, Comparative
Art and anthropology	Art,Modern—17th-18th centuries—History
Art and industry	Art—Themes, motives
Art treasures in war	Art treasures in war

Subject Headings
for Works of Imagination

The treatment of subject headings for literary works of all kinds—novels, plays, stories, poetry, etc.—also called works of imagination, should be considered carefully. For the most part, policies at LC, NLC, and other large libraries limit the assignment of subject headings to nonfiction works unless they are collections of texts by more than one author, texts augmented by literary criticism, or works on historical or biographical topics. The rationale for this practice is that people are thought to seek works of fiction in the catalog by their authors or titles, not by the subjects they cover. However, this has not been the case with children and youth, who often choose (or are guided to choose by parents, teachers, media specialists, and librarians) to learn about something by reading about it in stories. In the 1960s, in response to many requests from librarians and media specialists, new policies were established at LC for children's fiction under which they receive both subject headings and summary notes (see Figure 7.4). The program is described in greater detail in Chapter 9.

FIGURE 7.4

This example is an illustration of:
- edition statement
- publishing date not listed, copyright date given
- edition and history note
- summary
- Library of Congress annotated card subject headings
- fiction subject headings
- Library of Congress classification in CIP
- Library of Congress annotated card program CIP
- 2nd level cataloging

```
Calvert, Patricia.
    Sooner / Patricia Calvert. -- 1st ed. -- New York : Atheneum,
c1998.
    166 p. ; 22 cm.

    Sequel to: Bigger.
    Summary: With the realization that his father may not return
now that the Civil War is over, thirteen-year-old Tyler finds
himself the man of their Missouri farm and the master of a new
dog, the strikingly colored Sooner.
    ISBN 0-689-81114-4.

    1. Farm life -- Missouri -- Fiction.  2. Missouri -- Fiction.
3. Dogs -- Fiction.  4. Reconstruction -- Fiction.  5. United
States -- History -- 1865-1898 -- Fiction.  I. Title.
```

(chief source of information)
    (title page)

PATRICIA   CALVERT

SOONER

ATHENEUM BOOKS FOR YOUNG READERS

(information on verso)

Atheneum Books for Young Readers
An imprint of Simon & Schuster Children's Publishing Division
1230 Avenue of the Americas
New York, New York 10020

Copyright © 1998 by Patricia Calvert

Library of Congress Cataloging-in-Publication Data
Calvert, Patricia
Sooner / Patricia Calvert.—1st ed.
p. cm.
Sequel to: Bigger.
Summary: With the realization that his father may not return now that
the Civil War is over, thirteen-year-old Tyler finds himself the man of
their Missouri farm and the master of a new dog, the strikingly-colored
Sooner.
ISBN 0-689-81114-4
[1. Farm life—Missouri—Fiction. 2. Missouri—Fiction. 3. Dogs—Fiction.
4. Reconstruction—Fiction. 5. United States—History—1865-1898—
Fiction.] I. Title.
PZ7.C139So   1998
[Fic]—dc21
97-28007
CIP   AC

As a result, searchers have come to expect subject headings for children's fiction. More recently, practitioners have lobbied successfully for the assignment of headings for literary genres to adult fiction, for which ALA's Subject Analysis Committee published guidelines and terminology.[10] LC began experimenting with the new genre headings and encouraged others to do the same. Thus, local policies for subject access to children's and adult fiction need to be established based on estimates of the needs of searchers and practical considerations of time and money.

Caveats for Public Librarians and Media Specialists

There is a temptation in small media centers and public libraries with limited collections of materials to dispense with traditional modes of assigning and filing subject headings. It seems much easier and less troublesome to make up appropriate headings than to buy expensive tools like Sears or LCSH and to be bound by whatever terms are offered by published lists, whose intended audience includes much larger general libraries. Why should one invest time and money in them?

Several considerations offer answers to this question. First, consider the people using the catalog. Students, young people, and adults who use a catalog eventually go to larger libraries and use their catalogs. Those who go on to higher education will use the catalogs of their college or university libraries. They will benefit from the ability to use a library catalog following standard practices effectively. The transition from one catalog to another is easier when standard lists of terms are used in all of them.

Second, consider the need to control the list of terms. Making up one's own subject headings puts the burden of keeping track of what terms are selected, how they are defined, how they should be applied, and what cross-references should be made for them entirely on the librarian's or media specialist's shoulders. It can take a great deal of time to create and maintain a subject authority for the catalog; time that costs something in terms of other work one does not have time to do as well as the dollars and cents paid for the hours spent. If volunteers, clerical staff, or student aides are employed to help do subject cataloging, then the list of headings must be made available to them in a form they can use. Even if all the work is done alone, a properly written list will be needed for searchers to consult when they do not find what they want using their own search terms.

Third, one cannot use subject headings assigned by other catalogers, nor can they benefit from the work one does. Should one decide to enter a network environment, the terms probably can be accommodated as locally defined headings, but no one else will use them. Also, because the headings are unique to one's catalog, one cannot take advantage of copying the work of other network partners, most of whom use standard subject authorities.

Fourth, suppose one suddenly decides to take a leave from one's job or take another job altogether. The catalog should be seen as an ongoing tool, not as the individual expression of a single collection at one point in time, managed by one librarian or media specialist. How will one's successor understand and deal with the unique subject heading system? Complete, explicit instructions on how headings have been chosen, used, and managed, as well as a complete list of terms and cross-references, would have to be provided. Another person might have no interest in continuing the system or decide that it is not the best use of time and money, opting to change to a standard system. Then the entire collection would require conversion to that standard system.

Subject headings from standard authorities are used by commercial cataloging services, networks, and many centralized and cooperative services. Helpful manuals designed to make the assignment of subject headings easier for catalogers in school and public libraries, such as Joanna F. Fountain's *Subject Headings for School and Public Libraries*,[11] assume that standard authorities are being used and are based on them. Establishing a unique set of subject headings should be undertaken only after one has clearly assessed the alternatives and rejected them for well-defined reasons, because a nonstandard subject authority could result in less effective overall service than might have been provided using standard systems.

In the next two chapters, the structure and application of the *Sears List of Subject Headings* and *Library of Congress Subject Headings*—the most widely used standard subject authorities in North America—are described in greater detail.

Recommended Reading

Aluri, Rao et al. *Subject Analysis in Online Catalogs.* Englewood, CO: Libraries Unlimited, 1991.

Cochrane, Pauline Atherton, and Eric H. Johnson, eds. *Visualizing Subject Access for 21st Century Information Resources.* Urbana-Champaign, IL: Graduate School of Library and Information Science, University of Illinois at Urbana-Champaign, 1998.

Conway, Martha O'Hara. *The Future of Subdivisions in the Library of Congress Subject Headings System: Report from the Subject Subdivisions Conference Sponsored by the Library of Congress, May 9-12, 1991.* Washington, DC: Cataloging Distribution Service, Library of Congress, 1992.

Drabenstott, Karen M., ed. *Subject Authorities in the Online Environment: Papers from a Conference Program Held in San Francisco, June 29, 1987.* Chicago: American Library Association, 1991.

Ferguson, Bobby. *Subject Analysis: A Blitz Cataloging Workbook.* Englewood, CO: Libraries Unlimited, 1998.

Foskett, A. C. *The Subject Approach to Information,* 5th ed. London: Library Association, 1996.

Hennepin County Library. *Unreal! Hennepin County Library Subject Headings for Fictional Characters,* 2nd ed. Jefferson, NC: McFarland, 1992.

Hjørland, Birger. *Information Seeking and Subject Representation: An Activity-Theoretical Approach to Information Science.* Westport, CT: Greenwood Press, 1997.

Thesaurus Database. [online database] Amsterdam: Commission of European Communities, 1985- . (Maintained by Eurobrokers of Luxembourg; available via ECHO.)

Notes

1.   Library of Congress, Subject Cataloging Division, *Subject Cataloging Manual: Subject Headings,* 5th ed. (Washington, DC: Library of Congress, 1996-).

2.   Library of Congress, Subject Cataloging Division, *Library of Congress Subject Headings,* 23rd ed. (Washington, DC: Library of Congress, 2000), 5 volumes. This is the latest edition of

the printed list available at this writing. Examples of subject headings discussed in this and subsequent chapters are taken from this edition, unless identified as originating in another source.

3. A good example is Association for Library Collections & Technical Services, Subject Analysis Committee, *Guidelines on Subject Access to Individual Works of Fiction, Drama, Etc.,* 2nd ed. (Chicago: American Library Association, 2000), a pamphlet-sized publication.

4. Joseph Miller, ed., *Sears List of Subject Headings,* 17th ed. (New York: H. W. Wilson, 2000), 105.

5. David Judson Haykin, *Subject Headings: A Practical Guide* (Washington, DC: U.S. Government Printing Office, 1951), 7-9.

6. Joseph Miller, ed., *Sears List of Subject Headings,* 17th ed. (New York: H. W. Wilson, 2000); Lighthall, Lynne, ed. *Sears List of Subject Headings: Canadian Companion,* 5th ed. (New York: H. W. Wilson, 1995); Library of Congress, Subject Cataloging Division, *Library of Congress Subject Headings,* 23rd ed. (Washington, DC: Library of Congress, 2000); National Library of Canada, *Canadian Subject Headings,* 3rd ed., ed. Alina Schweitzer (Ottawa: Canada Communication Group—Publishing, 1992). Author's note: A new edition of Sears *Canadian Companion* is expected in spring 2001, and was not available as of this writing.

7. Carol Mandel, *Multiple Thesauri in Online Library Bibliographic Systems: A Report Prepared for Library of Congress Processing Services* (Washington, DC: Library of Congress, Cataloging Distribution Service, 1987); and Toni Petersen and Pat Molholt, eds., *Beyond the Book: Extending MARC for Subject Access* (Boston, MA: G. K. Hall, 1990).

8. John C. Rather, *Library of Congress Filing Rules* (Washington, DC: Library of Congress, 1980).

9. *ALA Filing Rules* (Chicago: American Library Association, 1980). An earlier set of rules issued by ALA is followed in libraries that still have card catalogs: *ALA Rules for Filing Catalog Cards,* 2nd ed. (Chicago: American Library Association, 1968).

10. Association for Library Collections & Technical Services, Subject Analysis Committee, *Guidelines on Subject Access to Individual Works of Fiction, Drama, Etc.,* 2nd ed. (Chicago: American Library Association, 2000).

11. Joanna F. Fountain, *Subject Headings for School and Public Libraries: An LCSH/Sears Companion*, 3rd ed. (Englewood, CO: Libraries Unlimited, 2001).

8

Sears List of Subject Headings

Background

The original title of *Sears List of Subject Headings* (Sears) was *List of Subject Headings for Small Libraries: Compiled from Lists Used in Nine Representative Small Libraries.*[1] It was initiated by its original compiler, Minnie Earl Sears, in response to requests by librarians for subject headings that were not as complex or difficult to understand and use as those found in the Library of Congress's published list, titled *Library of Congress Subject Headings* (LCSH). Sear's popularity was assured when H. W. Wilson, its publisher, adopted it for use on the catalog cards produced for its commercial card distribution service, which catered mainly to small public and school libraries.

From the start, Ms. Sears recognized the value of maintaining a uniform structure between LCSH and her list. Not only was it convenient to retain the same basic structure, but it was also then possible to coordinate terms from both lists. If a cataloger wanted to use a heading that Sears did not have but LCSH did, the heading could be added to the catalog without fear of conflicting with the structure of existing headings. If a small library grew large enough that Sears's headings were no longer effective in providing subject access for its patrons, it could "graduate" to LCSH without much trouble. The LCSH structure was not unacceptable by itself, but the terminology chosen for the headings was sometimes too technical, and the breakdown of subjects into categories was too specific for these smaller institutions with their limited collections of materials and unsophisticated searchers. Figures 8.1 and 9.1 demonstrate both the similarity between Sears and LCSH and LCSH's greater range of specificity.

The fact that Sears was designed from its inception to coordinate with LCSH made it attractive to librarians familiar with LCSH, who immediately grasped the advantages of Sears's simpler and broader terminology, and who could apply it easily. Sears's smaller size and simpler terminology also appealed to librarians who thought LCSH was too difficult to learn to use. H. W. Wilson kept Sears up-to-date for its customers. From 1923 to 1988, when LCSH began issuing new editions annually, new editions of Sears were issued about every five to seven years, whereas new editions of LCSH appeared only about once a decade. However, the most recent edition of Sears followed its predecessor by just three years.

At this writing, Sears is in its 17th edition.[2] Joseph Miller, its current editor, is only the fifth in the series of editors who followed Minnie Earl Sears. *Sears List of Subject Headings: Canadian Companion* (SearsCC) is in its 5th edition, compiled by Lynne Lighthall, although a new edition is expected soon.[3] It provides headings for items containing Canadian subject matter.

Format of the List

Sears is contained in one volume of nearly 800 pages. The headings are listed in two columns per page, thus the list contains between 15,000 and 16,000 authorized subject headings and cross-references. Before 1992, Sears's headings were listed in one column on the left-hand side of each page, and the second column on the right-hand side was left blank for the addition of cataloger's notes, cross-references, and new headings. This seems like a welcome feature, but when a new edition appeared, catalogers faced the burdensome task of transcribing their notes from the previous edition unless they had the foresight to maintain their policies and departures in a separate file. The practice of leaving a blank column was discontinued in the 15th edition.

FIGURE 8.1

Immigrants—*Continued*
  BT Minorities
  RT Aliens
      Immigration and emigration
Immigrants—United States   325.73
  UF United States—Foreign population
  NT Mexican Americans
  RT United States—Immigration and emigration
Immigration and emigration   304.8; 325
    Use for materials on migration from one country to another. Materials on the movement of population within a country for permanent settlement are entered under Internal migration.
  UF Emigration
      Foreign population
      Migration
  SA names of countries with the subdivision *Immigration and emigration,* e.g. **United States— Immigration and emigration;** and names of immigrant minorities and national groups, e.g. **Mexican Americans; Mexicans—United States;** etc. [to be added as needed]
  BT **Population**
  NT **Children of immigrants**
      Human geography
      Illegal aliens
      Naturalization
      Refugees
      United States—Immigration and emigration
  RT **Aliens**
      Americanization
      Colonization
      Immigrants
      Internal migration
Immortality   129
    Use for materials on the question of the endless existence of the soul. Materials on the character and form of a future existence are entered under **Future life.** Materials on the philosophical concept of eternity are entered under **Eternity.**
  UF Eternal life
      Life after death
  BT **Eschatology**
      Soul
      Theology
  RT **Future life**

Immune system   616.07
  UF Immunological system
  BT Anatomy
      Physiology
  RT Immunity
Immunity   571.9; 616.07
  NT Allergy
      Immunization
  RT Immune system
Immunization (May subdiv. geog.)   614.4
    Use for materials on any process, active or passive, that leads to increased immunity. Materials on active immunization with a vaccine are entered under **Vaccination.**
  BT **Immunity**
      Public health
  NT **Vaccination**
Immunological system
  USE **Immune system**
Impaired vision
  USE **Vision disorders**
Impeachment
  USE types of public officials and names of individual public officials with the subdivision *Impeachment,* e.g. **Presidents—United States—Impeachment** [to be added as needed]
Impeachments (May subdiv. geog.)   342
  SA types of public officials and names of individual officials with the subdivision **Impeachment** [to be added as needed]
  BT **Administration of justice**
  NT **Recall (Political science)**
Imperialism   325
  UF Colonialism
  SA names of countries with the subdivision *Foreign relations* or *Colonies* [to be added as needed]
  BT **Political science**
  NT **Colonies**
      Colonization
Implements, utensils, etc.
  USE **Agricultural machinery**
       Household equipment and supplies
       Stone implements

357

The book begins with an extensive introductory chapter in which the history of the list is described. It explains the principles on which the list is based and methods for applying it properly, along with a bibliography of basic sources for more information. Both of these elements are very helpful for media specialists and public librarians who may find doing any kind of cataloging a new experience.

Headings authorized for use in the catalog are always printed in boldface type, whether they are in the main filing order of headings or represent cross-references beneath other headings. Roman print is used for terms that may not be used as headings but for which cross-references are supposed to be made, whether they appear in the regular order of headings or beneath other headings as cross-references. For example, CARNIVOROUS PLANTS appears in boldface print as a main heading in the "C's", while INSECT-EATING PLANTS appears in Roman print under it. In the "I's", INSECT-EATING PLANTS appears in Roman print as a main heading with the cross-reference "USE CARNIVOROUS PLANTS" following, with CARNIVOROUS PLANTS in boldface.

A nice feature in Sears is the presence of a list of canceled and replacement headings; that is, headings from the previous edition that have been changed, immediately preceding the first page of subject headings. Some changes are minor, such as the replacement of ART FORGERIES with ART—FORGERIES; others are more far reaching, such as the replacement of BUYING with PURCHASING. The former change involved only adding a dash between the two parts of the term that, although primarily cosmetic, also changes the way the term is filed. The latter change alters the word used for the concept and shifts the file for it from the "B's" to the "P's." Some changes are even more extensive, such as the change from GRANDPARENT AND CHILD to GRANDPARENT-GRANDCHILD RELATIONSHIP. The list of changed headings expedites identifying the revisions that should be made in the catalog when adopting the new edition. Changed headings are also identified in the list as "Former headings."

In addition to the subject headings and cross-references, many of the headings have numbers next to them. These are classification numbers associated with the subjects, taken from the 13th edition of *Abridged Dewey Decimal Classification and Relative Index* (DDC-Abridged).[4] Using Sears alone, a cataloger could assign subject headings and classification numbers to an item at the same time, although they are cautioned about accepting recommended Dewey numbers without checking in the classification itself. When a subject has more than one viewpoint, more than one classification number can be suggested for a particular topic, depending on which one is represented in an item.[5] For example, COMPUTER BULLETIN BOARDS is followed by two numbers—004.693 and 384.3, depending on whether the focus is computer science or commerce. The classification numbers in Sears change to reflect changes in recommended viewpoints of subject matter as well as in new editions of DDC. For example, in the 15th edition, COMPUTERS was followed by three numbers: 004, 338.4, and 621.39, representing the viewpoints of computer science, communication, or electronic engineering. In the current, 17th edition, only two numbers follow COMPUTERS: 004 and 621.39. A number representing the communication viewpoint is no longer recommended. The editor states also that Dewey numbers are not assigned to very general topics and explains that numbers in Sears are deliberately kept short, but can be extended if desired by the addition of subdivision numbers in DDC tables.[6] (For a more comprehensive description of how DDC classification numbers are built with the addition of subdivisions, see Chapter 11.)

Some headings are followed by instructions on how to apply or subdivide them. For example, under the heading MAGNET SCHOOLS, it states: "Use for materials on schools offering special courses not available in the regular school curriculum and designed to attract students without reference to the usual attendance zone rules, often as an aid to voluntary school desegregation";[7] and under DIRECTORIES, it states: "Use for materials about directories and for bibliographies of directories. S[ee]A[lso] subjects and names of countries, cities, etc., with the subdivision *Directories,* for lists of persons, organizations, objects, etc., together with addresses or other identifying data [to be added as needed]."[8] The instructions may include information about when *not* to use a subject heading and furnish alternatives for similar works with different emphases. For example, under DINNERS, the instruction states: "Use for materials on menus and recipes for dinners. Materials on dining customs and gastronomic travel are entered under **Dining**."[9]

Sears (and most other subject authorities) does not list certain kinds of headings, like personal names, that would be difficult to anticipate and incorporate into the list. In addition to personal names, the omissions include other proper nouns—places, corporate bodies, events, etc.—and common names, such as the names of particular animals, birds, fruits and vegetables, flowers, diseases, chemicals and minerals, organs of the body, etc. An example of such an addition is the heading shown in Figure 8.2. A list of these categories is given to help guide catalogers adding these headings as needed.[10]

FIGURE 8.2

This example is an illustration of:
- other title information
- publishing date not listed, copyright date given
- detailed pagination statement
- descriptive illustration statement
- bibliography and index note
- Library of Congress subject headings
- Sears subject headings
- abridged and unabridged Dewey classification numbers. (See page 218 for a discussion of other possible classification numbers)
- Canadian CIP
- two levels of cataloging

2nd level cataloging

```
Ayre, John.
   Northrup Frye : a biography / John Ayre. -- Toronto : Random
House, c1989.
   472 p., [8] p. of plates : ill., ports. ; 24 cm.

   Includes bibliographical references (p. 453-458) and index.
   ISBN 0-394-22113-3.

Tracing with Library of Congress subject headings:

   1. Frye, Northrop -- Biography.  2. Scholars -- Canada --
Biography.  3. Critics -- Canada -- Biography.  4. College
teachers -- Canada -- Biography.  5. Victoria College (Toronto,
Ont.) -- Faculty -- Biography.  I. Title.

Recommended unabridged DDC: 801.95092
   801 (philosophy and theory of literature)
      .95 (criticism)
         092 (treatment of persons)
```

1st level cataloging

```
Ayre, John.
   Northrup Frye. -- Random House, c1989.
   472 p., [8] p. of plates.

   ISBN 0-394-22113-3.
```

Tracing with Sears subject headings:

```
   1. Frye, Northrup. 2. Colleges and universities -- Canada --
Faculty -- Biography.  3. Victoria College (Toronto, Ont.) --
Faculty -- Biography.  I. Title.
```

Recommended abridged DDC: 801.92

(chief source of information)
(title page)

(information on verso)

A
Biography

JOHN AYRE

Random House
Toronto

Copyright © 1989 by John Ayre

All rights reserved under International and Pan-American Copyright Conventions

Published in Canada by Random House of Canada Limited, Toronto.

Canadian Cataloguing in Publication Data
Ayre, John
   Northrop Frye: a biography
ISBN 0-394-22113-3

1. Frye, Northrop, 1912-   – Biography.
2. Scholars – Canada – Biography. 3. Critics – Canada – Biography. 4. College teachers – Canada – Biography. 5. Victoria College (Toronto, Ont.). – Faculty – Biography.   I. Title.
PN75.F7A9 1989   801'.95'0924   C89-094447-4

The headings in Sears are arranged according to the 1980 edition of filing rules sponsored and published by the American Library Association.[11] These rules, based on the principle of filing subject headings as they appear and without taking account of punctuation, were simplified from a more complicated edition of filing rules published previously, to facilitate automated filing in computerized catalogs. In the current method of alphabetizing, subject headings are filed word by word, with digits preceding letters, and punctuation ignored. Figure 8.3 shows how these rules would be applied to a list of hypothetical subject headings consisting of a single word followed by multiword headings starting with the same word. The multiword headings use different types of punctuation found in Sears, including inverted modifiers with commas (now largely obsolete), subdivisions with dashes, and a parenthetic qualifier.

Figure 8.3   Alphabetization According to the 1980 ALA Filing Rules

(the following terms are not real subject headings)

Children

Children, Adopted

Children and strangers

Children—Books and readings

Children in literature

Children—Research

Children (Roman law)

Children—United States

Children, Vagrant

The 17th edition contains only one authorized heading beginning with a digit—4-H CLUBS—but two others are included as cross-references. Regarding inverted terms requiring commas, the editor states: ". . . in Sears, the direct form of entry has replaced the inverted form, on the theory that most library users search for multiple-word terms in the order in which they occur naturally in the language."[12] One can argue that ignoring the punctuation in filing disperses some headings more closely related to one another than to those filed next to them; however, it is a boon to patrons who do not know the significance of the different types of punctuation.

Types of Headings

According to Cutter and other theorists, the perfect subject heading is a single noun with one precise meaning. Many subject headings do consist of a single word, usually a noun, but sometimes a verb form is used as a noun (for example, CONDUCTING). Single-word noun headings can have different meanings depending on whether the noun is in the singular or plural: PRAYER is used for the act of praying, whereas PRAYERS is used for the words, images, and thoughts of the act of praying. Similarly, ESSAY is used for materials about the literary form, whereas ESSAYS is used for collections of this genre. Sometimes a single noun is not intelligible alone, and an explanatory term or phrase is added in parentheses to define it clearly and precisely, such as BUSING (SCHOOL INTEGRATION). In such cases, the parenthetic word or phrase is called a "qualifier."

Another type of heading is composed of a single noun modified by an adjective or a second noun used as an adjective, such as MINIATURE GARDENS or CAREER CHANGES. As mentioned previously, earlier editions of Sears contained headings in which the adjective was inverted, following a comma (in the previous examples this would be CHANGES, CAREER and GARDENS, MINIATURE). With the 15th edition, all but a few of inverted terms were changed to natural word order; that is, the order in which we would speak or write them in texts. Among the few remaining inverted terms is STATE, THE, which is inverted to ensure that it is filed under "S," not "T," where it would be if it were filed under the initial article. However, ignoring the punctuation and filing this heading as if it were solely the two words "STATE THE" puts this heading on a different page of Sears than if the initial article was ignored, as is usually done with the initial article in titles, and the heading was filed as if it were solely "STATE."

A third type of heading is composed of two nouns connected by the conjunction *and,* such as LANDLORD AND TENANT. Sometimes, the two words represent opposites, such as GOOD AND EVIL; other times, the word pairs link similar concepts, such as LANGUAGE AND LANGUAGES or CARTOONS AND CARICATURES. More complicated compound headings (that is, multiword headings) of this type may include modified nouns; for example, ELECTRONIC APPARATUS AND APPLIANCES.

A fourth type of heading is composed of two nouns connected by a preposition. A few examples include: EMOTIONS IN CHILDREN; PSYCHOLOGY OF LEARNING; COOKING FOR THE SICK; and BIBLE AS LITERATURE. Many more headings in this category were included in earlier editions of Sears, but they have been eliminated for various reasons. Some described activities or functions seemed incongruous, such as CHILDREN AS ARTISTS or WOMEN AS AUTHORS. The wordings implied a disdainful attitude toward children and women and have been changed to neutral language. Now the authorized headings are CHILD ARTISTS and WOMEN AUTHORS, respectively. Other headings of this type have been shortened; for example, LEGAL ASSISTANCE TO THE POOR is now LEGAL AID.

The most complex headings involve linking two concepts that both require more than one word for expression, such as ILLUMINATION OF BOOKS AND MANUSCRIPTS or OVERLAND JOURNEYS TO THE PACIFIC.

Some multiword headings have been simplified in the current edition; for example, CHRISTIAN ART AND SYMBOLISM has been changed to two simpler headings, CHRISTIAN ART and CHRISTIAN SYMBOLISM. Other changes have eliminated words from multiword headings; for example, YOUNG ADULTS' LIBRARY SERVICES is now YOUNG ADULTS' LIBRARIES; and WORLD WIDE WEB SERVERS is now WEB SERVERS. Some terms have been made plural (LEMON is now LEMONS, referring to the fruit) or singular (BOOK INDUSTRIES is now BOOK INDUSTRY), presumably for clarity. A number of changes reflect changes in usage, such as the major change from INDIANS OF NORTH AMERICA to NATIVE AMERICANS and adding the word "RELATIONSHIP" to combinations of types of persons; for example, FATHER AND CHILD is now FATHER-CHILD RELATIONSHIP, and MOTHER AND CHILD is now MOTHER-CHILD RELATIONSHIP, etc.

Some subject headings are formulated with explanatory qualifiers to ensure their correct interpretation, such as MARS (PLANET) or LEFT AND RIGHT (DIRECTION). Other times, scope notes take the place of a qualifier to clarify meaning, as in the heading CLIMATE, used for materials on climate in general, whereas WEATHER is used for materials on conditions in a particular place and time.[13]

Cross-References

Sears has six kinds of cross-references: USE; UF (Use For); BT (Broader Term); NT (Narrower Term); RT (Related Term); and SA (See Also), explained next.

1. A USE reference leads both the subject cataloger and catalog searcher from an unauthorized word or phrase to the subject heading authorized to represent that concept. The unauthorized word(s) will appear in Sears in roman print, while the authorized heading that follows "USE" is in boldface type. The catalog should display the unauthorized word(s) and its USE cross-reference. An example is the word SKETCHING, which is followed by the instruction to USE DRAWING.

2. A UF (Use For) reference is furnished in Sears as an instruction to the subject cataloger to make a USE reference for unauthorized words that might reasonably be thought by a searcher to be the correct heading. It is the reciprocal of a USE heading. When an authorized subject heading that has UFs is assigned, references should be made in the public catalog from the word or words following the UF to the authorized heading being assigned, followed by the words USE [AUTHORIZED HEADING]. An example is found at the authorized heading DRAWING, which has a UF reference instructing the subject cataloger to make a USE reference to DRAWING from SKETCHING.

3. A BT (Broader Term) reference is furnished in Sears as an aid to the subject cataloger to consider authorized headings with broader meanings than the one at which it appears. Sears never shows the entire hierarchy of a subject at any one point, but, instead, lists headings one level broader and one level narrower than each authorized heading. An example is the heading BOTANICAL GARDENS, which has two BT references, GARDENS and PARKS. Subject catalogers are expected to give instructions at those BT references to also see the heading to which they refer. It is assumed that searchers will know the broader terms if they have identified a narrower one, but not vice versa. Practically, this means that when BOTANICAL GARDENS is assigned, the cataloger need not add cross-references to GARDENS or PARKS from it, because the searcher may be assumed to know them. Instead, the cataloger should add cross-references *to* BOTANICAL GARDENS *from* GARDENS and *from* PARKS, because it is more specific and might be overlooked by a novice in that subject area.

4. An NT (Narrower Term) reference is furnished in Sears as an aid to the subject cataloger to consider headings at narrower levels of hierarchy than the heading at which it appears. As a practical matter when assigning an authorized heading, subject catalogers should create displays in the catalog leading from that heading to any NTs already present in the catalog with materials listed under them, but not to NTs having no material listed under them.

5. An RT (Related Term) reference is furnished in Sears as an aid to subject catalogers and lay searchers to consider other authorized headings related to one at which it appears. For example, at HEALTH INSURANCE, there is an RT to HEALTH CARE REFORM. The cataloger might consider the latter heading in addition to or in place of the former. Additionally, when HEALTH INSURANCE is assigned, a cross-reference to HEALTH CARE REFORM may be made if there are any materials

listed under it. Similarly, when HEALTH CARE REFORM is assigned, a cross-reference should be made to HEALTH INSURANCE, if the latter has any materials listed under it.

6. An SA (See Also) cross-reference leads to a group of related headings, or gives an instruction to the subject cataloger about making groups of headings, as in the following two examples: at GODS AND GODDESSES, it notes, "SA names of gods and goddesses,"[14] pointing to a group of possible headings consisting of the names of individual deities; at MARKETING it notes, "SA subjects with the subdivision *Marketing* . . . to be added as needed,"[15] thus permitting the cataloger to use the authorized subject heading MARKETING as a subdivision under other authorized headings.

The addition of cross-references to the catalog gives searchers a chance to find words that might not be authorized for use as subject headings, but are commonly used for the concepts they represent. Cross-references contribute to the "user friendliness" of the catalog by enriching what is known as the "entry vocabulary," that is, the number of words and phrases providing a "hit" of some kind when searched. Depending on the type of catalog in which it is used, a USE cross-reference might retrieve nothing more than an instruction to use the authorized heading, requiring the searcher to do a second search using the correct heading. If programmed appropriately, however, a computer-based catalog can display the message about the correct heading and show the items listed under it, also, enabling the searcher to retrieve the requested materials even though an unauthorized word was entered. This saves the patron the time it takes to do another search.

A cross-reference that leads to a heading that either does not appear in the catalog at all or, if it appears, does not have any materials listed under it, is called a *blind reference.* It is frustrating for searchers to be led to another heading, only to fail to find any materials listed there. This should be avoided, as mentioned before. Some theories claim that by listing recommended references, even if they are blind references, the searcher is taught the correct words to use. Because local policies govern the matter, one can choose not to frustrate one's patrons even if that means the catalog does not teach them the correct vocabulary.

Despite the advantages of cross-references, called the catalog's *syndetic structure,* catalogers recognize that creating and maintaining them takes time and is costly. Working on syndetics is more costly than ordinary cataloging for two reasons: First, because decisions about the reference structure should be made by highly skilled people having profound knowledge and understanding of search options and behaviors; and second, as references are added, the network of headings and references rapidly becomes very complex, and the number of individual operations required to keep it up multiply exponentially.

Subdivisions and Subdivision Practices

When narrower subject headings are desired, authorized terms can be subdivided in one of three ways: by the presence of authorized subdivisions under the heading; by following instructions to subdivide a heading in specific ways; or by the application of one of nine subdivision patterns, called *key headings,* provided in the "Principles" section that precedes the list.[16] These are discussed next, in slightly different order than enumerated. The 17th edition eliminated a list of "commonly used subdivisions," which used to provide a fourth method of subdividing authorized headings. Instead, it has incorporated these subdivisions into general references within the list itself and provided instructions on how they are to be used. An example is

PSYCHOLOGICAL ASPECTS, which has a USE reference directing catalogers to apply it to subject headings as a subdivision to be added as needed.[17]

Key Headings: Any heading that fits the categories of the key headings can use all the subdivisions given under the designated model. For example, for countries of the world, UNITED STATES is the key heading, and any of the subdivisions listed under it can be used under all other countries, with one obvious exception—no other country can use the historic periods that further subdivide UNITED STATES—HISTORY. Countries about which collections are likely to be large enough to warrant the subdivision of history to the period level have their own historic periods listed in Sears, for example, CANADA (see next paragraph, for an example) or FRANCE. Sears does not list historical periods for countries, such as BRAZIL or DENMARK, where collections about their histories are likely to be small.

Jurisdictions smaller than countries also have key headings: states and provinces follow the model of OHIO; cities follow the pattern of CHICAGO (ILL.). The rest of the key headings are PRESIDENTS—UNITED STATES (for chief executives of nations); SHAKESPEARE, WILLIAM, 1564-1616 (for prolific authors); NATIVE AMERICANS (for ethnic groups or native peoples); ENGLISH LANGUAGE (for languages); ENGLISH LITERATURE (for literatures); and WORLD WAR, 1939-1945 (for wars or battles).

Authorized Subdivisions: Because Sears is intended for small collections, it provides relatively broad headings that tend to collocate rather than divide the parts of a concept; therefore, subdivided headings are not typical. Nevertheless, numerous examples are found throughout the list, from ABILITY—TESTING on page 1 to ZOOLOGICAL SPECIMENS—COLLECTION AND PRESERVATION, on page 770. A small minority contain more than one subdivision, such as UNITED STATES—CIVILIZATION—FOREIGN INFLUENCES and CANADA—HISTORY—1763-1867. Authorized subdivisions can change from edition to edition, but there does not seem to be a pattern to the changes. In the transition from the 15th to the 16th editions, many subdivided headings that were formerly [PLACE]—[TOPIC] were changed to [TOPIC]—[PLACE]. Still, the general instructions about subdividing topics by place versus places by topic are sufficiently vague as to allow catalogers much latitude to make their own choices. In searching for authorized subdivisions, catalogers should keep in mind that the method of alphabetizing can cause other multiword headings to file between a main heading and its subdivision. They will not be found in the same entry, or even in the same column or page of the list.

Instruction to Subdivide: Many topical subject headings are followed by an instruction that states: "(May subdiv. geog.)," meaning that the heading can be subdivided by the name of a place. Sometimes, the instructions are quite detailed, as for BRIDGES, which says: "This heading may be subdivided by the names of rivers, lakes, canals, etc. as well as by the names of countries, states, cities, etc."[18] Occasionally, an instruction will furnish limits on the types of places that can be used as subdivisions, as with RECONSTRUCTION (1939-1951), where it states: "(May subdiv. geog. except U.S.),"[19] indicating that UNITED STATES would not be an appropriate subdivision for this concept. The best strategy in dealing with geographic subdivision is to follow the instructions as stated and do not apply it if the instruction is absent.

When it is likely to be needed often, a subject heading can be authorized as a subdivision under other terms, and permission to use it in this way will be given. The subject heading MARKETING can be used both as a main heading or a subdivision under other topics, as noted previously.

Subdivisions can be used to make a subject heading match the precise subject of an item being cataloged—that is, to turn a broader subject heading into a coextensive heading. They also are useful in dividing a long list of entries into smaller groupings for more effective searching. Generally speaking, however, subdivision should not play an important role for collections using Sears because of their small size. To bring together several works on a topic, broad headings must be used. Subdivision, by definition, narrows topics and would, thus, cause fewer works to collocate under an individual heading. Thus, subdivision is limited to topics collected heavily, even by small libraries and media centers. Examples include United States and Canadian history, or children, both of which have numerous subdivisions.

Rules for Applying Sears's Headings

Instructions for using Sears's subject headings at the beginning of the book include the following generally accepted methods of application (paraphrased, not quoted, from Sears's text):[20]

1. Determine the subject(s) of the item being cataloged and write it down. Consider the item from the user's point of view as far as it is possible to do so. Then, assign up to three headings authorized by the list to represent the identified concepts. Assign more than three headings only after careful thought.

2. The most specific heading authorized to represent each identified subject should be applied. For example, if a videorecording is about cotton, assign the heading COTTON, not FIBERS, which is a broader heading that includes other substances as well as cotton.

3. Use the most specific heading directly, not indirectly as a subdivision of a broader heading. An electronic resource about cotton should be entered directly under COTTON, not indirectly under FIBERS—COTTON, as if COTTON were a subdivision of the broader heading FIBERS.

4. Remember that the purpose of subject headings is to bring like materials together. Think beyond the item being cataloged to items already in the collection and likely to be added that would share a particular heading.

5. Select words as subject headings that people using the catalog will be most likely to look up. In choosing between a scientific or technical term and a simpler, commonly used term, choose the former and make a cross-reference to it from the latter. For example, between FREE ENTERPRISE and LAISSEZ-FAIRE, choose FREE ENTERPRISE as the authorized heading and refer to it from LAISSEZ-FAIRE, the term used by economists.

6. Generally, treat items first by topic, then by geographical focus or form, although some types of subject are excepted.

7. Use subject headings that represent major literary forms or genres such as POETRY and FICTION for collections by several authors; do not use these headings for individual examples of the genre or for collections by a single author. Searchers will look up individual novels, collections of stories by a single author, or collections of poetry by an individual poet by the author's name or the title, not by subject. Minor literary forms are treated differently (see additional discussion in the following pages).

Catalogers using Sears to index materials are given guidance in treating selected types of material, including literary works, biographies, and works with a geographical focus. These are explored in greater detail here.

Literary Works: The broad term "literature" covers two distinct types of material: (1) works of literature (poetry, plays, novels, essays, etc.), and (2) works about literature. These two types are treated differently in subject analysis. Works about any of the literary forms consist of their names: POETRY, DRAMA, FICTION, ESSAY. Because this kind of item is *about* the literary form, the heading represents its topic, not the form in which it treats its topic. When an item is about only French poetry, not German or Dutch poetry, or only Japanese drama, not English or Brazilian drama, the geographical focus is included as a adjectival modifier: FRENCH POETRY, JAPANESE DRAMA. Whenever the work is historical or critical, or both, the subdivision —HISTORY AND CRITICISM is added to the main heading. Other subdivisions can also apply, and the key heading ENGLISH LITERATURE provides the model for any national literature.

Examples of any of the literary forms are divided into two types, those by individual authors and collections by multiple authors. Works by one author, especially individual examples of an author's works (one novel, one play, one poem) are not usually assigned any headings at all. Librarians believe that people search these items by their authors or titles, not by subject headings. Furthermore, even small libraries have many novels and plays, which would result in retrieving hundreds or thousands of items under the subject heading if it were used for individual examples of the genre. However, subject catalogers may want to assign topical headings to reflect what the novel or poem is about, and Sears recommends following the guidelines prepared by the Subject Analysis Committee of the Association for Library Collections & Technical Services (the division of the American Library Association concerned with cataloging issues).[21] Sears allows the use of the subdivision —FICTION.

In keeping with those guidelines, Sears allows genre subject headings to be assigned to individual examples (or collections by individual authors) of minor genres, such as science fiction or fairy tales, undoubtedly assuming that there are fewer such items in small collections. As mentioned previously, LC is experimenting with these kinds of assignments, hoping to learn whether they enhance retrieval.

Subject headings representing examples of literary forms or genres usually are reserved for collections by many authors; for example, ESSAYS—COLLECTIONS. (Note that the singular form, ESSAY, is used for the genre as a topic; the plural form, ESSAYS, is used for examples of the genre. Of the major genres, drama, fiction, literature, and poetry are the same for both types of use, whereas essay(s), parody(ies), and short story(ies) differ.)

Biographies: Biographies about one, two, or three individuals (called the "biographees") are considered "individual" biographies. For such works, each biographee is assigned a subject heading consisting of that biographee's name in authorized AACR2-98 form. A second subject heading can be assigned if the item contains a great deal of information about the person's work or field of interest. For example, if a biography of Georgia O'Keeffe contained the details of her life, but very little about her art, one subject heading—her name in its AACR2-98 form—would be enough. But if the biographer devoted a great deal of the contents to details about her artworks, their reception by art critics, and comparison with the works of her peers, a second subject heading, AMERICAN PAINTERS—BIOGRAPHY, could also be assigned. Catalogers are cautioned against overdoing the assignment of two headings.[22] On the other hand, a few people have so much information produced about them that it is useful to separate the biographies from other types of works. The key heading for these few individuals (Shakespeare, William) includes the name subdivided by the term—BIOGRAPHY.

When a work is about four or more persons, it is deemed a "collective" biography. If there is no limitation on the kinds of biographees (for example, they do all types of work, come from all places, etc.), the main heading BIOGRAPHY is assigned. When all the biographees come from a particular place, such as, British Columbia, the heading assigned would reflect that common focus: BRITISH COLUMBIA—BIOGRAPHY. If all the biographees were poets or baseball players, the headings assigned would reflect it: POETS—BIOGRAPHY or BASEBALL PLAYERS—BIOGRAPHY, respectively.

Works with Geographical Focus: Works with a geographic focus are treated in different ways, depending on the topic. Topics in the fields of history, geography, and politics tend to be treated from a specific locationally focused point of view. For this reason, many of the subject headings for these topics put the name of the location first and topical subdivisions following it, rather than the general rule, which dictates topic first and geographical focus second. This is not to say that one doesn't encounter general works about history or politics, only that a far larger number of items in those fields are likely to be specific to one place, such as Canadian history or New Hampshire politics. It makes sense to treat them differently than works on chemistry, which do not tend to have a geographic focus. Topical headings that may have geographic focus are so indicated by the instruction to subdivide geographically. In doing so, as discussed previously, one simply adds the name of the location as a subdivision under the topic; but, sometimes, catalogers are instructed to use the adjectival form of the name, such as GREEK LITERATURE. Guidance in bringing out geographic focus is offered in several places in the text.[23]

Sears recommends using the same principles to assign subject headings to videos, electronic resources, and material formats other than books. If one wanted to assign subject headings to the video version of the film *Gone with the Wind,* for example, one could find no better topical heading than UNITED STATES—HISTORY—1861-1865, CIVIL WAR, perhaps adding a final form subdivision for the literary genre or imaginary nature of the work, —DRAMA, —PERSONAL NARRATIVES, or —FICTION. "Videorecording" is not an authorized subdivision and catalogers are warned, specifically, not to use form subdivisions to describe physical format.[24]

Sears's Canadian Companion

The 5th edition of *Sears List of Subject Headings: Canadian Companion* (SearsCC) is a one-volume work with 99 pages. It is similar to the 17th edition of Sears in its design and structure with one small exception; it lists the meaning of BT, NT, RT, SA, and UF at the bottom of each page. SearsCC expands and adapts Sears where the larger work does not adequately cover Canadian topics. For example, Sears has 14 headings for Canadian history with one UF reference; SearsCC has 24 headings and lists many references.

In the introduction to SearsCC written in 1995, Lighthall lists six headings in SearsCC that do not follow Sears practice. Five of these have been changed in the 17th edition of Sears to the terms used in SearsCC, making Sears and SearsCC more compatible. This compatibility will be even greater when the 6th edition of SearsCC is published in spring 2001. A significant difference will be in Sears's use of NATIVE AMERICANS whereas SearsCC will list FIRST NATIONS, the term used in Canada for its native peoples. Examples of other differences that reflect Canadian usage are FRENCH-SPEAKING CANADIANS (SearsCC) rather than FRENCH CANADIANS (Sears) and QUEBEC (PROVINCE)—SEPARATIST MOVEMENTS (SearsCC) rather than QUEBEC (PROVINCE)—HISTORY—AUTONOMY AND INDEPENDENCE MOVEMENTS (Sears).[25]

Why Use Sears?

Two of the most important reasons one would choose to adopt Sears are (1) that it authorizes simpler words to represent topics than LCSH, and (2) it provides broader terms under which to bring together more items in a topical area, rather than differentiate them under many narrow headings. If one's public library or school library media center caters to young people and adults who are not experts in the subjects they search, then Sears's simpler terminology is more likely to match the words chosen for subject searching than sophisticated words for the same concepts. Also, if a collection is very small but general in scope, it is likely that few items would be gathered under a single heading if extremely narrow subject headings are used. Librarians and media specialists can feel confident that Sears's headings are at the right level of specificity when most searches produce manageable groups of items; and begin to worry when searches usually produce more hits than patrons want to view.

Some librarians and media specialists choose Sears because it is used by their peers—other schools in a school district, or other libraries in a system or consortium. Conforming to the same practices employed by one's colleagues is a valid basis for their choice. Also, a library or media center may choose to adopt Sears if it buys catalog records from a supplier that provides Sears's headings.

One might choose to use Sears because it is contained in one volume and does not require the purchase of additional tools for its application, as is the case with LCSH (see Chapter 9). Sears also furnishes guidance for assigning Dewey classification numbers, which is helpful, even if the numbers printed in Sears are not definitive.

Despite these advantages, there are good reasons why some media centers and small public libraries prefer to use LCSH. These reasons are explored, with a more detailed explanation of LCSH, in the next chapter.

Conclusion

The process of assigning Sears's subject headings to materials is simple, but requires care and thought in determining what an item is about and which authorized heading best represents the concept. As one works with Sears and becomes familiar with its vocabulary, assigning subject headings becomes easier. Try your hand at assigning one Sears's subject heading to the hypothetical titles in Figure 8.4. In addition to checking the accuracy and relevance of the subject headings the authors believe are correct, the answers note the type of heading each assignment represents. Answers are in Appendix C.

Figure 8.4

1. Title: *Digging for our roots*
   Summary: Tells how archaeologists excavate a site to uncover evidence of cultures that predate our own.

2. Title: *The pros and cons of bilingual education*
   Summary: Teachers, politicians, parents, and students explore major issues in bilingual education.

3. Title: *Database searching : a bibliography*
   Summary: A bibliography of source materials covering databases, search techniques, searching software, and related subjects.

4. Title: *Historical sketches of colonial America*
       Summary: Brief overviews of ten landmark episodes in the history of the American colonies from the landing at Plymouth to the battles at Lexington and Concord.

5. Title: *The miracle of the human hand*
       Summary: Description of the unique features of the human hand and how these features enabled early human ancestors to succeed despite their disadvantages in size and speed in comparison with other species.

6. Title: *Rock music : a 20th century phenomenon*
       Summary: Describes the rise of rock music and its subgenres, and the structural, harmonic, and melodic conventions it employs.

7. Title: *Don Quixote and his peers : portraits of early literary heroes*
       Summary: Explores the concept of the hero in early Spanish fiction.

8. Title: *A "yellow submarine" album*
       Summary: Songs from the Beatle's famous animated film with easy-to-play accompaniments.

9. Title: *The biological clock*
       Summary: The pros and cons of childbearing after age 40.

10 Title: *The Quebecois*
       Summary: Daily life, culture, heritage, and religion of French Canadians.

Notes

1.   Minnie Earl Sears, *List of Subject Headings for Small Libraries: Compiled from Lists Used in Nine Representative Small Libraries* (Bronx, NY: H. W. Wilson, 1923).

2.   *Sears List of Subject Headings,* 17th ed., ed. Joseph Miller (New York: H. W. Wilson, 2000). Hereafter called Sears.

3.   *Sears List of Subject Headings: Canadian Companion,* 5th ed., comp. Lynne Lighthall (New York: H. W. Wilson, 1995). Hereafter called SearsCC.

4.   Melvil Dewey, *Abridged Dewey Decimal Classification and Relative Index,* 13th ed., eds. Joan S. Mitchell et al. (Albany, NY: OCLC-Forest Press, 1997). Author's note: In 1999, Forest Press moved its operations to Dublin, Ohio, headquarters of its parent firm, OCLC, Inc.

5.   Sears, xi.

6.   Ibid.

7.   Sears, 423.

8.   Sears, 208.

9.   Sears, 207.

10.   Sears, xxxviii.

11.   *ALA Filing Rules* (Chicago: American Library Association, 1980).

12.   Sears, x.

13.   Sears, 146.

14.   Sears, 314.

15.   Sears, 431.

16.   Sears, xxxix.

17.   Sears, xl, 573.

18.   Sears, 98.

19.   Sears, 592.

20.   Sears, xv-xxx.

21.   Association for Library Collections & Technical Services. Subject Analysis Committee. *Guidelines on Subject Access to Individual Works of Fiction, Drama, Etc.,* 2nd ed. (Chicago: American Library Association, 2000).

22.   Sears, xxvi.

23.   Sears, xx, xxii-xxv, xxvii.

24.   Sears, xxx.

25. Material in this section is based on e-mail correspondence to Jean Weihs from Lynne Lighthall, August 21, 2000.

9

Library of Congress Subject Headings

Background

Library of Congress Subject Headings (LCSH) began publication in 1909, under the title *Subject Headings Used in the Dictionary Catalogues of the Library of Congress.* Parts of the first edition were issued over a period of five years and supplements continued updating it until a second edition was published in 1919. In 1975, the eighth edition appeared with the now-familiar title for the first time—*Library of Congress Subject Headings.* In 1988, as a result of LCSH's conversion to a computerized database and the ease with which updates can be cumulated and printed, new editions in book form began to be issued annually, instead of irregularly about once a decade, while versions in other forms are also available.

LCSH originally was based on a list of subject headings compiled and issued by the American Library Association (ALA), called *The List of Subject Headings for Use in Dictionary Catalogs.* In using the ALA list to catalog books for the collection, LC's subject catalogers adopted many of the headings the way they appeared in the ALA list, modified others, and created new ones when they did not find what they needed. This resulted in a pragmatic compilation of subject headings (also called "descriptors") derived from the contents of the books in LC's collection. LCSH's wide appeal is attributable to three factors: (1) that LC collects many more books in nearly all subjects than other general libraries; (2) that it does a fine job of maintaining and distributing the ever-growing list of authorized subject headings and cross-references; and, (3) that it charges very little for doing all of this work.

David Judson Haykin and Richard S. Angell, two of LC's cataloging heads during the middle of the twentieth century (Haykin led the Subject Cataloging Division from 1941-1952; Angell from 1952-1966), did much to influence, interpret, and explain the theory and practice of LCSH's terminology. Their writings and speeches about LCSH helped a growing community of users understand and use it more effectively.

Because LCSH's vocabulary grew, and continues to grow, based on the contents of items in LC's collection, it lacks headings for topics not included in that collection. Moreover, LCSH has lacked one consistent set of rules for creating new headings during nearly a century of growth. Subject headings have been created according to the theories and ideas of many catalogers and heads of subject cataloging at LC. One staff member approved one mode of syntax (such as inverted adjectives) while another preferred something else (such as direct word order). Catalogers within and outside LC have interpreted meanings differently, leading to some inconsistency in the application of headings to items with similar subject content. It is not surprising that LCSH fails to suit each of its non-LC users equally well. Most agree, however, that using LCSH is better than expending the effort, time, and cost of making up one's own list of headings "from scratch" for all materials cataloged.

The computer-based LCSH, part of a periodical CD-ROM titled *Classification Plus,*[1] contains few instructions about applying the headings, but the book version gives basic explanations on their use. To obtain detailed instructions about LCSH application, one can consult a lengthy reference manual titled *Subject Cataloging Manual: Subject Headings,* which, in its printed form, consists of hundreds of pages of text issued in oversized, red three-ring binders designed to look like LCSH. It is also available on the *Cataloger's Desktop* CD-ROM disk.[2] *Subject Cataloging Manual: Subject Headings* is an accumulation of policy decisions and interpretations made at LC for use by its subject catalogers. It was published and released to the library community in response to requests over the years for guidelines that everyone who uses LCSH could follow.

The manual takes a little effort to use, because it is made up of an open-ended series of memorandums numbered according to an internal LC system. Thus, although page numbers run from lower to higher numbers, they are not sequential. It is a good idea to use the detailed table of contents to find the pages that apply to the topics, headings, or subdivisions in which one is interested. It quickly will become obvious that the first sections cover general issues, followed by sections on the treatment of selected types of topics, and, last of all, sections that cover the use of general subdivisions known as *free-floating* subdivisions (see later), arranged alphabetically.

Format of the List

LCSH contains approximately 185,000 topical subject headings, more than 60,000 name headings, and nearly 500,000 cross-references. Some individual libraries and members of cataloging networks, such as the Research Libraries Group and OCLC have access to the online subject authority file maintained at LC, but most public libraries and school library media centers do not. Instead, they can choose to purchase LCSH in offline formats. It is available in book format, on microfiche, and on the *Classification Plus* CD-ROM disc issued by LC. A new edition of the book version is published every year. New editions of the microfiches and CD-ROMs are available every three months.

The book version of LCSH has well over 5,000 pages bound into five massive volumes with distinctive red covers. These covers have given LCSH its nickname, the Red Book. Volume 1 includes headings from A to C; Volume 2 those from D to H, Volume 3 those from I to M, Volume 4 those from N to R, and Volume 5 those from S to Z. The Red Book alone is not complete, however. It does not contain the list of general subdivisions, called "free-floating" subdivisions, that can be added to topical descriptors to give them greater specificity. Free-floating subdivisions are found in *Subject Cataloging Manual: Subject Headings* as well as in a separate publication titled *Free-Floating Subdivisions: An Alphabetic Index,* issued annually.[3] Rules for their use are found in both publications.

To use the book version of LCSH properly, its updates are a necessary accompaniment. Updates are available in electronic form posted on the World Wide Web at http://lcweb.loc.gov/catdir/cpso/wls.html, and issued in printed form in weekly lists[4] and quarterly *Cataloging Service* bulletins (CSB).[5] Together, the Red Book, the manual and subdivision guide, and the updates constitute a complete LCSH subject heading authority system.

Authorized headings are given in bold print; unauthorized headings and all cross-references are given in lightface print. LCSH prints headings in three columns to a page (see Figure 9.1).

FIGURE 9.1

BT Chronic diseases
    Kidneys—Diseases
NT Balkan nephropathy
    Chronic renal failure in children
    Renal anemia
Chronic renal failure in children
(May Subd Geog)
    [RJ476.R46]
UF Renal insufficiency in children
    [Former heading]
BT Chronic diseases in children
    Chronic renal failure
    Pediatric nephrology
Chronic renal insufficiency
USE Chronic renal failure
Chronic simple glaucoma
USE Open-angle glaucoma
Chronic toxicity testing *(May Subd Geog)*
UF Chronic toxicology testing
BT Toxicity testing
NT Carcinogenicity testing
    Mutagenicity testing
    Teratogenicity testing
Chronic toxicology testing
USE Chronic toxicity testing
Chronically ill *(May Subd Geog)*
UF Chronic diseases—Patients
BT Sick
NT Asthmatics
    Diabetics
    Epileptics
    Hemophiliacs
    Lepers
    Nursing home patients
    Silicotics
— Care *(May Subd Geog)*
    UF Chronically ill—Care and
        treatment *[Former heading]*
    BT Long-term care of the sick
    NT Life care planning
— Care and treatment
    USE Chronically ill—Care
— Economic conditions
    UF Chronically ill—Socioeconomic
        status *[Former heading]*
— Home care *(May Subd Geog)*
— Institutional care *(May Subd Geog)*

RT Anagrams
Chronograph
    [QB107 (Astronomical instruments)]
    [UF830-UF840 (Ballistic instruments)]
BT Astronomical clocks
    Astronomical instruments
    Time measurements
NT Le Boulengé chronograph
    Photochronograph
Chronology
    [CE]
UF Eras
    Hours (Time)
BT Auxiliary sciences of history
RT Calendar
    Time
SA *subdivision* Chronology *under names*
    of individual persons. sacred works.
    literatures, wars, and topical
    headings that are inherently
    historical; and subdivision History—
    Chronology *under names of*
    countries. cities, etc., and individual
    corporate bodies, and under ethnic
    groups and topical headings that are
    not inherently historical
NT Aztec chronology
    Chronograms
    Clocks and watches
    Cosmochronology
    Day
    Dendrochronology
    Geological time
    Indian chronology
    Maya chronology
    Months
    Night
    Rabinal Achi chronology
    Week
Chronology, Armenian *(May Subd Geog)*
    [CE36.5]
UF Armenian chronology
Chronology, Assyro-Babylonian
(May Subd Geog)
    [CE33]
UF Assyro-Babylonian chronology
    Chronology, Sumerian

USE Chronology, Historical—Charts.
    diagrams, etc.
— Charts, diagrams, etc.
    [D11-D11.5]
UF Charts, Historical
    Chronology, Historical—Charts
    [Former heading]
    Historical charts
Chronology, Indian
USE Indian chronology
Chronology, Indonesian *(May Subd Geog)*
UF Indonesian chronology
Chronology, Islamic *(May Subd Geog)*
UF Chronology, Muslim
    Islamic chronology
    Muslim chronology
Chronology, Japanese *(May Subd Geog)*
UF Japanese chronology
Chronology, Jewish *(May Subd Geog)*
UF Chronology, Hebrew
    Hebrew chronology
    Jewish chronology
RT Calendar, Jewish
    Jews—History—Chronology
Chronology, Maori *(May Subd Geog)*
    [DU423.C56]
UF Maori chronology
Chronology, Maya
USE Maya chronology
Chronology, Mexican *(May Subd Geog)*
UF Mexican chronology
Chronology, Muslim
USE Chronology. Islamic
Chronology, Oriental *(May Subd Geog)*
UF Oriental chronology
— Terminology
    UF Era names
        Reign names
Chronology, Palauan *(May Subd Geog)*
UF Palauan chronology
Chronology, Rabinal Achi
USE Rabinal Achi chronology
Chronology, Roman *(May Subd Geog)*
    [CE46]
UF Roman chronology
NT Secular games
Chronology, Slavic *(May Subd Geog)*
UF Slavic chronology

Names appear in the list (see Figure 9.2), but LCSH is not intended to control name headings even when they are used as subjects. Most of the headings and cross-references are topical terms. Names of people, geographic locations, and corporate bodies, and all titles used as subject headings in the catalog are controlled by means of a separate name authority file, apart from the subject authority file. (LC's name authority file can be used for this purpose by any institution.) Catalogers are directed to add name and title headings as needed, using the form prescribed by AACR2-98. With a few exceptions, catalogers cannot add more topical headings; instead, they must use the most appropriate authorized heading *already present* in the list, and hope that LC will add the desired ones before long.

Coded instructions for making cross-references appear with the subject headings, and catalogers must pay close attention to them: UF, BT, RT, SA, and NT (discussed later). Cross-references are given in that order and, within each category, in alphabetical order.

FIGURE 9.2   Library of Congress Subject Headings

Cheeseburgers   *(May Subd Geog)*
  UF Burgers, Cheese
      Cheese burgers
  BT Cookery (Cheese)
      Hamburgers
Cheesecake (Cookery)
      ₁TX773₁
  UF Cheese cake (Cookery)
  BT Cake
      Cookery (Cheese)
Cheesecake photography
  USE Glamour photography
Cheesecloth   *(May Subd Geog)*
  UF Butter muslin
      Cheese-cloth   ₁Former heading₁
  BT Cotton fabrics
Cheesemakers   *(May Subd Geog)*
  UF Cheese-makers
  BT Dairy workers
Cheeseman family   *(Not Subd Geog)*
  UF Cheasman family
      Cheesman family
  RT Chisholm family
Cheeseman Lake (Colo.)
  USE Cheesman Lake (Colo.)
Cheesequake State Park (N.J.)
  BT Parks—New Jersey
Cheeses
  USE Cheese—Varieties
Cheesman family
  USE Cheeseman family
Cheesman Lake (Colo.)
  UF Cheeseman Lake (Colo.)
      Cheesman Reservoir (Colo.)
      Lake Cheesman (Colo.)
  BT Lakes—Colorado
      Reservoirs—Colorado
Cheesman Park (Denver, Colo.)
  BT Parks—Colorado
Cheesman Reservoir (Colo.)
  USE Cheesman Lake (Colo.)
Cheeta
  USE Cheetah
Cheetah   *(May Subd Geog*
      ₁QL737.C23₁
  UF Acinonyx jubatus
      Cheeta
      Cheetahs   ₁Former heading₁
      Cheta
      Chetah
      Chita
      Chittah
      Hunting leopard

Cheezum family
  USE Chisholm family
Chefs
  USE Cooks
Chehalis Indian Reservation (Wash.)
  USE Chehalis Reservation (Wash.)
Chehalis Indians   *(May Subd Geog)*
      ₁E99.C49₁
  BT Coast Salish Indians
      Indians of North America—British
      Columbia
Chehalis language
  USE Upper Chehalis language
Chehalis Reservation (Wash.)
  UF Chehalis Indian Reservation (Wash.)
      Chehalis Reserve (Wash.)
  BT Indian reservations—Washington
      (State)
Chehalis Reserve (Wash.)
  USE Chehalis Reservation (Wash.)
Chehalis River (Wash.)
  BT Rivers—Washington (State)
Chehalis River Watershed (Wash.)
  BT Watersheds—Washington (State)
Cheherazade (Legendary character)
  USE Scheherazade (Legendary character)
Cheilanthes   *(May Subd Geog)*
      ₁QK524.A29₁
  BT Adiantaceae
Cheilobranchidae
  USE Alabes
Cheilodactylidae   *(May Subd Geog)*
      ₁QL638.C536₁
  BT Perciformes
Cheilodipteridae
  USE Apogonidae
Cheilosia   *(May Subd Geog)*
      ₁QL537.S9 (Zoology)₁
  BT Syrphidae
Cheilostomata   *(May Subd Geog)*
      ₁QL398.C5₁
  UF Chilostomata
  BT Gymnolaemata
  NT Adeonellidae
      Adeonidae
      Bicellariellidae
      Catenicellidae
      Cribrilinidae
      Hiantoporidae
      Metrarabdotosidae
      Onychocellidae
      Orbituliporidae
      Reteporidae

Cheiromancy
  USE Palmistry
Cheiroptera
  USE Bats
Cheirosophy
  USE Palmistry
Cheirostemon
  USE Chiranthodendron
Cheiver family
  USE Cheever family
Cheju Haehyŏp (Korea)
  USE Cheju Strait (Korea)
Cheju horse
  USE Cheju pony
Cheju pony   *(May Subd Geog)*
      ₁SF315.2.C35₁
  UF Cheju horse
      Chejuma
      Saishu pony
  BT Horse breeds
      Ponies
Cheju Strait (Korea)
  UF Cheju Haehyŏp (Korea)
      Jeju Strait (Korea)
      Saishū Kaikyō (Korea)
  BT Straits—Korea (South)
Chejudo Rebellion, Korea, 1948
  USE Korea—History—Chejudo Rebellion,
      1948
Chejuma
  USE Cheju pony
Cheke family
  USE Cheek family
Cheke Holo language   *(May Subd Geog)*
  UF A'ara language
      Aara-Maringe language
      Hograno language
      Maringe language
  BT Melanesian languages
      Solomon Islands—Languages
Cheke language
  USE Gude language
Chekeré   *(May Subd Geog)*
  UF Agbe
      Aggué
      Shekeré
  BT Musical instruments—Cuba
      Percussion instruments
Chekiri (African people)
  USE Itsekiri (African people)
Chelae
  UF Chelipeds
  BT Arthropoda—Anatomy

If a subject heading's meaning could be in question, instructions about how it is to be used are given in LCSH, beginning with the words "Here are entered . . ." The instructions usually are framed in positive language, but occasionally will add what should *not* be entered, as well. Figure 9.3 includes such an instruction under the heading BUSINESS COMMUNICATION.

LC classification numbers are listed for many of the headings and some of the subdivisions as well. These are just suggestions and should never be assigned to items being cataloged without consulting the full classification schedules. They can be a useful shortcut alternative to the sometimes tedious process of consulting page after page of numbers in crowded portions of the schedules, or as a guide in unfamiliar territory.

FIGURE 9.3   Library of Congress Subject Headings

Business and education
  USE Industry and education
Business and parapsychology
  USE Parapsychology and business
Business and politics *(May Subd Geog)*
  UF Politics and business
  BT Politics, Practical
  NT Corporations—Political activity
Business and social problems
  USE Industries—Social aspects
Business angels
  USE Angels (Investors)
Business announcements *(May Subd Geog)*
  UF Announcements, Business
      Business etiquette—Stationery
      Commercial announcements
  BT Business—Forms
      Commercial correspondence
      Stationery
Business anthropology *(May Subd Geog)*
  ₍GN450.8₎
  UF Business—Anthropological aspects
      Corporate anthropology
      Industrial anthropology
      Management anthropology
      Private sector anthropology
      Public sector anthropology
  BT Anthropology
  RT Corporate culture
Business Arabic
  USE Arabic language—Business Arabic
Business arithmetic
  USE Business mathematics
Business associations
  USE Trade associations

Business community participation in
  architectural conservation and restoration
  USE Architecture—Conservation and
        restoration—Business community
        participation
Business conditions
  USE *subdivision* Economic conditions *under
        names of countries, cities, etc., and
        under classes of persons and ethnic
        groups*
Business consultants *(May Subd Geog)*
  ₍HD69.C6₎
  UF Efficiency engineers
      Management advisory services
      Management consultants
  BT Consultants
  RT Interim executives
  NT Hospital consultants
      Marketing consultants
      Risk managers
  — Training of *(May Subd Geog)*
      ₍HD69.C6₎
Business corporations
  USE Corporations
Business correspondence
  USE Commercial correspondence
Business creativity
  USE Creative ability in business
Business credit
  USE Commercial credit
Business cycles *(May Subd Geog)*
  ₍HB3711-HB3840₎
  UF Economic cycles
      Economic fluctuations
  BT Cycles
  RT Financial crises

Business education (Internship)
  (May Subd Geog)
  UF Business interns
      Interns (Business)
        ₍Former heading₎
  BT Employees—Training of
      Interns
Business education graduates
  (May Subd Geog)
  BT College graduates
Business English
  USE English language—Business English
Business enterprises *(May Subd Geog)*
    Here are entered works on business concerns re-
    gardless of form of organization.
  UF Business organizations
      Businesses
      Companies
      Enterprises
      Firms
      Organizations, Business
  BT Business
  NT Architectural firms
      Black business enterprises
      Branches (Business enterprises)
      Business enterprises, Foreign
      Business enterprises, Trade-union
      Consulting firms
      Corporations
      Drive-in facilities
      East Indian business enterprises
      Economic interest groupings
      Executive search firms
      Family-owned business enterprises
      Gay business enterprises
      Government business enterprises
      Handicapped-owned business
        enterprises

Types of Subject Headings

LCSH uses a variety of grammatical constructions, from simple one-word headings to complex headings made up of several words. Many one-word headings consist of a single word, usually a noun, but sometimes a verb form is used as a noun; for example, BLEACHING. Single-word noun headings can have different meanings depending on whether the noun is in the singular or plural; for example, BONE is used for the generic material from which skeletons are formed, whereas BONES is used for skeletal structures of humans and animals. Similarly, ART is used for works about the visual arts whereas ARTS is used for works about the arts in general (including but not limited to visual arts) and about specific arts other than visual arts, such as literature and performing arts.

Another type of heading is composed of a single noun modified by an adjective or a second noun used as an adjective, such as CABLE TELEVISION and CARBON COMPOUNDS. LCSH sometimes reverses the order in which the words appear to bring the more important word, generally the noun in a noun-adjective dyad, to the filing position; for example, CARBOHYDRATES, REFINED. With computer-based keyword searching, the order of words is not critical, but in card files where only the initial word is searchable, it is an issue of importance.

A third type of heading is composed of two nouns connected by *and,* such as CARRIAGES AND CARTS or ART AND SCIENCE. Sometimes the two words represent opposites; sometimes they link similar things. More complicated compound headings (that is, headings made up of more than one word) in this category can include modified nouns, such as LANDSCAPE ARCHITECTURE and ENERGY CONSERVATION.

Prepositions link two nouns or modified nouns in another type of heading construction. Examples of this form include HISTORY IN ART, TITLES OF BOOKS, COOKERY FOR THE SICK, and BIBLE AS LITERATURE. Use of the word "as" to link categories of people to activities with which they usually are not associated (for example, CHILDREN AS ARTISTS) has been criticized by the library community for many years as demeaning to the people. Most have been eliminated, simplified, or revised to sound more neutral in tone. In particular, objections were raised over subject headings that seemed to connote that women professionals are unusual.

The most complex headings can involve both multiword concepts and combinations of concepts, such as DO-IT-YOURSELF PRODUCTS INDUSTRY or INFORMATION STORAGE AND RETRIEVAL SYSTEMS. Sometimes these are simplified by the removal of parentheses, rewordings, or both; for example, ERRATA (IN BOOKS) was changed to ERRATA, and CONVENTS AND NUNNERIES, BUDDHIST is now BUDDHIST CONVENTS. Sometimes, however, revisions add to headings to clarify them or expand their scope. For example, some years ago PETER'S DENIAL IN ART became JESUS CHRIST—DENIAL BY PETER—ART, and the one-word heading CLARET was changed to WINE AND WINE MAKING—FRANCE—BORDELAIS.

Some headings are formulated with explanatory qualifiers to ensure their correct interpretation, such as EQUILIBRIUM (ECONOMICS) and EQUILIBRIUM (PHYSIOLOGY). Not all terms that could benefit from such assistance, however, have it. BORING, although including a "Here are entered" instruction that clarifies its meaning as a word meaning cutting holes in the earth, does not have a qualifier to prevent its being interpreted erroneously as "dull." (The closest term to the latter seems to be BOREDOM.)

Cross-References

After the publication of the eleventh edition of LCSH in 1988, cross-references have been identified by the standard mnemonic abbreviations used for decades by specialized thesauri: BT (Broader Term), RT (Related Term), NT (Narrower Term), UF (Use For), SA (See Also), and USE. One helpful device found in some published thesauri, TT (Top Term), designating the highest term in a subject hierarchy, is not provided by LCSH, nor is there any hierarchical listing of descriptors showing the entire range of steps in a subject area from the broadest to the narrowest term such as those found in the National Library of Medicine's *Medical Subject Headings*.[6] Cross-references in LCSH lead a searcher one level of hierarchy upward (BT) or downward (NT), but the application policy is to make only the downward references in the catalog display. BT references are given for consultation only. Related headings at the same level of hierarchy will have reciprocal cross-references.

The cross-references fall into six categories:

1.   *Those directing a searcher from an unused heading to a used heading.* This type of reference is called a *Use* reference, but is also known as a *See* reference. The unused heading is found in the main file of descriptors in roman (plain) type, showing that it is not authorized for use, followed by the word USE and an authorized heading. The unused heading is also found in roman print beneath the authorized heading, preceded by the acronym *UF,* meaning Used For. An example is the reference at INTOXICATION, which is not authorized, to use ALCOHOLISM instead.

2. *Those directing a cataloger from a used heading to an unused heading.* As just mentioned, these references, known as *UF* or *Used For* references, do not appear as such in public catalogs. However, UF references help the indexer add to the public catalog cross-reference words that will direct searchers to the correct entry with an instruction to go to the authorized heading.

3. *Those directing a searcher from a broader used heading to a narrower, but also usable heading.* Two different cross-references fit this definition. The first is described here; the second in No. 6, later. The first is called an *NT* or *Narrower Term* heading, and is one of several types of reference that might all be known generically as *see also* headings. It leads searchers to more specific topics. Many NT cross-references appear under BUSINESS, leading to ACCOUNTING, ADVERTISING, BOOKKEEPING, CUSTOMER RELATIONS, and dozens of more narrow descriptors.

4. *Those directing a searcher from a narrower used heading to a broader, but also usable heading.* Called a *BT* or *Broader Term* heading, this is another of the *see also* headings. It leads the searcher to broader topics that also might be of interest. An example is the cross-reference given under ASPHALT to BITUMINOUS MATERIALS. Indexing theorists believe that BT references are less important than NT references because searchers can be expected to know broader topics without help, whereas they might not be aware of narrower categories. To illustrate with the example given here, searchers who know enough to search ASPHALT can be expected to know that it is a bituminous material, but those who search BITUMINOUS MATERIALS might be unaware of the names of specific ones such as asphalt.

5. *Those directing a searcher from one used heading to another at the same level of topical hierarchy.* Two different cross-reference types fit this definition. The first one is described here; the second in No. 6, next. The first is called an *RT* or *Related Term* heading. As its name implies, it leads searchers from the heading they are examining to related descriptors at similar levels of hierarchy in which they also might be interested. A person searching for AESTHETICS might also be interested in ART. Someone searching CHANCE might also be interested in materials to which the subject heading PROBABILITIES is assigned.

6. *Those directing a searcher from one used heading to a group of other headings at the same or narrower levels of hierarchy.* These are the final type of *see also* references, and they are designated *SA* or *See Also.* They can also carry instructions for the indexer to consult other headings or add headings that are not present in the list. Examples of such instructions appear at BOOKS, which notes: "SA *headings beginning with the word book*" and at COMMERCIAL PRODUCTS, which notes, "SA *names of individual products.*"

Figure 9.4 illustrates what these cross-references look like in LCSH and the discussion that follows illustrates some of the differences among the five types of cross-references.

FIGURE 9.4   LCSH Heading Bibliography with All Cross-References

Bibliography   *(May Subd Geog)*
  [Z1001-Z9000]
  Under this heading, when subdivided by place and appropriate topical subdivision, are entered works which discuss the theories, methods, history, etc. of the discipline of bibliography practiced within a particular region or country, e.g. Bibliography—United States—History; Bibliography—United States—Methodology.
  Works on the technique of compiling national bibliographies, i.e. lists of titles produced in one country, lists of titles produced in the language of one country without regard to place of publication, lists of titles produced by citizens of one country whether residing in that country or elsewhere, or lists of titles about one country, are entered under Bibliography, National with country subdivision, e.g. Bibliography, National—United States.
  Actual lists of titles published in a particular country are entered under the name of the country with subdivision Imprints, e.g. United States—Imprints.
  Actual lists of titles published in the language of one country without regard to place of publication are entered under phrase headings of the type English imprints.
  Actual lists of titles about a particular country are entered under the name of the country with subdivision Bibliography, e.g. United States—Bibliography.
  UF Book lists
      Lists of publications
      Publication lists
      Publications
  BT Documentation
      Information resources
  RT Abstracts
      Books
      Codicology
      Library science
  SA *names of literatures, e.g.* American literature; *and subdivision* Bibliography *under names of persons, places and subjects; also subdivision* Bibliography—Methodology *under specific subjects, e.g.* Medicine—Bibliography—Methodology; *and subdivision* Imprints *under names of countries, states, cities, etc.*
  NT Abstracting and indexing services
      Anonyms and pseudonyms
      Archives
      Best books
      Bibliometrics
      Bio-bibliography
      Book collecting
      Editions
      Electronic publications
      Errors and blunders, Literary
      Exchange of bibliographic information
      Gay press publications
      Indexes
      Indian imprints
      Lost books
      On-demand publications
      Periodicals—Indexes
      Personal bibliography
      Searching, Bibliographical
      Series (Publications)
      Titles of books
      Unfinished books
      Universal bibliography

If one looks up a word or phrase that is not authorized, such as ACCELERATED EROSION, that person will see a Use reference, such as "USE SOIL EROSION," identifying the heading that should be used instead. Under SOIL EROSION, a corresponding Used For reference to ACCELERATED EROSION will appear. In practice, this means that when the descriptor SOIL EROSION is first assigned to an item, the cataloger should also make a reference for the phrase that will not be used, ACCELERATED EROSION. The reference should look like this:

ACCELERATED EROSION. *Use* SOIL EROSION

The cross-reference can be a computerized entry if you have a computer catalog, or on a card, if the library or media center uses card files. The format of the catalog should not affect the entry of cross-references.

The Use reference will remain in the catalog until the last item on the subject SOIL EROSION is removed from the collection and that heading is removed. Accompanying the removal of SOIL EROSION, the cross-reference ACCELERATED EROSION, which would then be obsolete, also is removed. Otherwise, the cross-reference would lead to a heading with no materials under it, known as a *blind reference*. Blind references frustrate searchers because they fail to retrieve relevant materials, although some believe that just learning the proper subject heading to use for future searches is a sufficiently productive result.

Instructions direct that cross-references should be made for the public catalog display only from a given heading to the narrower and related headings listed with it, and not to the broader headings, which are provided mainly for the cataloger's use. For example, at BOAT LIVING there is an NT reference to SAILBOAT LIVING and at SAILBOAT LIVING there is a BT reference to BOAT LIVING. When the first item is cataloged under the narrower heading, SAILBOAT LIVING, no cross-reference is made to the broader heading, BOAT LIVING; but when the first item is cataloged under the broader heading, BOAT LIVING, a cross-reference should be made to the narrower heading, SAILBOAT LIVING (provided materials are listed under it). It will look like the following:

> BOAT LIVING. *See also* SAILBOAT LIVING

Among related headings, references are reciprocal. For example, at CONCERTS there is an RT reference to MUSIC FESTIVALS; at MUSIC FESTIVALS, there is an RT reference to CONCERTS. Each has a reference to the other. They look like this:

> CONCERTS. *See also* MUSIC FESTIVALS

> MUSIC FESTIVALS. *See also* CONCERTS

These cross-references are made on the assumption that someone interested in works on the subject of concerts might also be interested in works on the subject of music festivals, and vice versa.

Subdivisions

Not only does LCSH have a very large number of subject headings and references, it also has a great many subdivisions. Generally, one level of subdivision is sufficient to represent topics in detail, but some headings require two, three, or, even four subdivision levels.

Subdivisions are listed following the cross-references for a heading, each with the scope notes, classification numbers, and cross-references that pertain to that particular subdivision. Each subdivision is indented and printed with a long dash preceding it to indicate that it is not to be used alone, but only as a subdivision of the heading under which it appears. Subdivisions of a subdivision, necessary for very large topics that have several kinds of subdivisions (e.g., topical, chronological, and geographic) are indented further and are given additional dashes, depending on their level in the hierarchy. For example, a topic such as the history of Chinese calligraphy in the 20th century would be expressed by the LCSH heading CALLIGRAPHY, CHINESE—HISTORY—20TH CENTURY, which is a two-level hierarchy; and a topic such as the attribution of Chinese calligraphy from the Sui dynasty would be expressed as CALLIGRAPHY, CHINESE—HISTORY—THREE KINGDOMS—SUI DYNASTY, 220-618—ATTRIBUTION, which is a four-level hierarchy. Figure 9.5 shows how these hierarchies appear in the red book.

Very general topics such as art, music, science, etc., are likely to have many cross-references and, often, many subdivisions, some of which have their own subdivisions as well. This makes for confusion in locating a particular one, because it can be pages away from the main heading. LCSH has a large number of subdivisions because it is used to organize very large files under topics about which a great deal has been and still is being written.

FIGURE 9.5   Library of Congress Subject Headings subdivisions

---

Calligraphy, Chinese *(May Subd Geog)*
    UF Chinese calligraphy
    — Sung-Yüan dynasties, 960-1368
        USE Calligraphy, Chinese—History—
            Sung-Yüan dynasties, 960-
            1368
    — **Appreciation** *(May Subd Geog)*
        UF Appreciation of Chinese
            calligraphy
        BT Art appreciation
    — **Attribution**
        UF Attribution of Chinese calligraphy
            Calligraphy, Chinese—
            Reattribution
        BT Calligraphy, Chinese—Expertising
    — **Expertising** *(May Subd Geog)*
        NT Calligraphy, Chinese—Attribution
    — **History**
    — — **To 221 B.C.**
    — — **Three kingdoms-Sui dynasty, 220-618**
        UF Calligraphy, Chinese—History—
            Three kingdoms, six
            dynasties-Sui dynasty, 220-
            618 ₍Former heading₎
    — — Three kingdoms, six dynasties-Sui
        dynasty, 220-618
        USE Calligraphy, Chinese—History
            —Three kingdoms-Sui
            dynasty, 220-618
    — — **Three kingdoms-Sui dynasty, 220-618**

— — — **Attribution**
    UF Attribution of Three
        kingdoms-Sui dynasty
        Chinese calligraphy
        Calligraphy, Chinese—
        History—Three kingdoms-
        Sui dynasty, 220-618—
        Reattribution
    BT Calligraphy, Chinese—
        History—Three kingdoms-
        Sui dynasty, 220-618—
        Expertising
— — — **Expertising** *(May Subd Geog)*
    NT Calligraphy, Chinese—
        History—Three kingdoms-
        Sui dynasty, 220-618—
        Attribution
— — — **Reattribution**
    USE Calligraphy, Chinese—
        History—Three
        kingdoms-Sui dynasty,
        220-618—Attribution
— — **Ch'in-Han dynasties, 221 B.C.-220 A.D.**
— — **T'ang-Five dynasties, 618-960**
— — **Sung-Yüan dynasties, 960-1368**
    UF Calligraphy, Chinese—Sung-
        Yüan dynasties, 960-1368
        ₍Former heading₎
    NT Yün-chien school of calligraphy
— — **Ming-Ch'ing dynasties, 1368-1912**
    NT Yün-chien school of calligraphy
— — **20th century**

Three types of subdivisions predominate in LCSH: topical, chronological, and geographical. A fourth variety, form subdivision, also is present in the list, but these terms could be construed as a special type of topical subdivision. Subdivisions are indicated in the list in several ways, so catalogers must be alert to all the possibilities. To conform to standard practice, individual subdivisions must be assigned according to LC's established policies, given in *Subject Cataloging Manual: Subject Headings.* In particular, beginning catalogers should be aware that two main headings cannot be combined in a heading-subdivision relationship, unless one is listed specifically as a subdivision under the other, or unless one heading functions both as a main heading and a subdivision, and is permitted as a subdivision under the second heading. A useful rule-of-thumb is to avoid making any assumptions that the absence of an instruction *not* to subdivide is permission to go ahead. Quite the contrary—if there is no clear indication of permission to subdivide a heading, it probably cannot be subdivided. An important exception to the rule is the group of pattern headings listed in the preface to LCSH, discussed next.[7]

LCSH headings can be subdivided in four ways:

(1)   The subdivision can appear in the list under the heading.

(2)   An instruction to subdivide can be given with the heading in the list.

(3) The heading can be one of the designated pattern headings to which subdivisions may be added.

(4) The heading can be a term to which particular free-floating subdivisions can be added.

   The easiest and most straightforward method of providing for subdivisions is listing them under the headings to which they can be assigned, but doing so for all possible subdivisions would cause the Red Book to expand far beyond its already considerable proportions. Thus, although this method is used freely, alternative methods are also employed for reasons of economy and flexibility.

   Geographic subdivision instructions: The fact that a heading can be subdivided geographically usually is noted by the parenthetic instruction *(May Subd Geog)* after either a primary heading or a subdivision. The preferred method of subdividing geographically is to put the name of a country after the heading being subdivided. Geographic entities larger than countries, such as continents or other multicountry regions may be given the same way, but entities wholly within a country are preceded by the name of the country in which they are located. This practice is called *indirect geographic subdivision*. For example, headings and their geographic subdivisions assigned to books about agriculture in North and South America, the Amazon Region, the Andes Mountains, Argentina, Brazil, and Ecuador, the Andes mountains of Venezuela, and the cities of Buenos Aires and Rio de Janeiro, would create the following file:

> AGRICULTURE—AMAZON RIVER REGION
> AGRICULTURE—ANDES REGION
> AGRICULTURE—ARGENTINA
> AGRICULTURE—ARGENTINA—BUENOS AIRES
> AGRICULTURE—BRAZIL
> AGRICULTURE—BRAZIL—RIO DE JANEIRO
> AGRICULTURE—ECUADOR
> AGRICULTURE—NORTH AMERICA
> AGRICULTURE—SOUTH AMERICA
> AGRICULTURE—VENEZUELA—ANDES REGION (VENEZUELA)

   The resulting file intermingles geographic entities at different hierarchical levels by interfiling countries and continents with regions that span more than one country, but it places cities and localities within the files for their countries. This makes it possible to search localities either by browsing their country files or by requesting the desired locality in a key word search. The alternative—*direct* subdivision—would take Buenos Aires away from Argentina and place it between Brazil and Ecuador, move Rio de Janeiro to a spot between North and South America, and put the Andes Region of Venezuela between the whole Andes range and Argentina. Venezuela would disappear as a subdivision altogether. The directly subdivided file would look like this:

> AGRICULTURE—AMAZON RIVER REGION
> AGRICULTURE—ANDES REGION
> AGRICULTURE—ANDES REGION (VENEZUELA)

AGRICULTURE—ARGENTINA

AGRICULTURE—BRAZIL

AGRICULTURE—BUENOS AIRES

AGRICULTURE—ECUADOR

AGRICULTURE—NORTH AMERICA

AGRICULTURE—RIO DE JANEIRO

AGRICULTURE—SOUTH AMERICA

Three countries—the United States, Canada, and Great Britain—have special rules for indirect subdivision. (Although *United Kingdom* is the proper name of the country and should be used in place of *Great Britain,* LCSH uses Great Britain because of the difficulty of making the change.) For them, the names of states, provinces, and constituent countries, respectively, are used. Thus, materials on agriculture in Iowa City, education in London, and advertising in Toronto are assigned the following subject descriptors:

AGRICULTURE—IOWA—IOWA CITY
not AGRICULTURE—UNITED STATES—IOWA CITY

EDUCATION—ENGLAND—LONDON
not EDUCATION—GREAT BRITAIN—LONDON

ADVERTISING—ONTARIO—TORONTO
not ADVERTISING—CANADA—TORONTO

Policies for geographic subdivision have changed more than once over the years, sometimes favoring direct subdivision, sometimes indirect, and sometimes accepting both, depending on the country. The current policy favoring indirect subdivision results in a file gathered first at the country level, and then at the local level. Even the three exceptions gather records first at the state, province, or constituent country level before grouping them at the local level. Because much of the geographically distinctive material in our libraries and media centers is about these countries, this strategy avoids collocating for them at the country level and collocates at the state or province level instead.

Current LC policy is to subdivide indirectly, but older headings that were subdivided directly remain. LCSH is not governed solely by one policy, but is an amalgam of many policies implemented throughout the century that the list has been in existence. However, new direct geographic subdivisions will not be established under the current policy.

Other subdivision instructions: Instructions to use a particular nongeographic heading as a subdivision under other descriptors can be given with it in the list; for example, under BASEBALL, it says: "SA *subdivision* Baseball *under names of individual schools, e.g.,* Harvard University—Baseball."[8]

Pattern headings: LCSH's makers identify 23 groups of headings as *pattern headings.* Each member of a pattern heading group can be expected to need the same set of subdivisions; but instead of repeating the whole set under each, one heading is fully subdivided in the list and catalogers are instructed to use this pattern for all the others. For example, all plants and crops can be subdivided with the same terms as those given under CORN and all sacred works can be subdivided exactly like BIBLE. Some heading groups are provided with more than one pattern; for example, subdivision of diseases may follow the pattern under CANCER or the one under

TUBERCULOSIS. The list of the pattern headings is given in the introductory pages of the Red Book.

Free-floating subdivisions: A different kind of pattern is created by the designation of some subdivisions—all topical terms, including many representing literary forms—as *free floating*. Some terms have such widespread potential for use as subdivisions that it is difficult to anticipate and list them all. Instead, they can be assigned under a broad range of headings. LCSH gives specific guidance in how to assign free-floating subdivision terms. *Subject Cataloging Manual: Subject Headings* devotes many pages to these instructions.

Form subdivisions: Form subdivisions, mentioned previously in connection with the list of free floating terms, include terms that describe the format in which a work appears, such as —CATALOGS. This group of terms also includes literary genres, such as —DICTIONARIES and —BIOGRAPHIES. Most form subdivisions are free floating and are not given under each of the headings to which they may be added.

Chronological subdivisions: Chronological subdivisions, most of which are *not* free floating, are almost always given in the list of terms for those subject headings and subdivisions that can be subdivided by period. History is frequently subdivided by time period and historical topics are often specific to particular places. The introductory explanations warn catalogers not to use the historical periods developed for one place under other places. This is to be expected because each country, state, or province will have its own chronological landmarks as well as unique physical landmarks. Chronological periods that can apply to many topics, such as the names of the centuries, for example, —EIGHTEENTH CENTURY, appear in the list both as primary headings and as subdivisions.

Topical subdivisions: Topical subdivision is exactly what the name implies: a subdivision representing a topic; for example, BUILDINGS—MAINTENANCE. MAINTENANCE, the subdivision, does not represent a geographical, chronological, or form subdivision. It is a topical subdivision, but it cannot be used just anywhere, as the free-floating subdivisions can. If it was not given in the list under BUILDINGS, catalogers could not "make it up." They would have to use BUILDINGS alone or find another heading that was more appropriate.

Because subdivision must be done according to LC's established policies, uniform strings of headings and subdivisions are created that can be combined in only one way. It may be true that ARCHITECTURE—ARID REGIONS and ARID REGIONS—ARCHITECTURE mean the same thing, but LCSH only permits the former. Catalogers discover it by examining both terms and finding —ARID REGIONS listed as a subdivision under ARCHITECTURE, but no listing for —ARCHITECTURE as a subdivision under ARID REGIONS. LCSH strings are, thus, precoordinated.

Canadian Complement to LCSH

Canadian Subject Headings, third edition (CSH3)[9] is a one-volume work with 550 pages containing about 6,000 headings and many supporting references. It is neither a comprehensive list nor a substitute for LCSH. It is to be used for items containing Canadian subject matter; and LCSH is to be applied to all other materials. CSH3's headings and references expand and adapt LCSH where Canadian topics are not adequately covered or where LCSH headings are not acceptable in a Canadian context. The differences in the sociopolitical structure between Canada and the United States is an obvious area in which subject headings suitable to a Canadian topic are needed; for example, GOODS AND SERVICES TAX—CANADA. Figures 9.6 and 9.7 both illustrate the application of CSH3. Although the subject headings in Figure 9.6 could be built from LCSH, it is easier to use CSH3 where they are found fully constructed. Furthermore, for works dealing with specific aspects of prime ministers' activities, CSH3 provides many more subdivisions for prime ministers than LCSH and, therefore, a greater depth of analysis in this subject area.

FIGURE 9.6

This example is an illustration of:
- edition statement taken from outside prescribed sources (many libraries place such an edition statement in the note area, sometimes as a quoted note)
- publishing date not listed, copyright date given
- detailed paging
- edition and history note
- bibliography and index note
- Canadian subject headings (same in *SearsCC*)
- author/title added entries
- additional title added entries
- comparison between Library of Congress and National Library of Canada classification
- Canadian CIP data
- 2nd level cataloging

```
Donaldson, Gordon.
   The Prime Ministers of Canada / Gordon Donaldson. -- [4th ed.].
-- Toronto : Doubleday, c1994.
   x, 380 p. ; 22 cm.

   Previous eds. published as: Fifteen men (1969), Sixteen men
(1975), Eighteen men (1985).
   Includes bibliography (p. 370-373) and index.
   ISBN 0-385-25454-7.


   1. Prime ministers -- Canada -- Biography.  2. Canada --
Politics and government.  I. Donaldson, Gordon. Fifteen men.
II. Donaldson, Gordon. Sixteen men.  III. Donaldson, Gordon.
Eighteen men.  IV. Title.  V. Title: Fifteen men.  VI. Title:
Sixteen men.  VII. Title: Eighteen men.


Recommended DDC: 971.00922
Recommended LCC: F1005.D65 1994
Recommended NLC classification: FC26.P7D65 1994
```

(chief source of information)
(title page)

GORDON DONALDSON

Doubleday Canada Limited

(information on verso)

Copyright © 1994 Gordon Donaldson

Canadian Cataloguing in Publication Data

Donaldson, Gordon, 1926-
   The Prime Ministers of Canada

Includes index.
ISBN 0-385-25454-7

I. Prime ministers — Canada — Biography.
2. Canada — Politics and government. I. Title

FC26.P7D65 1994   971'.009'   C93-095409-2
FI005.D65 1994

Cover design by John Terauds
Printed and bound in the USA

Published in Canada by
Doubleday Canada Limited
I05 Bond Street
Toronto, Ontario
M5B IY3

Preface

This is a revised and extended version of *Fifteen Men*, which first
appeared in 1969, was updated in 1975, and became *Sixteen Men*,
and then *Eighteen Men*. *Twenty Persons* didn't have the same ring to it,
hence the new genderless title.

Figure 9.7 is an example of the difference in approach and terminology between CSH3 and LCSH.

FIGURE 9.7

The Government of Canada certification card received with the item provides the only information:

SIMANUK KILABUK
BIRDS ON BASE (walrus tooth)

This example is an illustration of:
- art original
- general material designation
- date not listed on item
- source of title note
- difference in Library of Congress Subject Headings and Canadian Subject Headings
- 2nd level cataloging

```
Kilabuk, Simanuk.
  Birds on a base [art original] / Simanuk Kilabuk.
[19--]
    1 sculpture : walrus tooth ; 6 x 13 x 3 cm.

  Title from certification card.

Tracing with Library of Congress Subject Heading:
  1. Inuit sculpture -- Canada.  I. Title.

Tracing with Canadian Subject Heading:
  1. Inuit -- Canada -- Sculpture.  I. Title.


Recommended DDC: 730.9719
```

CSH3 provides more user guidance in its text than LCSH (which has a separate manual) with 53 preliminary pages of introductory explanation and many more scope notes. The headings conform to LCSH patterns and directives, but an earlier cross-reference structure (x = see from, xx = see also from, sa = see also) once also used by LC has been retained. Cumulative supplements to CSH3 are published semiannually and a list of the changes since the last supplement are available on NLC's Web site at www.nlc-bnc.ca/csh/csh-e.htm. Subject authority records for *Canadian Subject Headings* are also available on AMICUS, NLC's bibliographic and authorities database, a fee-based service.

Although the subject heading list itself is composed of English-language terminology, the introduction to CSH3 is in English and French, and there are four indexes: English to French and French to English for both the main headings and subdivisions. The indexes link CSH3 to French-language headings found in *Répertoire de vedettes-matière*.[10]

NLC has been contributing new subject concepts identified in Canadian publications to LCSH since 1994. LC also uses CSH3 as a basic source when considering new headings.

Problems with LCSH

Until recently, LCSH evolved very slowly and its critics claim that LC has resisted important and necessary changes in spelling and terminology. In theory, LCSH is constantly under revision, with LC's subject catalogers (or catalogers outside LC) able to propose new or altered headings at any time. A slow pace of change in any list this large is understandable. LC has a great many more items cataloged under any one heading than smaller libraries do; therefore, the number of operations needed to update LC records whenever there is a change to an existing heading is considerable, running, for some descriptors used also as subdivisions, into the tens or hundreds of thousands. Thus, subject catalogers at LC resisted for many years changing the now-obsolete heading NEGROES to AFRO-AMERICANS and BLACKS (the former referring to Black people in the United States and the latter to Black people outside the United States) even though they acknowledged that the word *Negroes* had negative connotations in then-current usage. (*Canadian Subject Headings* does not have a heading for "Afro-Canadians," using instead BLACK CANADIANS.) Similar problems occurred with topical headings as well as the names of peoples. LC resisted changing MOVING PICTURES to MOTION PICTURES until 1989, which necessitated the change of many derivative headings, all published in the 12th edition. In the 1990s, however, the transfer of LC's catalog records and authority files to an online environment was completed and speeded up the process of change. New printed editions appear every year; greater flexibility in revising old headings and introducing new ones is an encouraging trend.

Many problems of LCSH have been or are being addressed by committees of the American Library Association. Its Subject Analysis Committee, a standing committee of the Cataloging and Classification Section of one of the divisions, appoints and maintains many subcommittees and task forces, each devoted to a particular problem or issue. Members are appointed on the basis of their interest and expertise, and their reports often are instrumental in adding new headings to LCSH, changing older ones, or modifying its application policies. A subcommittee of the Subject Analysis Committee succeeded in ridding the list of sexist headings intimating that it is unusual for women to be doctors, authors, or other kinds of professionals. The offensive "WOMEN AS" headings were deleted from the list and, instead, headings for such topics are constructed on the model WOMEN AUTHORS, WOMEN PHYSICIANS, etc. In the course of their work, the subcommittee studying this issue prepared a list of nonsexist subject headings demonstrating how to represent topics without sexual prejudice.[11] Since then, other nonsexist thesauri have been published.[12] Catalogers sensitive to gender issues also saw the presence of heading pairs that singled out only the female sex (such as "authors" and "women authors") as unequal treatment of women in subject headings. They lobbied to have gender-specific headings for both sexes, and LC has complied; for example, LCSH now has two headings: MALE AUTHORS and WOMEN AUTHORS.

Other groups have also lobbied LC successfully to create needed headings (e.g., the Music Library Association) or, alternatively, created their own thesauri to augment or supplement LCSH (e.g., the film archivists who jointly sponsored the publication of *Moving Image Materials: Genre Terms*). These terms also have been accommodated by special MARC fields in LC's computer encoding system.

NLC presents changes proposed for CSH3 to the Canadian Committee on Cataloguing for discussion. From time to time, the National Library forms ad hoc committees with membership drawn from the cataloging community to advise on special aspects of subject analysis.

LCSH has informative scope notes and instructions for the application of some of its descriptors, but there are not nearly enough of them. When using the Red Book, one wishes there were more. With so many headings appearing over such a long period of time, there are bound to be overlaps; for example, CONFORMITY and COMPLIANCE; COMPUTERS, ELECTRONIC DIGITAL COMPUTERS, MINICOMPUTERS, and MICROCOMPUTERS (but there is no heading for "mainframes," not even as a cross-reference). Sometimes the distinctions LC makes between similar headings can be missed by searchers unfamiliar with the terminology; for example, AFRO-AMERICANS and BLACKS differ only in whether the people to whom they refer live within or outside the United States. Subject cataloging specialists who work with LCSH will be aware of the distinction, but a student searching the catalog at school or an ordinary person searching the catalog in the public library may not.

Why Use LCSH?

Though LCSH may cover a large number of topics beyond the scope of a particular institution, use terminology in nonspecific ways, and suffer from other problems, public libraries and media centers may find, nevertheless, that using LCSH is cost-effective if they rely on cataloging services that use it, either for most or all of their cataloging. If LCSH is used for one's collection, several strategies can be employed to minimize the work:

- If technical terminology creates problems for searchers, who may not understand them, and the number of items using technical terms is not large, these materials can be given local subject headings in addition to or in place of the LCSH term. If the number of items affected is large and the work involved is too costly and time-consuming, an added locally assigned USE reference for a more understandable term might be more effective. Patrons would have to do two lookups; first for the local USE reference, which would lead them to the LC term, and then for the LC term, but at least they would not be stymied by terms they cannot understand.

- If LCSH uses inverted word order when the library or media center prefers direct word order, locally assigned USE references or local subject headings also will solve this problem. It all depends on how much original work it requires and whether it is cost-effective. The more one customizes LCSH, the lower its economic value to the agency will be.

- A user-friendly subject thesaurus might be used for alternatives to inappropriate LCSH terms. To minimize the work involved, a database of the substitutions and other local subject cataloging policies could be maintained.

One could do all original subject cataloging if customized subject access is important, but everything would have to be documented, which is a very costly business. Librarians and media specialists can consult a manual such as *Subject Headings for School and Public Libraries*, which combines a subset of LCSH terms, names, and titles that can be used to catalog a general collection of these materials.[13]

LC's Annotated Card Program

In 1965, LC responded to an expressed need on the part of librarians working with children and youth for modifications in subject headings for children's materials by initiating its "Annotated Card" (AC) program. Four modifications were made to the materials treated under the program: first, subdivisions referring to age level, such as —JUVENILE LITERATURE were dropped; second, selected terms were added, revised, or simplified; third, subdivision practice was altered; and, fourth, summaries were provided in the descriptive cataloging to inform searchers about the content of the materials (ergo, the name "annotated").

Examples of AC headings that differ slightly from LCSH form to simplify them are ALPINE ANIMALS, used instead of LCSH's ALPINE FAUNA, and BEDWETTING, used instead of LCSH's ENURESIS. Clearly, "animals" and "bedwetting" will be recognized and understood by youngsters more easily than "fauna" and "enuresis," respectively. In other cases, the modification is subtler, for example, ROBOTS is used in the AC program for materials about androids as well as other kinds of robots, whereas ANDROIDS is acceptable in LCSH for materials specifically about that type of robot.

Several modifications are made in subdivision practice in addition to the obvious one of omitting age-related terminology. Most important of these was the use of —BIOGRAPHY for individual biographies in subject fields in which LCSH had no term for persons in that field, and —FICTION, which could be added to all topical headings. Although LC is experimenting now with the assignment of topical subject headings to adult fictional works, they have been doing it for juvenile works for decades.

The list of Annotated Card Program headings, known colloquially as "AC" headings, immediately precede the regular list of headings, and appears exactly like the regular list, three columns to a page, with similar scope notes, cross-references, subdivisions, etc.; however, AC headings do not have recommended classification numbers.

AC headings are not made in place of LCSH headings, but in addition to them. For example, in the CIP for an illustrated edition of *The Jungle Book,* the CIP gives the first subject heading as CHILDREN'S STORIES, ENGLISH, followed by four AC headings: JUNGLES—FICTION, ANIMALS—FICTION, INDIA—FICTION, and SHORT STORIES. One can recognize the AC headings in CIP because they appear within square brackets following the regular LCSH headings. The summary or annotation appears in its usual place in the description.

The AC Program has been a great help to parents and teachers seeking relevant literature as well as to young searchers trying to find "something about steamboats" or other topics of interest. And who can say that a book intended for youngsters might not be equally interesting to adults, if the catalog helps them to discover that it exists?

Conclusion

Despite its problems and idiosyncrasies, LCSH remains the subject heading list in widest use among U.S. and Canadian libraries. Network records almost always contain LCSH subject headings. The need to exploit the power of cataloging networks is causing many librarians and media specialists to rethink their adherence to systems that are little used in computerized databases. There is no requirement that narrow headings be used when broader ones will do an acceptable job. If a library or media center has only a few books on a subject, the cataloger could decide not to distinguish them and put them all under a broad heading that contains them all. These decisions should be based on a clear idea of how the collection will grow in the future. Subject headings must bring together enough material so that someone looking under a particular heading will find all the materials relevant to that topic collocated there. At the same time, they must not bring together too many items, or the file will be rendered useless to all but the most persistent searchers. If a public library or media center uses a cataloging network as its source for cataloging data, then decisions must also weigh the cost of changing headings on derived cataloging against tolerating more or less collocation than would be optimal. Maintaining a local subject authority file that describes one's unique practices has its costs.

The delicate balance between gathering and distinguishing materials by subject shifts according to the needs of individual groups of materials and individual searchers. The best one can do is to try to please *most* of the searchers *most* of the time, while working toward an ideal subject catalog in which all users find exactly what they need under whatever headings they choose to use.

Try assigning a single LCSH heading to the hypothetical titles in Figure 9.8. The answers are in Appendix C.

Figure 9.8

1. Title: *Digging for our roots*
    Summary: Tells how archaeologists excavate a site to uncover evidence of cultures that predate our own.

2. Title: *The pros and cons of bilingual education*
    Summary: Teachers, politicians, parents, and students explore major issues in bilingual education.

3. Title: *Database searching : a bibliography*
    Summary: A bibliography of source materials covering databases, search techniques, searching software, and related subjects.

4. Title: *Historical sketches of colonial America*
    Summary: Brief overviews of 10 landmark episodes in the history of the American colonies from the landing at Plymouth to the battles at Lexington and Concord.

5. Title: *An illustrated guide to California's wildflowers*
    Summary: An illustrated guide to 250 varieties of wildflowers commonly found in California's deserts, mountains, and valleys.

6. Title: *Rock music: a 20th century phenomenon*
    Summary: Describes the rise of rock music and its subgenres, and the structural, harmonic, and melodic conventions it employs.

7. Title: *Ace 'em : gaining the winning edge in tennis*
    Summary: Discusses mental exercises and outlooks that provide the tennis player with a psychological edge over opponents.

8. Title: *A "yellow submarine" album*
    Summary: Songs from the Beatle's famous animated film with easy-to-play accompaniments.

9. Title: *The biological clock*
    Summary: The pros and cons of childbearing after age 40.

10. Title: *The Quebecois*
    Summary: Daily life, culture, heritage, and religion of French Canadians.

Recommended Reading

Chan, Lois Mai. *A Guide to the Library of Congress Classification.* 5th ed. Englewood, CO: Libraries Unlimited, 1999.

DeZelar-Tiedman, Christine. "Subject Access to Fiction: An Application of the Guidelines." *Library Resources & Technical Services* 40, no. 3 (July 1996): 203-210.

The Future of Subdivisions in the Library of Congress Subject Headings System: Report from the Subject Subdivisions Conference, Airlie, VA, May 9-12, 1991. Ed. Martha O'Hara Conway. Washington, DC: Library of Congress Cataloging Distribution Service, 1992.

Intner, Sheila S. et al. *Subject Access to Films and Videos.* Lake Crystal, MN: Soldier Creek Press, 1992.

LC Period Subdivisions under Names of Places. 4th ed. Washington, DC: Library of Congress Cataloging Distribution Service, 1990.

LC Subject Headings: Weekly Lists. Washington, DC: Library of Congress Cataloging Distribution Service, 1993- .

OCLC CatCD for Windows: LC Subject Authorities. Dublin, OH: OCLC, 1996- .

Olderr, Steven. *Olderr's Fiction Subject Headings: A Supplement and Guide to the LC Thesaurus.* Chicago: American Library Association, 1991.

Stone, Alva T. "The LCSH Century: A Brief History of the Library of Congress Subject Headings, and Introduction to the Centennial Essays." *Cataloging & Classification Quarterly* 29, issues 1 and 2 (2000). [theme issue about LCSH]

Studwell, William E. *Library of Congress Subject Headings: Principles, Theory, and Application.* Englewood, CO: Libraries Unlimited, 1991.

Winston, Iris. "Canadian Subject Headings: Making Information Retrieval Most Effective." *National Library News* 26, no. 12 (December 1994): 4-5.

Notes

1.   Library of Congress, Subject Cataloging Division, *Classification Plus: Library of Congress Classification and Library of Congress Subject Headings* (Washington, DC: Cataloging Distribution Service, 2000-).

2.   Library of Congress, Subject Cataloging Division, *Subject Cataloging Manual: Subject Headings,* 5th ed. (Washington, DC: Library of Congress, Cataloging Distribution Service, 1996-); *Cataloger's Desktop: Library of Congress Rule Interpretations, Subject Cataloging Manual: Subject Headings, Subject Cataloging Manual: Classification, USMARC Format for Bibliographic Data, USMARC Format for Authority Data, and Other Cataloging Tools* (Washington, DC: Library of Congress, Cataloging Distribution Service, 1999-). Whenever this work is cited, the entire title must be given, because LC publishes companion volumes titled *Subject Cataloging Manual: Shelflisting* and *Subject Cataloging Manual: Classification,* with which it would otherwise be confused.

3.   Library of Congress, Subject Cataloging Division, *Free-Floating Subdivisions: An Alphabetic Index,* 11th ed. (Washington, DC: Library of Congress, Cataloging Distribution Service, 1999). This tool is a compilation of and index to the free-floating subdivisions found in *Subject Cataloging Manual: Subject Headings* pages H1095 to H1200.

4.   *Library of Congress Subject Headings Weekly Lists* (Washington, DC: Library of Congress, Cataloging Distribution Service, 1984-).

5.   *Cataloging Service* bulletin (Washington, DC: Library of Congress, Cataloging Distribution Service, 1978-).

6.   National Library of Medicine, *Medical Subject Headings: An Annotated Alphabetic List* (Bethesda, MD: National Library of Medicine, 1975-); National Library of Medicine, *Medical Subject Headings: Tree Structures* (Bethesda, MD: National Library of Medicine, 1975-).

7.   Library of Congress, Subject Cataloging Division, *Library of Congress Subject Headings,* 22nd ed. (Washington, DC: Library of Congress, Cataloging Distribution Service, 1999), vol. 1, xiii-xv.

8.   Ibid., vol. 1, 515.

9.   National Library of Canada, *Canadian Subject Headings,* 3rd ed., ed. Alina Schweitzer (Ottawa: Canada Communication Group—Publishing, 1992).

10.   *Répertoire de vedettes-matière,* (Quebec: Université Laval, 1989-). *RVM* is cumulative and published twice a year on microfiche and on CD-ROM. It also is updated each month on NLC's Web site. For information in English, see www.nlc-bnc.ca/rvmweb/index-f.htm.

11.   Joan K. Marshall, comp. *On Equal Terms: A Thesaurus for Nonsexist Indexing and Cataloging* (Santa Barbara, CA: ABC-CLIO, 1977).

12.   Mary Ellen S. Capek, ed. *A Women's Thesaurus: An Index of Language Used to Describe and Locate Information by and about Women* (New York: Harper & Row, 1987); Ruth Dickstein, Victoria A. Mills, and Ellen J. Waite, *Women in LC's Terms: A Thesaurus of Library of Congress Subject Headings Relating to Women* (Phoenix, AZ: Oryx Press, 1988).

13.   Joanna F. Fountain, *Subject Headings for School and Public Libraries: An LCSH/Sears Companion*, 3rd ed. (Englewood, CO: Libraries Unlimited, 2001).

10

Classification Systems

Introduction

An important method of organizing materials is to arrange them in a useful order on the shelves. The famous library at Alexandria in the ancient world was supposed to have been classified by literary genres—all the poetry in one place, all the speeches in another, plays in a third, and so on. In medieval libraries, books were shelved by size (folios, quartos, octavos, etc.) in fixed locations, a practice that was also followed in the United States and Canada at one time. Size and genre classifications are still in use. Special shelves for oversized books are common, as are separate sections for genres such as mysteries, biographies, etc.

Media specialists and public librarians could arrange their materials in alphabetical order by their titles or authors, or their main entries; they could be arranged in the order they are acquired; they could be arranged by subject, by physical format, or by combinations of these methods. The one thing that never is done is to shelve materials randomly. A system always is used to arrange materials.

Classification is the name applied to the arrangement of materials, but that is not the only definition of the term. Classification is an inherently human activity, one that people perform constantly in interacting with the environment. Classification may be defined as the act of systematically arranging sets of objects or phenomena. Humans have categories for everything. Weather is categorized by the day's temperature into freezing, cold, cool, mild, warm, and hot, to which we can add dry, humid, or wet; sunny, hazy, overcast, or cloudy; and breezy or calm. Food is categorized by the time of day it is eaten into breakfast, brunch, lunch, dinner, supper, and snacks, or by type of food into proteins, starches, sugars, and fats, etc., or appetizers, soups, salads, entrees, side dishes, condiments, beverages, and desserts. Two ways to categorize clothing are by the part of the body a garment covers or by its material. A familiar classification is the arrangement of a supermarket, with its sections for dairy products, groceries, meats, fresh produce, frozen foods, paper goods, etc. In each of these examples, some attribute (or group of attributes) of the set of things to be classified is selected to divide the whole into manageable parts.

In the same fashion, knowledge can also be categorized. One familiar way to classify knowledge is by dividing it according to its focus of study; that is, the humanities (subjects that focus on human culture, such as religion and philosophy, literature, the arts, and history), social sciences (subjects that focus on society's organized activities, such as sociology, political science, law, and economics), and natural sciences (subjects that focus on natural phenomena and activities, such as chemistry, physics, mathematics, geology, biology, etc.). Sir Francis Bacon divided knowledge according to his notion of the origin of different types of studies. He related some subjects to people's imagination (literature and arts), some to their memory (history), and others to their reason (philosophy and religion, social and natural sciences).

Often, knowledge is classified by commonly recognized disciplines or fields of study. One way to decide what constitutes a field of study is to examine the curriculum of universities. One division into disciplines is based on the medieval university's liberal arts curriculum: the trivium (grammar, rhetoric, and logic) and quadrivium (arithmetic, music, geometry, and astronomy). Other divisions or classifications of knowledge include the disciplines with which we are familiar today, from archeology to zoology.

What is important about the division is that it must be exhaustive—no areas of knowledge can be left out—and its categories must be unambiguous and mutually exclusive. Arithmetic and geometry are unambiguous because they both are clearly defined (arithmetic deals with the computation of numbers and geometry deals with areas in space); they are mutually exclusive because they deal with different areas of the larger subject called mathematics. They are not exhaustive, however, because they leave out many other areas of study in mathematics, such as algebra, trigonometry, calculus, topology, etc. But if mathematics is divided into geometry and the mathematics of solids, there is a problem, because geometry includes the study of solids in space and one would never know where to put an item about spheres, for example. The difficulty is the lack of mutual exclusivity of these two categories.

The discussion of subject headings established that ambiguity is a problem of insufficient definition. The same problem can occur with classifications because they rely on words to express their categories as well as on the coded representations of subjects—the *symbolic notation*—associated with them. Subject cataloging and classification share two important aspects: (1) the categorization of subject matter, and (2) its expression according to predefined conventions. They differ primarily in the means they employ for displaying designated categories to end users, subject headings using words (subject headings or descriptors), and classifications using symbols (class "numbers" or notation) for this purpose. To be understood by the classifier, however, the symbols must be linked to recognizable identifications and these, like their subject authority counterparts, consist of words.[1]

Library Classifications

Most library classifications divide knowledge into disciplines or main classes. The ones with which we are most familiar—Dewey Decimal and Library of Congress classifications (DDC and LCC)—do this. DDC divides all knowledge into 10 main classes based roughly on the Baconian model. LCC divides it into 21 main classes,[2] deriving more main classes by choosing as separate disciplines some fields of study that DDC subsumes under a broader class; for example, political science, law, and education are each main classes in LCC, but in DDC, all three are part of the main class of social sciences.

Library classification is used primarily to place materials on library shelves. We are accustomed to having all copies of each title, whether it is a book, sound recording, video, or any other kind of physical medium, shelved together in one place in the library. This concentration on physical location of materials in a line on shelves, from the first classification number to the last, is a feature called *linearity*. Typically, library classifications are linear, although they do not have to be. Theoretically, they could be nonlinear or multidimensional. Similarly, in theory, if a video is about Mozart and Beethoven, it could be given two classification numbers, one for each composer, and copies could be placed at each location. However, although nonlinear classifications, called *faceted* or *synthetic* classifications, are available, and although multiple classifications for a single work are possible, they are rare in U.S. and Canadian libraries.

Faceted classifications are systems in which all possible components of a group of subjects are given and classification numbers are built by combining the appropriate components, usually in a predetermined citation order. Examples of faceted classifications include the Universal Decimal Classification (UDC), a transformation of the Dewey classification often used in Europe; the Bibliographic Classification of Henry E. Bliss, used for decades in the library of the City College of New York; and the Colon Classification devised by library theorist S. R. Ranganathan, used to some extent in India, his home country. The concept of main classes is present even in these faceted classifications; for example, UDC retains DDC's structure of ten main classes and Colon Classification divides the universe of knowledge into 41 main classes before applying the principles of faceting to the subdivisions of each class.

In contrast, *enumerative* classifications list all possible topics and subtopics with their classification numbers. Instead of building a number from the parts available for the task, in an enumerative system the best number from the list is chosen for each title being classified. Both DDC and LCC are enumerative classifications.

Neither type of classification is quite as simple as it sounds, but both types are functional, furnishing shelf arrangements that bring materials on the same subjects together.

Classification in North America

DDC and LCC are the most popularly used classifications in the United States and Canada. Public libraries of all sizes and school library media centers generally use DDC. Libraries in colleges and universities often choose LCC, but some public libraries use it as well; for example, Boston Public Library and some smaller public libraries in the state of Massachusetts. However, some colleges and universities use DDC—even large ones such as the University of Illinois at Urbana-Champaign and Northwestern University Libraries—making it hard to generalize about users of the two systems. DDC and LCC share many characteristics as well as having certain fundamental differences.

Similarities of DDC and LCC

DDC and LCC consist of schedules of numbers representing all topics in all disciplines in the universe of knowledge. These systems are called enumerative because all the classes are enumerated and the classifier examines the array to find the slot that fits each item being classified. By contrast, to classify an item in a nonenumerative or faceted system (also called a synthetic system), the appropriate numbers are taken from the different facets and combined (or synthesized) to build the number.

Other characteristics shared by DDC and LCC are their history and outlook. Both systems were devised in the United States; both are products of late-nineteenth or early-twentieth-century perceptions of the relationships between disciplines; and both display similar biases toward the United States and Western culture in general, and a white, male, Anglo-Saxon, Christian view of the universe. DDC is the product of Melville Dewey (who liked to spell his name Melvil Dui, although we now frequently find it spelled partly one way and partly the other: Melvil Dewey), who devised the scheme to arrange the books in the Amherst College Library, where he worked as assistant librarian. The first DDC was published in 1876. LCC is based loosely on the Expansive Classification of Charles Cutter, who also formalized the objectives of the catalog. Dewey and Cutter were contemporaries, and their classifications share some common notions; for example, that psychology is part of philosophy, not science, bearing a closer relationship to the occult than to medicine, and that women as a topic belong with marriage and the family, whereas men are equated with society in general. Topics for the United States—in language, literature, politics, geography, etc.—almost always precede those of the rest of the nations, are subdivided more extensively, or both. In part, this is because both classifications rely on literary warrant (i.e., the existence of literature on a topic) for their structure. It is also attributable to the nature of their environments. Rearranging the classifications to reflect a more modern outlook would require major relocations of materials, a suggestion that never is received enthusiastically by either library administrators or catalog department heads.

Both classifications are updated more or less continuously. The 1996 21st edition of DDC current at this writing will be superseded soon, but incremental changes can occur at any time and are reported on the publisher's Web site. LCC's revisions, which can occur any time the classifiers at LC dictate, are reported in *Additions and Changes,* a publication issued quarterly by LC.

LCC and DDC employ some similar devices to save the space of printing repetitious subdivisions for groups of topics. Tables of subdivisions are common to both, although they appear and are applied differently. In both classifications, instructions direct the classifier to use the numbers assigned to the first of a group of similar topics to each of the others.

Differences Between DDC and LCC

The major difference between DDC and LCC is their size, and, therefore, how narrowly topics are subdivided. LCC is much larger than DDC and has many more classes, dividing knowledge into narrower categories. It was implemented early in the 1900s, when LC's collection passed one million volumes, and it was intended to facilitate the shelving of a very large collection of materials with relative ease.

Another fundamental difference is the presence of a single structural principle for the system. DDC is based on the decimal principle. This means that all knowledge is divided into 10 main classes that are, in turn each divided into 10 more subclasses, and so on ad infinitum. LCC, on the other hand, has no such unifying structural rule. Each of LCC's schedules, representing a discipline of knowledge, was developed independently of the others according to the needs of LC's existing collections in each area as well as the expectations of experts for their growth in the future. No single method of subdivision was imposed on all of the developers, so in some cases they used different structures to represent the same kind of topical division; conversely, in other cases they used the same structure to represent different topical divisions.

More apparent to users of the two systems are differences in their notation. DDC uses only Arabic numerals, with the decimal placed after the third number, no matter how long the whole classification number might be. The use of only one type of character is called *pure notation.* LCC uses alphabetical characters—single capital letters to distinguish the main classes and double letters for most of the subclasses—and Arabic numerals, sometimes extended decimally, to subdivide them further. The use of different types of characters is called *mixed notation.* In addition, LC classes that require further subdivision may be *cuttered,* that is, divided by means of an alphanumeric code added to the initial groups of letters and numbers. Figure 10.1 shows the DDC and LCC numbers for public ownership of land, including a full range of notational possibilities for the LCC numbers.

Figure 10.1

DEWEY DECIMAL CLASSIFICATION

333.1	Public ownership of land
.11	Acquisition and disposal of specific kinds of lands
.101-.109	Standard subdivisions
.13	Acquisition
.14	Nationalization
.16	Disposal
.18	Public land surveys

LIBRARY OF CONGRESS CLASSIFICATION

	Public lands
HD216	History
221	Description, guides, etc.
239	Town sites, etc.
240	Bounty lands
241	Grazing lands
	Cf. HD1635+, Pasture lands
	Mineral lands
242	General works
.3	Coal lands
.5	Oil and gas lands
	Including oil rights
.9	Rights of way
	Inducing power translation, telegraph, etc.
	For railroad rights, see HE1063+
	Railroad land grants, see HE1063+
	School lands, see LB2827
	Swamp lands, see HD1665+
243	By region or state, A-Z
	Cf. HD196, United States history of land (Local)
	By city, see HD1291

——————

As a result of the decimal notation and Dewey's conscious efforts to provide them, there are many memory aids (called mnemonics) in DDC. The number for the United States, for example, is -73, whether it is part of a number for political parties (324.273) or history (973). DDC has tables of standard subdivisions that can be applied at will to any topic, and for peoples, geographic areas, languages, etc., that are applied as directed to many different topics. These are known as auxiliary tables. Thus, numbers from tables become intelligible to those familiar with them, and classification numbers become a familiar code language. In contrast, mnemonics are not possible between LCC's schedules, and even within a single schedule, few memory aids are to be found.

DDC's single set of tables for all the schedules is not matched by LCC, which has many different kinds of tables, some used for several subschedules within a division and others used only for a single number or a small group of numbers. The LCC classification relies on alphabetization to a great degree, unlike DDC, which rarely employs it as a means of dividing a large topic.

To sum up, differences between DDC and LCC include the following:

1. *Size*: DDC, although theoretically capable of infinite expansion, enumerates a more limited number of topics than LCC. In its massive array of more than 40 volumes and related updates, tables, etc., LCC is much larger than the compact four-volume DDC.

2. *Specificity*: LCC provides greater explicit specificity than DDC. Few librarians use the full capacity of DDC for specificity, and some opt to use broader classes than required.

3. *Structural principles*: DDC observes a number of overarching principles, including decimal division and mnemonic notations, which govern the entire system. In contrast, LCC's schedules were originally developed separately and each continues to be updated and expanded independently of the others.

4. *Notation*: DDC employs Arabic numbers in a pure notation; LCC employs both Arabic numbers and alphabetic characters in a mixed notation. One result of this difference is that LCC can achieve greater specificity than DDC with the same number of characters. Conversely, DDC numbers with the decimal placed after the third digit seem easier to remember by classifiers, patrons, shelvers, and other library staff. With DDC, one can move from brief classification numbers to more complex ones if the collection grows unexpectedly. One can begin with the abridged DDC and move to unabridged.

5. *Tables and subdivision practices*: DDC has seven auxiliary tables intended for use throughout its schedules, although some are used primarily with specific main classes (for details about DDC tables, see chapter 11). In contrast, LCC has hundreds of tables of which only three are used in multiple schedules. For the most part, LCC's subdivision tables have "local" applications in a single schedule or part of a schedule. In addition, many LCC tables require the creation of cutter numbers, and only LC itself can establish authoritative ones. Thus, non-LC classifiers needing a new cutter might have to wait until LC classifies the item first, or risk establishing a local cutter that conflicts with one LC establishes at a later time.

6. *Indexing*: One of DDC's best attributes is its Relative Index. LCC lacks a single index in which all topics are brought together regardless of their main class. The inability to see the whole array of topics in one place is a great drawback. Several decades ago, compilers tried to remedy this lack,[3] but most of the resulting indexes were incomplete and none have been kept up-to-date. Individual LCC schedules have indexes to their volume contents, but there is no guarantee that the terms used in one schedule will have the same meanings when they appear in another.

Call Numbers:
Other Shelving Elements

Depending on the system chosen for arranging the materials in a public library or media center, a classification number for each item will be chosen, but it is not the only element in the locational codes known as *call numbers.* In addition to the class number, one or more *book numbers,* also called *shelf marks,* will be added to aid in shelving many items that share a single classification number, because they cover the same topic. (These added elements are called book numbers even when they are applied to materials other than books.)

Usually, the first of the book numbers is, by an unofficial agreement, an alphanumeric code representing the main entry of the item called a *cutter number.* The name derives from the fact that Charles A. Cutter was the first to publish a list of the codes, later revised by a librarian named Margaret Sanborn, into tables called Cutter tables or Cutter-Sanborn tables.[4] This cutter number should not be confused with the cuttering done as part of LCC class numbers, although their origins and the principles on which they are derived are exactly the same. The difference is simple: DDC-classed materials use cutter numbers solely as shelf marks, but LCC-classed materials use the device of cuttering both as shelf marks and as part of its classification numbers, to subdivide large groups of materials within a class. Call numbers for DDC-classed materials generally have one cutter, the shelf mark; LCC-classed materials may have two or even three cutters, the last of which is the shelf mark.

Unique call numbers are generally considered essential in large collections and can be useful in some automated systems. However, unique call numbers may not be necessary in collections in which there are only a few items in each classification category. Some small public libraries and school library media centers add call letters (one or several) rather than cutter numbers to their classification numbers to form call numbers, because call letters are easier to apply. The first letter, first two, or first three letters of the main entry are used as call letters. If the main entry is a title, the call letters are not taken from initial articles, but from the word following the initial articles. Call letters for a book by Jane Austen could be A, AU (or Au), or AUS (or Aus), depending on the size of the collection and the type of lettering preferred. Call numbers resulting from this system may not be unique for each item, because items with the same classification number and with the same second or third initial letters will have the same call number; for example, books on the same subject by authors named Rose, Rosen, Rosenberg, Ross, or all. Nevertheless, in a small collection this will not hinder retrieval and will save money both in the classifier's time and the purchase of special tools for cuttering.

Other elements in a call number include a symbol, usually a letter of the alphabet, for the particular collection to which an item belongs, such as "R" for reference materials or "J" for children's materials. Within a collection, other symbols can be used to distinguish more categories. Popular collection marks also include special designations for biography ("B"), fiction ("F," "FIC," "Fic"), oversized materials ("O"), and audiovisual materials ("AV").

Audiovisual materials are not always designated AV or given mnemonic initials for the individual media formats. Other devices can be used. Codes have been published for different types of media.[5] Color coding—using a distinct color bar above the call number for each different physical format—was popular at one time. Although it is still done in some places, color coding has several disadvantages, principally that the number of media formats has proliferated to the point that dozens of colors have to be used to give each one its own unique identification. Fading can cause shades of colors to lose their distinctiveness, and it can be difficult to obtain the exact shade in new stock. It is also difficult to implement color coding in an automated system.

There are advantages to using spelled out words for media or other specially shelved collections, such as oversized books, microforms, photographs, and others. The most important advantage is instant understanding on the part of persons using them, which codes cannot guarantee. Spelled out words are unlikely to be misunderstood as being part of a mixed notation classification number, and more likely to be remembered during a trip to the shelves. (Studies show that meaningful strings of letters or numbers are remembered more easily than nonsense strings of letters or numbers of equal size. Think, for a moment, about which is easier to remember: Reference/Bibliography/Beethoven or R/016.78/B228a.)

A popular addition to a cutter number symbolizing an author main entry for an author who wrote more than one title is a letter or two from the first significant word in each title. This addition results in arranging the author's works on the shelf in alphabetical order by title without having to look beyond the call number to read the entire title. Although this is an ingenious method, it tends to lengthen call numbers and make them quite complicated to assign as well as to use in retrieving desired items from the shelves.

Other call number elements frequently encountered in libraries are dates, used particularly to distinguish two or more editions of the same title. Thus, a copy of the 21st edition of DDC shelved in the reference collection might have the complex LCC call number R/Z696/.D519/1996, in which the meaning is as follows:

R   =   Reference collection

Z696   =   LCC classification number for classifications

.D519 =   The cutter number for Dewey, the author main entry

1996   =   Date of the edition

Complex call numbers such as this one can be useful for staff members in large libraries who have to shelve many items with similar or possibly, even, identical classification numbers, cutters, and other shelf marks, but they are hard to remember when the user goes from the catalog to the shelf, and difficult to write down without making mistakes.

Policy Issues

One of the key policy issues to be decided in any library or media center is the classification to be used to organize and shelve its materials. In making the choice, a number of factors should be considered:

1. *Size of the collection.* If the collection is small, it may not require a fully developed classification. Dewey has an abridged version that might be sufficient for the collection's needs. The classification numbers in the abridged Dewey are matched to many of the headings in *Sears List of Subject Headings.*

If one has a small collection that is likely to grow larger, one will want to begin with an easily expanded classification. If that is the case, starting with abridged Dewey and expanding to the full Dewey might be the most effective solution.

If one has a very large collection (e.g., if it is a district-wide media center or public library system with main library and neighborhood branches), a fully developed classification might be needed to divide many similar materials into manageable groups of subject-related items. Full DDC or LCC might look attractive as a means of accomplishing the task of organizing and shelving so many materials.

If a classification system is already in use and you are considering changing to a different one, think about how older materials will be reclassified. Otherwise, the library or media center could end up with a significant proportion of materials in the old scheme and two sets of shelving to worry about.

2. *Knowledge level of the users.* The use of a complicated set of codes to shelve materials is not an effective choice for serving students and community members, teachers, and school administrators. The most effective system will be straightforward, easy to remember, and able to promote good browsing at the shelf. In most small public libraries and school library media centers, patrons are expected to find materials by browsing the open shelves as well as by finding call numbers in the catalog for specific titles.

Often, schools are smaller at the lower grade levels and larger at the secondary school level, making it easier to move both collections and users from simple to complex classification as one progresses through the grades. This transition may also apply in public libraries as young people change their selection of materials from the children's to the adult departments.

3. *Source of the classification numbers.* To devise a local classification and call numbers, all the work must be done from scratch. Opportunities to obtain classification or call numbers from sources such as cataloging-in-publication or a central service make it more practical to follow DDC or LCC, the systems these sources use. However, before accepting any classification simply because it saves money by eliminating original work, the cost of a reference librarian's or a media specialist's time spent helping patrons use a unique local system or the lost opportunities for successful searching if someone is not there to help must be balanced against the cost of using a better, but unique, local system.

4. *Networking obligations.* If the library or media center is part of a network, consortium, or other cooperative group, common use of a classification system can be of great benefit to all the participants. It is particularly important when the clients of some or all of the libraries and media centers in the network are permitted to borrow from other libraries or centers in the network. If so, all members would want to follow the same or similar classification practices to make it easier for their overlapping audiences to browse anywhere in the network. Altering the classification to satisfy the idiosyncrasies of a single agency might not be worth the cost of doing unique classification, and the value to one's own clients of having a common system would be destroyed.

Choosing an appropriate classification system is not the whole story, however. When the system is translated to the shelves, one may desire to make exceptions for certain materials, such as over- or under-sized items that do not fit on shelves designed for ordinary books. Typical examples are unbound materials and nonbook materials, such as soundtapes, computer disks, and other electronic media, which might be shelved near the equipment needed to use them. The fewer exceptions made to the classification, the more likely it is that clients will find materials, and the less time staff will have to spend explaining where particular materials are stored.

Once the classification scheme to be applied is determined, other desired shelf marks should be identified. These may include cutter numbers, dates to distinguish different editions of the same item, and volume numbers for multivolume works. They may also include copy numbers (copy 1, copy 2, etc.), but, today, these are being assigned less frequently. Now, copies are more likely to be given computer-readable bar codes. Bar codes do represent copy-unique numbers, but they rarely are considered part of an item's shelf address. When multiple copies with bar codes are shelved, no effort is made to put them in numeric sequence. It is sufficient that computer scanners will be able to tell them apart for circulation or inventory purposes.

An important policy issue to be decided is whether to require that each title in the collection be given a unique call number or permit the same call number to be assigned to more than one title. When several titles share a call number, materials within a single number can be placed on the shelf at random or shelvers can be asked to impose a subarrangement not reflected in the call number. The advantage to this is that closely related materials are brought together at the same point on the shelves. The disadvantage is that shelf location is not reflected precisely by the call number. In some computer-based systems, unique call numbers enabling precise retrieval of desired titles are a requirement for programming the call number as an access point. The advantage of establishing unique call numbers is that the call number serves as a unique identifier useful for online retrieval as well as indicating precise shelf location. The disadvantages of maintaining unique call numbers are that the numbers may get quite long and they require more steps to assign and decipher.

Whatever decisions are made should be carefully documented in writing and maintained in a file of all cataloging, indexing, and classification policies and procedures, so that other members of the staff and public can follow them. Whenever the person responsible for policy moves on to another position, that person's successor can understand existing practices and the rationale behind each one.

Let us look more closely at the details of the two major classification systems in use in the United States and Canada today. The next two chapters cover the Dewey Decimal and Library of Congress classifications in greater depth.

Recommended Reading

"Classification: Options and Opportunities." Ed. Alan R. Thomas. *Cataloging & Classification Quarterly* 19, nos. 3 and 4 (1995).

Comaromi, John P. *Book Numbers: A Historical Study and Practice Guide to Their Use.* Littleton, CO: Libraries Unlimited, 1981.

Marcella, Rita, and Robert Newton. *A New Manual of Classification.* Aldershot, England: Gower, 1994.

McIlwaine, I. C., with A. Buxton. *Guide to the Use of UDC: An Introductory Guide to the Use and Application of the Universal Decimal Classification.* The Hague, Netherlands: International Federation for Information and Documentation, 1993.

Scott, Mona L. *Conversion Tables: LC-Dewey; Dewey-LC; Subject Headings—LC and Dewey,* 2nd ed. Englewood, CO: Libraries Unlimited, 1999. [May be obtained in three print volumes or on IBM-compatible ASCII disks.]

Taylor, Arlene G. *The Organization of Information.* Englewood, CO: Libraries Unlimited, 1999.

Notes

1.   Experiments conducted by Karen Markey Drabenstott and her associates supported the theory that subject access for users of library catalogs is enhanced if the vocabulary of the Dewey Decimal classification is entered into the catalog and made searchable. Karen Markey [i.e., Drabenstott], "Analysis of a Bibliographic Database Enhanced with a Library Classification," *Library Resources & Technical Services* 34 (April 1990): 179-198.

2.   Determination of the number of main classes in the LC classification depends on what one considers a "main" class. If one assumes each separate volume constitutes a main class, there are now more than 40; but if one counts categories assigned a single letter, there are 21. Neither method of counting is perfect, although the B (Philosophy and Religion), K (Law), and P (Languages and Literatures) schedules each comprise several volumes, the E and F schedules (American, Canadian, and Local History) are combined into one and, with C and D (Auxiliary Sciences of History and Old World History), might be interpreted as a single subject area, History.

3.   The most ambitious attempt to create a unified index was done by Nancy B. Olson, *Combined Indexes to the Library of Congress Classification Schedules* (Washington, DC: U.S. Historical Documents Institute, 1974). Others are James G. Williams et al., *Classified Library of Congress Subject Headings,* 2nd ed. (New York: Marcel Dekker, 1982); and J. McRee Elrod et al., *An Index to the Library of Congress Classification; with Entries for Special Expansions in Medicine, Law, Canadiana, and Nonbook Materials,* preliminary ed. (Ottawa: Canadian Library Association, 1974).

4.   Charles Ammi Cutter, *Two-Figure Author Table* (Chicopee Falls, MA: H. R. Huntting; distr. Littleton, CO: Libraries Unlimited, 1969-); Charles Ammi Cutter, *Three-Figure Author Table* (Chicopee Falls, MA: H. R. Huntting; distr. Littleton, CO: Libraries Unlimited, 1969-); *Cutter-Sanborn Three-Figure Author Table,* Swanson-Swift revision (Littleton, CO: Libraries Unlimited, 1969). These tools are available also, if preferred, on CD-ROM from Libraries Unlimited.

5.   Alma M. Tillin and William J. Quinly, *Standards for Cataloging Nonprint Materials,* 4th ed. (Washington, DC: Association for Educational Communications and Technology, 1976), 25-28.

11

The Dewey Decimal Classification

Introduction

The Dewey Decimal Classification (DDC) is an all-inclusive, enumerative, hierarchical classification system. It employs the system of decimal division; that is, all knowledge is divided into 10 main classes, each of which is subsequently subdivided into 10 more subclasses and so on, theoretically, ad infinitum. Forest Press, the publisher, claims that it is the most popular classification system in the world.[1] DDC is used widely in the United States, Canada, and more than 100 other countries. NLC uses DDC to classify its collection, and *Canadiana* (the national bibliography now arranged by register number with one of its indexes by DDC) was arranged by DDC until its paper edition was discontinued at the end of 1991. DDC is the basis for arrangement of the *British National Bibliography* and other national bibliographic agencies in the Commonwealth and elsewhere, unlike the U.S. *National Union Catalog,* which was arranged alphabetically by main entry until it was automated; now, it is arranged by index number.

These two approaches to materials, the classified and the alphabetical, have more than just philosophical differences. The classified approach assumes that searchers know the arrangement of topics, whereas the alphabetical does not. Conversely, alphabetical main entry listings assume that a searcher knows the main entry of a work being sought (usually the author, but otherwise the title), which may not be true. As a result, the classified listing requires alphabetical indexes for authors and titles, and the main entry listing requires an alphabetical subject index. (The current *National Union Catalog* arrangement by index number assumes that users will find what they need in one of various indexes before going to the main tool.)

Principles Underlying the DDC

Seven principles underlie the organization and structure of DDC:

1. *Decimal division.* This was mentioned in the previous chapter, but it cannot be emphasized too often, because this is the primary method of division used by DDC. It merits notice in part because it is a familiar and useful method of dividing—division by tens is something people refer to as using "round" numbers; and, in part because it is at the root of some of DDC's most troubling limitations.

2. *Classification by discipline.* The primary attribute applied in dividing knowledge is discipline, represented by the 10 main classes. That may seem natural to readers of this book, because it is so familiar to most of us, but it is not the only possibility. Knowledge could be divided first by a different element, such as time period or geographic location, and only after that, by discipline, genre, or form, and other attributes.

3. *Hierarchy.* Although the principle of moving from the broadest categories to narrower ones and from these to still narrower ones until the narrowest possible category is reached is encountered frequently in classification, DDC emphasizes it and uses it obviously in complex numbers. Ideally, the hierarchy built into DDC numbers identifies topics at the same level and clarifies which are broader and narrower, merely by noting the number and character of the digits in the class. In practice, this works out only part of the time, because not all topical areas divide neatly into 10 elements. In areas such as literature, a number with three digits (e.g., 813, American fiction) might be at the same level as a number with five or more (e.g., Russian fiction, 891.43).

4. *Mnemonics.* Dewey was enamored of time-saving devices and incorporated them into his classification. Specific groups of numbers can represent the same topic in many places throughout the classification. A familiar example is the number "-73," which stands for the United States in geography (917.3), cookery (641.5973), political parties (324.273), etc. Mnemonic devices, however, should not be over-interpreted; for example, the number 730 does not mean United States anything. It stands for sculpture.

5. *Literary warrant.* This principle dictates that classes are created only after materials exist that require them. DDC purports to be a classification of all knowledge and it does an outstanding job of including topics. However, no classification of limited size can anticipate or list all topics, and DDC is no exception. "Computers" is a good example of a topic that was added when the need for it became clear. If one looks at the 19th and earlier editions of DDC, computers occupy a tiny category (001.64) under the larger topic of "Research" (001). In the 20th edition, computers expanded to occupy three newly established sections of their own (004 - 006).

6. *Enumeration.* This principle dictates the listing of potential class numbers in contrast to the principle of faceting or synthesis, that is, providing topical elements and allowing classifiers to put them together to build complex topics. Although this principle still generally guides DDC, recent editions incorporate more instances of number building and fewer instances of enumeration because it is more economical of page space. Enormous expansion of some subject areas in recent years would

require great increases in enumerated numbers to represent them, whereas instructions to apply existing expansion techniques without actually enumerating each of them does not.

7. *Relative location.* At one time in the United States, Canada, and elsewhere, library books were shelved in fixed locations. Once an item was given its place on the shelves (for example, the second book on the third shelf of the fourth stack), it would never be moved to any other, no matter what new materials were added to the collection. DDC assumes that as new materials are added and shelved, existing items will be moved as well, to maintain the subject relationships among them. The DDC number merely identifies a place relative to other items in the collection.

None of the seven principles operates perfectly throughout the DDC system, or, in all probability, any other classification system. They are observed as far as possible when they do not conflict, create unwanted juxtapositions of subjects, or interfere with practical considerations. Enumeration can be abandoned to save space; mnemonics are superseded when necessary; and other principles can be modified when it is important to do so. Nevertheless, the principles govern many of the decisions taken by DDC's editors with regard to class numbers and relationships.

An eighth principle—integrity of numbers—was promised by Dewey to DDC users in the early days of the classification. This meant that numbers assigned to represent a particular topic would not be changed. Changed numbers create significant work in a library trying to keep all of its materials shelved in a consistent, up-to-date manner. At the least, call number labels and markings in or on materials must be changed; catalog records must be altered to display new call numbers; and materials must be moved to their new locations. Sometimes, whole spans of numbers have been changed to reflect profound changes in a subject area, a practice called "phoenixing." A "phoenixed" schedule was entirely discarded and rebuilt (one might say, risen from its ashes, like the mythical bird). At several points in DDC's history, users rebelled at having to absorb too many phoenixed schedules. In recent years, "phoenix" was replaced by the milder term "complete revision" and the practice was modified, though not entirely abandoned.

Format of the Classification

DDC may be purchased in book or CD-ROM form. The book version of DDC is contained in four volumes of varying size totaling more than 4,000 pages. The first volume contains the introductory matter and seven auxiliary tables used to expand class numbers derived from the main schedules. Part of the introductory matter is a manual explaining generally how to use the classification, which is augmented by a very detailed manual in the final volume.[2] In the brief manual are many helpful instructions on accepted methods of building numbers using all the resources at hand: the schedules, tables, instructions, and conventions. The schedules themselves are contained in the second and third volumes. The Relative Index, the detailed manual on the use of specific numbers, and the policies and procedures of LC's Decimal Classification Division are in the fourth volume. At this writing, DDC is in its twenty-first edition.

"Electronic Dewey," or *Dewey for Windows*™ as the computer-based version is called, was in version 2.00 at this writing. It contains the Schedules, Tables, Manual, and Relative Index, as well as a User Guide explaining how to use program functions to assist in operations. The software offers flexible, efficient computerized retrieval using words or phrases, numbers, index terms, and Boolean combinations. This edition also offers an automatic cuttering function and provision for individual libraries to annotate their disks with local notes.

The principal advantages of the electronic version over the more familiar book version, aside from its computerized retrieval, are the inclusion of frequently used LC subject headings associated with a class number, taken from LC records in OCLC's database; the ability to verify a classification number application by sampling a catalog record that uses the number, also drawn from OCLC's database; a popular, easy-to-use "windowed" user interface; cut-and-paste functions that help minimize keying; and online help screens. All published updates to DDC are issued on updated CD-ROM disks, issued annually every January, without waiting for the printing of a new book version. Updates also appear on the DDC Web site, available to any user with Internet access.

The DDC's Relative Index was Melvil Dewey's original contribution to classification. Its great value lies in its bringing together all of the various aspects of a topic under the term used to represent it, no matter where they would be classified. For example, if you look up COMPUTER in the Relative Index, you will find 144 references to classes as far apart as musical composition employing computers (781.34) and computer science (004) or computer-assisted printing (686.22544) and computer sorting for library catalogs (025.3177).[3] If you looked up HEALTH, you would find dozens of references, including health care facilities (362.1) and their architecture (725.51), health foods (641.302), and health services in the United States during the Civil War (973.775).[4] The Relative Index does more than just list topics in alphabetical order with their associated class numbers. It also collocates the different contexts in which a single term might be used, or the different classes or disciplines in which a single topic might be found.

DDC is also available in an abridged edition suitable for general collections totaling up to 20,000 volumes.[5] Over the years, the abridged version has contained about one-tenth as many classification numbers as the unabridged. At this writing, the abridged version is in its 13th edition, published in one volume of just over 1,000 pages. Numbers in the abridged edition, although broader in meaning and shorter in total numbers than the full edition, are intended to be compatible with those in the full edition. Thus, this edition incorporates changed numbers for public administration, education, life sciences, plants, and animals, and new table numbers for the countries of the former Soviet Union.

DDC's main classes, based to some degree on an inversion of Bacon's classification of knowledge, include:

000	=	Generalities	500	=	Natural Sciences & Mathematics
100	=	Philosophy & Psychology	600	=	Technology (Applied Sciences)
200	=	Religion	700	=	The Arts
300	=	Social Sciences	800	=	Literature & Rhetoric
400	=	Language	900	=	Geography & History

In covering knowledge in only 10 main classes, DDC forces some odd companions into a single class. For example, in the 100s, philosophy, psychology, and the occult are found grouped together. Statistics, etiquette, commerce, and war share the 300s with sociology, economics, political science, law, and education. The 700s, primarily covering the arts, also include sports and games, played both indoors and outdoors. Geography and history are grouped together in the 900s in one large main class, even though they are quite different topics. One might expect to find library science with the social sciences, education, or both, but, instead, it is located in the 000s (read this as *zero hundreds*) along with research, publishing, and other generalities.

At the start of the second volume are three summaries of numbers: the 10 main classes; the one hundred divisions; and the thousand sections. (These summaries are also available as a separate pamphlet.[6]) This is a good place to begin when one is trying to assign a Dewey number for an unfamiliar topic. The first and most important decision made in the process (after deciding about the topic itself, of course) is the choice of an appropriate main class.[7] It would be much easier to have only one place to put a book on computers, for example. But if the book emphasizes the machinery, it is classified with other books on machinery, in the 600s, applied science and technology. If it emphasizes the mathematics of programming, it is more logically classed with other books on mathematics, in the 500s. If it emphasizes the programs and applications, it is classed nearer to research in the 000s. A video about trucks might emphasize the truck as a machine or a type of vehicle (600s) or it might emphasize transportation via truck (300s).

In some cases, a classification number will be chosen to reflect the interests of a library or media center's users. For example, the book in Figure 11.1 concerns the Canada-United States free trade agreement. Depending on the library, either 382.971073, stressing Canada's agreements with the United States, or 382.973071, stressing the United States's agreements with Canada, are equally applicable. In both cases, assigning the full nine-digit number enables the classification to reflect an item involving both countries, no matter which of them comes first. The source of information for Figure 11.1 is on the next page, 218.

FIGURE 11.1

This example is an illustration of:
- joint authors
- other title information listed on title page before title proper
- detailed pagination
- bibliography and index note
- Library of Congress subject headings
- joint author added entry
- difference in Dewey decimal classification number according to emphasis desired
- 2nd level cataloging

```
Doern, G. Bruce.
   Faith & fear : the free trade story / G. Bruce Doern & Brian W.
Tomlin. -- Toronto : Stoddart, 1991.
   xi, 340 p. ; 24 cm.

   Includes references (p.319-333) and index.
   ISBN 0-7737-2534-2.

   1. Free trade -- Canada.  2. Free trade -- United States.  3. Canada
-- Commercial policy.  4. United States -- Commercial policy.  5. Canada
-- Commerce -- United States.  6. United States -- Commerce -- Canada.
I. Tomlin, Brian W.  II. Title.


Recommended DDC: 382.971073 (for Canadian emphasis)
                 or
                 382.973071 (for U.S. emphasis)
```

Fig. 11.1—Continues

FIGURE 11.1 *(continued)*

(chief source of information)
          (title page)

                                        (information on verso)

THE FREE TRADE STORY

FAITH
&FEAR

G. BRUCE DOERN & BRIAN W. TOMLIN

Copyright © 1991 by G. Bruce Doern and Brian W. Tomlin

First published in 1991 by
Stoddart Publishing Co. Limited
34 Lesmill Road
Toronto, Canada
M3B 2T6

ISBN 0-7737-2534-2

Cover Design: Leslie Styles
Typesetting: Tony Gordon Ltd.

Printed and bound in the United States of America

DDC allows options in classification for some topics. Biography is one of these. DDC states that the preferred method is to place a biography with the topic for which the person is well known. The biography of Conrad Black in Figure 11.2 has been classified in economic production. However, DDC provides an alternate series of numbers in the 920s for libraries that want to shelve all biographies together. DDC suggests the following options:

a) Use the 920-928 schedule, for example, 923.871 (biography of Canadian persons in commerce, communication, transportation).
b) Use 92 for individual biographies.
c) Use B (indicating Biography) for individual biographies.
d) Use 920.71 for biographies of men, 920.72 for biographies of women.

In addition, the following practice is found in many libraries:

e) Use 920 for collected biographies, and 921 for individual biographies.

A good rule of thumb to remember about classification is that it aims to bring related works together. To do this, one can look in the library or media center's shelflist or on the shelves to see what kinds of subjects were assigned to any particular number under consideration. If they do not appear to be related to the work in hand, one should look elsewhere for the classification number.

FIGURE 11.2

This example is an illustration of:
- other title information
- publication date not listed, copyright date given
- work containing illustrations of specific types
- index note
- two ISBNs (one that applies to item in hand given)
- ISBN qualified
- DDC explained
- DDC prime mark
- 2nd level cataloging

```
Newman, Peter C.
    The establishment man : a portrait of power / by Peter C. Newman. --
Toronto : McClelland and Stewart, c1982.
    349 p. : genealogical table, port. ; 25 cm.

    Includes index.
    ISBN 0-7710-6785-2 (trade).

    1. Black, Conrad.  2. Businessmen -- Canada -- Biography.
3. Capitalists and financiers -- Canada -- Biography.  I. Title.


Recommended DDC: 338'.092
                 338 (production)
                   092 (biography)
```

(chief source of information)

(title page)

The Establishment Man
A Portrait of Power

BY
Peter C. Newman

(information on verso)

© 1982, Power Reporting Limited

All rights reserved. The use of any part of this publication reproduced, transmitted in any form or by any means, electronic, mechanical, photocopying, recording, or otherwise, or stored in a retrieval system, without the prior consent of the publisher is an infringement of the copyright law.

The Canadian Publishers
McClelland and Stewart Limited
25 Hollinger Road
Toronto, Ontario M4B 3G2

McClelland and Stewart

Throughout the schedules, selected numbers are left blank (or "unoccupied") to allow for future expansion without disturbing the existing classes. In the 000s, for example, 007-009, 024, 029, and 040-049 are unoccupied. Although many areas of the 500s and 600s are very crowded, having classes with seven or more digits, 517, 518, 524, 626, 654-656, and 699 are unoccupied. Each of the main classes has two or more unoccupied sections; the 000s and 200s have entire divisions that are not assigned.

"Copy" Classification

Many people use the Dewey numbers provided by LC in the CIP information located on the verso of the title pages of books, or they find Dewey numbers in computer network records, such as OCLC. If so, certain conventions followed by larger institutions should be understood. The most important is the method used to show where numbers have been expanded. An apostrophe (also called a *prime* or *hash* mark) is placed at the end of the basic number and again after each complete expansion of a number (see Figure 11.2 for an example of a prime mark).

Some agencies prefer that numbers not become too long and institute policies to limit them. Such policies should involve the addition or omission of expansions; for example, to limit a classification number to the basic number, or to one or more expansions beyond the basic number. They should not dictate a stated number of digits, such as no more than four digits after the decimal point, because for some numbers, the meaning of the categories that digits in an expansion represent would be lost. For example, the correct DDC number for slavery in ancient Athens is 306.3620385. This is a very long number that would only be necessary if a library or media center has (or expects to have) many items about ancient Athenian slavery in its collection. The length assigned to the number can be limited in the following ways according to the needs of the collection:

306	culture and institutions
306.3	economic institutions
306.36	systems of labor
306.362	slavery
306.36203	slavery in the ancient world
306.362038	slavery in ancient Greece
306.3620385	slavery in ancient Athens

A second convention that should be noted is the fact that some libraries furnish more than the class number, adding shelf marks such as cutters, call letters, etc., to it. When using another library's catalog records, shelf marks should be ignored unless it is a local policy to follow these practices, also. If so, then one must be careful about *whose* practices are followed. In some places, the initial letter of the main entry is used in place of a cutter number. In others, two- or three-digit cutters are used. It might be confusing to adopt all of these practices simultaneously. Letters or numbers that indicate an item is part of the reference collection or a departmental or branch collection, and dates indicating different editions of a work, are not part of their Dewey classification numbers.

A Closer Look at the Schedules

In this section, DDC's main classes are explored in greater detail, noting the subjects each includes for materials typically found in public libraries and school library media centers; however, no attempt is made here to list all the subjects included in the main classes. Familiarity with the schedules is best acquired by using them, together with one's shelflist and common sense.

000s: Generalities includes works about knowledge in general; research; communication in general; computers; controversial knowledge such as UFOs, the Loch Ness monster, and the Bermuda Triangle; reference materials such as bibliographies and catalogs; library and information science, including reading in general; encyclopedias and other encyclopedic works; organizations; publishing; and collections that cover many topics.

100s: Philosophy, Paranormal Phenomena, and Psychology, concepts and schools of thought are covered here in detail, as well as the occult; the entire field of psychology; logic; and ethics (subtitled *moral philosophy*).

200s: Religion is one of the most straightforward classes, dealing entirely with this one subject area. Two changes were made to the 21st edition in an effort to address longtime criticism that the great majority of numbers represent topics in Christianity, leaving few sections for all topics relating to all the other religions of the world. The bias is traceable to literary warrant in nineteenth-century U.S. college libraries, where collecting was largely confined to books about the Christian religion, and it has persisted for more than a century. First, the most general numbers, 201-209, which were devoted to generalities of Christianity only, were relocated to 230-270 with other topics in Christianity. Second, 296 and 297 covering Judaism and Islam, respectively, were revised and expanded.

300s: Social Sciences, in keeping with its label, covers sociology, political science, economics, law, public administration, and social problems. It also includes statistics (but in this case referring to demographic statistics, not probability theory, which is found in mathematics); military science, education; commerce; and an odd group of topics headed "Customs, Etiquette, and Folklore," under which subtopics such as marriage, death, war, holidays, chivalry, suicide, and cannibalism are subsumed. A major revision was made in public administration (351-354) in the 1996 21st unabridged edition, followed by a similar update in 1997 in the 13th abridged edition.

400s: Language is a perfectly straightforward class. Language in general (i.e., linguistics) is covered first, followed by individual languages beginning with English and other Western European languages. Preferential positioning of English and European languages probably is due to literary warrant and the fact that this is an American scheme, but the schedules include an instruction explaining how classifiers can give local emphasis to any other language of their choice.

500s: Natural Sciences and Mathematics includes mathematics, astronomy, chemistry, physics, geology, the sciences of the ancient world, paleontology and paleozoology, and the life sciences, first in general and then the separate subjects of botany (called "Plants" in the 1996 edition) and zoology (called "Animals" in the 1996 edition). The life sciences (560-590) underwent a major revision in the 1996 unabridged and 1997 abridged editions. As mentioned previously, computer programming will be found at 519.7, immediately after probability theory and statistical mathematics. Examining the subdivisions of computer programming, however, shows that materials classed here really are concerned with the mathematical process of programming, not the applications themselves; that is, *computer programs,* which are found in the 000s.

600s: Technology (Applied Sciences) includes medicine, engineering, agriculture (both raising plant crops and animal husbandry), management, manufacturing, and buildings (but not architecture, which is found in the next main class, fine arts) as well as home economics and family living. Popular topics for users of public libraries and media centers found here include parenting, pets, cookbooks, gardening, and automobiles. Many very fine distinctions must be made between pure and applied sciences, necessitating careful examination of other works in one's collection to bring together related items; for example, between botany (580) and horticulture (630), or between immunity in animals (591.29) and immunity in human beings (616.079).

700s: The Arts, Fine and Decorative Arts, as previously mentioned, combines the familiar topics of art in general, architecture, painting, sculpture, crafts, etc., and music, with performing and recreational arts. Thus, one finds circuses, movies, and television at 791, titled generically "Public performances"; theater, vaudeville, and ballet, called "Stage presentations" are at 792; and other kinds of dancing are grouped at 793 as "Indoor games and amusements," together with puzzles, riddles, magic, etc. The characterization of television as a "public performance" and folk dancing as an "indoor amusement" may be leftover nineteenth-century perceptions. We might be more inclined to think of television as an indoor amusement, and in some small towns folk dances are held outdoors as public events even if they are not professional public performances. Games of skill, including computer games and chess, are classed in 794, whereas games of chance (where some might prefer putting computer games) are in 795. Bowling is classed as an "indoor game of skill," in 794, whereas baseball and football are at 796 with other "Athletic and outdoor sports and games." The distinctions are, perhaps, transparent to those who watch all three sports and more on their television sets. "Aquatic and air sports" are at 797, and outdoor sports that bring people closer to nature—horseback riding, animal racing, hunting, and fishing—are found at 798 and 799. An interesting placement in the 700s is photography. One might expect that photographic art and techniques would be found under different main classes, in much the same way computer software and hardware are separated, but the entire section 770-779 is devoted to the art of photography, its techniques, and its processes. Specialists who see film and television art as a subset of photographic arts in general might be critical of the separation of these topics. The music schedule (780-789), although it resembles all the other schedules in outward appearance, was revised completely in the twentieth edition, and is, in actuality, a faceted scheme based on the British Classification for Music.

800s: Literature (Belle-Lettres) and Rhetoric in general is followed in this class by the individual literatures of different countries, beginning, as one might expect, with American literature in English. An instruction here similar to the one for languages enables a different national or language's literature to be assigned the preferential position, if desired. English and Anglo-Saxon literatures are followed by European literatures, including Latin and Greek, both ancient and modern, consuming all but the final 10 sections, 890-899. Into these last few numbers are squeezed all of Asian, Middle Eastern, and African literature as well as Russian, Polish, and other languages less familiar to North Americans. Shakespeare is the only author with his own number, 822.33. The citation order in the 800s is strictly observed: country or language first, followed by genre and chronological period, but only the most popular literatures have defined periods. Three tables for literature (see later) augment what can be represented.

900s: Geography, History, and Auxiliary Disciplines, the final class, begins with three divisions for general works on both geography and history (900-909), general works on geography alone, including travel books (910-919), and biography (920-929). Regarding biography, however, application policies given in the manual and used at LC's Decimal Classification Office recommend using the 920s solely for collective biographies, and classing the life stories of individuals in the subjects with which each is associated. Thus, biographies of mathematicians Gauss and Lobachevski, who pioneered non-Euclidian geometry, would be in 516.9 with that subject, and a biography of Sigmund Freud would be in 150, with other works on psychology. The other seven divisions (930-999) are devoted to history alone, beginning with a division for the ancient world and followed by one each for the continents of Europe, Asia, Africa, North America, and South America. All other countries and regions are grouped into the final division, including the final section, 999, for extraterrestrial worlds.

A Closer Look at the Tables

Because many instructions require use of the tables, a closer look at them may be helpful. Each number in the tables is preceded by a dash to show that it may not be used alone, but must be attached to a number from the schedules.

Table 1: "Standard Subdivisions" is the table most frequently used, because applying it does not require an explicit instruction in the schedules. There are frequent instructions in the schedules, however, to apply the standard subdivisions in special ways. These instructions must be heeded and supersede the unfettered application of numbers from Table 1. The entire list is preceded by a table of precedence directing classifiers on how to handle items having several applicable subdivisions.

DDC's mnemonics are recognizable to a great degree in the standard subdivisions. The philosophy of a subject is designated -01, just as the 100s represent that field; -06 stands for organizations and management, just as the 650s stand for management; -09 stands for historical and geographic treatment, just as the 900s stand for those fields. The analogies are not complete, however. -05 stands for serial publications, not scientific aspects, -08 stands for history and description of a subject among groups of persons, not literary treatments, etc.

Table 2: Table 2 "Geographic Areas, Historical Periods, Persons" and all other tables that follow can be used only when an explicit instruction in the schedules directs classifiers to do so. Table 2 gives numbers for geographic areas, beginning with general areas such as frigid zones at -11 (-113 if they are north of the equator and -116 if they are south of it), or land and landforms at -14. Locations in the ancient world are identified by -3 in this table, whereas those in the modern world are assigned numbers between -4 and -9. Some locales, particularly in the United States, have their own specific numbers; for example, the borough of Manhattan in New York City is -7471. Other much larger areas do not. The entire continent of Antarctica is represented by -989 and the whole universe of worlds outside of Earth has just one class, -99. Table 2 has another major use. When standard subdivision -09 is added to a number to show that a topic is limited to a particular place, the cataloger is instructed to go to Table 2 for a number to represent the area, and add it to the -09. For example, if an item is about forestlands in France, the number is 333.75'09'44. The first five digits represent forestlands in general, and the addition of -09 from Table 1 represents geographical treatment, and, following the instruction there, the addition of -44 from Table 2 represents France. Major changes to this table in the 21st edition and subsequent updates, some available at the DDC Web site, *Dewey for Windows,* or both address the breakup of the Soviet Union (-47) and Yugoslavia and other political changes affecting jurisdictions and boundaries.[8]

Table 3: Numbers from this table, titled "Subdivisions for the Arts, for Individual Literatures, for Specific Literary Forms" are designed to be used with 810-890 from the main schedules, namely, the numbers for various individual literatures. Table 3 is made up of three subordinate tables: Table 3-A, "Subdivisions for Works by or about Individual Authors;" Table 3-B, 700.4, 791.4, "Subdivisions for Works by or about More than One Author;" and Table 3-C, "Notation to Be Added Where Instructed in Table 3-B and in 808-809." In Tables 3-A and 3-B, the general categories of genre and criticism are subdivided finely for arranging very large collections of literary materials about authors. In Table 3-C, different categories with their subdivisions are found, such as literary qualities, themes, etc., to be used for arranging very large collections of general literary criticism.

Table 4: Titled "Subdivisions of Individual Languages and Language Families," its numbers are used, according to instructions, with numbers 420-490 from the main schedules. Among the most frequently used numbers from this table are -3, which represents dictionaries, and -86, which stands for readers. The numbers in this table do not all represent publication forms, however, but various other characteristics of language materials; for example, -5 is "grammar of the standard form of the language."

Table 5: This table, titled "Racial, Ethnic, National Groups," contains numbers for racial, ethnic, and national groups, organized more-or-less by geographic origins; for example, -1 stands for North Americans, -2 for people of the British Isles, -3 for Nordics, etc. There are some interesting divisions in this table; for example, Modern Latins (-4) does not include Italians, Romanians, and related groups, who have their own numbers beginning -5, or Spanish and Portuguese peoples, whose numbers begin with -6. The -6s do, however, include all Spanish-Americans at (-68) as well as Brazilians, subsumed under Portuguese-speaking peoples at -69. The number for groups not previously given their own numbers, -9, includes Semites, North Africans, Asians, Africans, and all native peoples (this is DDC's terminology, not the authors') of America and Australia. Individual peoples within this large grouping are given their own numbers, also; for example, Sri Lankans are at -91413 and Gypsies are at -91497. There is an option in Table 5 to class a group other than North Americans at -1 if a library or media center wishes to give local emphasis to that group.

Table 6: The table for "Languages" contains numbers for languages of the world, but is not intended to be used with the 400 class. Instead, it provides for representing the language characteristics of materials classed in other schedules. If, for example, one is classifying a translation of the Bible into Dutch, the notation for Dutch language, -3931, is added to the number for the Bible, 220.5, to form the precise class for Dutch-language Bibles, 220.53931. Here, as in the 400s, 800s, and elsewhere, there is an option to class a particular language first, at -1. English (-2) and European languages (-3 to -8) are given preference, and all the African, Asian, etc., languages are found in -9. Table 6, similar to several of the others, is a tiny encyclopedia of the world's languages, enumerated in just 25 pages.

Table 7: The final table, "Groups of Persons," identifies types of persons, with each section of the table representing a particular characteristic such as age, sex, race, ethnicity, nationality, etc. The category for young adults, interestingly, covers persons from 12 to 20 years of age, not the teenage years from 13 to 19 as one might expect. Children are divided into three groupings: infants, birth to two years of age; preschool, three to five years of age; and school ages, six to eleven. This is a curious division, because it cuts off sixth-graders from other elementary school-aged children and promotes them to young adulthood. (Because most schools group children into grades Kindergarten (K) through 4 or K through 6, or, occasionally, K through 8, but rarely K through 5, one wonders how DDC arrived at their decisions. And if age is the primary distinguishing feature, why are the terms *preschool* and *school children* used at all?) The specificity in this table is quite deep, with numbers assigned to subgroups such as Black Muslims at -2977 and insurance agents at -368.

New classifiers are reminded to use Tables 2 through 7 solely when instructions for a number from the main schedules tells them to do so. Only the numbers from Table 1 (standard subdivisions) can be used without explicit directions in the main schedules. At the same time, classifiers must be alert to instructions limiting or changing the normal pattern for standard subdivisions. They may be directed to use -001 to -009 in place of the usual -01 to -09; or they may be instructed to use -03 to -09, which means the first two standard subdivisions (-01 and -02) cannot be used for the particular number or number span to which the instruction applies. Although situations sometimes arise for which there are no instructions in either the schedule or the manual, the editors try to give as much guidance as possible about the way table numbers should be assigned.

Conclusion

DDC is widely used all over the world. It is the basis for the Universal Decimal Classification and some national classifications as well (for example, in Korea and Japan). Its popularity in the United Kingdom is assured by its use in the *British National Bibliography* and all the British Library's authoritative online cataloging. Its flexibility is sufficient to serve many purposes, and its ease of use is enhanced by the mnemonics, the Relative Index, and its easily grasped overall logic.

In the next chapter, a brief look is given to DDC's only major rival in U.S. and Canadian libraries—the Library of Congress classification. However, before going on readers may want to try their hands at assigning DDC numbers to the examples in Figure 11.3. Answers are in Appendix C.

Figure 11.3

1. TITLE: *Distance learning : a list*
    SUMMARY: Correspondence schools operating in Ontario, Canada, are listed and described with details of their degree programs and curricula.

2. TITLE: *Birds of a feather*
    SUMMARY: Interesting facts about birds are revealed in the letters of famous ornithologists.

3. TTLE: *Mythology and the Conquistadors*
    SUMMARY: An examination of Spanish-language mythology in Spain, Mexico, and Peru.

Fig. 11.3—Continues

FIGURE 11.4 *(continued)*

4.   TITLE: *Food from the sea*
        SUMMARY: A description of the life cycle of crabs and oysters.

5.   TITLE: *More food from the sea*
        SUMMARY: A description of the life cycle of lobsters, clams, and eels.

6.   TITLE: *Training your new poodle*
        SUMMARY: Illustrated guide to training pet poodles.

7.   TITLE: *New England's small-town treasures*
        SUMMARY: Text and pictures about the museums in the small towns of New England.

8.   TITLE: *The way things work*
        SUMMARY: Description of simple and complex mechanical devices from the inclined plane to microcomputers and flight simulators.

9.   TITLE: *Forest Hills : an illustrated history*
        SUMMARY: History of the New York City community and its West Side Tennis Club, formerly the site of the U.S. Open tennis tournament from 1874 to 1975.

10.   TITLE: *House*
        SUMMARY: Detailed description of the building of a house, from the initial concepts to the day the owners move in.

—————

Recommended Reading

Chan, Lois Mai, John P. Comaromi, Joan S. Mitchell, and Mohinder P. Satija. *Dewey Decimal Classification: A Practical Guide.* Dublin, OH: OCLC-Forest Press, 1996.

Davis, Sydney W., and Gregory R. New. *Abridged 13 Workbook for Small Libraries Using Dewey Decimal Classification Abridged Edition 13.* Dublin, OH: OCLC-Forest Press, 1997.

Dewey Decimal Classification [Web site]: http://www.purl.org/oclc/fp.

Green, Rebecca, ed. *Knowledge Organization and Change: Proceedings of the 4th International ISKO Conference, Washington, D.C., 1996.* Frankfurt: INDEKS Verlag, forthcoming.

Holley, Robert P., ed. *Dewey: An International Perspective: Papers from a Workshop on the Dewey Decimal Classification and DDC 20 Presented at the General Conference of the International Federation of Library Associations and Institutions (IFLA), Paris, France, 1989.* Munich: Saur, 1991.

Liu, Songqiao. "The Automatic Decomposition of DDC Synthesized Numbers." Ph.D. diss., University of California at Los Angeles, 1993.

Mitchell, Joan S. "Options in the Dewey Decimal Classification System: The Current Perspective." *Cataloging & Classification Quarterly* 19, nos. 3 and 4 (1995): 89-103.

Mitchell, Joan S., and Mark A. Crook. "A Study of Libraries Using the Dewey Decimal Classification in the OCLC Online Union Catalog: Preliminary Findings." In *Annual Review of OCLC Research 1994,* 47-50. Dublin, OH: OCLC, 1995.

Mortimer, Mary. *Learn Dewey Decimal Classification (Edition 21).* Lanham, MD: Scarecrow Press, 2000.

O'Neill, Edward T., and Patrick McClain. "Copy Cataloging Practices: Use of the Call Number by Dewey Libraries." In *Annual Review of OCLC Research 1995,* 11-15. Dublin, OH: OCLC, 1996.

Sifton, Pat et al. *Workbook for DDC 21: Dewey Decimal Classification Edition 21.* Ottawa: Canadian Library Association, 1998.

Vizine-Goetz, Diane, and Joan S. Mitchell. "Dewey 2000." In *Annual Review of OCLC Research 1995,* 16-19. Dublin, OH: OCLC, 1996.

Winkel, Lois. *Subject Headings for Children: A List of Subject Headings Used by the Library of Congress with Abridged Dewey Numbers Added.* 2nd ed. 2 volumes. Dublin, OH: OCLC-Forest Press, 1998.

Notes

1.   Lois Mai Chan et al., *Dewey Decimal Classification, A Practical Guide* (Albany, NY: Forest Press/OCLC, 1996), 8.

2.   The manual for the 19th edition of DDC was published as a separate title: *Manual on the Use of the Dewey Decimal Classification,* ed. John P. Comaromi et al. (Albany, NY: Forest Press, 1982). Its incorporation into the classification proper was made with the 20th edition, also edited by Comaromi.

3.   *Dewey Decimal Classification and Relative Index,* 21st ed., ed. Joan S. Mitchell et al. (Albany, NY: Forest Press/OCLC, 1996), vol. 4, 172-174. (Hereinafter DDC21.)

4.   Ibid., 352-353.

5.   *Abridged Dewey Classification and Relative Index,* 13th ed. (Dublin, OH: Forest Press/OCLC, 1997).

6.   *DDC 21 Summaries.* Dublin, OH: OCLC-Forest Press, 1999.

7.   "The guiding principle of the DDC is that a work is classed in the discipline for which it is intended rather than in the discipline from which the work derives." DDC21, vol. 1, xxx.

8.   DDC issued the following update to table 2: *Table 2. Geographic Areas: Great Britain and Republic of South Africa* (Dublin, OH: OCLC-Forest Press, 1999).

12

Library of Congress Classification

Introduction

The Library of Congress classification (LCC) is the result of applying very practical solutions to practical problems. When the library's collections were destroyed by fire during the War of 1812, Thomas Jefferson sold Congress his personal library, then numbering about 7,000 volumes, as the basis for establishing a new collection. Along with the materials came Jefferson's own classification system, which remained in place until the turn of the twentieth century. Herbert Putnam, then the new Librarian of Congress, implemented many changes at LC, including the launching of a new classification. The choice was not an easy one. DDC was in its fifth edition at the time, and Cutter's Expansive Classification, a popular rival, was in its sixth. But, after consideration of these and other alternatives, Putnam and Charles Martel, LC's chief cataloger, decided to devise a new and different scheme having as its primary objective solely the orderly arrangement of LC's current and future holdings. They wanted to avoid adopting an existing scheme into which LC's holdings had to conform.

One result of the main objective—organizing LC's holdings for effective retrieval—was to release LC from any obligation to a higher authority, such as the DDC's editors. (LC has total control over the classification.) Another was to permit literary warrant to govern the scheme, which evolved into a loose federation of schedules, each fitting a particular subject area according to what LC owned and expected to add in the years to come. Although several overarching principles are found throughout LCC, each schedule is an individual entity in which the breakdown and organization of the subjects need not relate to any other schedule. Thus, some schedules are in their fourth or fifth editions, whereas others may be in a third, and the most recently developed schedules (for the law of particular countries) are still in their first editions (for example, KDZ, KG, KH, Law of the Americas, Latin America, and the West Indies, was first published in 1984; KE, and KJ-KKZ, Law of Europe, was first published in 1989). Toward the end of the twentieth century, LC abandoned numbered editions in favor of dated editions.

LCC is updated on a continual basis. The latest decisions on new or revised classification numbers are disseminated between editions through publication in *Additions and Changes* (A&C), a quarterly newsletter from LC's Subject Cataloging Division, via LC's Web site, and in the classification's computer-based version, *Classification Plus*. Printed cumulations of newly established, dropped, and altered numbers are published irregularly by Gale Group, formerly known as Gale Research.

Other aids to using LCC for original classifying include LCSH (for general guidance only; numbers listed there should never be used without consulting the schedules themselves) and the *Library of Congress Shelflist in Microform,* a listing of LC's holdings by call number, including official cutter numbers and other shelf marks (available from University Microfilms International, the United States Historical Documents Institute, or both). Several indexes to the scheme as a whole have been marketed commercially.[1] Textbook-style explanations of LCC (similar to what follows in this chapter) are available in several basic cataloging texts, but the most complete guide is Lois Mai Chan's *A Guide to the Library of Congress Classification.*[2]

Principles Underlying the LCC

Eight principles underlie the organization and structure of LCC:

1. *Classification by discipline.* Like DDC, LCC divides knowledge first into disciplines, but there are 21 rather than 10, and the concept of what constitutes a "discipline" differs considerably from Dewey (see Figure 12.1).

2. *Literary warrant.* This principle, which dictates that classes be created only when materials exist that require them, operates much more importantly in LCC than it does in DDC. In DDC, literary warrant acts more as a priority check, because DDC attempts to classify all knowledge, not just the knowledge covered by existing documents. (Even DDC does not include all potential subjects, because to do so would require an infinite number of classes.) LCC aims only to classify all of LC's holdings, not all knowledge, as already explained. As a result, it is relieved of the need to anticipate and accommodate topics outside LC's collecting interests. The experts who devised the original schedule created numbers for existing holdings and for those topical areas in which they believed publication would flourish *and* LC would continue collecting.

3. *Geographical arrangement.* As might be expected in the course of legislative research, inquiries often involve particular places. As a result, subarrangement by geographical location often is preferred over subarrangement by other characteristics geared to a subject's "natural" hierarchy.

4. *Alphabetical arrangement.* A second subarrangement technique employed by LCC is cutter numbers, which alphabetize when they are applied. LCC cutters many elements throughout the schedules, including geographic names, topical terms, and personal names. Although cutters are thought of as mnemonic devices, they do not assist memory very much in LCC, because they are applied differently in different parts of the schedules; that is, there is no guarantee that the same term will be cuttered identically if it appears in different places, or, conversely, that the same cutter will represent the same word or name in different places in the classification.

5. *Economy of notation.* LCC uses mixed notation, employing both alphabetic and numeric characters. It can represent extremely narrow topics with a smaller number of characters than DDC uses for topics at the same level of specificity.

6. *Close classification.* LCC originated at a time when LC's collection contained more than one million books and was devised to handle not only this many items, but an ever-growing total. Thus, it assumes a deep specificity that DDC does not, even though DDC can be extended to accommodate equally deep levels of specificity. Classifiers are more likely to find in LCC a number that matches the topic of an item being classified than they are if they use DDC—provided, of course, that LC collects in this subject area.

7. *Enumeration.* Similar to DDC, LCC enumerates a very large proportion of the classes it provides and minimizes the use of number-building devices that allow classifiers to synthesize their own classes. The enormous size of LCC is evidence of its major reliance on enumeration.

8. *Relative location.* Like DDC, LCC employs the principle of relative location, although its use of geographic and alphabetic subarrangements tends to fragment materials related to one another in a topical hierarchy.

Like DDC, none of the principles operate perfectly throughout the whole LCC classification, but are observed as long as they do not conflict, create unwanted juxtapositions of subjects, or interfere with practical considerations. Enumeration sometimes is abandoned to save space; choices between geographic, alphabetic, and topical subarrangements may be forced; and other principles may be modified as LC's managers desire. Nevertheless, the operation of the principles can be observed throughout the schedules.

In addition to the eight principles, the following seven-point intellectual structure devised by Charles Martel may be seen in the arrangement of materials within classes and subclasses. However, current policies have abandoned it, so it will not be visible in newly created numbers.

1. *Form.* The first few numbers of classes and subclasses are allocated to general form subdivisions, including periodicals, often linked with society publications, yearbooks, congresses, documents, exhibitions and museums, and directories.

2. *Theory and philosophy.*

3. *History and biography.*

4. *Treatises and general works.*

5. *Law.* Until the completion of the K classes, legal materials focusing on a subject were classed with the subject; for example, building codes were classed in TH219 with building construction, TH9500 with fire prevention, etc. Since the publication of separate law classes, these numbers have been deleted and the materials relocated within K.

6. *Education.* Materials dealing with study, teaching, and research on a subject as well as textbooks on that subject, are included in this section.

7. *Specific subjects and subdivisions.* These numbers were likely to be the bulk of the schedules. Martel's seven-point structure was also applied to topics at each level of hierarchy. For example, TH1 is "Periodicals and societies" for building construction as a whole; TH1061 is "Periodicals, societies, etc." for systems of building construction; and TH2430 is "Periodicals, societies, congresses, etc." for roofing. Not every

topic has a number for periodicals; for example, floors and flooring, the topic following roofing, does not. The existence of a special number for periodicals depended not only on the logical structure, but on the likelihood that periodicals will be developed for particular subjects and that LC would collect and classify them. Note that the phrase used differs in each of the three instances in the example, combining different types of materials.

Format of the Schedules

More than forty separate volumes of schedules comprise LCC at this writing (also available on a CD-ROM, mentioned previously, titled *Classification Plus*). Although in general each volume represents a different discipline or subject area, some fields are divided among several volumes; for example, Class P, literature, is contained in 11 volumes plus a separate volume of tables. Each volume contains many, if not all, of the following parts:

1. *Preface.* Only a paragraph or two in length, the preface gives a history of the schedule's initial issue, name(s) of its originator(s), the dates of subsequent editions and, sometimes, their authors, and the contents of the current volume.

2. *Synopsis.* This overview lists the primary divisions of the class or subclass, and is, necessarily, very broad. For example, the synopsis of Class S, Agriculture, contains six divisions: S (General), SB (Plant culture), SD (Forestry), SF (Animal culture), SH (Aquaculture), and SK (Hunting sports).

3. *Outline.* A summary of the main subdivisions of the class, the outline will indicate the way topics in a particular field are arranged and can be very helpful in leading the classifier to appropriate parts of the schedule within the volume. From time to time, a cumulation of all the outlines has been published, which has proved very helpful both to classifiers and searchers.

4. *Schedule.* This is the complete enumeration, comprising nearly all of the volume itself.

5. *Tables.* Most LCC tables are designed to be used with one class number and are printed with it in the pages of the schedule, but selected tables intended for use with several parts of a schedule can be printed at the end of a subclass or at the back of a volume. Unlike DDC, which has seven auxiliary tables to be used throughout all of its schedules, LCC has only three interschedule (auxiliary) schedules: cutter numbers for countries of the world; states of the United States and provinces of Canada; and cities. The three auxiliary tables are not printed in all volumes, but appear in H, T, and Z. Other tables, such as those used with the P schedules, are published separately from the schedules.

6. *Index.* Originally, only some of the volumes were indexed, but now all have a volume-specific index. The lack of a combined index for the classification as a whole, however, is one of LCC's most serious drawbacks.

7. *Supplement.* Encountered in the past, supplements were small gatherings of new, deleted, or changed numbers not cumulated into the main part of the volume. Supplemental numbers usually had their own index, and the burden of consulting supplemental information, if present, was on the classifier.

Equally troublesome for classifiers as the lack of a combined index for LCC is the lack of coordination between LCSH and LCC. Not only are the classification numbers in LCSH simply suggestions, not prescribed for the topics where they are given, but the terminology for a topic may differ considerably between the two tools. Scope notes and helpful instructions are largely missing from LCC schedules, although there are a few cryptic aids for classifiers; for example, at S414 (Calendars. Yearbooks. Almanacs) it notes: "Popular farmers' almanacs in AY, e.g., AY81.F3."[3]

Originally, volumes of LCC were typeset and printed, attractively and sturdily bound in heavy-duty library bindings. In the recent past, they were issued in hastily reproduced type-scripts, bound in paper. Currently, computer processing has made the pages of newly issued volumes look neater, more attractive, and more consistent in their format, whereas the distinctive dark blue and white paper covers now used serve to identify them on the shelves, even if they fail to protect the pages as well as cloth bindings. Libraries often rebind them to ensure that they remain in good condition despite heavy use. Clearly, the CD-ROM version is far more convenient to store, search, and use, although it is costly. The CD-ROM version is also more up-to-date and does not require a shelf of supplements listing the new, changed, and deleted numbers between editions.

Main Classes of LCC

The main classes in LCC are designated by letters of the alphabet. Depending on how one counts, one or two letters can define a main class. For example, if one takes the broad view, P stands for languages and literatures, whereas PR is English literature, and PS is American and Canadian literature. The same idea is applicable to B (Philosophy and religion), H (Social science), and K (Law), which may be seen broadly as three individual classes or narrowly as several classes each. The other classes all are given one letter, with the exception of history, which encompasses four single letters (C, D, E, and F). A complete outline of LCC appears in Figure 12.1.

Figure 12.1   General outline of Library of Congress Classification

A	=	General works	M	=	Music
B	=	Philosophy and Religion	N	=	Fine arts
C	=	Auxiliary sciences of history	P	=	Literature
D	=	Old World history	Q	=	Science
E/F	=	New World history	R	=	Medicine
G	=	Geography	S	=	Agriculture
H	=	Social sciences	T	=	Technology
J	=	Political science	U	=	Military science
K	=	Law	V	=	Naval science
L	=	Education	Z	=	Bibliography

A quick perusal of the outline reveals several differences between LCC's and DDC's overall structures. First, several subjects grouped together in DDC are given their own schedules in LCC: agriculture and medicine are not part of technology; education, political science, law, and military and naval science are not part of social science; and generalities and bibliography are distinguished into two separate classes, A and Z, respectively, that are as far apart in the alphabet as possible. Second, the wide divergence between languages and literatures found in DDC is not present in LCC. Both are combined in P. Third, in LCC, music and fine arts each have their own schedule, separated from recreation, which is located at the end of the G schedule. Finally, history and geography, separated into several different schedules, are located toward the beginning of the scheme, immediately after religion, instead of at the end as they are in DDC. History and law are among LC's largest groups of holdings, so it is understandable that between them these two subject areas cover fifteen of the volumes, or nearly one-third of the scheme.

LC does not use the two schedules developed by NLC for materials relating to Canadian history and literature: FC (Canadian history) and PS8000 (Canadian literature). Canadian public libraries and school library media centers trying to assign more specific classification numbers to Canadian topics may prefer to use derived records from NLC rather than LC for those subject areas. Figure 9.6 demonstrates the difference in classification schedules for Canadian history.

Subdivision in LCC

The use of geographical location to subdivide a topic is frequently encountered in LCC. Geographic subdivisions can be arranged alphabetically or by area, and the latter arrangements often give preference to the United States, the countries of Europe, or both, and the western hemisphere. An example of this arrangement can be found at "Exploitation of timber trees" (S434-534). After a number for general works, the topic is further subdivided by country, beginning with the United States and followed by the rest of the Americas, Europe, Africa, Australia, New Zealand, Atlantic Islands, and, finally, Pacific Islands. Elsewhere, the countries are listed in alphabetical order, as can be seen in the next part of the schedule at "Plant culture: study and teaching" (SB51-52). In this case, SB51 is used for general works and SB52 is used to further subdivide the topic geographically with the instruction to add a cutter number, "By region or country, A-Z." This means that every country is assigned a cutter number using the initial letter of its name and one or more digits to represent a subsequent letter or letters, thus producing an alphabetical subarrangement.

Topical subdivisions under each geographic locality are sometimes represented by special number spans for different countries and sometimes by a different letter-and-number device resembling a cutter number. To subdivide the topic "Regulation, inspection, etc. of seeds" (SB114), one uses .A1 for the publications of societies, .A3 for general works, and .A4-Z for specific regions or countries. Although the first two subdivisions resemble cutter numbers, they do not represent words or names as ordinary cutters do. The United States has a special cutter number under the .A4-Z portion: .U6-7, where .U6 represents general works and .U7 is further subdivided by state, A-W. According to this instruction, a work about the inspection of seeds in the state of Georgia would be SB114.U7G+. (An additional level of subdivision allows the classifier to add a third cutter number to represent a specific locality within each state.)

Topical subdivisions of a subject unrelated to geographic locations also can be arranged alphabetically by means of the cuttering device. The S schedule is particularly rich in lists of cuttered subtopics such as different types of crops, ornamental plants, plant diseases, trees, etc. In the list of trees, some of the cuttering goes to five digits beyond the initial letter. Often, topical subdivisions are represented by numbers in a sequence of whole numbers. For example, in the HV schedule (Social pathology):

HV6085 = general works on the language of criminals

HV6089 = prison psychology

HV6093 = general works on intellectual and aesthetic characteristics of criminals

HV6097 = prison literature, wall inscriptions

HV6098 = tattooing

HV6099 = other forms of intellectual and aesthetic expression among criminals.

The lack of consistent treatments for similar subarrangements makes for an extremely complicated scheme. In addition, the lack of any major aids to its application makes LCC difficult to implement for original classification outside LC. Libraries and media centers that adopt LCC do so under the impression that they will find all or nearly all of the materials they buy already classified; they expect not to have to do much, if any, original classification.

Use of cutter numbers as part of the classification is one of the disadvantages of LCC for libraries other than LC; no one but LC can assign an official cutter number for anything—a location, a topic, or a book mark. Other libraries must wait until LC classifies an item requiring the appropriate cutter number before it is officially established. One might encounter a book on a particular type of tree that is not in the list given under SD397. If it is to be classified, you must guess at which numbers LC will use in the numeric portion of the cutter, and if there is any doubt as the proper name of the tree, the initial letter as well. (Take the following hypothetical example: Suppose you were assigning cutters for the different types of people who receive discount fares on public transit. Would you call student recipients "students" or "educational recipients," or would they be identified by their grade levels, "elementary" and "secondary"? Would older people be identified as "seniors," "aged," or "elderly"? Would civil servants be lumped into one group or divided into "police," "transit workers," "firefighters," etc.?)

LC establishes new cutter numbers after consulting its shelflist to see what already has been assigned. In doing so, its classifiers may decide that they should depart from their usual pattern, a simple formula with just a few rules (see Figure 12.2), because of some unique problem, or because of their expectation about future assignments likely to affect few libraries outside of LC.

The first element in an LC cutter number consists of the initial letter of the word to be represented, combined with one or more Arabic numerals chosen according to the following rules:

Figure 12.2   LC Rules for Creating Cutter Numbers

```
1. After initial vowels
        for the 2nd letter:  b   d   l,m   n   p   r   s,t   u,y
                use number:   2   3    4    5   6   7    8     9
2. After the initial letter S
        for the 2nd letter:  a   ch   e   h,i   m-p   t    u
                use number:   2    3   4    5     6   7-8   9
3. After the initial letters Qu
        for the 2nd letter:  a   e   i   o   r   y
                use number:   3   4   5   6   7   9
     for names beginning Qa-Qt
                        use:   2-29
4. After other initial consonants
        for the 2nd letter:  a   e   i   o   r   u   y
                use number:   3   4   5   6   7   8   9
5. When an additional number is preferred
        for the 3rd letter:  a-d   e-h   i-l   m   n-q   r-t   u-w   x-z
                use number:    2*    3     4    5    6     7     8     9
```

(*optional for 3rd letter a or b)

Subject Cataloging Manual: Shelflisting and *Subject Cataloging Manual: Classification,* the companion policy manuals to *Subject Cataloging Manual: Subject Headings,* are helpful for local classifiers in deciding on original cutters.[4] Another useful tool is LC's shelflist, which can be purchased on microfiche from University Films International.[5]

Comparison with DDC

Obviously, LCC has many more numbers and many more specific classes in which to place very narrowly defined topics. For example, LCC has individual numbers for most nineteenth-century English and American authors, and often individual numbers for each of their works. Contemporary U.S. authors are assigned numbers according to the first letter of their surnames. The difference is clear if you think about where to class Kurt Vonnegut. In DDC, he would join most of his contemporaries at 813.54 (U.S. writers of fiction working after 1945) and in LCC, he would join only those U.S. writers working after 1961 whose surnames begin with "V" at PS3572. That is quite a difference in specificity. The need for specificity is one reason large libraries such as the Boston Public Library and many university libraries turned to LCC.

Smaller libraries that made the change to LCC did so, however, not to achieve greater specificity, but to take advantage of the much larger proportion of titles classified in LCC than in DDC by the Library of Congress and other major originators of cataloging copy, freeing them from having to do as much original classification. Small- or medium-sized college libraries using OCLC thought that they would save a great deal of time (and, therefore, money) by copying the LCC numbers found online instead of doing original classification. The same advantage can accrue to public libraries and school library media centers, provided the titles they acquire are found in shared databases and have LC call numbers.

Another contrast is the nature of the classification number produced by each scheme. LCC numbers usually are shorter for topics of the same specificity, but their combination of alphabetic characters and numbers is not necessarily easier to remember or use. Some people may find the alphanumerics more understandable and logical, but others prefer the purely numerical system of DDC, particularly when libraries add cutter numbers as bookmarks and other marks in various alphanumerical sequences to the classification number to give each item a unique shelf location. This can result in very complicated combinations of all sorts of characters, including upper- and lowercase letters, whole and decimal numbers, and punctuation. To accommodate all of this information on books with narrow spines, libraries often break up the arrangement of the classification number into several lines. It may be hard to tell where the class numbers end and the bookmarks begin, or what follows what; for example, should JX1977.8.C53q1984 come before or after JX1977.D5b1987? (In the Simmons College library, it would come afterward.)

The general use of cutter numbers in all libraries as bookmarks or shelfmarks becomes confusing when they are also part of the classification numbers. It is especially confusing when an item has several cutter numbers, perhaps with one denoting geographic location, another denoting a topic subdivision, and a third for the shelfmark.

LCC's methods of subdividing are quite different from DDC's. One of LCC's favorites, shown in the previous examples, is to add cutter numbers for subtopics or geographical subdivisions (or, sometimes, for both). LCC also uses numerical expansions to subdivide topics; but they are added differently. When DDC instructs classifiers to add to a number, it means that some other number from a table or another section of the schedule will be tacked on to a base number from the schedules. For example, to expand the number for cooking, 641.5, to French cooking, one adds 9, representing geographic focus and 44 for France, to obtain 641.5944. In LCC, the instruction to add a number from a table to a base number in the schedules means to add the two numbers arithmetically. For example, to expand the number for classical art in countries other than Greece and Italy (N5801-5896), one adds a number from a designated table to the base number N5800. Using the number 13 for Canada, one adds it to 5800 to get N5813, representing classical art in Canada. Sometimes, when whole numbers are lacking to subdivide a topic as desired, LCC employs decimal numbers. In the previous example, to subdivide classical art in the United States for the colonial period, one adds 03.5 to 5800, to arrive at N5803.5.

LCC occasionally contains instructions to subdivide (or subarrange) a topic like some other in the schedule, but this is done far less frequently than in DDC. Rather, LCC simply lists various subarrangements in the schedules, and most of them differ from one another.

One final consideration is the browsability of collections that results from applying LCC or DDC. Because of its principle of hierarchy, which LCC does not employ, DDC produces arrangements that tend to be more satisfying to browse from a subject searcher's point of view. Use of alphabetical instead of hierarchical subarrangements, which LCC does by means of cuttering, tends to scatter materials on related topics and bring together topics at different levels of hierarchy. Even geographical subarrangement can be less browsable, despite its logic, for subject searchers who are more interested in topical issues than in locational ones.

Conclusion

LCC is much larger and more complex than DDC. Its overall arrangement of subjects is, perhaps, more logical and better organized for contemporary use than DDC, particularly in the fields of science and history. Using it to classify materials "from scratch," however, is difficult for librarians outside of LC, because it is controlled entirely by LC and devoted to the arrangement of LC's own collections.

Public libraries and school library media centers are less likely to consider adopting LCC because of its suitability for their collections than because they wish to conform to the choice of a central service or a shared cataloging network, and to take advantage of CIP or other outside sources of classification data, especially if that means avoiding original work. In making a decision to use external sources, the source database should be tested to see if all or most of the materials are, in fact, included in them. If not, it may prove more expensive to do original classification for the remainder than to do more original work with a simpler scheme, such as DDC.

LCC is a practical scheme. It requires less number building than DDC and provides shorter classification numbers than DDC (although they are made up of letters and numbers) for subjects of the same specificity. LCC seems more hospitable to new topics and allows for far greater subdivision of topics. In addition, it avoids trying to force differing disciplines into a single mold and allows every subject area to have the arrangement most "natural" to its literature.

The bias of LCC toward the United States, its neighbors, and traditional allies is, perhaps, even more pervasive than DDC's, but more understandable. LCC does not try to be a universal classification of knowledge, but only an orderly arrangement of LC's books. The difficulty of applying LCC to nonbook materials probably is no greater than applying DDC to them. Both schemes were developed to arrange books, not other forms of materials. In LCC's favor is the fact that there are more opportunities for close classification, a useful attribute because nonbook items often have very narrowly defined topics.

LC and other libraries using LCC are unlikely to change to DDC. LCC is equally unlikely to become ubiquitous in the United States or anywhere else. Rather, the dichotomy in the classification of library materials between DDC and LCC is likely to continue, with the choice depending on an agency's traditions, size, and orientation toward a particular source of cataloging and classification data. Heightened awareness of the workings of each system and an understanding of their differences and implications for use are valuable for all librarians and media specialists, and their patrons. Try your hand at assigning LC classification numbers to the following sample problems in Figure 12.3.

Figure 12.3   Original Classification Using LCC

Using the appropriate volumes of LCC, assign a classification number to each of the following titles. Use the rules in Figure 12.2 to create the cutter numbers, if necessary. Answers are in Appendix C.

1.   Item title: *J. P. Morgan and his peers: America's aristocracy.*
     Summary: Biographies of J. P. Morgan and the nineteenth century financiers with whom he competed.

2.   Item title: *Public funds and public buildings in Italy: Proceedings of the Fourth Annual Conference of the Association of Public Works Administrators, Rome, Italy.*
     Summary: Selected papers from the conference, comparing differences between the financing of public buildings by government sources and private groups.

3.   Item title: *How to fill out your Michigan income tax forms.*
     Summary: A guide to filling out Michigan state income tax forms.

4.   Item title: *An economic history of New York State.*
     Summary: Describes the changes in the primary industries in New York State, from agriculture and dairying to finance and tourism.

5.   Item title: *Saving the suburbs: can federal support save commuter trains?*
     Summary: Explores the financial losses of suburban rail lines and offers suggestions for federal support to keep them in operation.

6.   Item title: *Logan Airport: a study in inaccessibility.*
     Summary: Discusses roads and tunnels leading to Boston's Logan Airport and offers a plan to improve vehicle access.

Recommended Reading

C. A. Cutter's Three-Figure Author Tables [on CD-ROM]. Englewood, CO: Libraries Unlimited, 1995.

C. A. Cutter's Two-Figure Author Tables [on CD-ROM]. Englewood, CO: Libraries Unlimited, 1995.

Caster, Lillie D. *The Classifier's Guide to LCC: Subdivision Techniques for the Social Sciences (Class H).* New York: Neal-Schuman, 1986.

Chan, Lois Mai. *A Guide to the Library of Congress Classification,* 5th ed. Englewood, CO: Libraries Unlimited, 1999.

Cutter-Sanborn Three-Figure Author Tables [on CD-ROM]. Englewood, CO: Libraries Unlimited, 1995.

Dick, Gerald K. *LC Author Numbers.* Englewood, CO: Hi Willow, 1992.

Dittmann, Helena, and Jane Hardy. *Learn Library of Congress Classification.* Lanham, MD: Scarecrow Press, 2000.

FC: A Classification for Canadian Literature, 2nd ed. [Web site]: http://www.nlc-bnc.ca/pubs /abs/eclassfc.htm.

Library of Congress Subject Cataloging Division, Processing Services. *LC Classification Outline.* 6th ed. Washington, DC: Library of Congress, 1995; or, later versions may be accessed via the Web site: http://www.loc.gov/catdir/cpso/cpso.html.

Matthis, Raimund E., and Desmond Taylor. *Adopting the Library of Congress Classification System: A Manual of Methods and Techniques for Application or Conversion.* New York: R. R. Bowker, 1971.

Notes

1.   These indexes include James G. Williams et al., *Classified Library of Congress Subject Headings,* 2nd ed. (New York: Marcel Dekker, 1982); J. McRee Elrod et al., *An Index to the Library of Congress Classification; with Entries for Special Expansions in Medicine, Law, Canadiana, and Nonbook Materials,* preliminary ed. (Ottawa: Canadian Library Association, 1974); and Nancy B. Olson, *Combined Indexes to the Library of Congress Classification Schedules* (Washington, DC: U.S. Historical Documents Institute, 1974). A newer tool of value in this area is Mona L. Scott, *Conversion Tables: LC-Dewey, Dewey-LC.* (Englewood, CO: Libraries Unlimited, 1993). *Conversion Tables* is available also on CD-ROM.

2.   Lois Mai Chan, *A Guide to the Library of Congress Classification*, 5th ed. (Englewood, CO: Libraries Unlimited, 1999).

3.   Library of Congress, Subject Cataloging Division, Processing Services, *Classification: Class S: Agriculture,* 4th ed. (Washington, DC: Library of Congress, 1982), 8.

4.   Library of Congress, Subject Cataloging Division, *Subject Cataloging Manual: Shelflisting* (Washington, DC: Library of Congress, 1987); Library of Congress, Office for Subject Cataloging Policy, *Subject Cataloging Manual: Classification,* 1st ed. (Washington, DC: Cataloging Distribution Service, Library of Congress, 1992). A third tool with similar application is LC's Geography and Map Division's publication of geographic cutters: *Geographic Cutters,* 2nd ed. (Washington, DC: Library of Congress, 1989). These tools are also available on CD-ROM.

5.   Library of Congress, *The Library of Congress Shelflist in Microform,* microfiche ed. (Ann Arbor, MI: University Microfilms International, n.d.).

13

The MARC Formats

Introduction

The MARC formats are a series of codes and rules for marking bibliographic, authority, classification, holdings, and community information data into a form that can be understood and used by computers. As such, it is a type of markup language, similar in principle to SGML, HTML, and other markup languages used for transmitting electronic resources. MARC was intended to be used for library data.

The MARC formats are called *communications* formats, also, which means that once in this form, one computer can transmit the data to another computer. The term *bibliographic data* means all of the elements of a bibliographic record that have been described in this book so far: descriptions, access points, subject headings, and call numbers. *Authority data* means all of the elements of an authority record for names, titles, or subject descriptors, including the authorized form of the name or topic, cross-references to other name forms or topical terms, and the source material used in creating the authority record. *Holdings data* means the specific data relating to any item in a library's collection, including its copy number, cost, acquisition source, holding unit (such as a main library or branch library) or collection within a library or information center, etc. A fourth MARC format was developed for *classification data* and used to automate the LC classification. The fifth format is for *community information.*

Institutions outside LC, including NLC, were consulted during the development of the MARC formats and still contribute to their ongoing evolution, but they were initiated and devised primarily by LC, and they reflect the needs of its cataloging products and processes. This chapter concentrates on the format for bibliographic data.

History and Background

The first MARC format was devised for the bibliographic data of books in the 1960s. It went through several versions before being published as a national standard in the 1970s. Before long, a MARC format for serials was devised, followed by MARC formats for other types of materials for which LC produced bibliographies. After many years during which the number of separate MARC formats continued to grow, an integrated MARC format was implemented during the 1990s in which all fields were made uniform across all the physical forms of materials collected by libraries. All fields and codes still are not applicable to every type of material, but if they do apply, their meanings are the same, thereby simplifying the processes of learning and using the system of MARC protocols. The change in philosophy underlying the formats is profound, but changes in the practical applications are relatively transparent, especially to new catalogers who never used the earlier system of individual MARC formats for each type of material.

Individual bibliographic networks have issued their own manuals containing versions of MARC intended for use by their participants. Selected fields have been defined in unique ways by an individual network; for example, the coded version of the basic features of a document are known in the Online Computer Library Center (OCLC) and Research Libraries Information Network (RLIN) as *fixed fields* and in MARC 21 as field 008, shown in Figures 13.2-13.4 later in this chapter.

From 1994 to 1997, LC and NLC worked with their user communities through their MARC committees to reconcile the differences between the official Canadian and U.S. formats, known as CAN/MARC and USMARC, respectively. The result is MARC 21. MARC 21 is not a new format; it is the new name for the harmonized CAN/MARC and USMARC. MARC 21 consists of the five communications formats described previously: bibliographic data; authority data; holdings data; classification data; and community information. There also are concise formats for each of these.

Individual countries employing the MARC formats have their own official versions, including the United Kingdom's UKMARC; and a generalized or universal version also exists, called UNIMARC. Minor differences appear among the versions of MARC formats, but their fundamental structure is identical and the same principles apply to them all.[1]

It is equally important to know what the MARC formats are not. They are not a set of cataloging rules or a cataloging code. Instead, they are designed for use with data created by applying the standard cataloging rules, subject heading systems, and classification schemes discussed in previous chapters. Some allowances and special accommodations are made for local data, but there are limits to how far one can stretch the formats. For example, the bibliographic format is geared to AACR, so the library or media center that does not follow these rules will find itself having to create AACR-compatible records anyway in order to code them successfully.

The MARC formats are not computer systems, either. They are intended to be used *in* computer systems as templates for database structures, but, by themselves, they are not designed as information storage and retrieval systems. Additional programming is required to use the MARC protocols in creating functioning information storage and retrieval systems. There are places in the MARC formats for each part of the bibliographic, authority, classification, holdings, or community information record, and for the additional information needed to manipulate and retrieve the data.

Although ultimate authority over the MARC 21 formats rests with LC and NLC, other groups in the two countries play consultative roles. In the United States, a major influence is MARBI, the Committee on Representation in Machine Readable Form of Bibliographic Information. MARBI is an interdivisional committee of three American Library Association divisions: the Association for Library Collections & Technical Services (ALCTS), the Library and Information Technology Association (LITA), and the Reference and User Services Association (RUSA). MARBI's counterpart in Canada is the Canadian Committee on MARC (CCM), a committee with representatives from the English- and French-speaking national library associations (the Canadian Library Association and l'Association pour l'avancement des sciences et des techniques de la documentation, respectively). Major bibliographic networks, such as OCLC and RLIN in the United States and A-G Canada, also contribute important advice. The MARC Editorial Office at LC and MARC Office at NLC make and publish the final decisions.

The reason the MARC formats look very complicated is that they must include everything needed to identify every detail of a record to a machine that cannot understand any part of it by itself.

Elements of a MARC Record

Fields

Computer data generally are divided into parts called *fields,* and each field into *subfields.* Each catalog record (or bibliographic record, as it is called in the computer system) is composed of fields that correspond to each area of the catalog record (title, edition, publication information, physical description, series statement, notes, etc.). The subfields in each field, in turn, correspond to particular elements of the area; for example, subfields in the physical description field include one each for the extent, other physical details, dimensions, and accompanying materials; and the subfields in the Dewey Decimal call number field correspond to the classification number, the shelf marks, and the edition of the classification used.

Every MARC record has two kinds of information in it, contained in two kinds of fields: fixed and variable. The kind of information discussed in the preceding paragraph is variable in nature. The names of personal authors are an example. A person's name may consist of a forename alone (Homer); a forename and a surname (William Shakespeare); a forename and a compound surname (Walter de la Mare or Sir Alec Frederick Douglas-Home); or a family name (Adams family). Or, it may be another possibility, such as initials or descriptive phrases. The name can have 7, 17, or 27 letters. It could require the inclusion of numbers, frequently encountered for royalty (Elizabeth II or Louis XVI). Titles, too, may be short or long, contain letters, numbers, symbols, or all, and have one word or many. These data must be contained in fields that are flexible enough to admit all these different possibilities. Such fields have variable length and are called, appropriately, *variable fields.* Variable fields contain almost all of the data we have studied.

Some information in entries does not vary, but is always entered the same way, either because the data are naturally invariant or because they are intentionally coded to eliminate variation. An example of naturally occurring invariable bibliographic data is the ISBN. It always appears in the same form and sequence (10 characters, all digits or with a final "X"). An example of information deliberately coded in an invariant form is the geographic focus of a title. Geographic locations are reduced to seven characters representing the applicable continent, country, and locale. These kinds of information are contained in invariable or *fixed fields.*

Information from the variable fields can be coded and duplicated in the fixed fields to ease manipulation by the computer system. One such type of information relates to the physical description of materials. The physical description for nonbook materials is a good example. Each type of nonbook medium has its own kind of physical details. Films, videos, photographs, and electronic resources may have color or be in black and white. Sound recordings may be stereophonic or not. Microforms may be reduced to any one of several possible sizes. In each case, however, the number of possibilities is limited, so it is easy to use a few letters or numbers to reduce them to a short and invariable code and add it to the computerized record. It is useful to include the language of the item, its country of origin, the presence or absence of multiple parts, and a host of other important aspects of an item, some of which usually are not given in catalog records. All of these data, in fixed and unchanging form, are given in fixed fields.

The order of elements in the MARC format (see Figure 13.1) is very similar to the order of elements in a catalog record. The main exception is that the call numbers, standard numbers, and other coded elements, called *control fields,* appear first. Many would be missing on catalog entries in most libraries or, on LC printed cards, they would appear at the bottom of the card below the tracings. They are put first in the computerized record because they generally identify the record or item and, as such, are more efficiently used if they are read first; and they generally are in coded form, such as a single character or a short string of characters in fixed order, and are not understandable until they are translated. Therefore, it is better to have these identifying or controlling fields at the start of the record and not in the middle, where they would interrupt the bibliographic fields, or at the end, where a processing unit would have to scan through the first part of the record to reach them.

Subfields

Subfields are parts of fields. The title area in a bibliographic description generally is composed of four elements: title proper, general material designation, other title information, and statement of responsibility. The title field corresponds to the title area as a whole, whereas each of the four elements corresponds to a specific subfield within the title field. The title proper subfield is the first subfield in the title field, whereas the date subfield usually is the third subfield in the publication–distribution field, following two subfields for the place and name of the publisher–distributor.

Content Designators

Each field and subfield must be identified by a name, known as a content designator. In the MARC format, the fields are identified by three-digit codes called *tags* and subfields are identified by a single letter, number, or, occasionally, a symbol, all called *subfield codes*. Subfield codes are always preceded by a symbol called a *delimiter* that identifies the next character as a subfield code. In the OCLC network, the delimiter appears as a double dagger, whereas in the A-G Canada system it appears as a dollar sign. The function of the delimiter is the same—to identify subfields—even when various keyboards and printers interpret its symbol in different ways.

Figure 13.1   Summary of MARC Bibliographic Field Tags

0xx	Includes fixed fields and control numbers.
1xx	Main entries, including personal author, corporate body author, conference names, and uniform title main entries.
2xx	Transcribed titles, editions, material specific details, and publication–distribution information.
3xx	Physical descriptions.
4xx	Transcribed series statements.
5xx	Descriptive notes.
6xx	Subject descriptors.
7xx	Added entries for names of contributors and titles other than main entry titles and titles proper (the latter are coded by different means, described later).
8xx	Series added entries traced differently than transcribed.
9xx	Intended for local data.

The application of appropriate tags and subfield codes to cataloging data frequently is called *tagging and coding* a record, or sometimes just *tagging* or just *coding* it. All of these terms, as well as *encoding a record* or doing *content designation,* mean the same thing: that the protocols of the MARC format are being applied to cataloging data for entry into a computer system programmed to use it.

Fixed fields, usually the first fields in the record, are given a tag beginning with 0 (zero). Access points generally have tags beginning with 1 (main entries), 6 (subject descriptors), 7 (added entries), or 8 (series added entries). Title proper added entries are the main exception. They are identified as access points in the 245 field by the use of a special character called an indicator, described shortly. Fields relating to the descriptive elements have tags beginning with 2, 3, 4, and 5. Few MARC fields beginning with 9 are defined for use.

Indicators

Between the tags and the start of the data in the field itself are two numerical characters known as *indicators.* One or both of the indicators may be defined for a field or neither may be defined. When only one indicator is defined it may be in either the first or the second position. For the most part, indicators are values that instruct the computer system to treat the data within the field to which they are assigned in particular ways, such as how to index the character string, whether to print or not to print the data in the field on a catalog card or a screen produced from the computerized record, or whether to create or not to create an access point for the data in the field. In the fields in which personal or corporate body names are entered, the indicator informs the computer of the type of name being entered; that is, whether it is in the form of a surname followed by a forename (e.g., Einstein, Albert), a forename first (e.g., Leonardo, da Vinci), or the name of a whole family (e.g., Kennedy family). A computer system needs this information to file these names properly in its name indexes.

The most important thing to remember about indicators is that their meaning differs for each field in which they are used. Originally, they were a vital element in printing catalog cards from computerized data and they are equally useful to computer programmers working with online systems, who can use them to specify desired procedures having nothing to do with cards or printing.

Conclusion

Figures 13.2, 13.3, and 13.4 show bibliographic records for titles as they appear in three of the national bibliographic networks with their tags, indicators, delimiters, and subfield codes. (The networks are described in Chapter 14.) All are MARC formatted records even though there are recognizable differences in the way they look. Some of the differences occur because of the differing capabilities of various printers to print data from visual displays. Some occur because of the differing procedures followed by each network. Close inspection will reveal new MARC 21 data in the A-G Canada record.

Figures 13.5, 13.6, 13.7, and 13.8 show authority records from the LC Name Authority File and Subject Authorities for a personal name, corporate body name, geographic name, and an LCSH subject descriptor, respectively. Differences in the meanings of tags and subfield codes are obvious in these records when they are compared to the bibliographic records.

(Text continues on page 250)

FIGURE 13.2   MARC 21 Bibliographic Record from A-G Canada

#A3		59168708 07/10/00 12:47 cam a
001		59168708
003		CaOEAGC
005		20000626135547.0
008		000121s2000····mbc···········000·d·eng··
016	--	a 009001719
020	--	a 1896239633 : c$25.95
035	--	a (CaAEU)ANT-6968
040	--	a (CaOONL b eng c CaOONL d CaOONL d AEU
043	--	a n-cn-mb
055	-3	a PS8315.5.M35 b M36 2000
082	0-	a C812.54/08/097127 2 21
245	02	a A map of the senses : b [twenty years of Manitoba plays] / c edited by Rory Runnells ; with an introduction by Doug Arrell.
260	--	a [Winnipeg] : b Scirocco Drama, c 2000.
300	--	a 519 p. ; c 23 cm.
650	-5	a Canadian drama (English) z Manitoba.
650	-5	a Canadian drama (English) y 20th century.
650	-0	a Canadian drama z Manitoba.
650	-0	a Canadian drama y 20th century.
700	1-	a Runnells, Rory.

Owner: 9 ALBa PS 8315.5 M3 M36 2000b AEU

FIGURE 13.3   Bibliographic Record from OCLC

```
                                    ¶  CAT              SID: 09401      OL
Beginning of record displayed.


OLUC  ti "STANDARD CATALOGING FOR SCHOOL AND PUBLIC LI...   Record 2 of 2
   NO HOLDINGS IN OCL - 232 OTHER HOLDINGS
   OCLC: 33983358          Rec stat:    c
   Entered:    19951221    Replaced:    19970729     Used:    20000701
 ▶ Type:  a    ELvl:       Srce:       Audn:       Ctrl:       Lang:  eng
   BLvl:  m    Form:       Conf:  0    Biog:       MRec:       Ctry:  cou
               Cont:  b    GPub:       LitF:  0    Indx:  1
   Desc:  a    Ills:  a    Fest:  0    DtSt:  s    Dates: 1996,      ¶
 ▶  1  010       95-53186 ¶
 ▶  2  040       DLC ≠c DLC ≠d NLC ¶
 ▶  3  015       C97-10475-8 ¶
 ▶  4  020       1563083493 ¶
 ▶  5  043       n-us--- ¶
 ▶  6  050 00    Z693 ≠b .I56 1996 ¶
 ▶  7  055 02    Z693.3* ¶
 ▶  8  082 00    025.3 ≠2 20 ¶
 ▶  9  090       ≠b ¶
 ▶ 10  049       OCLC ¶
 ▶ 11  100 1     Intner, Sheila S. ¶
 ▶ 12  245 10    Standard cataloging for school and public libraries / ≠c Sheila
S. Intner and Jean Weihs. ¶
 ▶ 13  250       2nd ed. ¶
 ▶ 14  260       Englewood, Colo. : ≠b Libraries Unlimited, ≠c 1996. ¶
 ▶ 15  300       viii, 278 p. : ≠b ill. ; ≠c 27 cm. ¶
 ▶ 16  504       Includes bibliographical references (p. 211-213) and indexes. ¶
 ▶ 17  650  0    Cataloging ≠z United States. ¶
 ▶ 18  650  0    Public libraries ≠z United States. ¶
 ▶ 19  650  0    School libraries ≠z United States. ¶
 ▶ 20  650  6    Catalogage ≠x Normes ≠z ´Etats-Unis. ¶
 ▶ 21  650  6    Biblioth`eques publiques ≠x Normes ≠z ´Etats-Unis. ¶
 ▶ 22  650  6    Biblioth`eques scolaires ≠x Normes ≠z ´Etats-Unis. ¶
 ▶ 23  650  6    Catalogage ≠x Litt´erature de jeunesse ≠x Normes ≠z ´Etats-
Unis. ¶
 ▶ 24  700 1     Weihs, Jean Riddle. ¶
```

FIGURE 13.4   Bibliographic Record from RLIN

```
MC/PROD  Archival    FUL/BIB   DCLV00-A2572           Catalog          CRLG-EEG
IN ID DCLV00-A2572 - Record 1 of 1 - SAVE record

  ID:DCLV00-A2572          RTYP:d    ST:s    MS:       EL:5      AD:07-19-00
  CC:9554  BLT:pc     DCF:a    CSC:d   MOD:    PROC:              UD:07-19-00
  CP:mtu   L:eng      PC:i     PD:1879/1881  REP:                TOC:a
  010      00520290
  040      MtHi‡cDLC‡dDLC‡eappm
  100 1    Rose, John Baker,‡d1853-1884.
  245 00   John Baker Rose diary,‡f1879-1881.
  300      1 item.
  545      Helena, Montana, area rancher.‡bJohn Baker Rose was born in Hampstead
           Cedar Grove, Virginia, in 1853.  He left St. Louis, Missouri, with two f
           riends to set up a cattle business in Montana.  He settled near Helena,
           Montana, and remained there until 1881. He drowned in the Mississippi Ri
           ver near St.Louis, Missouri, on July 11, 1884.
  520 8    Diary of John Baker Rose.‡bCollection consists of a diary (July 1879-S
           ept. 1881) describing Rose's relocating to Montana, and his experiences
           operating a cattle business near Helena.
  555 8    Finding aid in the repository.
  650  0   Frontier and pioneer life‡zMontana.
  650  0   Overland journeys to the Pacific.
  650  0   Ranches‡zMontana‡zLewis and Clark County.
  651  0   Lewis and Clark County (Mont.)‡xHistory.
  797 2    NUCMC/Montana Historical Society
  797 2    NUCMC/MULP
  852      Montana Historical Society,‡bLibrary and Archives Dept.‡e(Helena)‡z(SC
           13).
```

FIGURE 13.5   Personal Name Authority Record

```
  ARN:     86904
  Rec stat: c      Entered:      19800903
  Type:     z      Upd status:   a      Enc lvl:    n      Source:
  Roman:           Ref status:   a      Mod rec:           Name use: a
  Govt agn:        Auth status:  a      Subj:       a      Subj use: a
  Series:   n      Auth/ref:     a      Geo subd:   n      Ser use:  b
  Ser num:  n      Name:         a      Subdiv tp:         Rules:    c
    1  010       n  50051972
    2  040       DLC   c DLC
    3  005       19840407101817.5
    4  100 10    Weihs, Jean Riddle.
    5  400 10    Riddle, Jean
    6  400 10    Weihs, Jean
    7  670       Her Non-book materials ... 1970.
    8  670       Her Accessible storage of nonbook materials, 1984:  b CIP t.p.
(Jean Weihs)
    9  678       Course Director, Library Techniques, Seneca College of Applied
Arts and Technology;  a b. 1930
```

FIGURE 13.6   Corporate Body Authority Record

```
ARN:    348749
Rec stat: n          Entered:      19791029
Type:      z         Upd status:   a     Enc lvl:    n     Source:
Roman:               Ref status:   a     Mod rec:          Name use: a
Govt agn:            Auth status:  a     Subj:       a     Subj use: a
Series:    n         Auth/ref:     a     Geo subd:   n     Ser use:  b
Ser num:   n         Name:         n     Subdiv tp:        Rules:    c
  1   010       n  79117036
  2   040       DLC  c DLC
  3   005       19840322000000.0
  4   110 20    Boston Public Library.
  5   410 10    Boston (Mass.).   b Public Library
  6   410 20    Public Library of the City of Boston
  7   410 10    Boston (Mass.).   b Boston Public Library
  8   410 10    Boston.  b Public Library.  w nnaa
  9   510 20    Mercantile Library Association (Boston, Mass.)
 10   667       AACR 1 form: Boston Public Library
 11   670       Its Monthly bulletin, 1896-
 12   670       Lectures for inventors, 1983:  b CIP t.p. (Boston Public
Library; Public Library of the City of Boston
 13   678       Opened to the public in 1854.
```

FIGURE 13.7   Geographic Name Authority Record

```
ARN:    2029822
Rec stat: n          Entered:      19860211
Type:      z         Upd status:   a     Enc lvl:    n     Source:
Roman:               Ref status:   n     Mod rec:          Name use: b
Govt agn:            Auth status:  a     Subj:       a     Subj use: a
Series:    n         Auth/ref:     a     Geo subd:         Ser use:  b
Ser num:   n         Name:         n     Subdiv tp:        Rules:    n
  1   010       sh 85136126
  2   040       DLC  c DLC
  3   005       19860211000000.0
  4   151  0    Toronto (Ont.)
```

FIGURE 13.8   Library of Congress Subject Authority Record

```
ARN:    2659069
Rec stat: c       Entered:      19891026
Type:     z       Upd status:  a      Enc lvl:    n      Source:
Roman:            Ref status:  a      Mod rec:           Name use: b
Govt agn:         Auth status: a      Subj:       a      Subj use: a
Series:   n       Auth/ref:    a      Geo subd:          Ser use:  b
Ser num:  n       Name:        n      Subdiv tp:         Rules:    n
   1   010      sh 89006162
   2   040      DLC   c DLC   d DLC
   3   005      19940422110444.5
   4   150   0  IBM-compatible computers
   5   450   0  Clones of IBM computers
   6   450   0  Compatible computers, IBM-
   7   450   0  IBM clones
   8   450   0  IBM compatibles (Computers)
   9   550   0  Microcomputers   w g
  10   670      Work cat.: Pilgrim, A. Upgrade your IBM compatible and save a
bundle, c1990.
```

In the next chapter, we will take a closer look at the national bibliographic networks based in the United States and Canada.

Recommended Reading

Byrne, Deborah J. *MARC Manual: Understanding and Using MARC Records.* 2nd ed. Englewood, CO: Libraries Unlimited, 1998.

Ferguson, Bobby. *MARC/AACR2/Authority Control Tagging: A Blitz Cataloging Workbook.* Englewood, CO: Libraries Unlimited, 1998.

Fritz, Deborah A. *Cataloging with AACR2R and USMARC for Books, Computer Files, Serials, Sound Recordings, and Videorecordings.* Chicago: American Library Association, 2000.

Furrie, Betty. *Understanding MARC: Bibliographic.* Washington, DC: Cataloging Distribution Service, Library of Congress, 1998.

Hagler, Ronald. *The Bibliographic Record and Information Technology.* 3rd ed. Chicago: American Library Association, 1997.

Library of Congress. *MARC Homepage.* Washington, DC: Library of Congress, 2000- . Available at http://www.loc.gov/marc/marc.html.

Library of Congress. Network Development and MARC Standards Office, in cooperation with Standards and Support, National Library of Canada. *MARC 21 Format for Bibliographic Data Including Guidelines for Content Designation,* 1999 ed. Washington, DC: Library of Congress Cataloging Distribution Service; Ottawa: National Library of Canada, 1999. [The concise format for bibliographic data is available online at http://www.lcweb.loc.gov /marc/bibliographic/. Formats for authorities data, holdings data, classification data, and community information, though not cited here, also have been published and are available from LC and NLC; concise versions also are available on the Web site.]

Millsap, Larry, and Terry Ellen Ferl. *Descriptive Cataloging for the AACR2R and the Integrated MARC Format: A How-to-do-it Workbook.* Rev. ed. New York: Neal-Schuman, 1997.

Truitt, Marc. "USMARC to UNIMARC/Authorities: A Qualitative Evaluation of USMARC Data Elements." *Library Resources & Technical Services* 36, no. 1 (January 1992): 37-58.

Notes

1.   Advantages for the British of harmonizing UKMARC with MARC 21 would be to broaden access to bibliographic records from North American sources, including a great deal of data for nonbook media. On the negative side, it could hinder cooperation with European neighbors based on compatibility with UNIMARC, which would not be possible with MARC 21. For discussion of this issue, see James Elliot, "MARC Harmonisation Moves to Major Consultation," *Select* 28 (Summer 2000): 1-2.

14

Computerized Cataloging
Shared Networks and Local Systems

Introduction

Many school library media centers and public libraries use computer systems to do their cataloging. Some of the computer systems are connected to databases shared with other libraries, media centers, or both, which can be located outside the local library or media center. Other systems belong to a local agency and serve only that one agency. When computerized cataloging systems are shared, the group and its joint databases fit the definition of a shared cataloging network. Cataloging networks come in all sizes, from global groups with thousands of members to a handful of neighboring agencies located within a few miles of one another. If a computerized cataloging system is not connected to groups beyond the local agency, it is called a local system. This chapter gives an overview of both types of computerized cataloging systems.

Shared Networks

During the 1960s, LC, NLC, and several far-sighted individual libraries initiated pioneering efforts to develop computerized bibliographic systems. A few of these early efforts grew into major computer-based networks supporting huge databases of bibliographic information shared by many member or consumer libraries.[1] They are called variously *bibliographic networks* or *bibliographic utilities*. Sometimes, the word *bibliographic* is dropped and they are called *networks* or *utilities*.

The name bibliographic utility comes from the fact that the networks appear to generate catalog records the way an electric utility generates electricity. Bibliographic utilities begin with catalog records created by their member libraries, which they incorporate into a shared network database. In addition, they can create new records as a service for members who cannot or do not wish to do original cataloging themselves. Shared cataloging could not exist without the contributions of the networks, because they provide the computer hardware, software, and communications systems that change individual catalog records into databases fitted with retrieval software. They also maintain the systems, produce desired bibliographic products, conduct research and development, and provide the organization in which all of these operations take place.

Three bibliographic networks based in the United States and Canada have large constituencies: OCLC, headquartered in Dublin, Ohio; A-G Canada Library Information Services, based in Toronto, Ontario; and Research Libraries Information Network (RLIN®), operated by The Research Libraries Group, Inc., with headquarters in Mountain View, California. Two other important networks are WLN, now part of OCLC, located in Lacey, Washington; and AMICUS, based at NLC in Ottawa, Ontario. All of these organizations have undergone fundamental changes since their inception and still operate in a dynamic environment.

OCLC, the largest provider of bibliographic records, has several offices and affiliates that serve individual libraries as their contact point for OCLC services. NELINET, in New England; SOLINET, in the southeastern United States; PACNET/OCLC Pacific, in California and the Pacific Northwest; and AMIGOS, in the southwestern United States, are examples of OCLC regional offices and network affiliates. OCLC also has service center offices outside the U.S. OCLC Canada, for example, serves libraries in Canada. The regional affiliates function as a local presence for training new members, introducing new products, distributing documentation, troubleshooting problems, and implementing services of all kinds for OCLC members in their region. Network affiliates can also provide their members with other non-OCLC services, such as local database licensing and consulting services. These vary from network to network; for example, SOLINET is known for its preservation services.

Brief History of the Utilities

OCLC

OCLC was established in 1967 as the Ohio College Library Center by the presidents and library directors of 54 Ohio colleges and universities seeking faster and less costly cataloging methods. The directors also hoped they would be able to share the cataloging and the resources it represented, but soaring processing costs and backlogs of uncataloged materials were their most pressing problems. The center began as an offline, batch-mode card printing facility, but under Frederick Kilgour's leadership, it introduced its online-based interactive cataloging system and online union catalog in 1971. Libraries connected to OCLC via specially designed terminals using dedicated leased telecommunication lines. Later, dial-access terminals were added as well as subsystems for acquisitions, serials, and interlibrary loans. Today, the organization's name is OCLC—Online Computer Library Center.

At first, OCLC confined its membership solely to Ohio libraries, but it later branched out to other states and regions, and eventually accepted members from beyond the borders of the United States. It is now global. OCLC is by far the largest utility, with more than 48,000,000 records in its WorldCat database, at this writing, representing the diverse collections of many thousands of libraries. The majority of OCLC member libraries are located in colleges and universities, but it has growing numbers of public libraries, government agency libraries, special libraries, and school library media centers.

Several advisory and user groups have been formed by members with special interests. The advisory groups are convened by OCLC, whereas the user groups are member initiated and directed. Type-of-library groups include advisory groups for public, college and university, and research libraries; and, user groups for health science, law, music, and theological libraries. Type-of-format user groups function for audiovisual or electronic resource catalogers, music catalogers, map catalogers, and archivists. Product-related advisory groups are available for cataloging, reference services, and resource sharing, and a user group for resource sharing also functions. These groups are primarily educational, providing newsletters, conference programming, and discussion forums, but some also initiate, consult, and lobby for improvements or special projects in their areas of interest. Mention should also be made of the OCLC Users Council, which is the direct link between member libraries and OCLC's Board of Trustees for governance.

OCLC markets a great variety of products, including archive tapes of each member's own cataloging; retrospective conversion services to turn noncomputerized records for items held before a library joined OCLC into machine-readable form; reference and document delivery services based on WorldCat and other databases; subsets of its huge database on CD-ROM disks; contract cataloging services for a library's current acquisitions; and more. In 1988, OCLC purchased Forest Press, publisher of the Dewey Decimal Classification system, and this subsidiary issues a variety of classification-related products of its own.

A-G Canada Ltd.

The roots of A-G Canada Ltd. began in 1965 when the University of Toronto Library became involved in an internal effort to automate its cataloging operations. Since its founding as UTLAS (University of Toronto Library Automation Systems), this bibliographic utility has had three other owners and names: Utlas International Canada, ISM Library Information Services, and presently, A-G Canada Ltd., a wholly owned subsidiary of Auto-Graphics of Pomona, California.

A-G Canada offers resource sharing, cataloging services, and proprietary database management with access to and from the database through Z39.50 search and retrieval protocols and World Wide Web facilities.

Libraries and media centers do not join A-G Canada as members with a voice in its governance, but purchase products and services from it as would the customers of any other commercial company. A-G Canada offers a broad range of services, and customers can choose to maintain a separate file of their own holdings or attach their holdings to an existing file.

A-G Canada is programmed to support English and French bilingual databases containing Canadian and Université de Laval French-language subject headings as well as LCSH. Its database includes catalog records from many sources, such as NLC, LC, and the U.S. National Library of Medicine. NLC has designated A-G Canada as a node on the NLC-sponsored Virtual Canadian Union Catalogue (vCuc).

In July 2000, A-G Canada had a database of more than 50 million records representing the collections of 600 libraries.

A-G Canada's database includes an authority control system that links bibliographic records with records in LC's name and subject authority files, the National Library of Medicine's MeSH file, NLC's name file, and the French-language *Répertoire de vedettes-matière*, permitting a local library's own authority files to be maintained and used in conjunction with all of these authority files.

RLIN ®

Four institutions—New York Public Library and Harvard, Yale, and Columbia universities—joined in 1974 to address mutual problems of sharing their materials and bibliographic information. They formed The Research Libraries Group (RLG), a not-for-profit membership corporation, the parent organization of RLIN®, which was launched in 1978. When a decision was made to select Stanford University's computer system, called Bibliographic Automation of Large Library Operations using a Time-sharing System (BALLOTS) instead of OCLC for RLG's network, Harvard left the group of four for a while and its place was taken by Stanford. Today, RLG is an international member alliance of more than 160 universities, national libraries, archives, historical societies, museums, and independent research collections, and public libraries.

RLIN® grew slowly and its membership is small in contrast to OCLC's membership of many thousands (how many there are depends on the way library systems and other group members are counted) and A-G Canada's customer base of many hundreds. However, non-members may opt to search RLG's databases and, at this writing, RLG counted nearly 10,000 active user accounts. RLG seeks unique or hard-to-locate data of particular value to its members and users, and its database is abundant in art, law, archival, visual, and area studies materials.

At this writing, the RLIN bibliographic database—now called the RLG Union Catalog—holds complete records and variant cataloging for some 37 million titles representing more than 100 million collection items. In RLIN®, every catalog record entered into its database is maintained intact and can be retrieved at any time. In contrast, in OCLC's database multiple records for the same title are not intentionally maintained online. Instead, duplicates are merged into a single master record per item, with cataloging from national libraries taking precedence over member-contributed original cataloging.

In addition to the original RLIN technical processing system, institutions can choose RLG's Zephyr®, a Z39.50 server that lets users of other online systems search using the commands and record displays of their own systems; and Eureka®, an interface designed for campus-wide access by students and faculty searching RLG's data resources through World Wide Web browsers.[2]

WLN (now OCLC/WLN)

WLN originated in the 1970s as a cooperative activity of the state library of Washington, and the acronym by which it was then known first stood for Washington Library Network. State decision makers sought sophisticated search capabilities with strict controls over data input, and engaged the Boeing Computer Services Corporation to program the network system. Computerized services began in 1977.

Subsequent decisions included extending network services to areas contiguous to the state, including the western Canadian provinces and Alaskan libraries and media centers, but not enlarging its constituency beyond this geographic region. Instead, WLN offered its software to interested parties in a remunerative package that included database sharing and encouraged replications of the network in other locations. The Australian National Library, the University of Illinois Libraries, and the Southeastern Library Network (SOLINET), an OCLC regional network, were among those that took advantage of the offer.

In 1985, the network's name was changed to Western Library Network. In 1990, it became an independent nonprofit corporation, changed its name to WLN, ended its previous relationship with the Washington state library, and moved to new headquarters. In 1999, WLN merged with OCLC and became the OCLC/WLN Pacific Northwest Service Center.

WLN was the first bibliographic utility to offer its members authority control services, in which the headings in bibliographic records were checked for accuracy before being added to the database. In April 1995, WLN added *Canadiana* authorities to its files.

Among WLN's popular products are CD-ROM-based library catalogs, LASERCAT and FASTCAT; MARS, an authority control and database preparation service; and ACAS, a collection assessment and analysis service. The systems are simple, hardy, and easy to run. The merged network continues to support these and other services.

AMICUS: Canadian Union Catalogue

AMICUS is an online union catalog containing the holdings of more than 500 Canadian libraries. With more than 22 million records and 38 million holdings, the AMICUS database is used primarily for interlibrary loans and resource sharing.

Originally established in 1983 as the DOBIS Search Service, NLC provides access to AMICUS 24 hours a day, 7 days a week via the World Wide Web and Z39.50. More than 800 institutions across Canada subscribe to AMICUS.

AMICUS functionality includes an integrated interlibrary loan function enabling users to request any item found in the database, MARC 21 downloading useful for copy cataloging, a bibliography creation and e-mailing function, and the ability to customize screens.

The bilingual service also contains NLC's name authority file and the subject authorities for *Canadian Subject Headings*. All records in AMICUS are MARC 21 compatible. AMICUS is the source of most of NLC's products, including the *Canadiana* CD-ROM. The database is growing at a rate of one million records annually.

Similarities and Differences
of Shared Networks

One important feature common to all of the bibliographic utilities is their use of the same communications format to enter and transmit their data: the *MA* chine-*R* eadable *C* ataloging (MARC) format devised originally by LC (see Chapter 13). Although each utility has adjusted the MARC format in some way to suit its particular needs, the basic structure is the same. Acceptance of the MARC format by the utilities helped to make it an international standard. Subsequent developments in bibliographic computing are transforming MARC into an essential system structure on which other important data sharing standards depend. It was the basis of the Linked Systems Project (LSP), which connected the utilities and LC's local computer system.

All the bibliographic utilities incorporate national library cataloging. LC's MARC records formed the nucleus and largest share of all utilities' databases when they started and continued to comprise a majority of records for several years. The relative balance between LC and member-contributed original cataloging shifted during the 1980s and, since that time, the proportion of LC and national library records has been shrinking. In the 1990s, LC began using the original cataloging of selected network member libraries as the basis for its own cataloging. Thus far, the project is proceeding smoothly, with appropriate caution and attention to quality. This puts real meaning into the phrase "cooperative cataloging," which formerly was defined as everybody else copying LC's original cataloging (hence, the phrase *copy cataloging*).

All utility records are not alike in quality and fullness, which has put limits on the acceptability of catalog records from libraries other than the national libraries, singling them out for more editing and revision. Some libraries and media centers are not as concerned about the quality of individual records as they are about getting cataloging done rapidly and preventing backlogs. Either way, a choice usually must be made between maximizing the use of the utility (greatest speed and least cost) and maximizing the quality of the cataloging (greatest accuracy and appropriateness for the individual library or media center). Such choices are never simple and are likely to differ from one library to another as well as from one cataloger to another.

Joining a utility will not mean that original cataloging no longer has to be done in a local information agency. That depends on whether the materials being acquired and cataloged are held widely enough to be found already cataloged by LC, NLC, or some other utility member. In general, the materials most likely to have cataloging available online are English-language trade books from publishers who participate in the CIP and ISBN programs. Materials least likely to have cataloging available online are nonbook and non-English-language items, and the publications of small presses and government agencies, especially at state and provincial or local levels.

Similarities and differences among the utilities include the following:

1. *Database design.* A major difference among the utilities is the design of their databases, called their *architecture* in computer jargon. A basic issue is whether every record entered into the database is retained or only one record per unique title.

   OCLC has one master record for each title in WorldCat, to which other libraries can attach their holdings symbols. A minicomplex of rules governs the source and content of master records. In the past, a catalog record contributed by a national library replaced a master record for the same item entered as original cataloging by a member library, but not the original cataloging of another national agency, in which case two duplicate records coexisted in the database. OCLC now merges information from all national library cataloging, resulting in records with information from many different sources.

   Duplicate records are identified by a detailed matching scheme (called an *algorithm*) that ensures against errors in matching. Corrections and additions to master records can be made by the inputting library or media center if no additional holdings symbols have been attached to the record, or by OCLC's quality control staff as well as a number of institutions designated "Enhance" libraries. All member libraries can enrich records by adding table of contents information, and call numbers and subject headings in schemes not already present in the record. Otherwise, edits made to master records by other member libraries are valid only for their own cataloging products (cards, disks, tapes, etc.). Master records save storage space in the computer system, but individual agencies cannot retrieve their records from the database.

   RLIN® has clusters of records for titles that include every individual record entered for each title regardless of its source. Any RLIN® library can retrieve its own records directly from the database at any time. The decision to make duplicate records part of the database required that the RLIN® system provide a great deal more storage space. Insufficient storage and computing power remained a problem for a long time.

   A-G Canada provides both options for its customers; that is, maintaining their records online separately, or attaching their holdings symbols to existing records.

2. *Searching/retrieval capabilities.* Differences in methods used to search the utility's database can give rise to important differences in efficiency and use.

   The original OCLC database was designed to be searched by *derived* author, title, and author-title search keys—that is, only parts of names, title words, or both that the searcher had to figure out from the whole name, title, or both[5] —and by selected control fields such as ISBNs, ISSNs, LC Control Numbers, etc. To improve retrievability for popular or generic titles and prolific authors, search keys can be qualified by physical format and publication date when these are known. Subject searching was not originally available in the cataloging mode (on the assumption that catalogers always have an item in hand to be cataloged and know the author's name and the title), but, several years ago, keyword access to subject information as well as to most of the rest of the bibliographic record was added, along with the Boolean "AND" capability. Title browsing is also available. OCLC's CD-ROM products are searchable by subject descriptors, keywords, and Boolean operators.[6]

   RLG wanted sophisticated retrieval capabilities because it intended its database to be used for research purposes and resource sharing as well as for cataloging, and built them into its original system. RLIN® can be searched by LCSH descriptors and keywords as well as by full titles, author names, and a variety of control numbers such as LC Control Numbers, ISBNs and ISSNs, SUDOC numbers, etc. Searchers can combine more than one search element using Boolean operators. A-G Canada and OCLC/WLN offer similarly sophisticated searching capabilities.

3.   *Authority control.* Automated authority control systems, now commonplace, went beyond programming capabilities in the early days of the utilities. Ideally, authority files are linked to the appropriate fields in bibliographic records and automatically reject unauthorized heading forms. Next best are unlinked-but-online authority files that human catalogers consult during the cataloging process, adding new authority records for missing names and series after researching and formulating them according to the rules of AACR2-98.

 WLN was the only network to adopt a system of strict authority control in the early 1980s, which ensured consistent headings. (Authority control is now present in some form in all the utilities.) However, it meant that headings had to undergo a lengthy verification process. Any record containing an unauthorized heading had to wait in a queue until verification was received, and during this time no one could retrieve it online, not even the contributing library. On the positive side, implementation of authority control enabled WLN to avoid the inadvertent entry of duplicate records with misspelled headings or the inclusion of headings that failed to conform to AACR2.

 UTLAS (now A-G Canada) mounted an authority control module in 1978 that permitted bibliographic headings to be linked to the appropriate authority records in a hierarchy of authority files and, as mentioned previously, has multiple linked authority files. OCLC and RLIN® had no such automatic verification systems and suffered in varying degrees from problems of unintended duplications and fragmentation of the works of individual authors or titles in series.[7] In the 1980s, LC began distributing its Name Authority File and, subsequently, its Subject Authorities File on MARC tapes. OCLC and RLIN® mounted them as unlinked files, mandating that catalogers consult them before entering a heading. As a self-regulating quality control measure, it relies on catalogers' willingness to comply with the mandate. It cannot protect against the entry of erroneous headings made by mistake, through ignorance, or because of careless research, but quality control measures eventually identify and correct the errors.

Joining a Shared Network

 The bibliographic utilities are employed directly by thousands of libraries and media centers and indirectly by many more of them to minimize the load of original cataloging that would otherwise burden them all. For many media centers and libraries, catalog records for virtually all the materials they purchase are available from the network, and nothing needs to be done "from scratch." For those with collections of unusual materials, catalog records for numerous titles are not available, and original cataloging is still necessary for those items.

 Maximizing use of the utility keeps the amount of costly, time-consuming original cataloging as low as possible for any individual library or media center, but it can involve incorporating records that contain errors, or that include more or less information than is preferred. Utility records are likely to contain some proportion of subject headings and classification numbers based on standards that are not used in a particular place (for example, not Dewey but LC numbers, or not Sears, but LCSH descriptors). Catalogers are faced with many decisions about how best to use the utility: Should all utility records be accepted or only those from designated libraries? How much time should be spent searching for existing cataloging before inputting an original record? (To minimize unwanted duplicates, bibliographic utilities expect a diligent search to be done before a new record is added to the database.) How much editing should be done to existing records to make them acceptable?

Care must be exercised in weighing the needs of the local agency against the potential savings of using imperfect cataloging from a utility database. Cataloging that truly is so undesirable that it is better to have nothing at all needs to be identified.

Each individual public library or media center that joins a utility or anticipates using one should clarify what it wants to accomplish and develop a policy governing the use of utility records that ensures its objectives will be met. If the idea is to save money or speed processing, a higher level of error and some differences from ideal cataloging probably will have to be borne. It would be wise to experiment using the utility to do copy cataloging (that is, using utility records as the cataloging source) with a representative sample of materials to anticipate problems *before* making these decisions.

In addition, benefits of joining a utility other than cataloging must be considered, such as gaining access to enormous amounts of bibliographic data for reference and resource sharing, and electronic communications with other agencies. For some, these benefits may have a higher priority than the suitability of its cataloging. Networks themselves share information, and some libraries or media centers might find it advantageous to join more than one network.

Individual libraries and media centers should understand the responsibilities they accept upon joining a utility. Any original cataloging contributed to the shared database must be consistent with the utility's input standards. The old adage "garbage in, garbage out" is highly relevant here. If catalogers want to take good cataloging out of online systems, they must put good cataloging into them. In the network environment, "good" cataloging means meeting national and international standards. Joining a network usually involves agreeing to follow network standards and minimizing the types of local deviations that might save time or effort in the local database, but may not be appropriate or beneficial in a shared system.

The utilities began their databases with a nucleus of authoritative machine-readable records created and distributed by LC and NLC. To be compatible with these data sources, they adopted the MARC format. Since then, MARC has become an international standard for the entry, manipulation, and transmission of cataloging data. Even small systems intended for individual libraries and media centers employ it to be compatible with larger networks. These local systems are described next.

Local Systems

To repeat the definition given at the beginning of this chapter, a local system is a computer-based bibliographic system under the control of an individual library or media center (or, possibly, a small group of them) that is not shared with groups beyond the local agency. The term *local,* used in this context, means that the system does not serve a broad constituency from different institutions spread over a broad geographic area, as the bibliographic utilities and their regional affiliates do. The exact meaning of *local* is difficult to interpret precisely. It is applied to limited groups that include more than one media center or library, one building, or one geographic location. A network linking media centers in the geographically dispersed buildings of a school district still is a local system because all participants are members of one district; and when a handful of public libraries share one "local" system, it may stretch the definition somewhat, but still contrasts sharply with bibliographic utilities.

Local systems employ microcomputers or slightly larger minicomputers.[8] To enlarge the amount of data storage and computing power while keeping costs low, microcomputers might add CD-ROM disk drives or links to larger computer systems, called *host* systems. These additions facilitate the cataloging process and also store local holdings data for a computer-based public catalog.

Computers can be used solely to assist the cataloging process by printing cards, or to perform both cataloging and display functions. Local systems that serve as public catalogs are called Online Public Access Catalogs (OPACs), even when the display itself is actually "offline" and not directly connected to the cataloging part of the system while the system is being used as a public display. For that reason, Public Access Catalog (PAC) is probably a more accurate name, even if it lacks the high-tech term "online." Capabilities for use as an online catalog depend on the computer and other equipment attached to it,[9] the size of the collections, and the type of online catalog desired.

Computer-based local systems and the software that runs them are undergoing constant change and will likely result in newer systems becoming larger, more powerful, and less costly. Local systems tend to be sold as a package of hardware and software with added system support that might include training, user support, software maintenance, ongoing upgrades, expansion potential, and other enhancements. If the desired software operates on "off-the-shelf" hardware, the agency might be encouraged to buy it separately from a local supplier. Vendors who market local systems to libraries and media centers have come to realize that offering customers flexibility in choosing package components is likely to meet with greater success than offering an all-or-nothing package.

Local System Components

To begin operations on a local system for cataloging or a public catalog display, a media center or library needs to obtain the following:

1. *Hardware.* One of the two central features in every computer system package is its machinery. Although it may not be obvious by looking at a computer, it contains at least three parts: a processor, an area for data storage, and devices for internal and external communication. In computer jargon, these are known as the CPU (central processing unit), memory, and input-output or I/O. The type of processor and its associated instructions, called its *operating system,* determines, in large measure, the quantity and method of operations that the equipment can be made (or *programmed*) to perform. These in turn determine the speed of operations experienced by users of the computer system primarily as response time, that is, the amount of time it takes for the computer to display a response to the user's commands. A system can have one CPU or several; it usually has multiple storage areas for primary and secondary storage of data; and it nearly always has more than one communication device—at least one (and often more than one) visual or screen display, keyboard, scanner, etc. as well as a modem, the unit used to transmit information outside the system via telephone lines or other electronic means. Hardware also includes the cables and connections needed to link the separate pieces of equipment together.

    In the early days of local computing, computer system vendors endeavored to supply customized hardware—that is, hardware that they designed and produced (sometimes by making small changes to standard items from a computer manufacturer), and that only they could supply. Today, this is not done very often. Some vendors simply charge their customers the cost (plus handling, overhead charges, or both) of equipment and supplies they obtain from third parties. Others add a surcharge for their services. Contracts usually can be negotiated that exclude hardware if a librarian or media specialist prefers obtaining the hardware from a local computer store.

2. *Software.* The other of the two central features in any computer system are the instructions needed to enter, manipulate, and delete data within the system, and to execute the operations for which the system is designed—cataloging, public catalog display, and, possibly, other bibliographic functions such as circulation control, acquisitions, or serials control. Development of the software that makes the system run is the vendor's major contribution, but, because it is performed "behind the scenes," out of the purchaser's view, it may not be recognized. Nevertheless, provision of the software is actually the most important single element in the package, and it should never be taken lightly or underestimated, let alone ignored.

3. *Documentation.* At one time, good documentation was very hard to obtain and purchasers of local systems were required to translate the documentation supplied by the vendor into something library or media center staff could understand and use. More recently, along with improvements in hardware and software, documentation was recognized as an important marketing feature and vendors have improved it. Documentation should explain how to operate the system and give step-by-step instructions for all activities the purchaser may be expected to perform. Some documentation comes in two versions: a full version to be used for reference, and a brief version outlining only the most commonly performed tasks.

    The quality of the documentation may vary widely, depending on the effectiveness of the writing, the presence of useful, understandable examples, finding tools such as tables of contents, indexes, etc., and its physical presentation, which frequently is in loose-leaf form so it can be updated easily. Documentation may not be provided on paper at all, but given in the form of online tutorials and help screens, programmed to be part of the computer system itself. When this is the case, the online documents usually can be printed out if the librarian or media specialist wants to work with paper materials. This can be especially important when documentation needs to be used away from the sites where computer terminals are located.

4. *Installation.* In the days when local systems involved minicomputers, vendors would arrange to install the equipment, which required expertise in cabling and the initial loading of system software. Today, because systems employing standard microcomputers use standard methods to load software with which purchasers are familiar, installation often is supplied in the form of a telephone call during which the vendor helps the purchaser perform the first software load and any unfamiliar cabling procedures.

5. *Staff training.* The need for staff training has diminished as local systems have become less complicated and computing in general has become more familiar to library and media center staffs. Staff training can be as minimal as ensuring that each staff member spends an hour or two learning the new system before using it, or it can involve a few sessions of longer duration with a knowledgeable guide. Many local systems are designed to obviate the need for training, aiming to be as "user friendly" as possible.

6. *Continuing maintenance and system support.* No matter how user friendly a local system may be, there always is a need for assistance with its maintenance and use, both for the hardware and the software. With the advent of standard microcomputers, hardware maintenance has moved out of the vendor's purview and usually is left to the purchasing library or media center, which should not overlook it.

    Routine hardware maintenance includes cleaning pieces of equipment with products approved by the manufacturer; keeping the area near the computer clean and dust free; using protective coverings (or, if necessary, removing them) when activities in the surrounding area might be dangerous to hardware components; and providing sufficient space around the equipment for its efficient operation. Cooling fans on units should never be blocked and papers or other library materials should not be piled on top of terminals, printers, etc.

Software maintenance and support continues to be an important function of vendor service. If an operation does not seem to work or if responses to designated commands are not as indicated, users must seek help and vendors, who created the software, usually are the sole source for it. Many vendors furnish toll-free telephone numbers with experts to answer the calls to accommodate this need, but hours of service and effectiveness of the experts varies widely.

7. *Ongoing research and development.* Of all the responsibilities vendors must bear, the duty to perform ongoing research and development is, perhaps, the most important, on a par with current system development. Not only are hardware capabilities always changing, which drives software development to take advantage of the new opportunities, but vendor competition is keen and retention of one's customers may depend on being able to produce desired new features regularly. Changes in computing occur so rapidly that systems are deemed obsolete in the marketplace long before their useful lives are over. Libraries and media centers benefit from the phenomenon, although they may sometimes feel as though it is a plot by vendors to pressure them to increase the size and power of their systems. In reality, it simply is a fact of life in the computer world.

Several other elements that figure importantly in the successful implementation of a local system rarely are supplied by vendors as part of their standard packages. These either are purchased separately as add-ons to standard packages, much like automobile accessories, or they must be supplied by the purchasing library or media center.

1. *Database.* The conversion of bibliographic information for holdings that pre-exist computerized operations must, sooner or later, be accomplished to obtain full value from a local system, especially if it serves as the public catalog. Until these older catalog records are entered into the computer database, searchers are forced to consult multiple catalogs to find what they want. Vendors may offer conversion services, or a separate vendor may be retained for the task. (Bibliographic utilities offer retrospective conversion services, and they are not the sole alternative.) To obtain the lowest cost for retrospective conversion service from the computer system vendor, it should be negotiated as part of the initial system contract; which means the purchaser should know the cost of using outside services.

2. *Physical site.* Microcomputers are more easily accommodated than larger minicomputers and mainframes, which often need controlled environments, special security measures, etc.; but even a microcomputer has to be placed in a proper setting, with room for associated equipment (cables, printers, scanners, etc.) and supplies (paper, disks, etc.). Conveniently located electrical outlets are needed to plug in computers and printers and any other peripheral equipment the library or media center chooses to add to them. Wiring must be able to carry the load. The range of acceptable heat, humidity, and other environmental conditions is very flexible, but there are limits the wise purchaser should not exceed. Tables should be large enough to provide workspace next to computers, with additional space for printers and their output. Furnishings used with computer hardware should be designed to avoid undesirable physical stress and strain (that is, be ergonomically correct). Lighting should not

create glare or cause other difficulties in reading screens. All physical site conditions are solely the responsibility of the purchaser, although vendors will help with good advice.

3. *Other hardware.* Not all hardware components are the vendor's responsibility. Equipment generally supplied by purchasers includes telephone lines and fax units, and might also involve specialized printers, speakers, or devices not handled by the vendor.

Purchasing a Local System

The local system marketplace changes rapidly and offers a wide array of products, services, product-service combinations, and options. Some vendors offer only one type of system package or component, whereas others offer an array of possibilities, from complete systems in several sizes and price ranges to a simple software package or module designed to run on a microcomputer supplied by the customer.

Books and articles that provide information and advice about the local system market place are listed in the recommended reading section at the end of this chapter. Although helpful, they date quickly and should be augmented with new readings. Some helpful hints about maneuvering effectively in this marketplace are:

1. Before you begin:

    • Prepare yourself with precise knowledge of existing holdings to be included in your system and the amount and costs of the cataloging work to be done.

    • Prepare a list of system capabilities you seek, divided into necessities (features you will not do without), desirable features (capabilities you might like to have, but are willing to do without), and luxuries (capabilities you neither need nor desire).

    • Be prepared to negotiate written contracts with all vendors, whether you buy a whole system from them or only a single component.

2. Before you buy:

    • Be objective and open-minded.

    • Prepare guidelines for evaluating and accepting a system so that each candidate is treated fairly and comparisons are as accurate as possible.

    • Talk to colleagues in similar agencies who use the systems you consider, asking each the same questions and making notes on their replies.

    • See each system or system component you plan to buy in operation and make sure it does what you think it can—most reputable vendors will supply the names of their customers.

    • Be prepared to calculate and compare *total* system costs and benefits over a year's time, not just the more obvious costs of starting up system hardware and software—sometimes the system that costs more at the beginning will be less costly to maintain over time.

    • Bear in mind that this will only be the first system you buy, but not the last—and the ability to transfer your database, etc., to other systems is an asset.

Local systems employing computers to assist catalogers and to serve the public service staff and patrons by performing catalog storage, retrieval, and display functions can be more flexible, efficient, and complete than noncomputerized systems. Just because a computer is used, however, does not mean that the media center or library will have a better catalog or better service. That depends on the type of local system and how it is used (as well as what kind of catalog it replaces). Media specialists and librarians have an important responsibility to make wise decisions in this aspect of bibliographic service.

Recommended Reading

Shared Cataloging Networks:

De Villers, Gisèlle. "AMICUS Overview." *National Library News* 26 (April 1994): 4-6.

Hannon, Hilary. *Discovering RLIN®: An Introduction to the Research Libraries Information Network Database.* Mountain View, CA: Research Libraries Group, 1992.

Kalb, Sam. "ISM and OCLC as Secondary Bibliographic Resources: Results of a TSIG-L Survey," *TSIG Newsletter* 5, no. 1 (spring 1994): 22-26.

Michalko, James, and John Haeger, et al. "The Research Libraries Group: Making a Difference." *Library Hi Tech* 12, no. 2 (1994): 7-32.

OCLC Newsletter. Columbus, OH: OCLC, 1978- .

RLIN ® Newsletter. Stanford, CA: Research Libraries Group, 1978- .

Schultz, Lois Massengale. *A Beginner's Guide to Copy Cataloging on OCLC/PRISM.* Englewood, CO: Libraries Unlimited, 1995.

Smith, K. Wayne. "OCLC: Changing the Tasks of Librarianship." *Library Hi Tech* 11, no. 3 (1993): 7-17.

Warwick, Robert T., and Kenneth Carlborg. *Using OCLC under PRISM: A How-To-Do-It Manual for Libraries.* New York: Neal-Schuman, 1997.

Wired Librarian's Newsletter. Freeport, IL: Micro Libraries, 1984- .

WLN Participant. Lacey, WA: WLN, 1981- .

Local Systems:

Barry, Jeff. "Automated System Marketplace 2000: Delivering the Personalized Library." *Library Journal* 124 (April 1, 2000): 49-60.

Breeding, Marshall. *PC-Based Integrated Library Systems.* Westport, CT: Meckler, 1994.

Cohn, John M. et al. *Planning for Automation: A How-To-Do-It Manual for Librarians,* 2nd ed. New York: Neal-Schuman, 1997.

Day, Teresa Thurman et al. *Automation for School Libraries: How to Do It from Those That Have Done It.* Chicago: American Library Association, 1994.

Howden, Norman. *Buying and Maintaining Personal Computers: A How-To-Do-It Manual for Librarians*. New York: Neal-Schuman, 2000.

Lighthall, Lynne. "The Sixth Canadian School Library Automation Survey." *Feliciter* 42, no. 5 (May 1996): 34-51.

Mayo, Diane, and Sandra Nelson. *Wired for the Future: Developing Your Library Technology Plan*. Chicago: Public Library Association, 2000.

Merilees, Bobbie. "Tenth Annual Survey of Canadian Installations of Integrated Library Systems." *Feliciter* 42 (June 1996): 24-29.

Morrill, B. "LION and the East Lyme Public Library: A Study in Resource Sharing." *Library Mosaics* 5 (July/August 1994): 12-13.

Nixon, Carol, and Heidi Dengler, compilers. *Computers in Libraries '99: 14th Annual Proceedings*. Medford, NJ: Information Today, 1999.

Patrick, Jill. "Automation in Small Libraries." *Access* 5, no. 1 (fall 1998): 33-34.

Saffady, William. *Introduction to Automation for Librarians,* 4th ed. Chicago: American Library Association, 2000.

Yee, Martha, and Sarah Shatford Layne. *Improving Online Public Access Catalogs*. Chicago: American Library Association, 1998.

Notes

1.   Only two of the bibliographic utilities actually predate 1970 as computer-based networks: OCLC and A-G Canada, originally known as UTLAS and, later, as ISM. AMICUS (originally DOBIS), RLIN, and WLN began later, in the late 1970s, although they built upon the research and development that went into the establishment of the older networks. RLIN employs a computer system developed in earlier years by Stanford University, and thus might be counted among the pioneering group, except for the fact that the network entity itself was a post-1970 phenomenon. WLN was begun as the Washington Library Network in 1967, but did not begin computing services until several years later.

2.   Details of this description were based on correspondence with Jennifer Hartzell, September 7, 2000, and data from the Research Libraries Group Web site, at http:www.rlg.org/toc .html, accessed 18 July 2000.

3.   http://www.wln.org/aboutwln.htm, accessed 29 June 2000.

4.   For a discussion of the problems of maximizing network benefits, see Sheila S. Intner's "Interfaces" columns, "Bibliographic Triage," and "Bibliographic Triage Revisited," *Technicalities* 7 (December 1987):10-12, and vol. 8 (October 1988):3-4.

5.   For example, if the title of a book to be searched is *Standard Cataloging for School and Public Libraries,* the best derived search key for retrieving it by title alone would be STA,CA,FO,S. There are several possible combinations of letters in derived title search keys, but the 3,2,2,1 combination contains eight characters, the largest number possible, and therefore is more likely to retrieve the correct item than alternatives with fewer characters. For example, STA,C,F,S (3,1,1,1), which also is acceptable, retrieves the correct title, but will also

retrieve titles such as *Stalking California's Flying Squirrels* or *Stains, Colors, Fibers, Mottles: A Book of Painting and Finishing Techniques.* The commas in the search keys are the parts of the program that indicate the index to be searched: three commas identify a search in the title index; two commas identify a search in the personal name index, and one comma identifies a search in the combined name-title index.

6.   Boolean operators are so named because their programming is based on the rules of Boolean algebra, a mathematical system invented by a scientist named Boole. Media specialists familiar with set theory will recognize it in the following examples:

> The Boolean AND: Searching for Diseases AND Children (two different subject headings) or for Einstein AND Relativity (author's name and a title word) retrieves that set of records containing both elements, not one or the other.

> The Boolean NOT: Searching for Diseases NOT Children or Einstein NOT Relativity retrieves that set of records containing the subject descriptor Diseases if they do not also contain a second descriptor for Children, or all of Einstein's titles except those containing the word "Relativity."

> The Boolean OR: Searching for Diseases OR Children or Einstein OR Relativity retrieves that set of records containing either Diseases or Children as a subject descriptor and all books by Einstein as well as all titles containing the word "Relativity."

Use of the Boolean OR will enlarge the set of retrieved records, whereas use of AND or NOT will diminish it, in different ways.

7.   OCLC was thought to have suffered the most from heading error and variation problems, possibly because only peer pressure could be brought to bear on a member that contributed incorrect or inconsistent headings to the database. RLIN demanded greater accuracy from its members, rewarding high-quality cataloging and penalizing errors. Nevertheless, in a study of member-contributed cataloging in both of these databases, Intner found that the differences in quality and fullness between a group of 215 matched pairs of catalog records were not statistically significant. Cataloging from both databases averaged more than two errors per record, although most of the errors were relatively minor and would not have affected retrieval. For additional details of the study and its findings, see Sheila S. Intner, "Quality in Bibliographic Databases: An Analysis of Member-Contributed Cataloging in OCLC and RLIN," *Advances in Library Administration and Organization* 8 (1989): 1-24.

8.   This and other computer terms used in this chapter are, for the most part, in common usage and understandable, or they are defined briefly in the text. The reading list at the end of this chapter includes several books that might be useful if one wants more explanation and elaboration than given here.

9.   Computers usually are divided into three types: microcomputers, minicomputers, and mainframe computers, generally known only as mainframes. The differences between the types used to be based on their size, processing speed, and the level of supportable activity, with microcomputers at the small, slow, single-user end of the scale and mainframes at the large, fast, multiple-user end, and minicomputers somewhere in-between. Although these are useful measures, they no longer are definitive. As developments in computer technology have progressed, smaller computers have become larger, faster, and able to support higher levels of activity, so it no longer is possible to point to a particular amount of data storage capacity, called memory, or a particular processing speed as being possessed only by one type of computer.

Relatively speaking, however, microcomputers still are at the small end of the scale in comparison with mainframes, and minicomputers still are in-between, but individual microcomputers can be larger in some respects than some minicomputers, and individual minicomputers can support as much activity as certain mainframes, etc.

Jonathan Intner offers an interesting discussion on differentiating among computer types in "Beasts in a Box: How to Choose Microcomputer Hardware," in *The Library Microcomputer Environment: Management Issues,* eds. Sheila S. Intner and Jane Anne Hannigan (Phoenix, AZ: Oryx Press, 1987), 78-79. Although the specifics are dated, the principles are valid and provide a warning to those who are not familiar with the computer marketplace that thinking about computers is quite different than thinking about other kinds of equipment used in libraries and information centers.

15

Cataloging and Classification Policies

The cornerstone of a public library or school library media center's cataloging and classification operations should be a policy manual containing a record of all of the decisions governing the bibliographic processing of materials and provision of bibliographic services to patrons. Developing such a manual takes time and effort, but the result is a document that can be helpful to all staff members, whether they perform cataloging and classification tasks or merely use these organizing systems to help patrons find what they want and need. A policy manual can also help highlight the way the mission of the media center or library is served by its cataloging and classification services.

Contents of the Policy Manual

As is true of all policy documents, a bibliographic policy manual should begin with a brief description of the library's community or the media center's school, or in other words, the organization being served; official mission statement; and a summary of its facilities, staff, collections, and patrons. Putting the description of these elements at the beginning of the policy clarifies the setting and context in which these policies must operate. Also, any obvious discrepancies between the setting, its mission, and the policies contained in the document might be made explicit at this point.

Next, a section for each part of the bibliographic system, arranged in any order that seems logical to the staff, should include the decisions pertaining to that part along with a brief explanation of why certain decisions were taken. There is no one right way to organize policy documents, although the most frequently encountered order is chronological, beginning with the first step in the process and concluding with the final steps of shelving, usage, deacquisition, or all. But it might be just as useful to divide the manual into decisions concerning descriptive cataloging, the assignment of subject descriptors, classification, shelflisting, and processing. Or it might be organized by medium, with decisions about books, videos, databases, etc., in separate sections or chapters.

If a manual is organized by the various aspects of bibliographic control, it might begin with a section on derived cataloging if it is done by the library or media center. Methods of searching, matching, capturing, and editing existing records from the source database should be outlined carefully and completely. Knowing that every change made to a derived record is an added cost, policy makers will try to use bibliographic records "as is" to the greatest extent possible. Any mandated changes written into the policy should be scrutinized to ensure that the benefits they produce exceed their costs.

The section on original cataloging might begin with descriptive cataloging, specifying the level of description for various types of materials, the authority control system, the way items that are part of a series will be treated (that is, cataloged and classified separately or as a collection at the series level), whether some or all series titles will be traced, if or when multipart items will be analyzed (that is, provided with separate catalog records for each part), and how uniform titles will be adopted. Catalogers might decide to furnish analytic records for electronic resources in which the individual files can be used singly, but only one overall record for electronic resources in which the files are used in concert. Different descriptive treatments for different types of materials might be specified; for example, collections of tests or college catalogs might be given first-level descriptions, whereas reference collections and research materials might be given second-level descriptions. Decisions about the inclusion or exclusion of identifying data, the addition or deletion of descriptive access points, etc., should be documented in the manual in this section.

The next section might deal with subject headings, explaining the source for descriptors, the minimum and maximum number of descriptors assigned, the desired depth of indexing, and any special treatments accorded to particular materials. For example, if broad headings are desired for a small collection, *Library of Congress Subject Headings* might be adopted as the source list for descriptors, but subdivisions (i.e., subheadings) might be omitted for all but a few subject areas in which holdings are relatively abundant. Some materials might be indexed analytically, with descriptors assigned for each part of a multipart item, for each chapter of a book, or for each cut on a sound recording. For example, a collection of Shakespeare's plays, which usually are wanted one at a time, is a candidate for such treatment.

The section on classification might indicate the chosen system used, the level of complexity within the system, and how hard-to-classify materials such as periodicals or databases are treated. The method of assigning cutter letters or numbers and methods of adding them and other shelf marks to the classification number to complete the call number should be described. The choice between creating unique call numbers for each item or allowing more than one item to share the same call number should be documented here. Any designated anomalies in the shelving arrangement should be noted, such as keeping new acquisitions in a prominent display for a month or two; housing oversized books on special shelves; or dividing materials by teacher, grade level, class, etc.

Explanations for the decisions recorded in the policy document will enable one's successors to understand the reasoning behind them and, as conditions change, to recognize when there is a need to make changes.

A wise addition to any statement of policies or procedures is the establishment of regular review and amendment processes. Although an annual or biennial policy review might seem unnecessary at the time new policies are instituted, it is a good idea. Frequent reviews head off crises caused by the continuation of outmoded policies. If the reviewer or reviewers take the responsibility seriously and are careful to examine every part of the document thoroughly—from the prefatory descriptions, through each section of the main text, to the closing amendment process—they might be able to anticipate the need for change before the kinds of problems that motivate change occur.

Writing the Policy Manual

One person should be charged with writing the manual to minimize the possibility that individual differences in style and language produce sections using different words for the same concepts and other potentially confusing linguistic problems. Over time, more than one person can write sections of the manual, but at any one time, one person should be assigned this responsibility.

A good way to begin writing the policy manual for the first time is to draw up a table of contents, then circulate it among staff for suggestions about additions or changes to be made. It might be wise to indicate that just because suggestions are solicited does not mean they automatically will be followed. If major differences arise, negotiation can produce an acceptable solution so that the manual is a source of agreement, not contention. The table of contents, once defined, establishes the scope of the manual and identifies the way that the whole bibliographic system will be divided.

Writing the manual might then begin by listing all the decisions and operations that should be covered within each section; for example, decisions and operations relating to materials issued in series could be listed under "Descriptive Cataloging," "Tracing Practice," "Indexing," and "Classification," if the manual is divided into types of operations, or under "Series," if it is divided into types of material. Either way, all the decisions and practices relating to the handling of series must be covered somewhere in the manual. For the user's convenience, an index can bring together related information that falls into different sections or chapters (that is, to bring together all the descriptive cataloging decisions when the division is by material type, or all the decisions relating to series when the division is by operation). Word processing software enables indexes to be created automatically, making this a relatively easy task.

When the decisions and operations to be covered are listed but before actual writing begins, questions about the style of the presentation need to be answered. Some of them are as simple as whether one or both sides of a page should be used, whether sources will be cited at the bottom of pages or as endnotes, and whether illustrative examples, flowcharts, tables, etc., will be given within text or as separate pages or sections. Although such decisions may sound trivial, they will impact the ease with which the manual can be updated; the size of the document ("document" is used as a generic term here; the manual need not be a book—it could just as easily be a database); the ease with which it can be consulted, excerpted, or duplicated; its applicability to the task of training new staff; and similar capabilities. Other decisions include the approach to describing operations as step-by-step procedures or straight narratives; the amount and types of illustration; the inclusion or exclusion of supporting material (such as quoting decisions from LC rule interpretations or simply directing the user to the page on which the interpretation appears); etc.

At this point, with the content, approach, and style clearly defined, writing can begin. If the person designated as the writer is knowledgeable in all the areas covered by the manual, that person should begin writing each part, section, and chapter, completing them according to an agreed-upon schedule. If the manual includes procedures and the writer does not know some of them well enough to describe them completely, these should be done jointly with a knowledgeable guide, or another person should submit a draft to the writer, who will put it into final format. Either way, as each portion is written, it is wise to circulate it among the staff who will be expected to implement the decisions, or who actually perform the procedures, to be certain the information given in the manual is clearly understood and usable. The writer should expect to edit the work not only to account for this solicited feedback from staff members, but also generally to enhance, clarify, sharpen, and polish the text and illustrative material, based on his or her own re-readings of the text.

When enough of the manual is completed to warrant its distribution, the first few months (or longer) of its use should be considered a "test run" to see how well it functions. It might be issued in chapters or sections, or upon completion of the whole. With actual use, however, unanticipated problems can be expected to arise, which usually must be resolved by revising the language, examples and illustrations, finding aids, etc. Occasionally, enough difficulty is encountered in using a new manual to prompt reconsidering its basic organization, formatting, or style, and to suggest doing a major overhaul. In this event, it is best to weigh the true need for a total revision versus continuing to try making the existing manual "work." The first version of a manual need not be the last, but the difficulties should be evaluated carefully and estimates made that changes in style or approach can achieve the desired improvement before discarding an existing document. It is realistic to expect several months of revision to follow issuing a new manual to discover and work out "bugs." These problems should not be perceived as anyone's fault or as an inadequate job of writing. Revision is inherent in the process of obtaining an effective manual.

Responses to Changes in Cataloging Standards

An important set of decisions that should be included in the policy manual is the response to major changes in cataloging and classification standards. When new versions of the descriptive cataloging code and the chosen subject and classification authorities appear, how will they be adopted and implemented? Such changes occur regularly, because their governing bodies all follow policies of continual revision, so they need to be acknowledged and strategies for their implementation developed.

Among several possible responses are

1. *Make all required changes for all holdings immediately.* This is the most desirable option for keeping the entire collection together in one style of organization and completely up-to-date, but it is the most costly alternative, both in terms of dollars and cents and the amount of staff time it will consume in the short run.

2. *Make no changes in existing holdings, but implement changes for new materials immediately.* This is the strategy followed by many librarians and media specialists, because it seems to do the best that can be done with limited resources. Its problem lies in the fact that over time, even just a few years, the organization of the agency will start to break down because what emerges from this option is not one unified collection, but several fragmented collections, each following different rules. It was the strategy of choice for many institutions when they automated, and when it finally became necessary to incorporate the older holdings into the automated system, it was a major job costing more than anticipated.

3. *Make all changes over a limited period of time.* This strategy seems to be the most reasonable when circumstances don't permit the first approach, because all the materials remain in one unified organizational structure, even though the structure will take on different aspects as various changes are implemented. It probably has the best payoff in the long run, because it will ultimately result in the same organizational effectiveness as the first option, but it will not require as large an investment at once.

4. *Make changes selectively.* This strategy also is popular with practitioners and may be the best overall strategy when changes in cataloging rules, subject descriptors, and classification schemes do not affect holdings to any great extent. For example, if a library does not buy many items about music and its collection consists solely of a few works about music appreciation and other general topics, then the library might choose not to implement the changes in the DDC music schedules that appeared in the 20th edition. This strategy can lead to future problems, however, if the discrepancies become more significant over time.

5. *Make no changes and continue using older editions.* This strategy is deceptively simple, easy, and inexpensive. Eventually, however, it breaks down because it doesn't have the capacity to keep up with changes in materials, subject matter, and user needs. It may be inexpensive in the short run, but when the moment arrives that "something must be done" to improve it, it will cost a great deal more than it would have to address the changes when they first occurred.

To summarize, each of these alternatives—and they are not the only ones possible—has some advantages and some disadvantages, and each will have a different result both in the short term and over the long term. Although the first option might be an ideal response, it also is the most costly; and although the last option is the least costly, it probably will result in the least effective service to patrons over the long term, even though problems might not become apparent for some time. The other options fall somewhere between these extremes, and each librarian and media specialist must weigh the alternatives in terms of the individual situation and its impact on budget and staff as well as on patron services.

Procedures

The bibliographic policy manual might also contain separate sections in which procedures are spelled out for accomplishing the specific tasks required to carry out each part of the bibliographic control system. These explanations of procedures, often comprising a separate manual or several separate manuals, should not be substituted for the policy manual. A procedures manual is quite different and does not set forth either the decisions that the designated procedures are intended to support or the reasons why those decisions were made.

Procedures seem best when they follow the chronological order of steps involved, but there is no reason why separate processes can't be arranged in any order one wishes. Thus, one way to arrange the procedures manual is by physical medium, another is by bibliographic function, and a third is simply to put them in alphabetical order according to their names. No matter what the arrangement of the procedures manual, it should be possible to locate an individual procedure in which one is interested very easily. Thus, if the manual is arranged by function, it should have an alphabetic index by title; and if it is arranged alphabetically by the names of the procedures or by physical medium, there should be a functionally organized list of contents provided as well. In a small library or media center, it is likely the same staff will handle all media, making arrangements by physical medium less efficient, although even a single staff member might choose to work with the media one format at a time.

Adoption of the Policy Manual

As a final step before a policy manual is adopted, it is essential for administrators to affirm the policies it presents. It will do little good to decide to put some bibliographic policy in place if those who are responsible for the media center or library are unwilling to support the idea it represents, to fund its implementation, and to appreciate its value to the organization being served.

In connection with seeking administrative approval for policies, media specialists and librarians must be prepared to document the needs served by particular policies, to know their costs, and to defend the expenditures. Whether or not a costly change is being contemplated, it is fair for an administrator to expect catalogers or media center managers to be able to answer questions about the costs and benefits of bibliographic policies, to argue persuasively on behalf of proposed policies, and to negotiate compromise positions, when necessary.

Conclusion:
Patron Service First and Foremost

Service to patrons is the ultimate objective of all bibliographic policies and procedures. A good policy manual should embody decisions that result in good patron service. Cataloging and classification policies that affirm the use of standard tools and processes are recommended in this book because the authors believe they furnish good service and benefit patrons.

The fact that they change over time, however, indicates that standards are not perfect and that the changes made to them contribute positively to their utility. Public librarians and school library media specialists can benefit also by developing a positive attitude toward change in bibliographic services that will allow the combination of creative ideas, increasing knowledge, and dynamic systems to come together in providing better patron services.

Recommended Reading

Intner, Sheila S. *Interfaces: Relationships Between Library Technical and Public Services.* Englewood, CO: Libraries Unlimited, 1993.

Larson, Jeanette, and Herman L. Totten. *Model Policies for Small and Medium Public Libraries.* New York: Neal-Schuman, 1998.

PLA Handbook for Writers of Public Library Policies. Chicago: Public Library Association, 1993.

Schmidt, William D., and Donald A. Rieck. *Managing Media Services: Theory and Practice.* 2nd ed. Englewood, CO: Libraries Unlimited, 2000.

Weihs, Jean. *The Integrated Library: Encouraging Access to Multimedia Materials,* 2nd ed. Phoenix, AZ: Oryx Press, 1991.

Weinberg, Bella Hass, ed. *Cataloging Heresy: Challenging the Standard Bibliographic Product: Proceedings of the Congress for Librarians, February 18, 1991, St. John's University, Jamaica, New York, with Additional Contributed Papers.* Medford, NJ: Learned Information, 1992. [Explains standards and the implications of departing from them.]

16

Managing the Cataloging Department

Someone must take responsibility for managing the public library or school library media center's cataloging and classification operations. In very small agencies, this role can be assumed by the same person responsible for reader's services and collection development, and all other information-related operations; or, in larger agencies, it may be assumed by one person as their primary job. The ultimate aim is the same: to ensure that someone sees to it that cataloging and classification operations are performed properly, in a timely manner, and according to established policies.

Management Tasks

The title "department head" or "department manager" carries with it the responsibility to perform a variety of tasks having less to do with cataloging and classification than with managing the library or media center as a whole, or, for that matter, managing operations of any kind. These tasks are connected with any or all of the following activities:

1. *Staffing*—recruiting personnel, training and integrating them into the staff, supervising their work, and evaluating both it and each staff member's overall performance (such as their reliability, promptness, adaptability, etc.) for the purposes of salary determination, promotion, etc.

2. *Budgeting*—preparing budgets periodically, monitoring expenditures, and supplying the library or media center director with a financial report at the end of the budget period (usually a year).

3. *Planning*—proposing departmental goals and objectives, the ways departmental operations should proceed, devising workflow routines and all procedures for accomplishing the work of the department, and, when necessary, thinking of and trying new methods for getting the work done.

4. *Decision making*—taking the risk of choosing among alternative goals and objectives, potential plans or proposals, policies, strategies, procedures, suppliers, staff members and staff assignments, budgets, etc., for the department, and ensuring that all decisions made are consistent with the policies set by those who govern the media center or library.

5. *Directing*—taking charge, assigning tasks, arranging for things to be done properly, ensuring that people are functioning effectively, and providing leadership for the department.

Needed Skills

Knowing how to catalog and classify materials purchased for the public library or school library media center has been the focus of this book, and this knowledge of how bibliographic data is created and used is essential for the cataloging department manager to perform the tasks previously listed. The manager must, however, have other skills as well—skills that do not involve bibliographic information at all. They include communication skills, political skills, financial skills, and leadership skills.

Communication skills—both speaking and writing—are important to convey one's ideas to the people with whom one comes into contact. Those who work in the cataloging department initially need training to do their work. Even if they are skilled at cataloging and classification, the local situation must be explained and any special rules and procedures described. This will be particularly important if the person has come from a different type of agency. Workers at all levels need to know what is expected of them, the meaning of policies, and how local procedures are to be followed.

When new staff are recruited and interviewed, the department manager may be expected to write or edit the job description. When selected candidates visit the institution for onsite interviews, the department manager will be one of the principal participants and usually is expected to ask questions of each candidate and describe to them the work of the department.

The department manager must be able discuss the department with other staff, with administrators, and with peers at other organizations. Often, the department manager must speak or write to suppliers, computer system vendors, and a variety of others who may be involved in its operations from time to time. The department manager is responsible for writing periodic reports, evaluations of staff and operations, proposals for new equipment, new policies, and new procedures, and maintaining correspondence for the department within and outside of the organization.

Political skills—defined as the skills needed to get things done with people—are important to the cataloging department manager in order to have the department's needs recognized and its programs and budgets approved. Political skills encompass being persuasive, putting forth ideas in ways that will appeal to decision makers, and being able to build support for new proposals. Political skills also aid the department manager in building consensus within the department, establishing and maintaining an *esprit de corps* that gives everyone in the department a sense of satisfaction, and helps the department run smoothly.

Financial skills are necessary for planning the department's budget, defending it successfully before higher authorities within the organization, monitoring expenditures, and evaluating the results at the end of the budget cycle. Computer software is available to assist with the statistical work involved, but even the best software cannot substitute for an understanding of basic financial management processes and techniques. The cataloging department manager should be able to determine the true costs and evaluate the total value of alternative expenditures, not just to learn the price of things.

Leadership skills combine envisioning goals and objectives for the department, imbuing others with the vision, and risking the decisions that make progress possible toward those goals and objectives. Any decision could prove to be right or wrong, and the department manager who makes decisions risks failure as well as success. If the cataloging department is to grow and change, develop and achieve, it must have a leader willing to take on the risks of making decisions because of the importance of achieving the goals.

Management Issues

After the 1980s, the biggest challenge facing cataloging department managers was introducing computers into their operations and upgrading them as new hardware and software were made available. Far from being a better producer of catalog cards, automation eventually required reorganizing the workflow, retraining the staff, and incorporating all previous bibliographic data into the new computer-based systems being implemented. Among the profound changes that resulted were new patron services made possible by linking catalogs electronically. If a library or media center catalog is linked to the Internet, searchers can go beyond the local agency's holdings to seemingly limitless resources located all around the world. Even without external links, a local computer catalog can be linked without much difficulty or expense to other internal information files within the organization, such as order files, circulation files, etc., enabling searchers to determine the exact status of a desired title, or who is using it when it isn't on the shelf.

As electronic resources become more sophisticated, the challenge to make wise use of them has not diminished, but increased, putting pressure on library and media center managers to continue making changes in the way locally owned holdings are cataloged, indexed, classified, and processed. The demand for high-quality standard cataloging is increasing. One of the newest topics for consideration is the cataloging of "virtual" resources; that is, materials accessible via electronic networks, to alert searchers to their availability. OCLC used the Internet itself to distribute its publication titled *Cataloging Internet Resources,* edited by Nancy B. Olson.[1]

Although computer-related issues occupy a great proportion of cataloging department managers' attention, they aren't the only ones to be addressed. Another important issue is whether maintaining an in-house cataloging operation is as effective as contracting with an outside service to provide the library or media center with cataloging for new acquisitions and to maintain the catalog system. Known as *outsourcing,* outside contracting has attracted much attention and prompted intense debate. Deciding whether to contract with a cataloging source outside the library or media center or do one's own cataloging requires careful consideration of many factors, including the cost, speed, and quality of available products, and the loss of control over local operations and in-house expertise.

Other issues of note at this writing are opportunities to use several subject authorities in the catalog of a single library or media center, made possible by the multiple subject fields in the MARC format; difficulties of recruiting well-trained catalogers, caused in part by the closing of a number of professional schools; development, by LC and others, of standards for minimal level catalog records called *core records;* and the continuing struggle to make limited budgets stretch to cover everything cataloging departments are called upon or would like to do.

It may be just a matter of time until expert systems using computerized cataloging tools are developed that create full standard records faster and more accurately than the best work human catalogers can do. Publishers could employ such expert systems to add full cataloging to every item they issue as part of the publishing process, much like Cataloging-In-Publication, but with greater control and accuracy. However, though the technological know-how for creating expert cataloging programs has been available for some time, the complexity of bibliographic variation has yet to be conquered. With the advent of this kind of automatic cataloging, the department manager can turn her or his attention to assisting searchers in taking full advantage of it to find what they want more quickly and efficiently than ever before. Patron service is, after all, the object of all of our efforts. In the meanwhile, the cataloging department manager must endeavor to employ computing and electronic access to accomplish the work that catalogers have performed in different ways since Callimachus classified texts in ancient times for the great library at Alexandria.

Ten Hints for
Good Cataloging Management

1. Make basic decisions about bibliographic control policies for your library or media center, then write them down and abide by them until they are changed. When you consider alternatives, keep in mind the needs of users, obligations to your network if you use one, and available budget and staffing.

2. Remember the tradeoffs between quality and quantity; trying to balance doing the best possible job with doing the whole job. In particular, beware of allowing uncataloged backlogs to build while the department's resources are invested in doing more complex or sophisticated work than necessary.

3. Have the tools you need to do a good job of cataloging. An expensive reference tool will pay off in the long run in the form of higher quality cataloging with less anxiety.

4. When you decide on a local rule interpretation or subject application, write it down and use it for all other cases of the same kind.

5. Try to use the cataloging information that others have prepared. Examine what you are cataloging "from scratch" and see how to expedite the work. If given the opportunity to outsource some or all of your cataloging to a reliable vendor, be objective in analyzing the costs and benefits of doing so.

6. Examine your problems and experiment with solutions. Own up to mistakes quickly and honestly, then move on to more successful options. Try not to promise output that you are not sure can be delivered.

7. Develop a support system, and work at both using it and contributing to it. Join the cataloging group in your state, regional, or national professional association and be active in it. Befriend colleagues in your library or media center, colleagues in peer agencies, nearby libraries of all types, network partners and network representatives, and cataloging experts. You can write for help to us and other authors of cataloging texts, to user group and association leaders, cataloging educators, etc.

8. Keep informed. Cataloging rules and tools are dynamic and are constantly accommodating new decisions. Read the literature, keep up on revisions, and take advantage of continuing education opportunities.

9. Inform those who use the library or media center, and public service staff members of your decisions and procedures, and seek their input before making your final decisions.

10.   *Trust yourself!* Undoubtedly, no one in your organization knows more about biblio-graphic issues than you do.

Recommended Reading

Belcastro, Patricia. *Evaluating Library Staff: A Performance Appraisal System.* Chicago: American Library Association, 1998.

Evans, G. Edward, and Sandra M. Heft. *Introduction to Technical Services,* 6th ed. Englewood, CO: Libraries Unlimited, 1993. [See, especially, Part 1, "Technical Services" and Part 3: "Cataloging."]

Evans, G. Edward et al. *Management Basics for Information Professionals.* New York: Neal-Schuman, 2000.

Gorman, Michael, and associates. *Technical Services Today and Tomorrow.* 2nd ed. Englewood, CO: Libraries Unlimited, 1998.

Hirshon, Arnold, and Barbara Winters. *Outsourcing Library Technical Services: A How-To-Do-It Manual for Librarians.* New York: Neal-Schuman, 1996. [Includes a computer disk containing relevant forms.]

Intner, Sheila S., and Josephine Riss Fang. *Technical Services in the Medium-Sized Library: An Investigation of Current Practices.* Hamden, CT: Library Professional Publications, 1991. [Now dated, but Chapters 2, 5, and 8 contain helpful information.]

Johnson, Peggy, ed. *New Directions in Technical Services: Trends & Sources, 1993-1995.* Chicago: Association for Library Collections & Technical Services, 1997.

Kascus, Marie A., and Dawn Hale, eds. *Outsourcing Cataloging, Authority Work, and Physical Processing: A Checklist of Considerations.* Chicago: American Library Association, 1995.

Larson, Jeanette, and Herman L. Totten. *Model Policies for Small and Medium Public Libraries.* New York: Neal-Schuman, 1998.

Leonhardt, Thomas W., ed. *Technical Services in Libraries: Systems and Applications.* Greenwich, CT: JAI Press, 1992. [See especially, Chapters 2 through 6, 12 and 13.]

McCue, Janet. "Technical Services and the Electronic Library: Defining Our Roles and Defining the Partnership." *Library Hi Tech* 12, no. 3 (1995): 63-70.

Ross, Catherine, and Patricia Dewdney. *Communicating Professionally: A How-To-Do-It Manual for Library Applications,* 2nd ed. New York: Neal-Schuman, 1998.

Stewart, Barbara. *Neal-Schuman Directory of Library Technical Services Home Pages.* New York: Neal-Schuman, 1997.

Sutton, Dave. *So You're Going to Run a Library: A Library Management Primer.* Englewood, CO: Libraries Unlimited, 1995.

Trotta, Marcia. *Successful Staff Development: A How-To-Do-It Manual.* New York: Neal-Schuman, 1995.

Warner, Alice Sizer. *Budgeting: A How-To-Do-It Manual for Librarians.* New York: Neal-Schuman, 1998.

Wilson, Karen A., and Marylou Colver, eds. *Outsourcing Library Technical Services Operations: Practices in Academic, Public, and Special Libraries.* Chicago: American Library Association, 1997.

Wilson, Lucile. *People Skills for Library Managers.* Englewood, CO: Libraries Unlimited, 1996.

Woolls, Blanche. *The School Library Media Manager,* 2nd ed. Englewood, CO: Libraries Unlimited, 1999. [See especially, Chapter 7, "Managing Personnel," and Chapter 9, "Managing the Budget."]

Notes

1.   Nancy B. Olson, *Cataloging Internet Resources: A Manual and Practical Guide,* 2nd, ed. (Dublin, OH: OCLC Inc., 1997). Also available via the OCLC Web site: http://www.purl.org/oclc/cataloging-internet.

Selected Bibliography

Materials included in this selected bibliography are of interest to school library media specialists and public librarians performing cataloging that conforms to the current U.S. and Canadian standards. Some items may duplicate those cited in the notes or reading lists following many of the chapters; however, no attempt was made to include all titles cited elsewhere in the book. In particular, basic cataloging tools described in the text are not duplicated here. With some exceptions, selections are intended to be up-to-date, published in 1996 or later, and general in scope and coverage.

General Works

AUTOCAT. Electronically accessed discussion group for catalogers available via the Internet. Subscriptions can be entered by sending a message to the discussion owner: AUTOCAT@UVMVM (you will have to add .BITNET or .EDU, as appropriate, to complete the Internet address), with a blank subject line, SUBSCRIBE [YOUR NAME].

Chan, Lois Mai. *Cataloging and Classification: An Introduction.* 3rd ed. New York: McGraw-Hill, 1999.

Cochrane, Pauline Atherton, and Eric H. Johnson, eds., with the editorial assistance of Sandra Roe. *Visualizing Subject Access for 21st Century Information Resources: [Papers Presented at the 1997] Clinic on Library Applications of Data Processing, March 2-4, 1997.* Champaign, IL: Graduate School of Library and Information Science, University of Illinois at Urbana-Champaign, 1998.

Cundiff, Margaret Welk. *Cataloging Concepts: Descriptive Cataloging. Instructor's Manual.* 2 vols. Ed. Matthew E. Gildea. Washington, DC: Cataloging Distribution Service, Library of Congress, 1993. [Course of study used at the Library of Congress for new descriptive catalogers; student's manual also available.]

Hagler, Ronald. *The Bibliographic Record and Information Technology.* 3rd ed. Chicago: American Library Association, 1998.

Harrod's Librarians' Glossary: 9,000 Terms Used in Information Management, Library Science, Publishing, the Book Trades and Archive Management. 8th ed. Comp. Ray Prytherch. Aldershot, England: Gower, 1995.

Intner, Sheila S., and Jean Weihs. *Special Libraries: A Cataloging Guide.* Englewood, CO: Libraries Unlimited, 1998.

Maxwell, Robert L., with Margaret F. Maxwell. *Maxwell's Handbook for AACR2R: Explaining and Illustrating the Anglo-American Cataloguing Rules and the 1993 Amendments.* Chicago: American Library Association, 1997.

Millsap, Larry, and Terry Ellen Ferl. *Descriptive Cataloging for the AACR2R and USMARC: A How-To-Do-It Workbook.* Rev. ed. New York: Neal Schuman, 1997.

Saye, Jerry D. *Manheimer's Cataloging and Classification: A Workbook.* 4th ed., revised and expanded. New York: Marcel Dekker, 1999.

Shearer, James R., and Alan R. Thomas, eds. *Cataloging and Classification: Trends, Transformations, Teaching, and Training.* Binghamton, NY: Haworth Press, 1997.

Taylor, Arlene G. *The Organization of Information.* Englewood, CO: Libraries Unlimited, 1999.

———. *Wynar's Introduction to Cataloging and Classification.* 9th ed. Englewood, CO: Libraries Unlimited, 2000.

Nonbook Materials

Audiovisual Librarian. London, England: Audiovisual Group of the [British] Library Association, 1973- . [quarterly]

Dreissen, Karen C., and Sheila A. Smyth. *A Library Manager's Guide to Physical Processing of Nonprint Materials.* Westport, CT: Greenwood Press, 1995. [This addresses the physical processing of nonprint items. We include it here because cataloging and processing can be combined in public libraries and media centers.]

Fritz, Deborah A. *Cataloging with AACR2R and USMARC for Books, Computer Files, Serials, Sound Recordings, Videorecordings.* Chicago: American Library Association, 1998.

Hsieh-Yee, Ingrid. *Organizing Audiovisual and Electronic Resources for Access: A Cataloging Guide.* Englewood, CO: Libraries Unlimited, 2000.

MC Journal: The Journal of Academic Media Librarianship. [electronic journal] Lori Widzinski, ed.; available via e-mail at *HSLLJW@ubvm.cc.buffalo.edu.*

OLAC Newsletter. Buffalo, NY: OnLine Audiovisual Catalogers, 1981- . [quarterly]

Olson, Nancy B. *Cataloging of Audiovisual Materials and Other Special Materials: A Manual Based on AACR 2.* 4th ed. Eds. Sheila S. Intner and Edward Swanson. DeKalb, IL: Minnesota Scholarly Press, 1998.

Robinson, Sally Mason. *Developing and Managing Video Collections in Libraries: A How-To-Do-It Manual.* New York: Neal-Schuman, 1996.

Urbanski, Verna et al. *Cataloging Unpublished Nonprint Materials: A Manual of Suggestions, Comments, and Examples.* Lake Crystal, MN: Soldier Creek Press, 1992.

Weihs, Jean, and Lynne C. Howarth. "Nonbook Materials: Their Occurrence and Bibliographic Description in Canadian Libraries." *Library Resources & Technical Services* 39, no. 2 (1995): 184-197.

Ongoing Publications

Cataloging & Classification Quarterly. Binghamton, NY: Haworth Press, 1980- .

Cataloging Service bulletin. Washington, DC: Library of Congress, 1978- . [quarterly]

CMC News. Cannon Falls, MN: CMC News, 1979- . [3 times a year]

Information Technology and Libraries. Chicago: American Library Association, 1982- . [quarterly]

International Classification and Bibliographic Control. Frankfurt: IFLA, 1972- . [quarterly]

Library Hi Tech. Ann Arbor, MI: Pierian Press, 1982- . [monthly]

Library Resources & Technical Services. Chicago: American Library Association, 1957- . [quarterly]

Technical Services Quarterly. Binghamton, NY: Haworth Press, 1983- .

Technicalities. Kansas City, MO: Media Periodicals Division/Trozzolo Creative Resources, 1981- . [bimonthly]

B

Glossary

This list of acronyms and cataloging terms includes those defined in the text compiled here in one place for convenience as well as for readers who encounter a term or acronym subsequently to its first mention (the definition of a term appears only at its first mention). The list also includes some terms not used in the text, but often encountered in the cataloging literature.

A&C. *Additions & Changes,* quarterly publication of the Library of Congress used to up-date the Library of Congress Classification.

AACR. *Anglo-American Cataloging Rules.* Cataloging rules cooperatively developed by the library associations and national libraries of the United States, United Kingdom, Canada, and, beginning in 1981, Australia. *See also AACR1, AACR2, AACR2R,* and *AACR2-98.*

AACR1. *Anglo-American Cataloging Rules,* 1967. The first edition of AACR, published in two versions, one for North Americans and one for the United Kingdom.

AACR2. *Anglo-American Cataloguing Rules,* 1978. The second edition of AACR, this time published in one version for all the participating nations.

AACR2R. *Anglo-American Cataloguing Rules,* second edition, 1988 revision. This edition was the standard until 1998, when an updated revision was published.

AACR2-98. *Anglo-American Cataloguing Rules,* second edition, 1998 revision. The current standard edition of rules for descriptive cataloging and access. One update, the "1999 Amendments to AACR2," has been issued since its publication, available as a free download from the American Library Association's Web site, at http://www.ala.org/editions/updates/aacr2.

AALL. American Association of Law Librarians.

AAT. *Art and Architecture Thesaurus.*

Access. The process of choosing and formulating headings for bibliographic records. Also refers to the larger processes of providing bibliographic access (that is, cataloging), intellectual access (that is, classification and indexing), and physical access to material.

Access point. Any name, word, or phrase by which a catalog record can be retrieved from the catalog, known also as an *entry, heading,* or *retrieval point.*

AC heading. Annotated Card heading. Subject heading from a special list of terms created by the Library of Congress for juvenile materials. *See also* Annotated Card Program.

Added entry. A secondary access point; any heading by which a catalog record can be retrieved other than the first (or *main*) entry.

A-G Canada Ltd. The Canadian bibliographic utility formerly known as ISM.

ALA. American Library Association.

ALCTS. Association for Library Collections & Technical Services. A division of the American Library Association called the Resources and Technical Services Division before 1989.

Alphabetico-classed catalog. A semiclassified catalog in which principal headings are in classified order, but headings at the same level of hierarchy are arranged alphabetically.

Alternative title. A title following title proper and preceded by the word "or," in any language. For example the underlined data in the operetta by Gilbert and Sullivan titled: *Trial by jury, or, The lass who loved a sailor.*

AMICUS. The resource-sharing database of the National Library of Canada. *See also* DOBIS.

Analytic(s). Catalog records or access points for a work that is part of a larger bibliographic unit; for example, one song on a sound recording containing several songs.

Annotated Card Program. Program initiated by the Library of Congress for cataloging juvenile materials that includes adding specialized subject headings and summary notes to the catalog records.

ANSCR. Alpha-Numeric System for the Classification of Recordings.

Area of description. One of the eight parts of a bibliographic description designated by ISBD and AACR2-98; for example, the Edition area (area 2) or the Series area (area 6).

ARLIS/NA. Art Libraries Society of North America.

ASTED. Association pour l'avancement des sciences et des techniques de la documentation. The professional association for French-speaking librarians in Canada.

Authority file. A file containing the official forms of names, uniform titles, series titles, subject headings, or all used as access points in a library catalog, and citations to sources used to establish them as well as cross-references to variant forms.

Authority record. One record in an authority file. *See also* Name authority, Subject authority.

Auxiliary table. In classification, a separate table of subdivisions intended to be used with numbers from the main schedules.

BALLOTS. Bibliographic Automation of Large Library Operations using a Time-sharing System. The forerunner of RLIN®.

Bibliographic description. The part of a catalog record that identifies the item it represents, exclusive of access points, call numbers, and other control numbers other than the ISBN and the ISSN.

Bibliographic identity. The name used on an item to identify the creator. One who uses more than one name on his or her works is said to have multiple bibliographic identities.

Bibliographic level. 1. One of three standard styles of description prescribed by AACR2-98, each containing varying amounts of bibliographic information from the least (level 1) to the most (level 3). 2. In OCLC's MARC format, a fixed field identified by the prefix "Bib lvl," that indicates whether an item is monographic or serial.

Bibliographic network. A group of libraries who share a computerized database of bibliographic information or whose individual bibliographic databases are electronically linked.

Bibliographic record. A catalog record.

Bibliographic unit. A cataloging unit; an entity capable of being cataloged, indexed, and classified, such as a book, a videorecording, a game, etc.

Bibliographic utility. A group of electronically linked libraries that generate new catalog records.

Blind reference. A cross reference used in a catalog that leads searchers to a term having no entries under it.

Book mark. *See* Cutter number, Shelf mark.

Book number. *See* Cutter number, Shelf mark.

Boolean operators. The words AND, OR, NOT, etc., used in combining subject terms for retrieval.

Boolean retrieval. Computer programs based on Boolean algebra that permit retrieval for combinations of search terms.

Call letter. *See* Shelf mark.

Call number. The shelf address of an item, usually consisting of its classification number and shelf marks.

CAN/MARC. CANadian MAchine-Readable Cataloguing.

Carrier. For selected nonbook materials, the container that carries the material on which the intellectual content of an item is recorded, such as a cartridge, cassette, disc, reel, etc.

Cast. In some nonbook media such as videorecordings, the performers. Also, a note naming the performers. *See also* Credits.

CCC. The Canadian Committee on Cataloguing, responsible for monitoring issues and standards in cataloging for the Canadian cataloging community.

CC:DA. Committee on Cataloging: Description and Access, a committee of the Cataloging and Classification Section of the Association for Library Collections & Technical Services, a division of the American Library Association. This committee is responsible for monitoring issues and standards in descriptive cataloging for the U.S. cataloging community.

CCM. Canadian Committee on MARC.

CD-ROM. Compact Disc-Read Only Memory. A storage device for computerized information; data are read from the discs by a scanner.

CDS. Cataloging Distribution Service. The marketing agency for the Library of Congress's bibliographic products.

Chief source. In descriptive cataloging, the main location from which bibliographic data are taken, such as the title page of a book, title screens of an electronic resource, etc. *See also* Prescribed source.

Citation order. In classification and indexing, a prescribed order in which the components of a topic are given; for example, Topic—Location—Period *versus* Location—Topic—Period.

CLA. Canadian Library Association.

Classed catalog. A catalog in which records are filed by subject, such as a shelflist. *See also* Dictionary catalog, Divided catalog.

Closed entry. Catalog record previously containing open dates, etc., for a publication in progress, that has been completed or "closed," presumably because the title is completed. *See also* Open entry.

CODEN. An internationally recognized identifier for a serial title, administered by the Chemical Abstracts Service.

Coding. The act or process of assigning MARC content designators to bibliographic data. Sometimes called *coding and tagging. See also* Tagging.

Coextensive. Exactly matching. In indexing and classification, an index term or a class that is neither broader nor narrower than the topic being represented, but exactly matches its breadth and depth.

Collocate. To bring related items together, such as titles written by the same author, editions and versions of the same title, or materials on the same topic.

Colophon. A page at the end of a printed item on which bibliographic information is given.

Command-driven. A computerized system requiring the entry of commands for operation. *See also* Menu-driven.

COMPASS. A computer-assisted system of indexing library materials used at one time in the United Kingdom and elsewhere. Originally developed by the British Library's Classification Research Group in the 1970s and named PRECIS, the system subsequently was simplified and renamed COMPASS. *See also* PRECIS.

CONSER. CONversion of SERials. A program originally administered at the Library of Congress but later shifted to OCLC, whose objective is to build a national database of catalog records for serials and holdings.

Content designators. In the MARC formats, all of the characters or combinations of characters identifying specific parts of bibliographic, authority, or holdings records, and the kinds of data held in them.

Continuation. A publication such as a serial, series, or frequently revised monographic title to which a library or information center subscribes on an ongoing basis.

Control field. A field in the MARC format identified by a tag beginning with the number zero. Control fields contain information such as call number, ISBN, LCCN, etc. *See also* Fixed field, Variable field.

Controlled vocabulary. A list of terms authorized for indexing, such as a subject heading list or thesaurus. *See also* Subject authority, Uncontrolled vocabulary.

Conventional title. *See* Uniform title.

Copy cataloging/classification. A method of cataloging or classifying library materials in which a source record is copied or edited instead of creating a new record. Also called "Derived cataloging/classification." *See also* Original cataloging/classification.

CORC. Cooperative Online Resource Catalog. A project sponsored by OCLC to compile a database of metadata for Internet resources.

Core record. A catalog record standard containing less data than that required for full-level status by national bibliographic input standards, but more than that required for minimal-level status. Core records include, in addition to minimal-level data, selected descriptive fields and access points that conform fully to national authority control requirements. *See also* PCC.

Corporate body. A named group of people that acts as an entity.

Credits. For some nonbook items such as videorecordings, a statement naming participants in the creation of the item. Also a note naming those participants. Credits can be divided into technical credits (those responsible for taping, filming, editing, etc.) and artistic credits (writers, directors, producers, etc.). *See also* Cast.

Cross-reference. A message in the catalog that links two or more related access points. For example, a message at *Clemens, Samuel Langhorne* referring searchers to *Twain, Mark.*

CSB. *Cataloging Service* bulletin. A Library of Congress periodical publication providing news of cataloging policy decisions, new subject authorities, etc.

CSH. *Canadian Subject Headings.*

Cutter letter(s). Alphabetic device similar to a cutter number in which one or more letters are used in place of combined letters and numbers to arrange items in alphabetical order. *See also* Cutter number, Shelf mark.

Cutter number. An alphanumeric code originated by Charles A. Cutter, designed to arrange items in alphabetical order. Sometimes called "book mark" or "book number." *See also* Shelf mark.

Cuttered, cuttering, cutters. A verb form of the word "cutter" naming the act of assigning a cutter number.

DC. *See DDC, Dublin Core.*

DC&. *[Dewey] Decimal Classification Additions, Notes and Decisions.* A Forest Press occasional publication, now discontinued, that provided news about classification policy decisions, etc.

DDC. Dewey Decimal Classification.

De facto. Literally meaning "in fact" or "in practice." A term applied to the Library of Congress functioning in the role of national library of the United States even though no legislation designates it as such.

De jure. Literally meaning "in law." A term that can be applied to the National Library of Medicine and National Agricultural Library functioning in the role of national libraries of the United States, because legislation legally designates them as such.

Delimiter. In the MARC format, a symbol identifying the start of a subfield. Delimiters can print variously as double daggers (‡), dollar signs ($), or "at" symbols (@). *See also* Subfield code.

Derived cataloging/classification. *See* Copy cataloging/classification.

Descriptor. A term consisting of one or more words indicating subject matter, often taken from a list of terms known as a thesaurus or subject heading list. *See also* Subject authority, Subject heading.

Dictionary catalog. A catalog in which all records are filed alphabetically. *See also* Classed catalog, Divided catalog.

Direct entry. 1. An access point in which the desired name or word is the first part of the heading, without naming a larger unit of which it is part. For example, the heading is ONTARIO, not CANADA—ONTARIO; or the heading is WHALES, not MAMMALS—WHALES. 2. A multiword heading given in the order in which it would be spoken (that is, "natural order") without reversing the order of the words. For example, LIBRARY CATALOGS, not CATALOGS, LIBRARY, or JAPANESE LITERATURE, not LITERATURE, JAPANESE. *See also* Indirect entry. 3. A corporate body name heading for a part of a larger body that is entered under its own name, not the name of the large body. For example, the heading is LIBRARY OF CONGRESS, not UNITED STATES. LIBRARY OF CONGRESS.

Distinctive title. A title consisting of words in addition to those naming a compositional or publication type, such as "Scottish symphony," or "Bulletin of healthy living." *See also* Generic title.

Divided catalog. A catalog in which different types of records are gathered into separate files; for example, author headings in one file, title headings in a second file, and subject headings in a third file; or, author and title headings in one file, topical subject headings in a separate file. *See also* Classed catalog, Dictionary catalog.

DOBIS. DOrtmunder BIbliotheks System. A bibliographic network originating at the University of Dortmund, adopted and administered in Canada until the 1990s by the National Library of Canada. *See also* AMICUS.

Dublin Core. A set of 15 identifying elements used to create metadata for electronic resources similar to the much larger number of elements used in library catalog records. Sometimes abbreviated "DC."

Dumb terminal. A video display monitor that does not contain a central processing unit.

Dumping. Automatic entry of data in a computerized system. Also called *loading* or *mounting* data.

EAD. Encoded Archival Description, a set of protocols for editing text for computer input and communication.

Emanate/emanation. To issue/issuing items by a corporate body.

Entry. Narrowly defined, an access point; broadly defined, a bibliographic record.

Enumerative. A classification or subject authority in which all topics, both simple and compound, are listed (or enumerated) for the cataloger, who merely selects the appropriate one(s) for each item. *See also* Faceted, Precoordinate, Postcoordinate, Synthetic.

Extent. The total amount of an item's physical manifestation, for example, the pages of a book, reels of microfilm, cassettes of a videorecording, disks of an electronic resource, etc. Data given in the extent can also include the number of frames, duration, etc., for some materials.

Faceted. A classification or subject heading list in which topical components (i.e., facets) are listed and the cataloger builds an appropriate class number or heading by combining the appropriate components. *See also* Postcoordinate, Synthetic.

Field. In the MARC formats, one part of a record corresponding to one area of description, one subject heading, one call number, etc. *See also* Control field, Fixed field, Variable field.

Fixed field. 1. Any field containing data of fixed length and in fixed format. For example, the 043 field contains codes representing geographic data given in eye-readable form elsewhere in the record: "na̅us̅ca" in the 043 field stands for "North America—United States—California." 2. In OCLC and RLIN records, this refers also to special formatting of the 008 field in which specially designed prefixes identify subfields in place of the usual subfield codes. *See also* Control field, Variable field.

Form subdivision. In subject cataloging or indexing, a term used as a subdivision that describes the form or genre of an item, such as -DICTIONARIES; in classification, a number or span of numbers assigned to materials having specific forms or genres; for example, in DDC, standard subdivision -05 means Serials.

Format integration. In the MARC formats, the process by which individual formats for books, serials, maps, and other material forms, each developed separately, were compiled into one unified group of protocols called an *integrated format*. *See also* Integrated format.

Free-floating subdivision. In subject authorities, a term that can be added to authorized subject terms as a subdivision without a specific listing or instruction.

Full stop. British term for the mark of punctuation called a "period" by North Americans.

Generic title. A title consisting of words naming a type of composition or publication, such as "Symphony," or "Bulletin." *See also* Distinctive title.

gmd. General material designation. Part of the first area of description naming the media group to which an item belongs.

General material designation. *See* gmd.

Heading. *See* Access point.

Help screen. A feature of computer systems in which an instructional screen (help screen) can be requested by the user.

Host/host system. A larger computer system to which a smaller computer system is linked.

HTML. HyperText Markup Language, a set of protocols for editing text for computer input and communication.

ICCP. International Conference on Cataloguing Principles, held in Paris in 1961.

IFLA. International Federation of Library Associations and Institutions.

Imprint. Publishing data for a book, including the location and name of the publisher, and date of publication. In AACR2, these data were expanded and renamed "publication, distribution, etc., information."

Indicators. In MARC format fields, special values that instruct the computer to manipulate data in a particular way. For example, in the 245 field, the first indicator value controls making an added entry for title proper and the second indicator value controls indexing of title proper.

Indirect entry. An access point—often a geographic or corporate body name—in which the desired name is not the first part of the heading. For example, the desired name is BOSTON, but the heading is MASSACHUSETTS—BOSTON, or the desired name is REFERENCE AND ADULT SERVICES DIVISION, but the heading is AMERICAN LIBRARY ASSOCIATION. REFERENCE AND ADULT SERVICES DIVISION. *See also* Direct entry.

Indirect subdivision. A subdivision of an access point in which the subdividing term is expressed indirectly. For example, to show agriculture in Canterbury, England, indirectly, the subdivision is AGRICULTURE—ENGLAND—CANTERBURY, not AGRICULTURE—CANTERBURY.

Input standards. Standards dictating the amount of data that must be included in catalog records that can be entered into the database of a bibliographic utility.

Integral label. A label permanently affixed to the carrier of a nonbook material by its publisher or distributor.

Integrated format. In the MARC format, the unified set of protocols applicable to all types of library materials now in use for encoding bibliographic data. *See also* Format integration.

Interactive multimedia. The gmd proposed by CC:DA for a new media group consisting of computer files combined with other media such as video, sound, graphics, text, etc., in which the user of the item is able to manipulate it to produce unique results.

International Serials Data System. *See* ISDS.

International Standard Bibliographic Description. *See* ISBD.

International Standard Book Number. *See* ISBN.

International Standard Music Number. *See* ISMN.

International Standard Recording Code. *See* ISRC.

International Standard Serial Number. *See* ISSN.

ISBD. International Standard Bibliographic Description. An international standard promulgated by IFLA for describing materials, which mandates sources for the descriptive data, the data elements, the order in which they are to appear, and punctuation to identify them.

ISBN. International Standard Book Number. An internationally used unique identifier for each title issued by publishers participating in the program.

ISDS. International Serials Data System. A program for identifying the world's serials using an individual symbol (CODEN) and title (key title) identifier for each unique title.

ISM. ISM Information Systems Management Corporation. The Canadian bibliographic utility formerly known as Utlas International, later changed to A-G Canada Ltd.

ISMN. International Standard Music Number. An internationally used unique identifier for each musical publication issued by publishers participating in the program.

ISRC. International Standard Recording Code. An internationally used unique identifier for each recording issued by publishers or distributors participating in the program.

ISSN. International Standard Serial Number. An internationally accepted unique identifier for each serial issued by publishers participating in the program.

Joint Steering Committee for Revision of AACR. An international body consisting of representatives of the library associations and national libraries of the United States (that is, the Library of Congress), Canada, the United Kingdom, and Australia, charged with determining the contents of the *Anglo-American Cataloguing Rules.* Also called "Joint Steering Committee."

JSC. *See* Joint Steering Committee for Revision of AACR.

JSCAACR. *See* Joint Steering Committee for Revision of AACR.

Key heading. In *Sears List of Subject Headings,* a designated subject heading whose subdivisions can be applied to any similar subject heading; for example, "Chicago" is the key heading for all cities. *See also* Pattern heading.

Key title. In the ISDS program, a title assigned to an individual serial to identify it uniquely.

Keyword. 1. A significant word in a title or subject heading. 2. A searchable word, such as a significant word in a title or subject heading. 3. Colloquially, any searchable subject word or term.

Keyword index. An index in which significant words from titles, subject headings, or other areas of a catalog record are access points. *See also* KWIC index, KWOC index.

KWIC index. KeyWord In Context index. An index of title or subject words in which the titles are given in natural word order. For example, the title *Managing the Library Automation Project* would appear as:

Managing the Library	AUTOMATION	Project
Managing the	LIBRARY	Automation Project
	MANAGING	the Library Automation
Project		
Managing the Library Automation	PROJECT	

KWOC index. KeyWord Out of Context index. An index of title or subject words in which the titles are given in indirect order, bringing the keyword to the filing position. For example, the title *Managing the Library Automation Project* would appear as:

AUTOMATION	Project, Managing the Library
LIBRARY	Automation Project, Managing the
MANAGING	the Library Automation Project
PROJECT,	Managing the Library Automation

LC. The U.S. Library of Congress.

LCC. Library of Congress Classification.

LCCN. Library of Congress Control Number. A unique number assigned by the Library of Congress to each catalog record it creates and by which its customers order cataloging on cards or in computer-readable format. Before the advent of computerized cataloging products, the acronym stood for Library of Congress Card Number.

LCRI. Library of Congress Rule Interpretation. A policy decision for the application of a rule appearing in AACR2-98 made by the Library of Congress.

LCSH. *Library of Congress Subject Headings.* A subject authority produced by the Library of Congress.

Linearity. A feature of library classification in which all subjects are perceived as being placed in a straight line (that is, in two dimensions) from beginning to end, as on library shelves.

Loading. *See* Dumping.

Local system. A computer system entirely within the control of a single library or library system. Occasionally, a local system is shared by a small group of libraries.

LSP. Linked Systems Project. A program linking the Library of Congress's computer system with the computer systems of other program participants.

Main class. In classification, the primary categories into which knowledge is divided.

Main entry. 1. The first and most important descriptive access point assigned to a catalog record by which the item can be retrieved. 2. In a single entry catalog, the access point for a record.

MARA. MAchine Readable Accessions.

MARBI. The Committee on Representation in MAchine-Readable Form of Bibliographic Information. An interdivisional committee of the American Library Association comprised of representatives from three of its divisions: Association for Library Collections & Technical Services, Library and Information Technology Association, and Reference and User Services Association.

MARC. MAchine-Readable Cataloging. A group of identifying codes used to communicate bibliographic and other types of data using computers, originally devised by the Library of Congress.

MARC format(s). The compilation(s) of codes used for identifying data for computer communication. Formats have been established for bibliographic data, authorities, holdings, classification, and community information. *See also* MARC.

MARC 21. A version of the MARC format that merges previously separate formats used by Library of Congress (USMARC) and National Library of Canada (CAN/MARC).

Material specific details. The third area of description. Also called "mathematical details."

Mathematical details. *See* Material specific details.

Menu-driven. A computer system that operates by presenting a list of options (menu) to the user from which a selection must be made. *See also* Command-driven.

MeSH. *Medical Subject Headings.* A thesaurus of terms for indexing medical information sponsored by the National Library of Medicine.

Metadata. 1. Data identifying other data, such as citations to documents. 2. Data identifying electronic resources, particularly Internet resources.

Minimal level cataloging. Catalog records containing less information than the minimum required by currently accepted standards.

Mixed notation. In classification, a system of symbols representing the subjects composed of more than one type of character; for example, numbers and letters of the alphabet. *See also* Pure notation.

Mixed responsibility. An item created by differing contributions of more than one responsible party, such as a book having an author, an editor, and an illustrator.

MLA. 1. Medical Library Association, 2. Music Library Association.

Module. In a computer system, a program segment or package designed to perform one function in a multifunction system.

Monograph. An item published or produced in full within a finite time period. *See also* Serial.

Monographic series. *See* Series.

Mounting. *See* Dumping.

MRDS. The MARC Records Distribution Service of the National Library of Canada.

Multimedia. 1. British gmd for multipart items in which the parts belong to more than one medium and no one part predominates, but not a synonym for and not to be confused with *interactive multimedia.*

NAL. National Agricultural Library [U.S.].

Name authority. An official record of the establishment of a name form for use as an access point in library catalogs, with its cross-references and data sources. *See also* Authority record.

NLC. National Library of Canada.

NLCRI. National Library of Canada Rule Interpretation. A policy decision for the application of a rule appearing in AACR2-98 made by the National Library of Canada for its catalogers.

NLM. National Library of Medicine [U.S.].

NLMC. National Library of Medicine Classification.

Notation. In classification, the system of symbols used to represent subjects. *See also* Mixed notation, Pure notation.

OCLC. Online Computer Library Center. A bibliographic utility headquartered in Dublin Ohio, formerly known as the Ohio College Library Center.

OCLC/WLN. A bibliographic utility headquartered in the state of Washington, originally called Washington Library Network, then renamed Western Library Network, and subsequently merged with OCLC.

Ohio College Library Center. *See* OCLC.

OLUC. OnLine Union Catalog. Former name of OCLC's bibliographic database, now known as WorldCat. *See also* WorldCat.

Online Computer Library Center. *See* OCLC.

OPAC. Online Public Access Catalog. *See also* PAC.

Open entry. Catalog record for a publication-in-progress in which selected elements are left incomplete, such as dates of publication, distribution, and extent of the item. *See also* Closed entry.

Original cataloging/classification. The process of creating a new catalog record for an item without the use of a previously created record for the same or related item. *See also* Copy cataloging/classification.

Other physical details. Data relating to the physical properties of an item being cataloged other than its extent, dimensions, and accompanying materials. For example, for a book, it includes illustrations; for an electronic resource, it includes the presence of sound, color, etc.

Other preliminaries. *See* Preliminaries.

Other title information. Title information other than the main title (title proper), alternative title (a title following title proper preceded by the word "or"), and parallel title (title proper in another language or script).

Outsourcing. The practice of contracting with an organization outside the library or media center, often but not always a commercial organization, for operations or services typically performed within the library or media center, such as cataloging.

PAC. Public Access Catalog. *See also* OPAC.

Parallel title. The main title of an item in another language or script.

Parenthetic qualifier. *See* Qualifier.

Paris principles. A statement of descriptive cataloging principles adopted by participants in the International Conference on Cataloguing Principles held in Paris in 1961.

Pattern heading. In *Library of Congress Subject Headings,* a set of subdivisions for a subject heading designated to be applied to all other subject headings of the same type without additional instruction. *See also* Key heading.

PCC. Program for Cooperative Cataloging; promulgator of the core record standard.

Periodical. 1. A serial title issued on a regular schedule, generally more frequently than once or twice a year. 2. Journal, magazine, or newspaper.

Postcoordinate. A classification or subject heading list in which class numbers or headings for topical components are given in the schedule or list to be assembled by the cataloger or searcher as needed. *See also* Faceted, Synthetic.

PRECIS. PREserved Context Indexing System. A computer-assisted system of indexing library materials once used in the United Kingdom and elsewhere, developed by the British Library's Classification Research Group in the 1970s. The system was later simplified and renamed COMPASS. In the 1990s, it was completely discontinued.

Precoordinate. A classification or subject heading list in which topical components are already preassembled (precoordinated) and given in the schedule or list. *See also* Enumerative, Postcoordinate.

Preliminaries. Pages in a book beginning with the cover and concluding with the verso of the title page. Also called "other preliminaries" to exclude the title page recto from the definition.

Prescribed source(s). Location(s) authorized by AACR2-98 for obtaining bibliographic data for a particular area of description. The locations vary by type of material. *See also* Chief source.

Primary entry. *See* Main entry.

Pure notation. In classification, a system of symbols representing subjects that use only one type of character; for example, only digits (as in DDC) or only letters of the roman alphabet (as in the Bliss Bibliographic Classification). *See also* Mixed notation.

PURL. Permanent Uniform Resource Locator, permanent address for an Internet resource that is maintained over time, eliminating retrieval problems caused by changing Internet addresses. *See also* URL.

Qualifier. A word or phrase that removes ambiguity from an access point, usually given in parentheses, such as Cambridge (Mass.) and Cambridge (England), or Kiss (Performing group).

Recto. The right-hand page of a book, always bearing an odd number. *See also* Verso.

Research Libraries Group. The parent organization of the RLIN.

Research Libraries Information Network. *See* RLIN.

Retrieval point. *See* Access point.

RLG. *See* Research Libraries Group.

RLIN. A bibliographic utility headquartered in Mountain View, California, established to serve the needs of research libraries.

RTSD. Resources and Technical Services Division of the American Library Association. Former name of the division known since 1990 as Association for Library Collections & Technical Services (ALCTS).

Rule of three. A library rule-of-thumb using three as the cutoff point for differing treatments; for example, if one, two, or three authors are equally responsible for an item, choose the first-named as the main entry, but if there are more than three, choose the title as the main entry.

SAC. The Subject Analysis Committee of the Cataloging and Classification Section of the Association for Library Collections & Technical Services, American Library Association. This committee is responsible for monitoring issues and standards used in subject analysis.

Search key. In computer systems, a combination of characters from parts of access points (for example, letters from an author's surname and the first significant title word). Search keys are used in place of the full access points to minimize the size of indexes needed by the computer system as well as to minimize the number of characters searchers must enter.

Secondary entry. *See* Added entry.

Separate bibliographic identity. *See* Bibliographic identity.

Serial. An item published or produced in parts intended to go on without end. Should not be confused with *Series. See also* Monograph.

Series. A group of discrete items having, in addition to their own titles, a common title identifying them as part of the group. Also called *Monographic series.* Should not be confused with *Serial.*

Set. A group of related materials that can be cataloged as a group.

SGML. Standard General Markup Language, a set of protocols for editing text for computer input and communication.

Shared responsibility. Applies when an item is created by more than one responsible party sharing the same type of contribution; for example, a book with two authors.

Shelflist. A catalog of items owned by a library arranged by call number.

Shelf mark. Any code or system of marks designed to arrange items on shelves, excluding the classification numbers. Also called *Book mark, Call letter. See also* Cutter letter, Cutter number.

SLA. Special Libraries Association.

smd. Specific material designation. Part of the fifth area of description, naming the physical manifestation of the item.

Specific material designation. *See* smd.

Specificity. The degree of broadness or narrowness of a term used for indexing materials; or, the degree of broadness or narrowness of a subject catalog.

Standard number. *See* ISBN, ISMN, ISRC, and ISSN.

Standard subdivision. In DDC, a number from auxiliary Table 1 that can be added to a number from the schedules without a specific instruction to do so.

Statement of responsibility. Part of the first area of description naming those with overall responsibility for the creation of the item.

Subfield. Part of a field in the MARC format.

Subfield code. A character identifying the subfield and the data it contains. *See also* Delimiter.

Subject authority. A record of the establishment of an acceptable subject term containing the term, the cross-references established with it, and the sources of the information. *See also* Controlled vocabulary.

Subject cataloging. The act of assigning subject headings to an item being cataloged.

Subject heading. 1. A word or phrase identifying the intellectual content of an item being cataloged and used as an access point. 2. A term from an authorized list of terms to be used as access points. *See also* Descriptor.

Subject heading list. A list of terms, usually including cross-references, for indexing items being cataloged. Subject heading lists usually cover all branches of knowledge unless they explicitly state otherwise.

Symbolic notation. *See* Notation.

Syndetics. The structure of cross-references that link related terms.

Synthetic. A classification or subject heading list in which components of class numbers or headings are given to be assembled (synthesized) by the cataloger or searcher. *See also* Faceted, Postcoordinate.

Tag. The three-digit code identifying a field in the MARC format.

Tagging. The act of assigning codes to bibliographic data in the MARC format. Also known as *tagging and coding. See also* Coding.

TEI. Text Encoding Initiative, a set of protocols for editing text for computer input and communication.

TGN. *Thesaurus for Geographic Names.*

Thesaurus. A list of terms, with cross-references that clarify the relationships among terms used for indexing. Thesauri often are limited to a single discipline or group of disciplines.

Title proper. The main title of an item.

Truncation. A feature of computerized retrieval in which searches can be performed on word roots; for example, LIBR- would retrieve records for LIBRA, LIBRARIAN, LIBRARIES, LIBRARY, etc.

Turnkey system. A computer system package comprising hardware, software, installation, training, and (usually) ongoing maintenance, support, and development.

UBC. Universal Bibliographic Control. A program of IFLA.

UDC. Universal Decimal Classification. An international classification system based on the Dewey Decimal Classification.

UKMARC. United Kingdom MAchine Readable Cataloguing.

Uncontrolled vocabulary. A system of indexing in which any terms, not just those on an authorized list, are used for retrieval, such as a title keyword index. *See also* Controlled vocabulary, KWIC index, KWOC index.

Uniform title. A title created and assigned by catalogers to collocate editions and versions of a work that appear under different titles proper. The uniform title assigned to an item may be the title by which it is commonly known, the original title of a work published in translation, or a title constructed by the cataloger.

UNIMARC. UNIversal MAchine Readable Cataloguing.

URL. Uniform Resource Locator. Address for an Internet resource. *See also* PURL.

USMARC. United States MAchine-Readable Cataloging.

Utility. *See* Bibliographic utility.

UTLAS. University of Toronto Libraries Automated Systems. The original name of the Canadian bibliographic utility currently known as A-G Canada Ltd.

Utlas International. Name of the Canadian bibliographic utility originally known as UTLAS when it was purchased by the Thomson Corporation. *See also* A-G Canada Ltd.

Variable field. A field in the MARC format containing data that varies in length and format. *See also* Control field, Fixed field.

vCuc. Virtual Canadian Union Catalog.

Verso. 1. Left-hand page of a book, always bearing an even number. 2. Back of the title page.

Washington Library Network. *See* OCLC/WLN.

Western Library Network. *See* OCLC/WLN.

WLN. *See* OCLC/WLN.

WorldCat. Name of OCLC's online shared bibliographic database. *See also* OLUC.

C

Answers to Exercises

Answers to Examples in Chapter 4

Completed description for FIGURE 4.25 (page 72)

This example is an illustration of:
- flash cards
- title main entry with no statement of responsibility listed on the item
- general material designation
- publication date not listed, copyright date given
- scope note
- audience level
- two levels of cataloging

2nd level cataloging

```
Subtraction 0-12 flash cards [flash card]. -- St. Paul, MN :
   Trend, c1997.
   91 flash cards : col. ; in container 8 x 15 x 4 cm.

   Can also be used for games.
   Audience level: Ages 6 and up.
```

1st level cataloging

```
Subtraction 0-12 flash cards [flash card]. -- Trend, c1997.
   91 flash cards

   Can also be used for games.
```

Completed description for FIGURE 4.26 (page 73)

This example is an illustration of:
- musical score
- uniform title
- optional placement of general material designation at end of title proper
- musical presentation statement not listed in chief source
- publication and copyright dates unknown
- numbered series statement
- two levels of cataloging

2nd level cataloging

```
Beethoven, Ludwig van.
  [Leonore overture, no. 3]
  Overture no. 3, Leonore, op. 72a [music] / Beethoven. -- New
York : M. Baron, [19--]
  1 miniature score (64 p.) ; 20 cm. -- (Baron orchestra scores ;
no. 42)
```

1st level cataloging

```
Beethoven, Ludwig van.
  [Leonore overture, no. 3]
  Overture no. 3, Leonore, op. 72a [music]. -- M. Baron, [19--]
  1 miniature score (64 p.)
```

Completed description for FIGURE 4.27 (page 74)

This example is an illustration of:
- item by one person with no collective title for its components
- alternative title
- statement of subsidiary responsibility
- multiple places of publication (Canadian library would have: Oxford ; Toronto)
- detailed pagination
- unnumbered series statement
- variations in title note
- bibliography note
- contents notes
- British Library CIP corrected
- two levels of cataloging

2nd level cataloging for a U.S. library

```
Jonson, Ben.
   Volpone, or, The fox ; Epicene, or, The silent woman ; The
alchemist ; Bartholomew Fair / Ben Jonson ; edited with an
introduction by Gordon Campbell. -- Oxford ; New York : Oxford
University Press, 1995.
   xxviii, 530 p.; 20 cm. -- (The world's classics)

   Cover title: The alchemist and other plays.
   Bibliography: p. xxiv-xxv.
   Chronology of Ben Jonson: p. xxvi-xxvii.
   Glossary: p. 516-530.
   ISBN 0-19-282252-7.
```

1st level cataloging for both

```
Jonson, Ben.
   Volpone, or, The fox ; Epicene, or, The silent woman ; The
alchemist ; Bartholomew Fair. -- Oxford University Press, 1995.
   xxviii, 530 p.

   Cover title: The alchemist and other plays.
   ISBN 0-19-282252-7.
```

Completed description for FIGURE 4.28 (page 75)

This example is an illustration of:
- other title information
- two joint authors
- publishing date not listed, copyright date given
- detailed pagination statement
- accompanying material (no specifications listed for CD-ROM disc)
- systems requirements note
- index note
- two levels of cataloging

2nd level description

```
Ready, Kevin.
   Hybrid HTML design : a multi-browser HTML reference / Kevin
Ready, Janine Warner. -- Indianapolis : New Riders, c1996.
   xxvii, 412 p. : ill., ; 23 cm. + 1 computer optical disc.

   System requirements for accompanying disc: CD-ROM drive.
   Includes index.
   ISBN 1-56205-617-4.
```

(Example for figure 4-28 continues on page 304.)

Example for FIGURE 4.28 *(continued)*
1st level description

```
Ready, Kevin.
  Hybrid HTML design / Kevin Ready, Janine Warner. -- New Riders,
c1996.
  xxvii, 412 p. + 1 computer optical disc.

  System requirements for accompanying disc: CD-ROM drive.
  ISBN 1-56205-617-4.
```

Completed description for FIGURE 4.29 (page 76)
This example is an illustration of:
- game
- title main entry with no statement of responsibility listed on the item
- general material designation
- publication and copyright dates unknown
- accompanying material given in the physical description area
- local details note
- two levels of cataloging

2nd level cataloging

```
Ladybird key words reading game [game]. -- Loughborough,
 Leicestershire : Wills & Hepworth, [19--]
   16 games (various pieces) : col. ; in container 25 x 19 x 4 cm.
+ 1 instruction booklet.

   Originally received in 36 pieces; 15 pieces have been cut as
instructed.
```

1st level cataloging

```
Ladybird key words reading game [game]. -- Wills & Hepworth,
 [19--]
   16 games (various pieces) + 1 instruction booklet.
```

Completed description for FIGURE 4.30 (page 77)

This example is an illustration of:
- a compiled/edited work
- title main entry
- other title information
- subsidiary responsibility
- complex publisher's statement
- work consisting mostly of illustrations
- black and white and colored illustrations
- width of book greater than height
- Canadian CIP
- two levels of cataloging

2nd level cataloging

```
Toronto's Toronto : a photographic collection / conceived
   and edited by J. Marc Coté Pouliot ; introduction by
   Barbara Frum. -- Toronto : Coach House Press [for] the
   Toronto Animation Partnership, c1988.
   97 p. : chiefly ill. (some col.) ; 27 x 28 cm.

   ISBN 0-88910-327-5.
```

1st level cataloging

```
Toronto's Toronto / conceived and edited by J. Marc Coté Pouliot.
   -- Coach House Press, c1988.
   97 p.

   ISBN 0-88910-327-5.
```

Completed description for FIGURE 4.31 (page 78)

This example is an illustration of:
- kit
- work emanating from a corporate body entered under title
- general material designation
- same organization responsible for intellectual content and publication
- probable date of publication
- systems requirements note
- title information note
- two levels of cataloging

(Example for figure 4.31 continues on page 306.)

Example for FIGURE 4.31 *(continued)*

2nd level cataloging

```
BioTech career kit [kit] / Biotechnology Human Resources Council.
  -- Ottawa : The Council, [2000?]
  1 computer optical disc : (sd., col. 4¾ in.)
  1 book (162 p. : ill. ; 22 cm.)
  1 poster (col. ; 69 x 49 cm.)
  1 teacher's guide (27 p. ; 22 cm.)
  All in container 24 x 21 x 3 cm.

    System requirements for CD-ROM: Pentium 166 or equivalent; 32
  MB RAM or Macintosh Power PC with 20 MB free disc space; Windows
  95/98 or MacOS 7.5; CD-ROM drive; 16-bit sound card video display
  capable of 32-bit color at 640 by 480.
    Title on CD-ROM: BioMars : a biotechnology career adventure
  game.
    ISBN on book: 0-9684482-0-8.
```

1st level cataloging

```
BioTech career kit [kit] / Biotechnology Human Resources Council.
  -- The Council, [2000?]
  1 computer optical disc, 1 book, 1 poster, 1 teacher's guide.

    System requirements for CD-ROM: Pentium 166 or equivalent; 32
  MB RAM or Macintosh Power PC with 20 MB free disc space; Windows
  95/98 or MacOS 7.5; 16-bit sound card video display capable of
  32-bit color at 640 by 480.
```

Completed description for FIGURE 4.32 (page 79)

This example is an illustration of:
- anonymous work given title main entry
- work with few sources of information
- other title information
- no place, publisher, or date of publication listed
- probable country of publication
- probable date of publication
- source of title note
- quoted note
- contents note
- because of the lack of appropriate information, all information should be given; only the glossary note could be omitted for libraries that practice 1st level cataloging

```
Wrought iron : its manufacture, characteristics, and
  applications -- [United States? : s.n., 1936?]
  59 p. : ill. ; 24 cm.

  Cover title.
  "J.A., E.B.S., Pittsburgh, Penna., June 15, 1936"—Pref.
  Glossary: p. 57-59.
```

Completed description for FIGURE 4.33 (page 80)

This example is an illustration of:
- marks of omission in other title information
- edition statement
- statement of responsibility relating to the edition taken from other than prescribed sources
- detailed pagination
- two levels of cataloging

2nd level cataloging

```
Thompson, Silvanus P.
  Calculus made easy : being the very simplest introduction to
... differential calculus and the integral calculus / Silvanus P.
Thompson. -- 3rd ed. / [revised by F.G.W. Brown]. -- London :
Macmillan, 1946.
  vi, 250 p.; 19 cm.
```

1st level cataloging

```
Thompson, Silvanus P.
  Calculus made easy. -- 3rd ed. -- Macmillan, 1946.
  vi, 250 p.
```

Completed description for FIGURE 4.34 (page 81)

This example is an illustration of:
- separate works with a collective title
- title main entry
- other title information
- no statement of responsibility
- detailed pagination
- work containing only one type of illustration
- nature and scope note
- original publications note
- two levels of cataloging

(Example for figure 4.34 continues on page 308.)

Example for FIGURE 4-34 *(continued)*
2nd level cataloging

```
The opera libretto library : the authentic texts of the
   German, French, and Italian operas with music of the
   principal airs, with the complete English and German,
   French, or Italian parallel texts. -- New York : Avenel
   Books, 1980.
   3 v. in 1 (470; 504; 481 p.) : music ; 24 cm.

   Musical excerpts in piano-vocal score.
   Reprint of: The authentic librettos of the Wagner operas  --
The authentic librettos of the French and German operas  -- The
authentic librettos of the Italian operas. New York : Crown,
1939.
   ISBN 0-517-318830.
```

1st level cataloging enriched

```
The opera libretto library. -- Avenel Books, 1980.
   3 v. in 1 (470; 504; 481 p.)

   Reprint of: The authentic librettos of the Wagner operas  --
The authentic librettos of the French and German operas  -- The
authentic librettos of the Italian operas. New York : Crown,
1939.
   ISBN 0-517-318830.
```

Answers to Examples in Chapter 5

Answer to FIGURE 5.13

MAIN ENTRY: Title proper
ADDED ENTRIES: Editor; Series

A title main entry was chosen for *Library Technical Services* because many contributors are responsible for the text, and Godden's contribution was editing. Rule 21.7B1 was applied here. Godden is an added entry, according to the same rule. An added entry is made for the series (rule 21.30L.1).

Answer to FIGURE 5.14

MAIN ENTRY: Corporate body that prepared the report
ADDED ENTRIES: Corporate body that commissioned the report; Title proper

A corporate body main entry was chosen for this earthquake study because it falls under rule 21.1B2c. Rule 21.30E1 mandates the added entry.

Answer to FIGURE 5.15

MAIN ENTRY: First-named author
ADDED ENTRIES: Second author; Third author; Title proper; Author/title with
first-named author and previous title

    The first-named author, Timothy Nolan, is chosen as the main entry for *Plan or Die!* Rule 21.6C1 states to enter a work under the first-named author if there is no indication in the layout or typography that one author is more responsible than the others, and to make added entries for the other authors. In addition to the added entry for the title proper, an author-title added entry is made for the previous title under rule 21.30G1.

Answer to FIGURE 5.16

MAIN ENTRY: Uniform title
ADDED ENTRIES: Responsible corporate body; Title proper; Series

    A uniform title main entry, *Mother Goose,* is chosen for *The Sesame Street Mother Goose.* This is an anonymous work entered under title according to rule 21.5A. However, because *Mother Goose* is a classic work appearing in numerous manifestations having varying titles proper, a uniform title is used instead of the title proper, according to rule 25.2A. LC practice is to omit the brackets, exercising the option in rule 25.2A. Added entries are made for Children's Television Workshop, title proper, and the series.

Answer to FIGURE 5.17

MAIN ENTRY: Title proper
ADDED ENTRIES: First-named compiler

    Rule 21.6C2 states that if responsibility is shared among more than three persons, and principal responsibility is not attributed to one, two, or three, the work is entered under title (generally called "The Rule of Three"). The same rule mandates an added entry under the person named first on the item.

Answer to FIGURE 5.18

MAIN ENTRY: First-named author
ADDED ENTRIES: Second author; Title proper; Corporate body

    The first-named author, L. McDonald, is chosen as the main entry. Rule 21.6C1 states to enter a work under the first-named author if there is no indication in the layout or typography that one author is more responsible than the others (and there are no more than three authors), and to make added entries for the other authors. In addition to the added entry for the title proper, a corporate body added entry is made for Health Canada under rule 21.30E1.

Answers to Examples in Chapter 8, Figure 8.4

1.   Subject heading: **Excavations (Archaeology)**
       Type: A noun with a qualifier

2.   Subject heading: **Bilingual education**
       Type: Multiword heading in natural order (compare with figure 9.8, No. 2)

3.   Subject heading: **Databases—Bibliography**
       Type: Use of a form subdivision of broad application

4.   Subject heading: **United States—History—1600-1775, Colonial period**
        Type: Use of multiple subdivisions; use of a chronological subdivision

5.   Subject heading: **Hand**
        Type: Name of body part not given in the list, but to be added as needed

6.   Subject heading: **Rock music—History and criticism**
        Type: Use of a topical subdivision of limited application

7.   Subject heading: **Spanish literature—16th and 17th centuries**
        Type: Use of a key heading (English literature) and chronological subdivision

8.   Subject headings: **Motion picture music**
                              Vocal music
        Type: Use of two headings to express different aspects of the subject

9.   Subject headings: **Childbirth**
                              Middle aged women
        Type: Use of two headings to express different aspects of the subject

10.   Subject headings: **French Canadians** (from Sears)
                              French-speaking Canadians (from SearsCC)
        Type: Name of people, showing that Sears and SearsCC headings differ

Answers to Examples in Chapter 9, Figure 9.8

1.   Subject heading: **Excavations (Archaeology)**
        Type: A noun with a qualifier

2.   Subject heading: **Education, Bilingual**
        Type: An inverted heading

3.   Subject heading: **Databases—Bibliography**
        Type: Use of a form subdivision

4.   Subject heading: **United States—History—Colonial period, ca. 1600-1775**
        Type: Use of multiple subdivisions; use of a chronological subdivision

5.   Subject heading: **Wild flowers—California**
        Type: Use of a geographic subdivision

6.   Subject headings: **Rock music—History and criticism**
                              Rock music—Analysis, appreciation
        Type: Use of a pattern heading using the category "Operas"; two subject
        headings seem to be appropriate for this example

7.   Subject heading: **Tennis—Psychological aspects**
        Type: Use of a free-floating topical subdivision, "Psychological aspects"

8. Subject heading: **Motion picture music—Excerpts—Vocal scores with piano**
Type: Heading with more than one subdivision

9. Subject heading: **Childbirth in middle age**
Type: Phrase heading

10. Subject headings: **French-Canadians** (from LCSH)
    Canadians, French-speaking (from CSH)
    Type: Name of people, showing that LCSH and CSH headings differ

Answers to Examples in Chapter 11, Figure 11.3

1. Classification: **374.4'713**
   Explanation: Use of a geographic subdivision (-713 means Ontario)

2. Classification: **598'.0922**
   Explanation: Use of a biographical subdivision (-0922 means biographical information about a group of persons, not just one individual)

3. Classification: **398.204'61**
   Explanation: Use of a language subdivision (-61 means Spanish language)

4. Classification: **594.4**
   Explanation: Example of an item containing two subjects, each given equal emphasis; the number assigned is the number that comes first in the schedules

5. Classification: **590**
   Explanation: Example of an item containing three or more subjects, all given equal emphasis classed in the number that covers all of the subjects

6. Classification: **636.728'35**
   Explanation: Use of a pattern number drawn from instructions to add to a base number; in this case, the base number is 636.728 and 35 means training

7. Classification: **069.09'74**
   Explanation: Use of an instruction for treatment of a geographic focus, plus addition of an area subdivision from Table 2

8. Classification: **600**
   Explanation: Use of a general number for all types of mechanical and technical devices

9. Classification: **796.34'2'09'747243**
   Explanation: Use of a geographic subdivision for a locale within New York City (-747243 means the borough of Queens County, where Forest Hills is located)

10. Classification: **690'.837**
    Explanation: Use of a pattern number drawn from instructions to add numbers to a base number; in this case, the base number is 690 and 837 is for separate houses

Answers to Examples in Chapter 12, Figure 12.3

1. Classification: **HG172.A2.B5**
   Explanation: A form subdivision found in the schedule (that is, biography)

2. Classification: **HD4186**
   Explanation: A form subdivision found using a table of subdivisions (that is, periodicals, societies, serials)

3. Classification: **HJ4655.M5**
   Explanation: A geographic subdivision using a cutter number

4. Classification: **HC107.N7**
   Explanation: A geographic subdivision using a table of cutters for U.S. states

5. Classification: **HE206.2**
   Explanation: A chronological subdivision found directly in the schedule

6. Classification: **TL725.3.A2**
   Explanation: A topical subdivision using a cutter number (that is, airport access)

Additional Cataloging Examples

The following 10 examples will provide additional practice for the beginning cataloger. For meaningful practice, we suggest covering the cataloging data with a sheet of paper, cataloging an item, and then comparing your work with the suggested answer. Remember that no two professional catalogers will necessarily interpret the same item in the same way.

Examples begin on page 314.

EXAMPLE 1

This example is an illustration of:
- statement of responsibility listed outside chief source
- all illustrations are in color
- index note
- LCSH and Sears the same
- unabridged and abridged Dewey decimal classification the same
- two levels of cataloging

2nd level of description

```
Wilkinson, Philip.
  100 greatest inventions / [text, Philip Wilkinson]. -- Surrey,
Great Britain : Dragon's World, 1995.
  110 p. : col. ill. ; 29 cm.

  Includes index.
  ISBN 1-85028-311-7.

  1. Inventions -- History.  I. Title.

Recommended DDC: 609
```

1st level of description

```
Wilkinson, Philip.
  100 greatest inventions. -- Dragon's World, 1995.
  110 p.

  ISBN 1-85028-311-7.

1. Inventions -- History.  I. Title.

Recommended abridged DDC: 609
```

(chief source of information)
(title page)

DRAGON'S WORLD

CHILDREN'S BOOKS

(information on verso)

DRAGON'S WORLD

CHILDREN'S BOOKS

Dragon's World Ltd
Limpsfield
Surrey RH8 0DY
Great Britain

First published by Dragon's World 1995

© Dragon's World 1995

Text:	Philip Wilkinson
Editor:	Kyla Barber
Copy Editor:	Claire Watts
Designer:	Mel Raymond
Design Assistants:	Karen Ferguson
	Victoria Furbisher
Picture Reseracher:	Susan Trangmar
Art Director:	John Strange
Editorial Director:	Pippa Rubinstein

The catalogue record for this book is
available from the British Library

ISBN 1 85028 311 7

EXAMPLE 2

Chief source of information (the item itself) has:

- -

- separate titles on each side of the chart
- a small inset map showing the Alaska, British Columbia,
  Washington, and Oregon coasts on the "Birds" side
- Printed by Dalgleish and Company 1994

- -

This example is an illustration of:
  • chart
  • no collective title for an item with two separate works
  • title main entry with no statement of responsibility listed on item
  • general material designation
  • no place of publication
  • no publisher, manufacturer only given note
  • contents note
  • "with" note
  • Sears and Library of Congress subject headings are the same
  • 2nd level cataloging

Northern Pacific coast birds [chart]. -- [S.l. : s.n.], 1994
   ([S.l.] : Dalgleish).
   1 chart : col. ; 74 x 90 cm.

   Includes inset map of the coast from Alaska to Oregon.
   With: Northern Pacific coast fish.

   1. Birds -- Northwest Coast of North America.

Northern Pacific coast fish [chart]. -- [S.l. : s.n.], 1994
   ([S.l.] : Dalgleish).
   1 chart : col. ; 74 x 90 cm.

   With: Northern Pacific coast birds.

   1. Fishes -- Northwest Coast of North America.

Recommended DDC: 597.097

EXAMPLE 3

This example is an illustration of:
- other title information
- edition statement
- publishing date not listed, copyright date given
- descriptive illustration statement
- dimensions where the width of the item is greater than the height
- bibliography note
- audience level note given as a quoted note
- summary
- two ISBNs; the one given applies to the item in hand
- ISBN qualified
- both Library of Congress and LC annotated card subject headings
- optional addition of fuller form of given names added to name in subject heading
- unabridged Dewey decimal classification with prime mark
- alternate classifications for biography
- Library of Congress classification in CIP
- Library of Congress annotated card program CIP
- 2nd level cataloging

```
Conrad, Pat.
    Prairie visions : the life and times of Solomon Butcher / Pat
Conrad. -- 1st ed. -- New York : HarperCollins, c1991.
    85 p. : ill., map ; 21 x 27 cm.

    "Ages 10 up"--Jacket.
    Includes bibliographical references (p. 85).
    Summary: A collection of photos and stories about photographer
Solomon Butcher and turn-of-the-century Nebraska.
    ISBN 0-06-021375-2 (lib. bdg.).
```

Tracing with Library of Congress subject headings
```
    1. Butcher, Solomon D. (Solomon Devore) -- Juvenile literature.
2. Photographers -- Nebraska -- Biography -- Juvenile literature.
3. Nebraska -- History -- Juvenile literature.  I. Title.
```

Tracing with Library of Congress annotaed card subject headings

```
1. Butcher, Solomon D. (Solomon Devore).  2. Photographers.  3.
Nebraska -- History.  I. Title.
```

Recommended DDC: 770.'92 or [B] or [92]

Example 3—Continues

EXAMPLE 3 *(continued)*

(chief source of information)
      (title page)

Prairie Visions:

The Life and Times of

SOLOMON BUTCHER

PAM CONRAD

▰ HarperCollins*Publishers*

(information on verso)

PRAIRIE VISIONS: *The Life and Times of Solomon Butcher*

Copyright © 1991 by Pam Conrad

All rights reserved. No part of this book may be used or reproduced in any manner whatsoever without written permission except in the case of brief quotations embodied in critical articles and reviews. Printed in the United States of America. For information address HarperCollins Children's Books, a division of HarperCollins Publishers, 10 East 53rd Street, New York, NY 10022.

Library of Congress Cataloging-in-Publication Data. Conrad, Pam. Prairie visions : the life and times of Solomon Butcher / by Pam Conrad.   p.   cm. Includes bibliographical references. Summary: A collection of photos and stories about photographer Solomon Butcher and turn-of-the-century Nebraska.   ISBN 0-06-021373-6. — ISBN 0-06-021375-2 (lib. bdg.)   1. Butcher, Solomon D. (Solomon Devore), 1856–1927—Juvenile literature.   2. Photographers—Nebraska—Biography—Juvenile literature.   3. Nebraska—History—Juvenile literature.   [1. Butcher, Solomon D. (Solomon Devore), 1856–1927.   2. Photographers.   3. Nebraska—History.]   I. Title.   TR140.B88C66   1991   770'.92—dc20   [B]   [92]   90-38658   CIP   AC

Designed by David Saylor

1 2 3 4 5 6 7 8 9 10

First Edition

EXAMPLE 4

This example is an illustration of:
- serial
- serial reproduced in microform
- general material designation
- open entry
- series statement
- frequency note
- numbering and chronological designation note
- publication, distribution, etc. note
- index note
- library's holdings note
- note relating to the original
- ISSN
- 2nd level cataloging

Catalog record for paper copy where information about 1st issue is known

```
Children's literature in education. -- 1 (Mar. 1970)-     .
   New York : Human Sciences Press, 1970-
      v. : ill. ; 25 cm.

   Three issues yearly, 1970-1974; quarterly, 1975-     .
   Parallel numbering begins no. 24 = v. 8, no. 1.
   Issues 1-72 published by: APS Publications/Agathon Press.
   Indexes begin v. 8.
   ISSN 0045-6713.
```

Catalog record for microform where information about 1st issue is known

```
Children's literature in education [microform]. -- 1 (Mar.
   1970)-     . -- Ann Arbor, Mich. : University Microfilms, 1979-
      microfilm reels : ill. ; 35 mm. -- (Current periodical
series)

   Library has: 20 (Spring 1976)-
   Reproduction of: New York : Human Sciences Press. Three issues
yearly, 1970-1974; quarterly, 1975-     . Parallel numbering
begins no. 24 = v. 8, no. 1. Issues 1-72 published by: APS
Publications/Agathon Press. Indexes begin v. 8.
   ISSN 0045-6713.
```

Example 4—Continues

EXAMPLE 4 *(continues)*

Catalog record for microform based on earliest issue in hand when information about 1st issue is unknown

```
Children's literature in education [microform]. -- 20 (Spring
   1976)-    . -- Ann Arbor, Mich. : University Microfilms, 1979-
      microfilm reels : ill. ; 35 mm. -- (Current periodical
series)

   Reproduction of: New York : Human Sciences Press. Quarterly.
Parallel numbering begins no. 24 = v. 8, no. 1. Issues 20-72
published by: APS Publications/Agathon Press. Indexes begin v. 8.
   ISSN 0045-6713.
```

NOTE: LC does not follow AACR2R-98 for microforms when the
content was originally published in another format. Records
derived from MARC records may have data about the original item
in the physical description area and about the item in hand, the
microform, in the note area. LC records and records of those
institutions using LCRIs for microforms will differ from similar
microform records found elsewhere which are cataloged according
to AACR2R-98.

(information from the first three title frames of the earliest edition in hand)

CURRENT PERIODICAL SERIES

PUBLICATION NO: 11,146

TITLE: CHILDREN'S LITERATURE IN EDUCATION

VOLUME: **ISSUES:** 20-23

DATE: Spring - Winter 1976

NOTICE: This periodical may be copyrighted, in which case the contents remain
the property of the copyright owner. The microfilm edition is reproduced by
agreement with the publisher. Duplication or resale without permission is
prohibited.

University Microfilms International, Ann Arbor, Mich.

MICROFILMED — 1979

Children's literature in education 20

Contents

Spring 1976

APS Publications Inc.

Children's literature in education is published four times a year in Spring, Summer, Fall and Winter by APS Publications, Inc. All correspondence concerning subscriptions should be addressed as follows:

APS Publications, Inc., 150 Fifth Avenue, New York, NY 10011.
Annual subscription: Individual, by personal check only: $12.00; Institutional: $15.00.
(Postage outside US, $2.00 additional)

EXAMPLE 5

This example is an illustration of:
- distributor (in Canadian record)
- publishing date not listed, copyright date given
- detailed pagination
- accompanying material with optional addition of physical description (in 2nd level)
- series statement
- systems requirements note
- index note (in second level)
- Library of Congress and Sears subject headings
- alternate Dewey decimal classification numbers
- two levels of cataloging

Example 5—Continues

EXAMPLE 5 *(continued)*

2nd level cataloging for a U.S. library

```
Vadnai, Noah.
   Travel planning online for dummies / by Noah Vadnai. -- Foster
City, CA : IDG Books, c1998.
   xxiv, 327 p. : ill., ; 24 cm. + 1 computer optical disc (sd.,
col. ; 4¾ in.) -- (For dummies)

   System requirements for accompanying disc: PC with a 486 or
faster processor or Macintosh OS with 68030 or faster processor;
8MB RAM (16 MB recommended); Windows 3.1 or later or Macintosh
7.5 or later; CD-ROM drive double speed or faster; sound card for
PC; monitor capable of displaying 256 colors or grayscale; modem
14,400 bps or faster.
   Includes index.
   ISBN 0-7645-0438-X.
```

2nd level cataloging for a Canadian library

```
Vadnai, Noah.
   Travel planning online for dummies / by Noah Vadnai. -- Foster
City, CA : IDG Books; Macmillan Canada [distributor], c1998.
   xxiv, 327 p. : ill., ; 24 cm. + 1 computer optical disc (sd.,
col. ; 4¾ in.) -- (For dummies)

   System requirements for accompanying disc: PC with a 486 or
faster processor or Macintosh OS with 68030 or faster processor;
8MB RAM (16 MB recommended); Windows 3.1 or later or Macintosh
7.5 or later; CD-ROM drive double speed or faster; sound card for
PC; monitor capable of displaying 256 colors or grayscale; modem
14,400 bps or faster.
   Includes index.
   ISBN 0-7645-0438-X.

Tracing with Library of Congress subject headings

   1. Tourism -- Computer network resources.  I. Title.  II. Series.
```

1st level cataloging for both countries

```
Vadnai, Noah.
  Travel planning online for dummies. -- IDG Books, c1998.
  xxiv, 327 p. + 1 computer optical disc.

  System requirements for accompanying disc: PC with a 486 or
faster processor or Macintosh OS with 68030 or faster processor;
8MB RAM (16 MB recommended); Windows 3.1 or later or Macintosh
7.5 or later; CD-ROM drive double speed or faster; sound card for
PCs; monitor capable of displaying 256 colors or grayscale; modem
14,400 bps or faster.
  ISBN 0-7645-0438-X.
```

Tracing with Sears subject headings

```
  1. Tourist rade -- Internet resources.  I. Title.
```

Alternate DDC depending on emphasis needed
```
025.0910'202 (if stressing computer aspect)

910.202 (if stressing travel aspect)
```

(chief source of information)
   (title page)

by Noah Vadnai

IDG Books Worldwide, Inc.
An International Data Group Company

Foster City, CA ♦ Chicago, IL ♦ Indianapolis, IN ♦ New York, NY

Example 5—Continues

EXAMPLE 5 *(continues)*

(information in text)

System Requirements

Before you try to access the programs on the CD, make sure that your computer meets the following minimum system requirements.

- A PC with a 486 or faster processor or a Mac OS computer with a 68030 or faster processor.

- Microsoft Windows 3.1 or later, or Mac OS system software 7.5 or later.

- At least 8MB of total RAM installed on your computer. For best performance, we recommend that Windows 95-equipped PCs and Mac OS computers with PowerPC processors have at least 16MB of RAM installed.

- For Windows, you need at least 120MB of hard drive space available to install all the software from this CD. For Macs, you need at least 60MB. (You need less space if you don't install every program.)

- A CD-ROM drive — double-speed (2x) or faster.
- A sound card for PCs. (Mac OS computers have built-in sound support.)

- A monitor capable of displaying at least 256 colors or grayscale.

- A modem with a speed of at least 14,400 bps.

If your computer doesn't match up to most of these requirements, you may have problems using the contents of the CD.

(information on verso)

Travel Planning Online For Dummies®

Published by
IDG Books Worldwide, Inc.
An International Data Group Company
919 E. Hillsdale Blvd.
Suite 400
Foster City, CA 94404
www.idgbooks.com (IDG Books Worldwide Web site)
www.dummies.com (Dummies Press Web site)

Library of Congress Catalog Card No.: 98-87911

ISBN: 0-7645-0438-X

Printed in the United States of America

10 9 8 7 6 5 4 3 2 1

1B/RV/RQ/ZY/IN

Distributed in the United States by IDG Books Worldwide, Inc.

Distributed by Macmillan Canada for Canada; by Transworld Publishers Limited in the United Kingdom; by IDG Norge Books for Norway; by IDG Sweden Books for Sweden; by Woodslane Pty. Ltd. for Australia; by Woodslane (NZ) Ltd. for New Zealand; by Addison Wesley Longman Singapore Pte Ltd. for Singapore, Malaysia, Thailand, Indonesia and Korea; by Norma Comunicaciones S.A. for Colombia; by Intersoft for South Africa; by International Thomson Publishing for Germany, Austria and Switzerland; by Toppan Company Ltd. for Japan; by Distribuidora Cuspide for Argentina; by Livraria Cultura for Brazil; by Ediciencia S.A. for Ecuador; by Ediciones ZETA S.C.R. Ltda. for Peru; by WS Computer Publishing Corporation, Inc., for the Philippines; by Unalis Corporation for Taiwan; by Contemporanea de Ediciones for Venezuela; by Computer Book & Magazine Store for Puerto Rico; by Express Computer Distributors for the Caribbean and West Indies. Authorized Sales Agent: Anthony Rudkin Associates for the Middle East and North Africa.

EXAMPLE 6

```
Chief source of information (the mount) has:
- - - - - - - - - - - - - - - - - - - - - - - - - - - - - - -
Cornelius Krieghoff, 1856
PLAYTIME, VILLAGE SCHOOL
Collection of K.R. Thomson, Toronto
A Canadart reproduction B 4
Printed in Canada
- - - - - - - - - - - - - - - - - - - - - - - - - - - - - - -
The accompanying sheet has:
C. Krieghoff
eight paragraphs about his work
Charles Macklem Nelles
CANADART copyright
- - - - - - - - - - - - - - - - - - - - - - - - - - - - - - -
```

A small slip giving the distributor's name and address has been inserted loosely into the plastic envelope. The distributor is not listed on the bibliographic record because this method of indicating distributorship is an indication of impermanence.

This example is an illustration of:
- art reproduction
- general material designation
- unknown place and date of publication and copyright date
- accompanying materials listed in note area
- note relating to numbers borne by the item (other than ISBN/ISSN) given as a quoted note
- note relating to the original
- Library of Congress subject heading
- Dewey decimal classification
- 2nd level cataloging

```
     Krieghoff, Cornelius.
       Playtime, village school [art reproduction] / Cornelius
     Krieghoff. -- [S.l.] : Canadart, [19--]
       1 art reproduction : col. ; 36 x 51 cm.

       Accompanied by: C. Krieghoff / Charles Macklem Nelles. 1 p.
       "A Canadart reproduction B 4".
       Reproduction of original: 1856. In collection of K.R. Thomson,
     Toronto.

       1. Painting, Canadian.  I. Title.


     Recommended DDC: 759.11
```

EXAMPLE 7

This example is an illustration of:
- other title information
- statement of subsidiary responsibility
- publishing date not listed, copyright date given
- series statement with subseries
- contents note
- summary
- two ISBNs; the one given relates to the item in hand
- Library of Congress annotated card program CIP
- Library of Congress subject headings and annotated card program headings the same
- 2nd level cataloging

```
Kittredge, Mary.
   The human body : an overview / Mary Kittredge ; introduction by
C. Everett Koop. -- New York : Chelsea House, c1990.
   144 p. : ill. ; 24 cm. -- (The encyclopedia of health. The
healthy body)

   Glossary: p. 126-131.
   Includes bibliography (p. 123-125) and index.
   Summary: Examines the human body and its systems, including the
nervous, digestive, and immune systems.
   ISBN 0-7910-0019-2.

   1. Human physiology.  2. Body, Human.   I. Title.   II. Series.
III. Series: The healthy body.

Recommended DDC: 612
```

(chief source of information)
(title page)

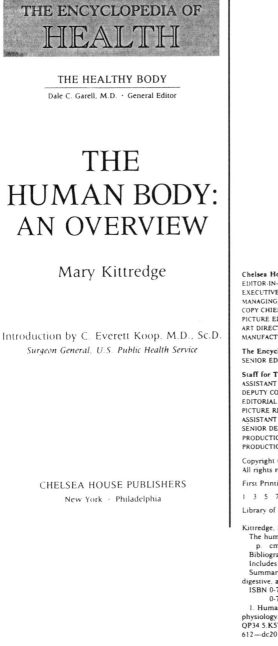

THE ENCYCLOPEDIA OF
HEALTH

THE HEALTHY BODY
Dale C. Garell, M.D. · General Editor

THE
HUMAN BODY:
AN OVERVIEW

Mary Kittredge

Introduction by C. Everett Koop. M.D., Sc.D.
Surgeon General, U.S. Public Health Service

CHELSEA HOUSE PUBLISHERS
New York · Philadelphia

(information on verso)

Chelsea House Publishers
EDITOR-IN-CHIEF Nancy Toff
EXECUTIVE EDITOR Remmel T. Nunn
MANAGING EDITOR Karyn Gullen Browne
COPY CHIEF Juliann Barbato
PICTURE EDITOR Adrian G. Allen
ART DIRECTOR Maria Epes
MANUFACTURING MANAGER Gerald Levine

The Encyclopedia of Health
SENIOR EDITOR Paula Edelson

Staff for THE HUMAN BODY: AN OVERVIEW
ASSISTANT EDITOR Laura Dolce
DEPUTY COPY CHIEF Nicole Bowen
EDITORIAL ASSISTANTS Navorn Johnson, Jennifer Klein
PICTURE RESEARCHER Debra P. Hershkowitz
ASSISTANT ART DIRECTOR Loraine Machlin
SENIOR DESIGNER Marjorie Zaum
PRODUCTION MANAGER Joseph Romano
PRODUCTION COORDINATOR Marie Claire Cebrián

Copyright © 1990 by Chelsea House Publishers, a division of Main Line Book Co.
All rights reserved. Printed and bound in the United States of America.

First Printing

1 3 5 7 9 8 6 4 2

Library of Congress Cataloging-in-Publication Data

Kittredge, Mary, 1949–
    The human body / Mary Kittredge; introduction by C. Everett Koop.
        p.   cm. — (The Encyclopedia of health. The healthy body)
    Bibliography: p.
    Includes index.
    Summary: Examines the human body and its systems, including the nervous,
digestive, and immune systems.
    ISBN 0-7910-0019-2.
        0-7910-0459-7 (pbk.)
    1. Human physiology. 2. Body, Human. [1. Body, Human. 2. Human
physiology.] I. Title. II Series.   89-9877
QP34 5.K57 1990   CIP
612—dc20   AC

EXAMPLE 8

```
Chief source of information (the box, size 18 x 12 x 8 cm.) has:
- - - - - - - - - - - - - - - - - - - - - - - - - - - - - - - - - - -
"Fisher-Price Marching Band" on 5 sides with "Fisher-Price" a
different color and a smaller size than "Marching Band"
- on one side "Marching Band" is at the top and "Fisher-Price"
  at the bottom
- one side has c1988 Fisher-Price / Division of The Quaker Oats
  Company / East Aurora, NY 14052 / Made in U.S.A.
- "2210" on all sides
  "3-7" on one side
- - - - - - - - - - - - - - - - - - - - - - - - - - - - - - - - - - -
```

The box contains a hat, a slide whistle, a glockenspiel, a drum with two drumsticks, two cymbals, a maraca, and a tambourine

This example is an illustration of:
- toy
- title main entry with no statement of responsibility listed on the item
- date of production not listed, copyright date given
- alternative title note
- audience level note
- note relating to number borne by the item other than ISBN/ISSN
- alternate Dewey decimal classification numbers
- prime mark in Dewey decimal classification
- two levels of cataloging

2nd level cataloging

```
Marching band [toy]. -- East Aurora, NY : Fisher-Price, c1988.
  2 cymbals, 1 drum, 2 drumsticks, 1 glockenspiel, 1 hat, 1
maraca, 1 slide whistle, 1 tambourine : col. ; in container 18 x
12 x 8 cm.

  Title also on container: Fisher-Price marching band.
  Audience level: age 3-7.
  2210.

  1. Rhythm bands and orchestra.
```

1st level cataloging

```
Marching band [toy]. -- Fisher-Price, c1988.

  1. Music toys.

Recommended DDCs (depending on emphasis wanted:
790.133 (Abridged: 790.1) - play with toys
796.13 (Abridged: 796.1) - singing and dancing games
372.87'044 (Abridged: 372.87) - teaching music in elementary
education
```

EXAMPLE 9

This example is an illustration of:
- work with no title page
- other title information
- second statement of responsibility and publisher the same
- edition statement
- statement of responsibility for edition
- joint publishers
- source of title note
- contents note
- prime mark in Dewey decimal classification
- Library of Congress CIP corrected
- two levels of cataloging

2nd level of description

```
Furie, Betty.
   Understanding MARC bibliographic : machine-readable cataloging
/ [written by Betty Furie in conjunction with the Data Base
Development Department of The Follett Software Company]. -- 5th
ed. / reviewed and edited by the Network Development and MARC
Standards Office, Library of Congress. -- Washington, DC :
Cataloging Distribution Service, Library of Congress in
collaboration with Follett, c1998.
   29 p. : ill. ; 24 cm.

   Cover title.
   Includes bibliographical references.
   ISBN 0-8444-0961-8.

   1. MARC formats -- United States.  I. Follett Software Company.
Data Base Development Department.  II. Library of Congress.
Network Development and MARC Standards Office.  III. Title.
```

1st level of description

```
Furie, Betty.
   Understanding MARC bibliographic. -- 5th ed. -- Cataloging
Distribution Service, Library of Congress, c1998.
   29 p.

   Cover title.
   ISBN 0-8444-0961-8.

1. MARC formats -- United States.  I. Title.

Recommended abridged DDC: 025.3
Recommended DDC: 025.3'16
```

Example 9—Continues

EXAMPLE 9 *(continued)*

(information on cover)

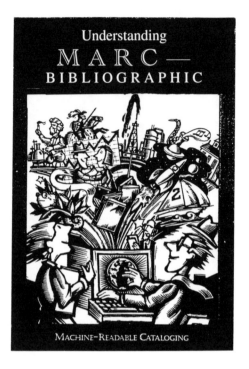

(information on back of cover)

Understanding MARC—*Bibliographic*

Written by Betty Furrie in conjunction with the Data Base Development Department of The Follett Software Company

Fifth edition reviewed and edited by the Network Development and MARC Standards Office, Library of Congress

Published by the Cataloging Distribution Service, Library of Congress, in collaboration with The Follett Software Company

Available from:

Follett Software Company	Library of Congress
A Follett Corporation Company	Cataloging Distribution Service
1391 Corporate Drive	Customer Service Section
McHenry, IL 60050	Washington, DC 20541-4912
1-800-323-3397	1-800-255-3666

Library of Congress Cataloging-in-Publication Data

Furrie, Betty.
   Understanding MARC : machine readable cataloging / [written by Betty Furrie, in conjunction with the Data Base Development Department of the Follett Software Company ; reviewed and edited by the Network Development and MARC Standards Office, Library of Congress]. — 5th ed.
      p. cm.
   Cover title.
   Includes bibliographical references.
   ISBN 0-8444-0961-8
—— —— Copy 3 Z663. 12 . U53 1998
   1. MARC formats—United States. 1. Follett Software Company. Data Base Development Dept. II. Library of Congress. Network Development and MARC Standards Office. III. Title.

Z699.35.M28F87 1998   98-2391؛
025.3' 16—dc21   CIl

ISBN 0-8444-0961-8

Copyright °1998 The Library of Congress, except within the U.S.A.
Understanding MARC: Bibliographic was a copyrighted work originally published by the Follett Software Co. in 1988 (second edition, 1989, third edition, 1990). Credit must be given when excerpting from this publication.

EXAMPLE 10

This example is an illustration of:
- slide set
- bilingual item
- title main entry for item issued by a corporate body
- same organization listed in statement of responsibility and as publisher
- date of production not listed, copyright date given
- accompanying materials listed in note area
- Library of Congress subject headings
- corporate body added entries
- Dewey decimal classification number
- 2nd level cataloging

```
The search for Franklin [slide] / National Film Board of Canada
    in co-operation with the New Brunswick Museum = A la recherche
    de Franklin / Office national du film du Canada en
    collaboration avec le Musee du Nouveau-Brunswick. -- Montreal :
    N.F.B.C., c1975.
    10 slides : b&w and col.

    Notes / Dona Atcheson. 1 p.

    1. Franklin, Sir John.  2. Northwest Passage.  3. Explorers.
4. Scientific expeditions -- Arctic regions.  I. National Film
Board of Canada.  II. New Brunswick Museum.

    Recommended DDC: 971.9
```

(chief source of information)
    (slide frame)

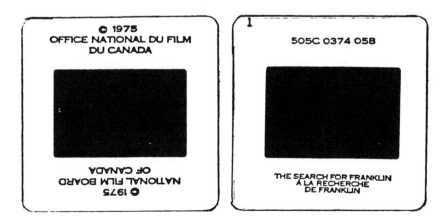

Example 10—Continues

EXAMPLE 10 *(continued)*

(information on accompanying notes)

575C 0374 058

. . . . .

5. Un baleinier amarré à un iceberg
En 1845, l'*Erebus* et le *Terror* levérent l'ancre. Ils Avaient 134 hommes à bord et étaient pourvus du meilleur équipement technique pour leur recherche du passage du Nord-Quest. L'expèdition fut aperçue pour la dernière fois le 28 juillet 1845, par un baleinier amarré à un iceberg; elle traversait alors le détroit de Lancaster. En 1847, on commença à se préparer pour porter secours à l'expédition de Franklin. Et en 1853, on envoya les deux navires *Assistance* et *Pioneer*, sous le commandement de Sir Edward Beecher, dans l'espoir de découvrir des traces de l'explorateur disparu.

L'Office national du film du Canada
Boite postale 6100, Montréal, Québec H3C 3H5 Imprimé au Canada

À la recherche de Franklin

Produit en collaboration avec
le Musée du Nouveau-Brunswick

. . . . .

audacieux d'Angleterre. Parmi les monuments commémoratifs élevés à ses exploits, on en trouve un à Londres, sur la Place Waterloo, dédié au commandant et à l'équipage de l'*Erebus* et du *Terror*.

Dona Atcheson
Traduction: Marie Normandin

575C 0374 058

. . . . .

5. Whaler Moored to an Iceberg
The *Erebus* and *Terror*, which set out in 1845, carried 134 officers and men, and were well equipped with every device then known to help in the search for the Northwest Passage. The expedition was last seen on July 28, 1845, as it was passing through Lancaster Sound, by a whaler which was moored to an iceberg. By 1847, preparations began to be made in the event help should be needed by the Franklin expedition. And in 1853, the two ships *Assistance* and *Pioneer* set out, under Sir Edward Beecher, in the hope of finding some traces of the vanished explorer.

National Film Board of Canada
P.O. Box 6100, Montreal, Quebec H3C 3H5 Printed in Canada

The Search for Franklin

Produced in Co-operation with the
New Brunswick Museum

. . . . .

companions on the *Erebus* and *Terror*.

Dona Atcheson

INDEXES

The three indexes that follow provide a detailed guide to the contents of the book. The first index is a topical guide to the text followed by an index of both personal and corporate names. The third index accommodates those who wish to study the figures and examples more systematically, and is divided into four subsections: Type of Media, Access Points, Description, and Classification. Problems encountered in normal cataloging and rule interpretations can be checked across figures and examples using these indexes. This should provide valuable additional practice in learning the rules.

TOPICAL INDEX TO THE TEXT

333

INDEX TO PERSONAL
AND CORPORATE NAMES

INDEX TO FIGURES AND EXAMPLES

TYPE OF MEDIA

ACCESS POINTS

Author/Creator Main Entry

Title Main Entry

Added Entry

Subject Headings

DESCRIPTION

Title and Statement of Responsibility Area (Area 1)

Edition Area (Area 2)

Material Specific Details Area (Area 3)

Publication, Distribution, Etc., Area (Area 4)

Physical Description Area (Area 5)

Series Area (Area 6)

Note Area (Area 7)